POWER, POLITICS, AND PRINCIPLES

Mackenzie King and Labour, 1935–1948

Why have Canadian union density rates remained relatively stable, in sharp contrast to the decline in American unionization since the 1960s? *Power, Politics, and Principles* traces the root of this question back to the passing of PC 1003 in 1944, a wartime order that protected the right of workers to organize and form unions and forced employers to negotiate at the collective bargaining table. In detailing the significance of this pivotal labour law, author Taylor Hollander brings a new perspective to bear on its creator and proponent, William Lyon Mackenzie King. While many scholars have characterized the former prime minister as politically calculating and opportunistic, Hollander argues that Mackenzie King's adherence to key principles – particularly his determination to preserve and enhance the cohesiveness of the country – resulted in the creation of a more favourable legal environment for Canadian workers and their unions than that which existed across the border. Through secondary sources as well as a wide range of primary materials collected from government departments, wartime agencies, labour organizations, and corporate offices, Hollander delves into the policymaking process, revealing how the passing of this wartime order marked a new stage in Canadian industrial relations.

TAYLOR HOLLANDER is a middle school history teacher at Orchard House School in Richmond, Virginia.

Power, Politics, and Principles

Mackenzie King and Labour, 1935–1948

TAYLOR HOLLANDER

UNIVERSITY OF TORONTO PRESS
Toronto Buffalo London

Toronto Buffalo London
utorontopress.com

ISBN 978-1-4875-0234-8 (cloth) ISBN 978-1-4875-2193-6 (paper)

Library and Archives Canada Cataloguing in Publication

Hollander, Taylor, author
Power, politics, and principles : Mackenzie King and labour, 1935–1948 / Taylor Hollander.

Includes bibliographical references and index.
ISBN 978-1-4875-0234-8 (hardcover). – ISBN 978-1-4875-2193-6 (softcover)

1. Labor policy – Canada – History – 20th century. 2. Labor laws and legislation – Canada – History – 20th century. 3. Labor unions – Canada – History – 20th century. 4. Collective bargaining – Canada – History – 20th century. 5. Canada – Politics and government – 1935–1948. 6. King, William Lyon Mackenzie, 1874–1950. I. Title.

HD8106.H65 2018 331.097109'044 C2018-900444-4

University of Toronto Press acknowledges the financial assistance to its publishing program of the Canada Council for the Arts and the Ontario Arts Council, an agency of the Government of Ontario.

Canada Council for the Arts Conseil des Arts du Canada

Funded by the Government of Canada | Financé par le gouvernement du Canada | Canada

Contents

Illustrations

Abbreviations

ACCL	All-Canadian Congress of Labour
AFL	American Federation of Labor
BNA	British North America (Act)
CAALL	Canadian Association of Administrators of Labour Legislation
CBC	Canadian Broadcasting Corporation
CBRE	Canadian Brotherhood of Railway Employees
CCF	Co-operative Commonwealth Federation
CCL	Canadian Congress of Labour
CFL	Canadian Federation of Labour
CIO	Committee for Industrial Organization (US, prior to 1938); Congress of Industrial Organizations (US, after the 1938 split with the AFL)
CLRB	Canadian Labour Relations Board
CMA	Canadian Manufacturers' Association
CSU	Canadian Seamen's Union
CTCC	Confédération des travailleurs catholiques du Canada
DMS	Department of Munitions and Supply
Dofasco	Dominion Foundries and Steel Company
DOL	Department of Labour
EAC	Economic Advisory Committee
IAM	International Association of Machinists
ICA	Industrial Conciliation and Arbitration (Act)
ICLC	Interdepartmental Committee on Labour Co-ordination
IDIA	Industrial Disputes Investigation Act
IDIC	Industrial Disputes Inquiry Commission
ILGWU	International Ladies' Garment Workers' Union

IRC	Industrial Relations Counselors, Inc.
IRDIA	Industrial Relations and Disputes Investigation Act
IWA	International Woodworkers of America
Mine Mill	International Union of Mine, Mill, and Smelter Workers
MP	member of Parliament
NASCO	National Steel Car Corporation
NIRA	National Industrial Recovery Act (US, 1933)
NLRB	National Labor Relations Board (US)
NLSC	National Labour Supply Council
NSS	National Selective Service
NWLB	National War Labour Board
RCMP	Royal Canadian Mounted Police
REL	Research Enterprises Limited
Stelco	Steel Company of Canada
SWOC	Steel Workers' Organizing Committee
TLC	Trades and Labour Congress
UAW	United Automobile Workers
UE	United Electrical, Radio and Machine Workers
UMW	United Mine Workers
URW	United Rubber Workers
USW	United Steelworkers
WEA	Workers' Educational Association
WLRB	Wartime Labour Relations Board
WPTB	Wartime Prices and Trade Board
WUL	Workers' Unity League
YMCA	Young Men's Christian Association
YWCA	Young Women's Christian Association

Orders in Council, Bills, and Acts

1939

War Measures Act – (25 August) reinvoked 1914 act, altered distribution of powers between federal and provincial governments, and set aside usual guarantees for civil liberties

PC 2483 or the Defence of Canada Regulations – (3 September) imposed severe constraints on what people could say or do during wartime

PC 3495 – (9 November) extended the Industrial Disputes Investigation Act (IDIA) of 1907 to all war production industries

1940

PC 2363 – (4 June) amended the Defence of Canada Regulations (PC 2483) to outlaw the Communist Party

PC 2686 – (19 June) established the bipartite Nation Labour Supply Council (NLSC) to advise the government on industrial relations problems

PC 2685 or the Declaration of Principles for Wartime Regulation of Labour Conditions – (19 June) endorsed but did not enforce the collective rights of workers

PC 5922 – (25 October) established the Interdepartmental Committee on Labour Co-ordination to attempt a more unified approach to labour issues among various departments and agencies

PC 7440 or the Wartime Wage Policy – (20 December) instructed conciliation boards to make wage recommendations below the highest level paid by an employer between 1926 and 1940; also reaffirmed PC 2685 with more assertive language

1941

PC 892 – (7 February) amended the Defence of Canada Regulations (PC 2483) to allow "good faith" criticisms of the government and peaceful picketing

PC 4020 – (6 June) established the Industrial Disputes Investigation Committee (IDIC) to conduct preliminary investigations into impending or ongoing strikes

IDIA Amendment – (14 June) prevented someone who had recently worked as either a labour or corporate lawyer from sitting on conciliation boards

PC 4844 – (7 July) amended PC 4020 to allow the IDIC to investigate union discrimination complaints

PC 5830 – (29 July) allowed the minister of munitions and supply to use federal troops in industrial disputes, a response to the Arvida strike

PC 7307 – (16 September) mandated a strike vote after a conciliation board report

PC 8253 or the Wartime Wages and Cost of Living Bonus Order – (24 October) fixed a wage ceiling or freeze at mid-November rates, created tripartite national and regional war labour boards to administer wage controls, and gave the National War Labour Board (NWLB) the authority to investigate and make policy recommendations to the labour minister

1942

PC 1426 – (24 February) ended the National Labour Supply Council

PC 10802 – (1 December) recognized but did not enforce the collective rights of workers in Crown corporations

1943

PC 1141 – (11 February) reconstituted the NWLB so that it became an independent three-member board of industrial relations experts

PC 9384 or the Wartime Wages Control Order – (9 December) imposed stricter wage controls for all workers, but allowed the NWLB to correct for unfair wage levels

1944

PC 1003 or the Wartime Labour Relations Regulations – (17 February) compelled employers to recognize and bargain with the representatives of their employees' choosing

PC 6893 – (1 September) amended PC 1003 to revoke PC 7307 or the strike vote requirement

1945

National Emergency Transitional Powers Act – (31 December) replaced the War Measures Act and extended PC 1003 until March 1947

1946

PC 3689 – (August 30) allowed the labour minister to order a strike vote before or during a strike

1947

Continuation of Transitional Measures Act – (31 March) replaced the National Emergency Transitional Powers Act and further extended PC 1003

Bill 338 – (17 June) submitted to House of Commons as a peacetime replacement for PC 1003, but didn't make it through the Industrial Relations committee

1948

Bill 195 – (6 April) submitted to House of Commons as a second effort at a peacetime replacement for PC 1003

Industrial Relations and Disputes Investigation Act – (1 September) put into effect a peacetime collective bargaining law; PC 1003 expired

Preface

Mackenzie King could not believe it. William Gladstone, the four-term Liberal prime minister of England, stood just a few feet away on the streetcar. Only a short while earlier, King had seen the "Grand Old Man" of British politics praying in an empty House of Commons. Although "anxious to meet him," he had "hesitated to interrupt." But then fate smiled kindly; here was another, more suitable opportunity to approach his hero. As the streetcar wound its way through London, King moved over to Gladstone and "told him who I was, [that I] had been P.M. of Canada over 20 years." The two men must have been a study in contrast. Besides increasingly wispy hair, they shared bright, penetrating eyes that conveyed intelligence and confidence. But Gladstone cut the more imposing figure with his ramrod posture, large head, and enormous sideburns, not to mention his chin-high collar and cravat. Unlike the Canadian prime minister, who had a short, stocky build and not much enthusiasm for physical exertion, the Victorian statesman's hobby of felling oak trees had kept him fit and trim, even gaunt. Curious onlookers would have also noticed how the two Liberal Party leaders were not on equal footing. Clearly in awe of the Scottish-born politician, King acted reverently, effusing that "he had been more anxious to meet him than anyone in the world." Gladstone remained silent, but reached out and "shook hands twice, very warmly." In such close proximity, the full force of the great man's "power and personality" swept over King and he became "quite overcome with emotion." He was struck how Gladstone appeared larger than life, more a demigod than an ordinary person. Although the British prime minister rode the streetcar, he acted transcendent or free from the limitations of reality.

And for good reason. Gladstone had died forty-nine years earlier. It was all a dream.[1]

When Mackenzie King woke up on the morning of 16 August 1947 at Kingsmere, his country estate in the Gatineau Hills, he immediately began to think about the significance of his dream. What seemed clear was that Gladstone's appearance was a spiritual vision. Like many well-educated women and men in the late nineteenth and early twentieth centuries, including pre-eminent political leaders like Gladstone, King often looked to the supernatural for guidance and reassurance. Trying to reconcile the tension between faith and science in an increasingly modern world, he believed that spiritual interactions provided a rational basis for the afterlife – that they empirically validated his religious beliefs. He especially cherished visitations from Gladstone. Greatly influenced as a young man by the writings of Thomas Carlyle, the Scottish historian who argued that "the history of what man has accomplished in this world, is at bottom the History of the Great Men," King regarded Gladstone as the role model and inspiration for his own political career.[2] "Oh God I want to be that man," he had exclaimed in 1900 when he began to follow purposefully, almost obsessively, Carlyle's call to "hero worship."[3] Over the next fifty years, King read and re-read nearly every biography written about Gladstone, especially John Morley's three-volume work entitled *The Life of William Ewart Gladstone,* originally published in 1903. When King commissioned J.W.L. Forster to paint his mother's portrait, which he later placed prominently in the library of Laurier House, his Ottawa residence, he arranged to have his favourite chapter in Morley's tome, "The Prime Minister," lying open on her lap. He also corresponded with one of Gladstone's sons, who sent a painting of his father to hang in the main hall of Laurier House; acquired a pair of Gladstone's cufflinks which, in 1944, he decided to wear every day to embolden himself; and even tried to emulate the ruins and gardens of Gladstone's estate in Wales at Kingsmere. More than all these material possessions, however, King valued his apparitions of the great statesman; they provided him with comfort, encouragement, and direction.[4]

Later in the day, while King walked across a field to visit the grave of his recently deceased dog, he decided that "Mr. Gladstone's vision may have to do with the last portion of my own parliamentary career."[5] Despite much equivocation on his part, a sign had finally arrived from the otherworld that he had fulfilled his life's work and it was time to retire from public service. For King, the presence of the illustrious

Gladstone in his dream confirmed his own status as a notable political figure in modern history – someone who had exhibited great wisdom and ability in directing the affairs of government. After all, just like Gladstone, his political accomplishments had spanned several decades. "I am the dean of the House of Commons," King reasoned, "as well as the longest in time of service as P.M. in Canada." Even more importantly, like Gladstone, King felt that he had managed to maintain his integrity. Inspired by his hero's moral courage in the face of failure, dissent, and upheaval, the Canadian prime minister had long ago resolved to adhere to a set of Christian-inspired principles throughout his career.[6] "My whole nature thirst[s] for the opportunity to do the work even as he did his," King wrote as a young man, "to be strong in my ideals, true to the most real purpose, [and] firm in the struggle for the right [and] true."[7] Now, nearly fifty years later, Gladstone's manifestation seemed to recognize, if not celebrate, his steadfast veracity. With these thoughts in mind, King reached the grave site and "quite involuntarily ... began to repeat aloud" the first verse of the hymn, "O Thou Who Camest from Above," a meditation on Leviticus 6:13 about the importance of righteousness and commitment – two qualities that he believed summed up the political lives of both Gladstone and himself.[8]

Acknowledgments

As a middle school teacher living in Virginia, I have fumbled my way through some unique challenges to complete this book. But I have not done it alone. Many people provided encouragement, assistance, and inspiration. In particular, I owe a large thank you to all the digital archivists who are democratizing the historical record. Given my limited resources, I could not have attempted to write *Power, Politics, and Principles* without online access to important archival materials like the King Diaries, *Labour Gazette*, wartime newspapers, and labour photographs. I am also grateful to everyone who researched and reproduced images for me at the Ottawa City Library, Library and Archives Canada, Jewish Public Library Archives, Archives of the Confédération des syndicats nationaux, Nova Scotia Archives, Dalhousie Archives, City of Vancouver Archives, City of Toronto Archives, Memorial University Archives, and Wayne State University Archives. Almost without exception, the responses of the archivists and librarians to my haphazard, sometimes frenetic requests were helpful, timely, and friendly.

The incisive comments and suggestions of the editors and anonymous reviewers at the University of Toronto Press greatly improved this book. I would particularly like to thank Carolyn Zapf, whose copy editing skills were invaluable. I greatly appreciate her close reading of the manuscript and thoughtful suggestions for changes. My thanks as well to Christine Robertson for carefully guiding the manuscript through the book production process. I am also indebted to Len Husband who first expressed interest in my writing and then later figured out alternative funding. As the years slipped by, his continued faith in my abilities was very reassuring. Even though it has been a long time since I attended university, I would like to acknowledge the lasting influence of two of my professors, Nick Salvatore and Melvyn Dubofsky. From these superb historians, I learned about the richness and messiness of history, as well as the virtues of clear, unpretentious writing. And the curiosity and exuberance of my students kept me grounded and engaged, as they pushed me to learn new skills, rethink assumptions, and, perhaps most importantly, not take myself too seriously.

The support and understanding of friends and family were vital to the completion of my manuscript. I am extremely fortunate to work with colleagues at Orchard House School who are enthusiastic, forward thinking, and selfless. It is a privilege to belong to such a committed, vibrant community of educators. For many years, my good friend Joe Grasso has been someone I can talk to and depend on. I cannot thank him enough for his steadfastness, advocacy, and humour. I am also grateful for the positive energy of many other friends, like Betsy Colwill, Peter Arnade, Marie Grasso, Jennifer Scanlon, and Michael Arthur. My sister, Andrée Hollander, and brother, Greg Hollander, and their respective families keep me rooted in Canada. It is always wonderful to travel back home and spend time with them. Barbara and Lincoln Blake have offered me love and guidance in countless ways. Generous in every sense of the word, their unselfish regard for others inspires us all to do better. Although my mom, Barbara Hollander, passed away before I began work on this book, her deeply intelligent, pragmatic way of thinking had a big influence on my analyses and writing. In our weekly phone calls, my dad, Lou Hollander, not only provided wise counsel, but also inspired me with his own personal commitment to lifelong learning. I am beholden to both my parents for the high value they put on education and their unconditional love.

This leaves the two people closest to my heart. My daughter, Emma Blake, became an adult as I worked on this book. Despite inheriting my genes, she has turned out to be very capable, kind-hearted, and genuine. I am particularly impressed with her perceptive intelligence, inner strength, and quick wit. Thank you Emma for making me laugh, giving me purpose, and really, as cheesy as it sounds, just being you. Finally, I owe my biggest debt of gratitude to my partner-in-life, Holly Blake. While I greatly enjoy writing history, it is a painstaking process for me, and Holly has had to endure many bouts of perfectionism and uncertainty. Indeed, if not for her love and affection, discerning comments, and slight impatience, I would still be sitting in front of an unfinished manuscript. For more than twenty-five years of ups and downs, she has been my principal source of strength and happiness. This book is dedicated to Holly.

POWER, POLITICS, AND PRINCIPLES

Mackenzie King and Labour, 1935–1948

Introduction

Power, Politics, and Principles chronicles the making of a path-breaking labour policy in Canada during World War II. Two somewhat distant personal experiences inspired this book. The first involved a plant shutdown. In the early 1980s, I worked on the floor of Goodyear Tire's large flagship plant in New Toronto, Ontario. My various duties, such as cleaning bathrooms, slinging tires, coating whitewalls, and testing samples, were demanding, especially with rotating shifts. All the heat, noise, and repetition made for long hours. Still, I was fortunate to have the job. The decent wages and benefits allowed me to live comfortably and even accumulate some savings. I became a shop steward and frequented the union hall around the corner from the plant. With the company in the midst of spending millions of dollars on plant improvements, our local union executives talked confidently about long-term material gains and, in particular, the construction of cooperative housing units for members across the street. Although I didn't realize it then, I belonged to what historian Joan Sangster and others refer to as "the first tier" of the labour force – mainly white, mainly male industrial workers who benefited from the growth and influence of unions after World War II.[1] I also didn't realize that the decades of security and stability were about to end. In 1986, not long after I quit my job to return to university, Goodyear announced that it was closing the plant. More than 1,500 workers lost their jobs. Management claimed that the cost of thwarting a hostile takeover necessitated the shutdown. Within three years, however, the company had begun to build a fully automated, non-union plant 250 kilometres away in Napanee, Ontario. In short, the debt load had been a convenient excuse for Goodyear to rid itself of an outdated facility and a well-entrenched union presence.[2] As one worker told the media: "They're kicking us out like we're nothing, just trying to clean house as cheap as they can."[3] Lucky to have left when I did, I was not directly or adversely affected. But the abruptness and severity of what happened – the sudden demise of this large, productive factory and what it meant for everyone I had worked with – did influence my world view.

The second personal experience had to do with the classroom. After earning my undergraduate degree, I moved to the United States to enter a graduate program in industrial relations. Sitting through courses on labour law, labour history, labour economics, and bargaining strategy, I learned how many companies south of the Canadian border were also taking steps to rid themselves of unions. The most influential book on industrial relations at that time, *The Transformation of American Industrial Relations* by Thomas Kochan, Harry Katz, and Robert McKersie, explained that heightened global competitiveness and escalating wage rates had pushed managements to find non-union alternatives, abandoning a New Deal model of industrial relations which "had worked well in the post–World War II years because it provided stability while also satisfying other basic economic and organizational needs."[4] A lot of classroom discussion involved the breakdown of the post-war or "Fordist" accord between organized labour and employers: the implicit understanding that unions would minimize production disruptions if companies provided regular wage increases and good benefits. Today, some historians question whether a post-war accord ever existed. "During the first two decades after World War II," writes Nelson Lichtenstein, "few unionists could have been found to declare their relationship with corporate America particularly agreeable or stable."[5] In the late 1980s, however, it certainly appeared that there had been a meaningful shift in managerial attitudes and behaviour: companies throughout Canada and the United States were adopting much more belligerent stances towards unionism. Whether implementing quality circle programs, hiring anti-union consultants, or moving production facilities, the corporate assault on unions seemed not only pervasive, but also oblivious to national boundaries.

There was one significant cross-national difference: union density rates. Although once comparable at around 30 per cent in the 1960s, the percentage of organized workers in the United States plummeted, while the Canadian rate remained fairly steady. Granted, public sector unionism accounted for much of the union density rate in Canada. Like the United States, most private sector unions in Canada had experienced significant membership declines. The Canadian section of the United Steelworkers, for example, lost 37,000 members between 1982 and 1990.[6] Still, Canada's private sector rate fell at a slower pace and stayed more than twice as high as that of the United States.[7] After witnessing the tactics of Goodyear Tire, I was surprised to learn that conditions for unionism in the United States were worse than in Canada. Besides some vague generalizations about political culture, however, I couldn't find satisfactory explanations for the relative resiliency of Canadian unions.[8] The insufficient comparative analysis was understandable. To borrow from the language of transnational historians, the labour histories of the two countries are remarkably "entangled."[9] In both Canada and the United States, there has been a striking overlap of employers and unions; the parallel passage of comprehensive labour legislation that protects the rights of workers; and, unlike more tripartite arrangements in Western Europe, the similar development of highly decentralized patterns of collective bargaining. Even Samuel Gompers, the inveterate, turn-of-the-century president of the American Federation of Labor, observed that Canadians and Americans are "more than neighbors; we are kin ... [O]ur labor problem with all its ideals, aspirations and ambitions is alike for both of us."[10] So why did the two labour movements begin to move along distinct trajectories in the late twentieth century? What substantive differences lay beneath all the similarities?

Although not as intentional as it sounds, these two formative experiences in the workplace and classroom pushed me to investigate the cross-national divergence in union density rates in a dissertation and now in this book. What I discovered was that Canada's collective bargaining regime – the legislative framework for determining union recognition, dispute resolution, and bargaining units – was in large part responsible for the difference. The legal rules and procedures for Canadian industrial relations date back to February 1944, when, after much hesitancy, Prime Minister Mackenzie King and his cabinet adopted Order in Council PC 1003 or the Wartime Labour Relations Regulations. PC 1003 was only a temporary wartime measure and would eventually expire in 1948. But the order marked the beginning of a new era in Canadian industrial relations, one that still endures today, more than seventy years later. For the first time, a federal labour policy forced employers to recognize and bargain with the representatives of their employees' choosing. After decades of avoidance, if not intransigence, corporate executives now had to sit down at the bargaining table with union leaders and negotiate the terms of the employment relationship.

It was no longer legally permissible to ignore the collective demands of workers; managerial prerogatives and arbitrary decision-making were curtailed. Covering all war production or most industries in the country, PC 1003 had an immediate impact. Within two years, the failure rate for contract negotiations dropped to 3.5 per cent, and the country experienced a 15 per cent jump in union membership. As one newspaper reported, "Canadian labour has stepped out of its short pants for good."[11]

It would be a mistake to attribute the divergent union density rates solely to labour law. Since the late 1980s, when I first began to look for explanations, scholars have offered an assortment of non-legislative reasons, such as leftist purges, political structures, nationalist attitudes, and union leadership, for the relative strength and power of Canadian unions or, conversely, the weak state of organized labour in the United States. What they often highlight is the debilitating impact of racial attitudes and practices in the United States. Although racism was also a constant in Canadian labour history, it did not impede union organizing to nearly the same extent. The most well-known example is "Operation Dixie" – the drive to organize the large industrial workforce of the southern states in the late 1940s. Despite the responsiveness of black workers to unionism, the Congress of Industrial Organizations (CIO) focused most of its resources on the predominately white textile industry and refused to push a civil rights agenda. Meanwhile, anti-union forces warned white workers that the CIO promoted racial equality. "By the end of the decade," writes historian Michelle Brattain, "it became clear to CIO leaders and outside observers that the campaign, by almost any standard, was a categorical failure."[12] And, as August Meier and Elliott Rudwick document in their history of the United Auto Workers in Detroit, this widespread racism was (and is) certainly not confined to white industrial workers in the American South.[13] In the recent words of an organizing director for Unite Here, "Racism is … the shoals upon which American labor has sunk for centuries."[14]

Still, most comparative studies of Canadian and US labour history agree that the current gap in union density rates reflects, at least in part, differences in labour law. In the words of labour historian David Brody: "The rights of workers to organize and bargain collectively are much more effectively protected under Canadian law ... Canadian law signals the legitimacy of collective bargaining."[15] What is particularly glaring about the legal framework for industrial relations in the United States is how the law makes it much more difficult for unions to win recognition. Unlike Canada, where union certification often depends on a simple count of membership cards, the United States requires that unions secure the majority of votes in representation elections. This stipulation allows, if not encourages, employers to mount vigorous campaigns to quash the union sympathies of their workers. Although mandatory elections are becoming more prevalent in Canada, there is still only a small window for counterattacks because the elections must take place expeditiously. South of the Canadian border, long delays separate initial petitions and actual elections. Given ineffective penalties and lengthy procedural delays for unfair labour practices, US employers have ample opportunity to discredit unions and intimidate workers. A study of over 1,000 elections between 1999 and 2003 discovered that US companies threatened to close plants in 57 per cent of the elections, and cut wages and benefits in 47 per cent of them.[16] Echoing Brody, an economic policy think tank in the United States arrived at the following conclusion a few years ago:

> Compared to Canada, many workers in the United States are not able to exercise their right to freely join and form unions and participate in collective bargaining, in large part due to employer opposition, which current labor policy fails to adequately address.[17]

As legal scholar Reuel Schiller points out, the historical irony is that the architects of the collective bargaining regime in the United States had a much different intention.[18] In 1935, Senator Robert Wagner and other liberal Democrats in Congress persuaded more moderate colleagues and a reluctant President Franklin Roosevelt to support the passage of the National Labor Relations or Wagner Act because they wanted to encourage the spread of unions. Worried about the recent upsurge in workplace conflicts, bolstered by the midterm elections of 1934, and supported by like-minded reformers outside the government, they believed that trade unions helped to stabilize the industrial order, prevent economic downturns, and promote more equitable income and wealth distribution. The act's advocates subscribed to what scholars today commonly refer to as "industrial pluralism," or the idea that a workplace can be a mini-democracy run jointly by workers and managers as equal citizens. They believed that to be treated as equal citizens workers needed to gain more power by organizing into unions and negotiating binding contracts. This notion of compulsory or legally obligated recognition and collective bargaining was a hard sell in Congress.

Many politicians wanted the government to stay out of the traditionally private realm of industrial relations. Borrowing from the Norris-LaGuardia or Anti-Injunction Act of 1932, which removed barriers to unionism because they interfered with a worker's "freedom of labor," Wagner and the other reformers used rights language – language that dates back to the Declaration of Independence – to win over critics. Rather than the tyranny of a monarchy, though, they focused attention on the tyranny of the workplace and how it undermined the individual rights of workers. Or, to put it another way, they argued that the individual rights of workers depended on the realization of their collective rights.[19]

The end result was one of the most far-reaching policies of the New Deal era. The Wagner Act strongly supported the growth of unions, prohibited unfair labour practices by management only, and established the National Labor Relations Board (NLRB) as the administrative agency to determine union certification and prevent employer intimidation. In 1937, two years after the passage of the act, the Supreme Court upheld its constitutionality in *NLRB v. Jones and Laughlin Steel Corp.* It was a surprising decision, because earlier the court had proven much less receptive to the breadth and scope of New Deal policies. This time, however, a majority of justices agreed that workers had a "fundamental right" to organize into unions and bargain collectively. A relieved Senator Wagner lauded: "A pathway to industrial accord and economic progress has been cleared."[20] Importantly, since the policymakers treated the workplace as a mini-democracy, they had included a provision for representation elections – a provision rolled over from the National Industrial Recovery Act of 1933 (an ill-fated effort to establish industry-wide codes of fair competition). It seemed a relatively benign requirement. The Wagner Act already prevented employer interference in elections. It also allowed for alternative methods of assessing union support, such as membership card checks, membership list inspections, and even the general impressions of NLRB officers.[21] At that point in time, it didn't seem likely that representation elections would diminish the uncompromising impact of the act. Certainly the business community was not hopeful. "Of all the one-sided, inequitable, trouble-causing, and ineffective pieces of legislation that was ever passed," lamented the president of the Connecticut Manufacturers Association in late 1937, "the Wagner Act is, perhaps, one of the worst."[22]

What the policymakers failed to anticipate was how the National Labor Relations Act contained the seeds of its own undoing. Almost immediately, a coalition of Republicans, Southern Democrats, and business interests, not to mention old-school labour leaders in the American Federation of Labor, mounted a relentless counterattack. These "conservative revanchistes," as labour historian Melvyn Dubofsky calls them, were particularly effective in turning public opinion against the new labour law.[23] In 1939, the Smith Committee in the House of Representatives conducted an exhaustive investigation of the National Labor Relations Board, eventually issuing a long list of recommendations to enervate the Wagner Act. The Senate failed to embrace the Smith amendments, but the hearings generated a lot of negative attention. When the Smith Committee uncovered correspondence between NLRB officials and union attorneys, for example, newspaper headlines shouted "NLRB Aides Assisted in Strike."[24] Although the labour movement grew in size and influence during World War II, the backlash continued unabated. In 1947, after regaining control of Congress and against the backdrop of a massive strike wave, Republicans used the same "rights talk" of ten years earlier to amend the Wagner Act. In order to "restore to American workers and employers alike, the rights guaranteed them by the Constitution," the Labor-Management Relations or Taft-Hartley Act allowed for decertification proceedings, established unfair labour practices for unions, imposed strike restrictions on workers, and invited states to pass right-to-work laws so that jobs did not depend on union membership. The new legislation also made representation elections compulsory, abolished card checks, and recognized the free speech right of employers to influence votes. Taft-Hartley made little immediate impact on strike or union density rates. But it further encouraged the general public to question the value, if not the legitimacy, of trade unionism.[25] Under the guise of redressing the pro-labour bias of the Wagner Act so that employers were now treated as "equal" citizens, the Taft-Hartley Act also created ample opportunity for anti-unionism in the future. From the vantage point of moderate observers, who felt the Wagner Act was too skewed towards organized labour, the Taft-Hartley Act confirmed Plato's dictum: "The excessive increase of anything causes a reaction in the opposite direction."[26]

There are other explanations for the breakdown of US labour law. Scholars influenced by critical legal studies place the blame squarely on New Deal policymakers, rather than on a conservative backlash. Borrowing from Antonio Gramsci, the Italian political theorist, they argue that these liberal Democrats purposively ensnared workers and their unions in a web of workplace rules and regulations so that shop floor activism and militancy – the lifeblood of the labour movement – were curtailed.[27] Although material benefits for union members increased, the ensuing system of "industrial legality" served to legitimate the dominant role of the employer in the workplace. As Christopher Tomlins writes in his history of US labour law, the Wagner Act offered workers "a counterfeit liberty."[28] While an important corrective to studies that glorify the Wagner Act, however, there are two problems with treating labour law as a hegemonic tool – a tool wielded by liberal Democrats to defuse the militancy of workers and protect the capitalist order. First, this approach downplays the complexities and ambiguities of the policymaking process. New Deal policymakers were not operating in isolation. Nor were they confident of the outcome. As political scientist David Plotke details, the Wagner Act transpired because a "political alignment" or "Democratic order" developed that "extended outside the administration" and "cut across a number of institutional lines." And, even then, he points out: "Passing the Wagner Act did not guarantee implementation."[29] When this Democratic alignment crumbled in the late 1960s, conservative forces inside and outside the government wrested back control of the legislative process. As a result, during Democratic presidencies and Democratic majorities in Congress, four drives to win minor improvements in labour law, like card check certifications, met with defeat.[30] Second, a hegemonic emphasis downplays the benefits of the Wagner Act for workers. Certainly the collective bargaining law curbed militancy. But the labour movement also won higher wages, better working conditions, and, perhaps most importantly, greater self-respect for its members. Without succumbing to a Whiggish history of sustained progress, these positive aspects of the Wagner Act should be recognized and understood. As labour studies scholar Richard Hurd suggests, the labour policy offered workers "a constrained liberty," not a "counterfeit liberty."[31]

Indeed, hegemonic arguments aside, it is difficult to overstate how a conservative backlash has weakened the framework for labour law in the United States. From the Landrum Griffin Act of 1959, which regulated the internal affairs of unions, to the introduction of right-to-work bills in twenty-one state legislatures in 2013, a plethora of new policy developments have redefined the rights of workers, reshaped power relations in the workplace, and reduced the scale and scope of organized labour.[32] "As a result," writes industrial relations scholar James Gross, "the current national labor policy favors and protects the powerful at the expense of the powerless."[33] Most remarkable is how the diminishing of labour law in the United States has not only resulted from but also contributed to a pervasive culture of anti-unionism. In particular, since the 1970s, several years before President Reagan's notorious confrontation with the Air Traffic Controllers' Union, employers have used permanent replacements to great effect. By 1990, 82 per cent of employers in the United States said they would use or consider using replacements.[34] With workers almost bound to lose their jobs if they stage walkouts, the bargaining leverage of union negotiators has been effectively undermined. Many unions no longer consider the strike to be a valuable weapon for winning concessions. "Replacement workers are poison to organized labor," writes former union representative David Macaray. "What's the advantage of having the right to strike if, by shutting down the operation, a worker winds up losing his job because he's been permanently replaced by a new hire?"[35] With more permissive laws, employer opposition to unions has become so aggressive and so widespread that union avoidance consulting is now a multimillion dollar industry. According to industrial relations scholar John Logan, union avoidance experts often run workplaces during anti-union campaigns, utilizing a long list of hardline strategies to reassert the superior position of employers. Claiming a success rate of 90 per cent, they are "brazen about encouraging employers to fight unionization to the bitter end and confident in their ability to preserve a union-free environment."[36]

This brief discussion about the framing and gradual weakening of the Wagner Act provides the backdrop for understanding how a fairly unique and contingent or unpredictable arrangement of historical constructs influenced the passage of PC 1003 in wartime Canada. The goal here is not to consecrate the Canadian experience or to make an argument for Canadian exceptionalism. As mentioned before, the collective bargaining regimes in Canada and the United States are more alike than different. Especially compared with labour laws in other countries, what we are discussing are significant, not fundamental, variances in the two legal systems. With the earlier US labour law serving as a model of sorts for PC 1003, scholars even refer to both sets of rules and regulations as "Wagnerism." There are seven main components: (1) protect the right of workers to organize and form unions; (2) certify unions on the basis of majority support; (3) require good faith bargaining from both unions and employers; (4) allow strikes or third party dispute resolutions if collective bargaining fails; (5) rely on compulsory arbitration to resolve differences during the life of a collective agreement; (6) prohibit strikes and lockouts during the term of an agreement; and (7) create administrative boards to enforce the laws and provide remedies for disputes.[37] In addition, both legal frameworks encourage firm-level rather than industry-wide bargaining and marginalize large numbers of workers, particularly female workers and workers of colour, who have remained, until fairly recently, unorganized.[38] What's more, Wagnerism faces just as questionable a future in Canada as it does in the United States. Since the 1980s, the legislative erosion of rights, heightened forces of globalization, and increased popularity of neo-liberal economic policies like deregulation and fiscal restraint have contributed to what legal scholar Eric Tucker calls "Wagnerism's shrinking dominion" in Canada.[39] *Power, Politics, and Principles* helps to explain why in relative terms the Canadian labour movement has fared better over time; it does not make an argument for the superiority of Canada's collective bargaining regime.

Few published, comprehensive histories of PC 1003 exist. The paucity is not for lack of recognition. Numerous scholarly works about Canadian history, legal process, and industrial relations mention, if not briefly discuss, the order. The regulations even have a dedicated entry in the *Encyclopaedia Britannica*. But there has been little effort to delve deeply or closely into why and how the collective bargaining policy actually happened. The reasons are many. Although industrial relations scholars are interested in changes over time and the evolution of new employment practices, they focus more on the present than the past to understand relationships between employees and employers. Despite a growing awareness that examinations of the nation-state can reveal a great deal about the activities of ordinary people, labour historians tend to eschew top-down, Ottawa-centred considerations of the historical process for studies of working-class culture, shop floor protest, and workers excluded from the collective bargaining regime. Sociologists, political scientists, and critical legal theorists connect the legacy of PC 1003 to theories of social change and capitalist accumulation, but often neglect the historical context of the policymaking process. The making of labour policy has largely escaped the attention of political historians, even if they have now expanded their definition of politics to include non-traditional sources of power. Although the secondary literature usually treats PC 1003 as a significant event in Canadian history, these studies reveal little about its formulation.[40]

This disregard has resulted in and contributed to misconceptions about the passage of the collective bargaining policy. The philosopher Bertrand Russell is often credited with writing: "In all affairs, it's a healthy thing now and then to hang a question mark on the things you have long taken for granted."[41] Whether or not the adage belongs to him, it certainly holds true for historical references about PC 1003. Instead of figuring out what happened during the passage of the order, most scholars reduce its origins to largely unsubstantiated generalizations about working-class power. Irrespective of their academic discipline or views on the submissive power of labour law, they assume that mounting social pressures in the form of labour disputes and left-wing politics forced the King cabinet to pass PC 1003. This misconception does have some basis in reality. During the war, the economic and political mobilization of workers was impressive. Between 1939 and 1944, for example, the number of union members in the country more than doubled, and the union density rate increased 7 per cent.[42] At first glance, there does seem to be a logical, straightforward connection between militancy, solidarity, and labour policy innovations; PC 1003 would appear to be a textbook case of how social movements influence the political process. Yet, is history ever that linear or unambiguous? Was the order mainly due to workers flexing their new organizational and political muscles? Not according to the leaders of the wartime labour movement. Just about a year before the passage of PC 1003, Patrick Conroy, the secretary-treasurer of the Canadian Congress of Labour, believed that organized labour's struggle for compulsory collective bargaining had reached an impasse. When asked whether a new labour policy was imminent, he replied: "We do not feel it worthwhile to raise people's hopes."[43] In an effort to "hang a question mark" on PC 1003, *Power, Politics, and Principles* dives into the messiness of the policymaking process and sorts out how the order, despite its less-than-captivating name, involved a complex array of real people and their clashing ideas, as well as the impetus of earlier policy initiatives and enduring bureaucratic forces. Working-class pressures were an important part of this unfolding drama, but there was nothing clear-cut or obvious about the path to PC 1003.

In particular, it is important to recognize Mackenzie King's influence in the development of the wartime regulations. When I first began my research into the order, it was not my goal to shine the spotlight on Canada's tenth prime minister. Trained as a social historian to take a "bottom-up" approach to understanding the past, I had anticipated writing about workers and their local unions, not leading members of the political establishment. The more I immersed myself in the historical record, however, the more I found it difficult to escape King's contributions to the moulding and shaping of Canadian industrial relations in the first half of the twentieth century. Although the prime minister often prioritized the exigencies of the economy and the war effort over labour relations, there is little doubt that he held the reins of power when it came to the future of the collective bargaining regime. No other individual or agency had as much sway over pursuing or retarding labour policy reforms. No one else had the decision-making authority and control to manipulate and coerce the movers and shakers who walked the halls of the parliament buildings. Imbued with the sensibilities of social history, *Power, Politics, and Principles* is not a political history in the conventional sense of a "great man" narrative. It recognizes how many different individuals and groups contributed to the making of PC 1003; ordinary people – people who lacked wealth and formal power – did have an impact on the policymaking process. But this book does argue that King's involvement in the creation of Canada's current collective bargaining regime was critical.

Which brings us to the most provocative claim in these pages: it was Mackenzie King's political principles that both directly and indirectly helped to determine the timing, content, and lasting impact of the order. Yes ... principles. Although most historians and commentators view King as one of the top prime ministers in Canadian history, they rarely associate his name with the word "principles." He is known as a highly skilled politician who took a very calculating, opportunistic approach to policy decisions. Most writers today emphasize his shrewdness and underhandedness, not his character and conviction. And it is hardly a new assessment. While in office, some newspaper reporters nicknamed Mackenzie King "Mr. Wait-And-See" because he always appeared hesitant to take action without widespread support. Others lamented his tendency to be "politically expedient [and] keep behind rather than ahead of public opinion."[44] After King's death in 1950, criticism became louder, bowling over more laudatory appraisals with statements like "King was a man who pushed clarity of thought aside the moment it threatened to interfere with day to day politics."[45] Or, as F.R. Scott pronounced in his famous 1957 poem entitled *W.L.M.K.*:

> He skillfully avoided what was wrong
> Without saying what was right,
> And never let his on the one hand
> Know what his on the other hand was doing.[46]

King's reputation as a political trimmer and temporizer hardened during the 1970s and 1980s, when scholars gained access to 30,000 pages of his diaries and produced such a plethora of books and articles that one reviewer observed: "He bestrides our past like a pudgy Presbyterian colossus."[47] The prime minister's intellectual abilities, leadership skills, and personal eccentricities were closely examined. He earned the somewhat unfair and ahistorical but lasting reputation as the "Weirdo PM." Most studies confirmed that he largely acted out of self-interest and for political advantage. In subsequent years, when scholarly interests in conventional political history waned, King receded into the shadows of the historical record, mainly appearing in works on trade and foreign policy. With only a few exceptions, though, the consensus remained intact. As one historian noted: "To him no policy was often the best policy, and a decision delayed was a mistake avoided. Principle was not an issue."[48] Rather than high-minded or virtuous, the secondary literature insists that King acted more Faustian, willing to sacrifice his ideals to preserve power.

Power, Politics, and Principles offers a different perspective. It argues that Canada's longest serving prime minister actually remained faithful to his particular political vision for the government and country during his many years in Ottawa, at least in the area of industrial relations. In the words of political scientist Joy Esberey, one of the few scholars to make a similar assessment, it is a "myth that he was an absolute pragmatist without political principles and a compromiser without parallel."[49] Of course, as intellectual abstractions, political principles are difficult to pin down. They present students of history with challenging questions of definition and method. Consider this diary entry written by King on 15 August 1941: "It curiously was sent to strengthen my determination not to yield to any conventions which ran counter to principles."[50] He was referring to a dream he had experienced the night before about meeting a political rival. But why did he mention his principles? Was it because he had just heard Winston Churchill and Franklin Roosevelt announce in their Atlantic Charter that the war was about fighting "to preserve the rights of man and justice"; learned about the death of Arthur Purvis, the high-minded industrialist, in a plane crash just days before King, himself, was to fly to England; or remembered that his beloved dog, whose "noble little spirit" was a source of "real inspiration," had died exactly one month earlier? Or was it some combination of these events? And what did the prime minister mean by "principles?" It is a remarkably ubiquitous, yet nebulous word. Although many political histories written since the 1800s refer to, if not venerate, principles, they tend to assume rather than to clarify their scope and purpose.[51] This conceptual vagueness cuts across disciplines. As one study revealed, five thousand articles listed in the *Philosopher's Index* between 1940 and 2009 used the word "principles," but few offered any explanation for the "meaning of principles or their actuality."[52] Perhaps little wonder that historians interested in social and material life are inclined to dismiss discussions of political principles, especially those of national figures, as ethereal and elitist.

For our purposes, Mackenzie King's political principles refer simply to his own personal, well-entrenched beliefs or imperatives about what he thought was best for Canada and Canadians. Influenced by both ideas and experience, he formulated these subjective truths as a young man and then used them to guide his political behaviour and actions throughout his remarkable career in Ottawa. To figure out what those principles were and how he adhered to them, I rely on his voluminous diary as a main primary source. But I do so cautiously. Like all diaries, King's self-writing examines, explores, and reflects, but also fashions and revises, idealizes and exaggerates, distorts and deludes. In his narration, he constructed his own reality – a reality that was more often about self-adulation and validation than authenticity. As King biographer Allan Levine writes: "He portrayed himself always in the best possible light, blaming others for the conflicts and problems he routinely encountered."[53] Given that the prime minister offered a skewed perception of his own existence in his diaries, I also draw on a wide range of other sources – correspondence, memos, and minutes – from government departments, wartime agencies, labour organizations, and corporate offices. King's diary is a tremendous resource, but to weigh and measure the validity and applicability of his political principles, we need to situate his thoughts within a more tangible and precise historical context. What were those principles? Three stand out. First, in response to the inequalities of industrial society and the possibility of perpetual class conflict, King believed that the less privileged deserved better living and working conditions. Second, well aware that Confederation was a rather tenuous agreement, he placed a great premium on reconciling regional, class, and religious differences to preserve or even enhance the cohesiveness of the country. Third, rejecting "conservative reaction" on the one hand and "extreme radicalism" on the other, King pushed for a moderate liberalism that avoided skewed policymaking and provided, in his words, "the greatest possible service to the largest number of people in our Land."[54]

The prime minister understood, of course, that he needed to play politics – to compromise and delay – so that he could remain in office and continue to pursue his political vision. This strategy meant deviating from his principles, sometimes in unsavoury, if not disturbing, ways to win votes or to undermine opponents. It also meant taking a slow, cautious approach to policy reforms. Rather than try to change conditions with one broad stroke, he believed that lasting improvement depended on incremental, well-understood, and politically feasible solutions. King couldn't just ignore the realities of power and influence. For his principles to prevail, he had to use his political expertise and guile to full advantage; he had to substitute short-term tactics for long-term vision by manoeuvring and manipulating, consenting and conceding. If he remained too rigid or forced the issue about the correctness of his viewpoints, he would lose support and his capacity to wield power, to push people in the right direction. So, in the face of political challenges and uncertainty, it was often necessary to abandon or at least dampen down his principles until he could turn conditions to his favour. As King put it, "History would condemn a [government] standing for certain principles if it allowed itself to be defeated."[55] Although routinely criticized – then and now – for "vague, maddening, and oblique" behaviour, he viewed politics as a means to an end, the way to accomplish his ideals.[56] Egocentric, ambitious, and insecure, King was hardly selfless when it came to motives. But he genuinely and presumptuously believed his political tactics and actions benefited the greater good in the long run. The prime minister also proved astute at adapting his principles to changing conditions. This tactic didn't mean that he abandoned them when new circumstances demanded; his essential principles remained unaltered throughout his life. When necessary, however, King adjusted and accommodated. He considered this flexibility to be a hallmark of his political philosophy, once dismissing a proposal for a charter of liberalism as "a great mistake" because it committed ideals to paper. "The principles ... remain the same," he lectured, "but their application and policies ... have to change with time."[57] There is no disguising how, in the words of one wartime journalist, Mackenzie King "could be ruthless, procrastinating, evasive, uncreative, uninspiring, and, in the end, resistant to change."[58] But readers are urged to look beyond commonly held assumptions about the prime minister. Even if his actions were opportunistic and his principles problematic, he did adhere to a well-conceived political vision throughout his career; he did demonstrate commitment and courage in the face of adversity.

By holding fast to his principles, King influenced Canada's collective bargaining regime in two decisive ways. Both had to do with limiting backlash, maintaining unity, and furthering the public good. First, he delayed any consideration of a labour policy that circumscribed or compelled employer behaviour until late 1943, nearly nine years after his good friend, Franklin D. Roosevelt, signed the Wagner Act into law. The lag wasn't for lack of political muscle. King not only won the federal elections of 1935 and 1940 with significant majorities, but also obtained incredible wartime powers in 1939. He probably enjoyed more leverage over the policymaking process than any other prime minister in Canadian history. Despite the repeated demands of the labour movement and the lackluster opposition of the business community, however, King refused to think about the possibility of compulsory collective bargaining. Worried that "class legislation" would trigger reactionary responses from conservative forces, mire the country in industrial unrest, and ultimately hurt workers and their families, he insisted that the government play an ostensibly impartial role in industrial relations – that it not appear to favour unions over business.

Second, when King finally supported the idea of compulsory collective bargaining, he made certain that PC 1003 was not unabashedly pro-union like the Wagner Act. Building on the legacy of previous labour laws, his policymakers paid little attention to questions of industrial democracy and shop floor power. Instead, their focus was on process and peace. Under the guise of neutrality, they created a collective bargaining regime in Canada that not only outlawed unfair labour practices for both employers and unions, but also imposed extensive strike bans and grievance arbitration provisions. As Labour Minister Humphrey Mitchell explained, Canada made the decision "to travel down the middle of the road."[59] Although genuinely sympathetic to the plight of workers, the prime minister remained convinced that more forceful measures would incite demands for "corrective" legislation and divide the country. As time revealed, King was right. Unlike the more progressive Wagner Act, the moderate collective bargaining regime in Canada did not become a magnet for the hostility and antagonism of "conservative revanchistes" in the post-war period. Left relatively unscathed, PC 1003 and subsequent provincial laws proved more advantageous to workers and unions in the long run than the continually worked over, if not besieged, labour law of the United States. Or, to put it another way, King's sway over the policymaking process, which largely reflected his political principles, helped to create the cross-national divergence in union density rates at the end of the century.

Despite all the focus on the influence of Mackenzie King, the following pages treat PC 1003 as a largely positive development for industrial workers, not as an exercise in hegemony. Many scholars in Canada will disagree. Much like Christopher Tomlins and others in the United States, they view labour policy as calculated efforts by liberal governments to co-opt working-class pressures and protect private property rights. "What was distinctive about the Canadian compulsory collective bargaining regime," explain Judy Fudge and Eric Tucker in *Labour Before the Law*, "was the extent to which it substituted the rule of law for economic power."[60] This argument has merit. Mackenzie King and other policymakers certainly feared class upheaval and wanted to preserve the economic order. It is also evident that workplace contractualism encouraged union complacency and worker indifference in the long run. As the youngest member of my department at Goodyear Tire, for example, I became the shop steward by default; no one else wanted the position. Yet, there was nothing foreordained about PC 1003. Although I emphasize Mackenzie King's prominent role, the order was the product of protracted struggles within and between the labour movement, business community, government bureaucracy, and general public. It was not simply a strategic initiative by a liberal state to preserve the capitalist system in the face of collective action. Indeed, without the pivotal contributions of three labour law experts (including a socialist) on an independent government board, there is a good chance that the prime minister would have continued to ignore calls for a collective bargaining policy. It is also difficult to discount or overlook how PC 1003 redefined power relations in the workplace so that workers gained not only higher wages and better conditions but also more dignity and self-worth. Before unions and collective agreements, wages fluctuated wildly and jobs disappeared overnight. Foremen and supervisors also exacted demeaning and expensive tributes. As an auto worker from Windsor, Ontario, remembered, "We got the [pay cheque] and when we headed home the 'boss' was standing in front of the hotel, waiting. We had to buy him drinks until midnight. He didn't pay."[61] There is little question that PC 1003 established a collective bargaining regime that diminished the militancy of organized labour over time. But the making of the labour policy was also complex, uncertain, and beneficial – it defies neat theoretical conceptualizations.

Power, Politics, and Principles covers a thirteen-year period from 1935 to 1948. A conflation of events determined the beginning and end points of the book. In 1935, King not only won re-appointment as prime minister, but the US Congress also passed the Wagner Act. In 1948, King not only retired from the Liberal Party leadership, but the Canadian Parliament also passed the Industrial Relations and Disputes Investigation Act, which converted PC 1003 into a long-lasting, peacetime policy. During this remarkable period in Canadian history, economic travails, military exigencies, and communist intrigues reigned supreme. It was a tumultuous, unpredictable time that marked the maturation of Canada as a nation. And, through it all, Mackenzie King utilized his skills as a politician to win over or, at least, dominate competing visions and agendas about industrial relations and labour policies so that his principles informed the shape and direction of Canada's collective bargaining regime and, ultimately, the cross-national divergence in union density rates fifty years later.

Chapter One

The Unity of Our Country, Fall 1935–Fall 1939

"Strike, strike, strike!" shouted the audience as the curtain dropped. Clapping erupted around Mackenzie King, emanating from every corner of the packed theatre in Ottawa. The sixty-one-year-old prime minister had decided to spend the evening of 22 April 1936 at the Dominion Drama Festival before boarding the late night train to Toronto. Three productions were on the playbill, each competing for the coveted Bessborough Trophy, which was awarded to the best amateur company in the country. In the understated words of the judge, the audience members, who included King, the governor general, and two former prime ministers, were of a "comfortable" background. Yet, this last performance, an overtly political work called *Waiting for Lefty*, earned the most enthusiastic applause of the evening. There was nothing subtle about the play. Mainly taking place in a union hall, it provided a hard-hitting, gut-wrenching glimpse into working-class life, delivering a clear message about the baseness of capitalism and the virtues of collective action. With actors placed throughout the theatre, either wandering through the aisles or rising from their seats, the production also involved a good deal of audience participation, blurring the line between performers and spectators.[1] As the judge put it, "There was a direct emotional appeal ... that was very hard to resist."[2] It is difficult to imagine King, who was known for his reserved manner, joining other theatregoers as they called out loudly in support of the workers. With its raw, forceful acting, however, the play made a deep impression. "'Waiting for Lefty,' while extreme," he observed a little later, "was a true picture of the kind of life men are encountering today ... Parts of the play reminded me very much what I myself witnessed when dealing ... first-hand with industrial disputes some years ago."[3]

King's compassion for the trials and tribulations of wage-earners was genuine. Although not as forward-thinking as his grandfather, the infamous William Lyon Mackenzie, who had once argued that workers alone should enjoy the fruits of their labour, the prime minister firmly believed that a moral imperative existed to better conditions for working people.[4] As a devout Christian, one of his lifelong goals was to create "a better world to come when we shall all have been made equal in the sight of God."[5] Convinced that people faced with a hopeless future would resort to desperate measures, he had a great desire to ease the tensions between the "haves and have nots," which was, in part, fear driven. Like many educated, middle-class reformers from the turn of the century, King deemed it politically and socially dangerous to ignore the underlying problems of industrial society. When Mitchell Hepburn of Ontario took a hard line against striking workers in 1937, for example, King worried that the premier's "fascist" actions would swell the ranks of the Communist Party, much like in Spain. Still, the prime minister was not just worried about upheaval.[6] Clearly sympathizing with wage-earners and their families, he blamed "the accumulation of wealth under existing conditions" for the ills of Canadian society.[7] He also appreciated the appeal of the labour movement. Although some labour leaders, in his view, acted stridently and recklessly, he understood that trade unions were "the effort of the great mass of the people to realize the capacities of their natures, to fulfill the end of their being."[8]

Yet, during the late 1930s, Mackenzie King refused to consider the passage of compulsory collective bargaining legislation that would help workers gain better wages and greater respect. Unlike in the United States, where Congress had recently passed the far-reaching National Labor Relations or Wagner Act, labour laws north of the border remained weak and ineffectual, not forceful and comprehensive. At the federal level of government, nothing compelled employers to recognize and bargain with the representatives of their employees' choosing; nothing stopped employers or their shop floor supervisors from committing unfair labour practices to defeat union drives; and nothing created the administrative machinery to protect the collective rights of workers. Provincial labour policies were not much better. Although British Columbia and Nova Scotia had compulsory recognition and collective bargaining laws, workers found it difficult to win their battles because of judicial biases and broadly defined managerial prerogatives. In Ontario, the industrial heartland of the country, the collective rights of workers were barely acknowledged.[9] Why the policymaking inertia? Although many factors were at work, like a weak and divided labour movement, it was Mackenzie King's political principles that largely made a Canadian version of the Wagner Act not just unattainable, but inconceivable. Deeply committed to the ideal of a nation free of any kind of sectionalism, he believed that progressive labour policies, like the Wagner Act, would incite employer backlash and further rupture class relations. "The reason, above all others, which accounts for our success," the prime minister explained at a Liberal Party banquet shortly before the outbreak of World War II, "is that we have sought, above all else, the unity of our country."[10] As a result, Depression-era workers continued to face severe challenges when they wanted to join unions, win recognition, and bargain collectively; belligerent opponents enjoyed almost free rein.

The Prime Minister

For a head of state, Mackenzie King possessed an expertise in industrial relations that was unsurpassed. Truly a pioneer in the field, he helped develop the first strategies for resolving workplace conflicts, not just in Canada but also in the United States. As historian Margaret Bedore writes, the prime minister "approached industrial relations both as a social scientist and as a moralist."[11] Although King was not religious in the institutional sense, Christian beliefs played a central role in his intellectual development. While a young man at the University of Toronto in the early 1890s, he had found it difficult to reconcile the problems of an industrializing society, like urban poverty and vice, with his genteel Presbyterian upbringing. His concern pushed him to embrace a social Christianity, which emphasized reform and improvement over salvation and atonement. Inspired by forward-thinking Protestant ministers who linked the teachings of Jesus to a coming age of peace and abundance, he hoped to make the world a better place – one driven by fairness and harmony, not self-interest and conflict. During this time, King became "enraptured" with the writings of Arnold Toynbee, the British political economist who argued that industrial society must be premised on Christian principles.[12] As mentioned in the preface of this book, King also began to adulate William Gladstone, the British prime minister, whose early life he admired for "his deep religious nature, the reverence he had for God, himself, and his fellow men."[13] Attempting to translate his religious beliefs into action, King took breaks from his undergraduate studies to visit sick children in a Toronto hospital, work on a city mission committee, and, like Gladstone, provide assistance to prostitutes. Later, in 1896, he became a graduate student of political economy at the University of Chicago and spent two months living at Jane Addams's Hull House, where well-schooled, middle-class reformers offered support and guidance to the low-income residents of the Near West Side. While attending classes and working on his master's thesis, he organized clubs for teenage immigrants, visited the homes of the indigent, and gave talks to patrons. As King put it, "I am trying hard to make every moment of my life count."[14]

For reasons of temperament and ambition, King decided after a few months at Hull House that hands-on work with the less privileged was not his calling. Joining the new generation of social scientists who utilized the data collection techniques of the natural sciences to confront the human costs of industrialization, he began to engage in more formal academic studies of workplace conditions, soon publishing two scholarly papers on trade union history and methods. Later, while pursuing additional graduate degrees at the University of Toronto and Harvard University, King investigated sweatshop conditions in Toronto's garment industry for the *Mail and Empire*, prepared a legislative brief for the Consumer's League of Massachusetts on wage-earning women in Boston's sweatshops, and submitted a study to the Canadian government on sweatshops and government contracts.[15] Sociologist Kenneth Westhues explains that what mattered to turn-of-the-century social reformers like King "was the ability to write critical, empirical social analyses."[16] Rather than rely entirely on moral arguments to win reforms, they placed a heavy emphasis on the gathering of facts and figures to expose the sins of industrialization. By providing a scientific, rational understanding of social problems, by presenting unbiased, observed truths, they anticipated swaying public opinion and, ultimately, improving society.[17] "I look," King explained, "to education, the enlightenment of the masses, to accomplish permanent good."[18] This three-part, causal connection between objective investigation, public education, and social betterment would become a familiar refrain in his lengthy career, greatly informing his efforts to resolve industrial disputes and resist labour policy innovations. "[O]nce in possession of the facts," he told the House of Commons in 1910, "the public will find a way of seeing that any evil under which it may be wrongfully suffering will be removed and that no situation ... will prove too intricate for a satisfactory solution."[19]

Unlike earlier generations of Christian-inspired leaders, King didn't find it difficult to reconcile his religious beliefs with science. No doubt influenced by his friendship with Graham Taylor, the chair of the Department of Christian Sociology at the Chicago Theological Seminary, King treated religion as an ethical guide and science as the indisputable proof. Or, as Taylor put it, King pursued "sociology with God left in it."[20] He felt that the evolutionary concepts of Charles Darwin underscored the possibility of a more humane industrial order – that the Christian prophecy of a millennial kingdom of peace and abundance could be attained by using science to improve society. Referring to "science as an aid to faith," he also concluded that the "teachings of Christ" – the ideals of love and cooperation – were like a "statement of law." They were the key to social evolution. There would be no better world – no thousand year reign of the "saints on earth" – until the different social classes opted for empathy and harmony over apathy and hostility. To ignore the "teachings of Christ" – to let the poverty, inequality, and terrible workplace conditions prevail – was to put the country in peril.[21] As Haymarket Square in Chicago or the street railway strikes in Ontario had demonstrated, upheaval and chaos would be the end result. Importantly, King argued that this cataclysm would not be the fault of an unruly labour force, but of an increasingly industrialized workplace where "workers are mistaken as a means to an end, instead of being regarded as ends in themselves."[22] When an acquaintance questioned the drive and initiative of labourers, he retorted: "The mass of workers ... [are] doing their best all the time."[23]

Bolstered by faith and science, Mackenzie King became an internationally renowned industrial relations expert during the first two decades of the twentieth century. Despite earning two master's degrees and completing the oral exams for his doctorate at Harvard University, which he eventually earned in 1909, the future prime minister decided to forgo an academic career to wield influence in the less comfortable and more ruthless political and corporate world. Motivated by idealism, ambition, and earnings, King believed he could make his convictions mean something by gaining access to real power. In 1900, he joined the federal government as the editor of the *Labour Gazette*, a new government periodical that collected and reported data on industrial disputes and labour market conditions. Within a few months, he also became Canada's first deputy minister of labour and ultimately interceded in more than forty labour disputes throughout the country.[24] During this time, King drew on his experience with workplace conflicts to draft and lobby for the passage of a path-breaking labour law called the Industrial Disputes Investigation Act in 1907. Two years later, after winning election to the House of Commons, he became Canada's first full-fledged minister of labour and played a major role in resolving the Grand Trunk Railway strike of more than 8,000 workers. After losing his seat and office in the 1911 election, he eventually served for several years as an industrial relations advisor to the Rockefeller family in the United States, testifying at length before the US Commission on Industrial Relations and devising a widely adopted employee representation plan as an alternative to unionism. Finally, just before returning to politics as the new leader of the Liberal Party in 1919, King published a capacious work, entitled *Industry and Humanity*, where he argued that "an industrial system characterized by antagonism, coercion, and resistance must yield to a new order based upon mutual confidence, real justice, and constructive good-will."[25] Twenty years before Queen's University offered the first industrial relations courses in Canada, the future prime minister had established himself as an authority in the field.[26]

As deputy minister of labour, King developed an undying enthusiasm for the practice of conciliation. With conciliation, a third party, like a government official, helps adversaries, like employers and workers or their unions, identify their common interests. Unlike arbitration, conciliation does not impose solutions on the parties in conflict. Instead, it encourages dialogue, appeals to reason, and emphasizes the public interest. This consensual, tension-lowering approach to dispute resolution predated King. Confronted with crippling industrial strikes, federal officials had used conciliatory methods since the late 1800s to encourage good faith bargaining and try to bring about actual settlements. The goal was to reduce conflict in key developing industries, like mining and railways, without using more forceful methods that might increase unrest.[27] Convinced most industrial disputes involved "a certain blindness in human beings" and intent on creating a more harmonious industrial order, however, King quickly became the most outspoken champion of conciliation. Rather than compel workers, unions, or employers to accept rulings, he made it his mission to clear away misunderstandings and encourage goodwill. "If Reason can be brought to bear upon the merits of a dispute," he explained, "the result ... is certain to be the best attainable under any circumstances." In a now famous analogy, King likened the government's role in an industrial dispute to an "impartial umpire" or referee in sports; its responsibility was to ensure a fairly played game, not to exhibit preferences or to influence the final score. "Conciliation," he insisted, "is always the best of methods to employ in adjusting differences."[28]

In hindsight, it is difficult not to criticize King's embrace of conciliation as delusional or, even worse, disingenuous. The employment relationship at the turn of the century was hardly a level playing field; employers enjoyed considerably more power and leverage than workers living on the margin or unions with limited resources. Unrestrained by the voluntary features of the conciliation process, employers were free to reject bothersome negotiations and ignore undesirable outcomes. As legal scholars Judy Fudge and Eric Tucker discovered: "The vast majority of the disputes in which [King] was involved were settled on terms favourable to the employer."[29] Yet, the prime minister genuinely believed that conciliatory methods could help create a better, fairer, more righteous world. "Industry must be made to serve and to save Humanity through a recognition of common interests between men of all classes," he preached in *Industry and Humanity*. Since "it is in the image of God Himself, not after the patterns of some industrial model, that all men, from the humblest to the greatest have been created," conciliation will help to strip away bias and confusion to reveal the innate goodness in people and "promote [a] spirit of co-operation and constructive good-will." He insisted that this kind of government intervention created a more humane industrial order because it involved "the elimination of fear and the establishment of faith between the parties concerned." King also warned that government strong arming would have the opposite effect: "To apply Force in seeking to prevent and settle industrial differences is to destroy the very spirit that it is desired to create and maintain, namely, confidence and good-will." Compelling employers and workers to acquiesce and conform would only result in backlash, confrontation, and unrest; it would dash any hopes of achieving a penultimate age.[30]

Given that conciliation depended on the open-mindedness and cooperation of participants, King developed a strong antipathy for inflexible positions taken by either belligerent employers or radical labour leaders. A point of emphasis is needed here. Much has been made in the secondary literature about his preference for old-school, craft-based unions over newer, industrial unions that cut across skill levels. Rather than denigrating industrial organization itself, however, he deplored labour leaders who, for ideological and organizational reasons, refused to compromise or make concessions. Indeed the prime minister recognized the importance of collective action for all workers. Writing in *Industry and Humanity*, he noted:

> The right of association and of organization by workers is a fundamental right ... What the individual worker has lost of independence, through the transitions and the expansion of Industry, he is entitled to regain, so far as may be possible, through associated effort ... In collective security lies the elimination of the fears which individual isolation necessarily begets.[31]

Collective action didn't necessarily mean unions. As an advisor to John D. Rockefeller Jr in the United States, King did develop and actively promote the aforementioned representation schemes whereby committees of management and employee representatives jointly discussed working conditions and completely avoided unions. By 1924, his employee representation plans covered 1.25 million workers in some of the leading companies in the United States.[32] Still, King viewed his plan as complementing rather than supplanting unions.[33] He recognized that unions were not only a fact of industrial life, but also greatly improved conditions for workers. "[I]t must be conceded by all," he wrote, "that Labour owes to the Trade-union movement more than it is possible to express in words."[34] This acknowledgment included industrial unions. During the momentous General Motors strike of 1937, for example, King accepted the organizing campaign of the upstart United Auto Workers as legitimate. When more conservative colleagues expressed misgivings, he insisted that "labour has ... the right to sell its services in a way likely to be most beneficial to itself."[35]

In the early 1900s, the federal government enacted two lasting pieces of labour legislation that built upon the concept of conciliation. First, the Conciliation Act of 1900 (later incorporated into the Conciliation and Labour Act of 1906) allowed the labour minister, upon the request of one of the disputing parties or at the minister's own initiative, to dispatch a conciliation officer to investigate and mediate any anticipated or actual strike and lockout in the country. The government relied on ad hoc conciliators from various branches until the Labour Department created a formalized conciliation service in 1927. During the 1930s, eight permanent conciliators staffed offices in most of the major cities and employed a variety of methods and degrees of intervention to settle potential or ongoing conflicts.[36] Second, in 1907, King drafted the Industrial Disputes Investigation Act (IDIA), which allowed the labour minister, upon application from a disputing party, a municipality, or at the minister's own initiative (as later amended), to appoint an autonomous, ad hoc conciliation board. To make sure the conflict was worthy of government intervention, the workers could not make an application for a conciliation board until a majority had voted in favour of going on strike. Made up of an employee, an employer nominee, and a neutral chair, a conciliation board was used to resolve disputes and prevent stoppages in mining, railway, and public utility operations – those industries thought to be critical to the economy in the early 1900s. The chair was chosen by the disputing parties or by the minister if the two sides were unable to agree on a candidate. In a significant departure from previous labour policies, the IDIA forced the disputing parties to participate in the fact-finding proceedings of a conciliation board and prohibited strikes and lockouts prior to, as well as during, a board's tenure. The conditions of employment were also frozen. If, after numerous investigative hearings, the board failed to bring about a settlement, it issued a report of non-binding recommendations. Only then could a legal strike or lockout take place. Impressed with these two innovations, an official in the US Department of Commerce and Labor reported that the IDIA should serve as a "guiding star" to American policymakers.[37]

Despite King's aversion to forcing outcomes in industrial relations, he did not have a problem with compelling the disputing parties to meet and discuss their differences. With the IDIA, the government was not making workers and employers accept solutions. What it did do was "give Reason its chance"; it provided the opportunity for a third party to use its powers of persuasion to resolve the conflict. As for the strike restrictions in the IDIA, King claimed in *Industry and Humanity* that he "was not seeking to take away from Labour any right." Consistent with his loftier goal of creating a better world, he actually drafted the labour policy to help workers improve their lives. "It was the large purpose," he explained, "of providing an instrument that would be effective in uncovering industrial wrongs and exposing injustice in industrial controversies." Investigation was the instrument in question – what King called "a letting in of light." Drawing on his background in the social sciences, he drafted the IDIA so that a conciliation board had the power to "get at the truth" by examining documents, interviewing participants, and visiting premises. Once again, he formulated the three-part, causal connection between objective investigation, public education, and social betterment. The board members collected the facts and figures, not only to use in discussion with the disputing parties, but also to release to the general public; the heightened public awareness was supposed to encourage a change in attitudes among the disputing parties and assist in achieving positive results. "If I have sought to promote legislation which would make investigation available in many directions," he asserted, "it is because I have faith in the power of an intelligently formed Public Opinion to remove any injustice and to redress any wrong." Since the IDIA made it possible to expose intolerable workplace conditions and arbitrary managerial decisions, workers benefited and conditions improved. "If Industry is to serve Humanity," King concluded, "it can only be through general acceptance of the principle of investigation prior to the severance of relations."[38]

Encapsulating this notion of conciliation – settling differences without compelling solutions – was King's particular brand of liberalism. Like classical liberals, he believed in free trade and fiscal restraint. He agreed that the ultimate goal of liberalism should be "to extend and defend freedom." But King also recognized that "Canada is a very difficult country to govern" because it is divided regionally, culturally, and economically.[39] Applying the same concept of conciliation used in industrial relations, he believed it was the job of the government to bridge these divides by playing the role of an intermediary. The government needed to be "large enough and strong enough to bring together in common effort those who are of different racial origins and religious faiths, those who belong to different classes, those who come from different sections of the country." "Liberalism," he explained, "has always been anxious, not so much to emphasize differences, as, where it has been possible, to reconcile them."[40] Only then could complete freedom be achieved. This emphasis on national unity greatly influenced King's attitudes about policymaking. Although a reformer at heart, he nearly always took a slow and deliberate approach to policy innovations. Critics accused him of timidity, evasiveness, and expediency. While certainly guilty of political opportunism, he also feared that abrupt change would alienate a large segment of the population, heightening rather than smoothing over sectionalism. A case in point was when former prime minister Bennett, a Conservative, implemented a sweeping reform package in 1935. Not only did the Privy Council in England declare Bennett's effort "to force the pace," as King put it, ultra vires or outside the jurisdiction of the federal government, but the far-reaching program also alienated the provinces.[41] In contrast, King noted: "Liberalism in Canada has sought to put forward only policies which it believes [will] find acceptance in the minds of the people at large."[42] A cautious, religiously inspired policymaker who sought a more harmonious world, King refused to break new ground without widespread support. Given Canada's fragile existence, too much was at stake if part of the country rejected a new law. As he told Winston Churchill during World War II, "true Liberalism stands for ... 'inclusive' rather than 'exclusive' policies."[43]

Throughout King's lifetime, his principles remained fairly static. Certainly experience and circumstance varied their efficacy. He did become, after all, an adept politician who was skilled in the arts of compromise and adjustment. As he liked to say, running a government was similar to sailing a ship because "often you must tack and veer and run out storms." Yet, inspired by his hero William Gladstone, he also placed a high value on integrity. Regardless of the situation, King tried to stay true to an enduring set of ideals or, to extend his nautical analogy, "to keep in mind the port where you are going."[44] In other words, given his unwavering commitment to a unified country free of all sectionalism, there was no way he would consider far-ranging labour policies, like a Wagner Act, that forced employers to recognize and bargain with unions. Worried about aggravating class relations, worsening conditions for workers and their families, and sending the country into a tailspin, he could not fathom government intervention in industrial relations that went beyond conciliatory methods. "The nation that ... encourages its people to look to Force rather than to Reason," he counselled, "is helping to bring destruction ... upon itself."[45]

Before the onset of World War II, King believed that the New Deal administration of Franklin Roosevelt had edged dangerously close to this precipice. Over the course of eighteen meetings and numerous letters and phone calls in the late 1930s and early 1940s, the two heads of state would eventually form a close friendship. Not only did both men bond as Harvard alumni, but they also, as historian Elizabeth Elliot-Meisel writes, "found it easy to be in each other's company, to speak frankly, to hammer out ideas, and to get their staffs to work smoothly together."[46] Prior to developing this relationship, however, King expressed serious, if not angry, misgivings about Roosevelt's broad and intrusive recovery, reform, and relief efforts. "The mad desire to bring about State control and interference beyond all bounds makes one shudder," he wrote after attending a lecture on the New Deal program.[47]

Surprisingly, nothing in the historical record reveals King's reaction to the passage of the National Labor Relations or Wagner Act in June 1935. Although conjecture, it is hard to believe that he would have been unaware of this momentous legislative development. After all, twenty years earlier, he had made his name as an industrial relations expert in the United States. It also seems likely that the new labour law's aggressive, pro-union intervention into the traditionally private realm of the employment relationship would have dismayed him. The contrast with his more moderate approach to industrial relations, a "reliance on reason rather than force," was glaring.[48] Indeed, in early 1938, the prime minister appeared to be referring to the Wagner Act when he observed rather smugly that "the United States is wrestling as it never has before with problems of industrial relations."[49]

King's earlier criticism of the more benign National Industrial Recovery Act (NIRA) of 1933 certainly intimates that he would have been upset with the Wagner Act. As one of the cornerstones of the early New Deal, the NIRA made it possible for each industry to establish "codes of fair competition," which encompassed production, prices, and wages. To ensure the support of the labour movement, section 7a of the act also declared that the codes must include provisions for union recognition and collective bargaining. King applauded the Roosevelt administration's effort to enlist the cooperation of business and labour, noting that this collaborative strategy "might have been taken literatim et verbatim from my Industry and Humanity."[50] But he was shocked how Roosevelt and his administrators arbitrarily circumvented the US Constitution to give some of the codes, including union recognition and collective bargaining, the force of law. When the US president sided with John L. Lewis and the United Mine Workers against the "captive coal mines" of the steel companies, King worried that "govt. in the U.S. has become very much of a dictatorship" and that "no democracy can long respond to methods of the kind."[51] The upsurge in strikes during 1933 and 1934, which was partially due to employer backlash, confirmed his fears. In early June 1935, when the US Supreme Court declared the NIRA unconstitutional, King felt both vindicated and righteous. Meeting with William Elliott, a Roosevelt advisor, he talked about how his own "stand on the constitutional issue, and labour policies ... had been thoroughly sound and confirmed by experience."[52] Indeed, it is not difficult to imagine his consternation when the president signed the more far-reaching Wagner bill into law just a few weeks later.

That fall, Mackenzie King gained almost absolute authority as the gatekeeper of labour policy in Canada, squelching any possibility of a Wagner-like act. In the national election of October 1935, he not only became prime minister for the third time in fifteen years, but the Liberal Party also secured 173 of the 245 seats in the House of Commons, the largest majority since Confederation. The opposition parties, led by the decimated Conservatives with only 40 seats, lacked any chance of outvoting the government on policy proposals.[53] Moreover, under the Canadian system of parliamentary government, which emphasizes rigid party discipline, the prime minister and his cabinet allowed little input from backbenchers.[54] The main task of the Liberal members, aside from constituency business, was to support the draft bills of the cabinet. As Paul Martin, a newly elected Liberal member of Parliament from Windsor, Ontario, remembered: "We were ... called upon in parliament to approve measures without having had an opportunity to amend or influence them."[55] The party did meet regularly in caucus, where King explained the rationales for policies and listened to grievances. But he rarely asked for feedback or advice and, in the words of one staff member, he "never permitted the caucus to determine policy."[56]

Although some Liberal backbenchers called for a Canadian Wagner Act in the late 1930s, no one with real power or influence in the government was prepared to take up the cause. Most of the prime minister's colleagues in the cabinet, predominately middle-aged career politicians from small-town ridings, held strong anti-union views or were simply indifferent to industrial relations. King's closest associate, Ernest Lapointe, the minister of justice, was progressive for the French-Canadian wing of the Liberal Party, but had little tolerance for collective action. When Lapointe mistakenly thought sit-down strikes were underway at General Motors in Oshawa, Ontario, for example, he threatened to "utilize all the [government's] resources and agencies at its command ... to the end of restraining and eliminating this illegal mode of procedure." Just one cabinet member actually represented a working-class constituency: the newly elected transport minister, Clarence Decatur (C.D.) Howe, from Port Arthur, Ontario. But he believed that enlightened management, not unions, would solve the problems of workers.[57]

Only Norman Rogers, the minister of labour, who had served as King's personal secretary during the late 1920s and, more recently, on the faculty of the Political Science Department at Queen's University, consistently supported the collective rights of workers. Rogers announced in his New Year's message of 1938: "It is an obligation of government to uphold freedom of association and the right of workers to organize in unions of their choice."[58] But for three reasons the labour minister and his department weren't up to the challenge of

1.1 Mackenzie King, 1942

Source: National Film Board of Canada, Still Photography Division, Library and Archives Canada, PA-805705.

pushing politicians for a collective bargaining policy. First, Rogers was busy trying to convince the provinces to accept a constitutional amendment that brought unemployment insurance under the jurisdiction of the federal government. Second, the civil servants in the department, who mainly administered acts, collected labour statistics, and mediated labour disputes, were not prepared to make their own policy recommendations. "It is the function of the Department of Labour to render such assistance as lies within our jurisdiction," a high-ranking official affirmed, "and it is the function of government to place on our statute books such legislation as will work for social advancement and industrial peace."[59] Third, King considered the Department of Labour to be his personal domain. "No Minister of Labour, not even Norman Rogers in whom he had exceptional confidence, ever had a free hand," a close associate remembered.[60] Even though the prime minister held Rogers in

1.2 King Cabinet, 1939. Members involved in industrial relations: Norman Rogers, standing third from left; J.L. Ilsley, standing fourth from left; C.D. Howe, standing second from right; Norman McLarty, standing far right; Ernest Lapointe, sitting third from right

Source: National Film Board of Canada, Laurier House Collection, Library and Archives Canada, C-090191.

high regard, he sometimes found it necessary to temper the labour minister's enthusiasm for reform – to remind him about political realities. "There is a danger of Rogers going too far for principle," King reflected after a labour policy discussion, "destroying the opportunity to affect reform by persistent effort over a period of time."[61]

During the late 1930s, the prime minister remained confident that no further legislative action was needed to recognize and protect the collective rights of workers. Besides repealing sections of the Criminal Code and the Immigration Act, which had allowed the deportation of foreign-born labour organizers and radical activists, he failed to pursue any new labour policy initiatives, preferring to rely on turn-of-the-century conciliatory methods to resolve disputes.[62] What he didn't seem to realize was how industrial relations had changed since his tenure in the Labour Department – that his conceptual understanding of what it took to resolve conflicts was outdated. Unlike twenty to thirty years earlier, when relatively moderate craft unions were the norm, a fairly large number of nascent, left-leaning industrial unions were now trying to win recognition in the natural resource and mass production industries. Representing unskilled workers who wanted to recapture the prosperity and security of earlier decades, these unions felt little compunction about confronting employers who were saddled with excess capacity and wanted to maintain full control over the production process. In these kinds of emotionally charged, zero-sum disputes, conciliators found it next to impossible to engage in their conventional practice of "horse-trading."[63] There was no middle ground; unions either won recognition or they failed to win recognition. With neither side willing to make concessions and employers under no legal obligation to abide by recommendations, government officials often found themselves forced to let strikes and lockouts run their course. Preoccupied with deteriorating conditions in Europe, committed to his deeply rooted principles, and convinced the Wagner Act was to blame for a tumultuous 1937 strike wave in the United States, the prime minister perceived nothing different about these new developments in Canadian industrial relations – nothing that his three-part equation of conciliation, investigation, and public pressure couldn't remedy. "With confidence, goodwill, and co-operation, progress can be made in any direction," he told labour leaders in early 1938. "[W]ithout it nothing can be achieved."[64]

King also offered another reason for his policy inertia: constitutional limitations. It was a valid point. Contrary to the intent of the drafters of the British North America (BNA) or Constitution Act of 1867, the

Judicial Committee of the British Privy Council had ruled in a 1925 decision (*Toronto Electric Commissioners v. Snider*) that King's beloved IDIA was ultra vires. Except for interprovincial transportation and communication agencies or under conditions of national emergency, the field of industrial relations was a provincial responsibility.[65] In response, the federal government immediately passed a legislative amendment that allowed the provinces to extend the application of the IDIA to their jurisdictions. While nearly all the provinces complied, most limited the act's coverage to a few select industries, greatly diminishing the role of the federal government in industrial conflicts. A provision already existed in the IDIA that allowed disputing parties in an industry outside its scope to make a joint application for a conciliation board. But it was rarely pursued after the *Snider* decision; most industrial relations remained free of federal intervention.[66] As the Privy Council's ultra vires ruling concerning the "New Deal" program of former prime minister Bennett reaffirmed in 1937, revisions needed to be made to the constitution before the federal government could implement far-reaching socio-economic legislation of any kind. The BNA Act offered no specific formula for making amendments, so the accepted custom was for the federal government and the provinces to reach a unanimous agreement on changes before submitting a largely ceremonial request to the British Parliament for constitutional modifications. Not an easy task, even at the best of times, which these were not.[67]

In the late 1930s, federal-provincial relations were at a low point, making constitutional changes a remote possibility. Ottawa's effort to assume jurisdictional responsibility for unemployment insurance was a case in point. In November 1937, spurred on by Norman Rogers and the National Employment Commission, King sent a letter to provincial leaders asking for their agreement to a constitutional amendment. The positive replies fell well short of a consensus.[68] For both political and personal reasons, a great deal of animosity existed between King's administration and the provinces. In Alberta, William "Bible Bill" Aberhart's populist Social Credit government clashed repeatedly with Ottawa over monetary policies. In British Columbia, Duff Pattullo's Liberals demanded greater fiscal power so their province could implement its own socio-economic reforms. Maurice Duplessis in Quebec and Mitchell Hepburn in Ontario were so incensed with King's refusal to allow increased hydroelectric exports to the United States that they seriously considered forming their own national party. Indeed, as zealous advocates of provincial rights, the premiers of Ontario and Quebec deeply resented federal interference in any aspect of their governance, especially industrial relations. As Duplessis declared at a birthday party for Hepburn, the provinces "must have more autonomy or there can be no unity in Canada. The individual members of a nation must be given their rights or there can be no nation." King's feud with Hepburn went well beyond politics. Although members of the same political party, Hepburn routinely denounced King as incompetent and inane, while the prime minister derided the premier as an "alcoholic" and "gangster." "I am sick and disgusted with King and his whole outfit," Hepburn wrote to Pattullo in July 1937, "and want nothing more to do with them, politically or otherwise."[69]

Concerned about national unity, the prime minister was not about to push hard for any kind of constitutional amendment, even for unemployment insurance. His unwillingness to take action annoyed civil servants in the Departments of External Affairs and Finance, the Bank of Canada, and the Prime Minister's Office, who thought it ridiculous to kowtow to the aggressive territoriality of the premiers. Initially a repository for patronage appointments and unambitious administrators, the Canadian civil service had, in recent years, added a number of broadly educated, extremely competent individuals to its ranks. Shaken by the social and economic upheavals of the Depression, they were part of a larger intellectual movement that believed the federal government should become more involved in regulating the economy. Although mainly interested in fiscal issues, these proponents of a strong central government targeted a wide range of socio-economic policies, which for some included the field of industrial relations. In August 1937, they appeared to have achieved a major breakthrough when the King cabinet established the Royal Commission on Dominion-Provincial Relations, better known as the Rowell-Sirois Commission, to examine the division of powers in the BNA Act. But the civil servants had been outmanoeuvred. In an impressive display of Machiavellian misdirection, the prime minister appointed the commission to sidetrack the constitutional question, not to challenge provincial jurisdictions. Until the commission submitted its report, he refused to pursue any policy that expanded the powers of the federal government. Forced to conduct an enormous amount of research and to switch chairs midway through its investigation, the commission would not complete its work until February 1940.[70]

When it came to federal labour policy, the constitutional question was a real obstacle to change. At the same time, though, it was a convenient excuse for inaction. If King had been willing to push the issue, it seems likely that the jurisdictional constraints could have been circumvented. In a 1938 report for the Rowell-Sirois Commission, for example, Brooke Claxton, a future member of the King cabinet, and Léon M. Gouin, a Montreal law professor with strong Liberal Party connections, identified two loopholes in the BNA Act that would have allowed a greater policy role for Ottawa. First, they argued that the Dominion had the power to incorporate civil rights, like the right to organize, into the federal Criminal Code. Second, they observed that unions operating in more than one province could receive the same federal legal status as interprovincial companies.[71] With sectionalism running rampant, however, the prime minister was not about to confront the constitutional question without widespread national support. Even if he had, the passage of a Wagner-like act would have been highly unlikely. Given his passion for conciliation, King believed the government should intervene in industrial conflicts to investigate conditions and facilitate discussions, not to take sides or determine outcomes. "To apply Force in seeking to prevent and settle industrial differences," he liked to emphasize, "is to destroy the very spirit it is desired to create and maintain, namely confidence and good-will."[72] As King told his cabinet shortly before the onset of war in September 1939, the resolution of any kind of dispute, whether industrial, political, or international, required a neutral third party to recognize "that all things [have] two sides, and that there [is] a certain amount of truth in both sides, the effort being to finding the best way of harmonizing views." Rather than adapt to changing conditions and despite his concerns about the betterment of the working classes, he remained true to the principles he had first embraced as a young man.[73]

The Labour Movement

On the evening of 14 April 1937, hundreds of war veterans gathered at Memorial Park in Oshawa, Ontario. In the midst of the fifteen-day strike for union recognition and improved working conditions at General Motors, they had just marched through downtown, wearing medals pinned to their overcoats, waving Union Jacks, and singing "We'll Never Let the Old Flag Fall." Crowds had lined the streets, many people cheering them on with words of encouragement. Much of the community, including several local businesses, fully supported the strikers in their showdown against the corporate behemoth. It was hard not to be sympathetic; General Motors had just announced its largest profit in company history, while simultaneously cutting the wages of Oshawa workers for the fifth time in five years. Given the involvement of the United Automobile Workers (UAW), which belonged to the newly formed Committee for Industrial Organization (CIO) in the United States,[74] Premier Mitchell Hepburn insisted that the strikers were the pawns of "foreign agitators." But the parade left little doubt that the stoppage was Canadian born and bred: the workers had contacted the UAW, not the other way around. Now, standing in the park with friends and family, smoking cigarettes and rubbing hands together to stay warm as the wind blew in from Lake Ontario, the veterans waited with heightened anticipation for a speech that not only celebrated their patriotism, but also strengthened their resolve. Hugh Thompson, the tall, fedora-wearing organizer for the UAW, did not disappoint, connecting the walkout with Canada's entry into the Great War. "We demand the right of free men to live as they want to live," he shouted out to the crowd in his Ulster accent. "It's the duty of all good Canadians to fight for industrial democracy."[75]

After two weeks of peaceful picketing and newspaper headlines, the workers managed to win important concessions from General Motors, such as a shorter work week, an increase in wages, and a seniority system. As the first large foray into organizing mass production industries, their strike proved to be an important milestone in Canadian labour history. But it fell short as a "fight for industrial democracy." Throughout the strike, the company had made clear that it would not concede union recognition to the UAW. Mitchell Hepburn, the self-appointed mediator in the dispute, had also done everything, short of mustering "the entire resources of the province," to thwart the union.[76] He freely admitted to the press that his goal was to stomp out the CIO in Oshawa before its unions spread to other industries, especially the gold mines of wealthy supporters.[77] As a result, there was no formal recognition of the UAW in the final contract; General Motors was only required to deal with a local committee of union members, not the international union. Although workers continued to enjoy the support of the UAW, it would prove to be a tenuous arrangement that placed a great deal of responsibility on the shoulders of inexperienced local members and made it very difficult for the union to implement an industry-wide strategy for organizing and bargaining.[78] The Oshawa contract was a stark contrast to a recent agreement in Flint, Michigan, where General Motors agreed to recognize and bargain with the UAW. Confronted with organizing drives, other Canadian companies soon followed suit, signing contracts that were little more than ephemeral verbal agreements or letters of intent. Their phony compliance not only prevented the outbreak of strikes, but also weakened the grip of the unions.[79] As Hepburn boasted a little later at a life insurance conference, "the lawlessness of the CIO will never be tolerated in Canada."[80]

It would be several months before labour leaders realized the full significance of Hepburn's words because the time seemed ripe for organizing. After bottoming out in 1933, the economy had shown hesitant, but positive, signs of growth. "We have had nearly four years of fairly consistent recovery," the Bank of Toronto reported in early 1937, "[and] in the past two years stock-market values have nearly doubled."[81] The unemployment rate, while still three times as high as in 1929, dropped by 14 per cent between 1933 and 1937.[82] With the improved conditions, skilled workers were slowly returning to the fold of their badly decimated craft unions. At the same time, the CIO unions in Canada, which organized workers across skill levels, had begun to push energetically for gains. Led by extremely committed labour activists, these industrial unions usually traced their origins to the recently disbanded, Communist Party–led Workers' Unity League (WUL). In 1935, when the Communist International (Comintern) instructed the WUL unions to build a united front against fascism, most had joined the Trades and Labour Congress (TLC), a large, traditionally craft-based labour organization with a fifty-year history.[83] Within the TLC, some of the left-leaning unions merged with powerful craft union affiliates, while others established Canadian branches of the newly formed CIO unions in the United States. When labour leaders south of the border proved reluctant to divert scarce resources from the United States, Canadian activists (both inside and outside the TLC) appropriated the CIO name and the names of CIO-affiliated unions for their own locals. Every now and then organizers, like Hugh Thompson, arrived from the United States to lead organizing campaigns. The CIO executive in the United States also appointed a few regional directors in Canada. For better or worse, however, the Canadian CIO leaders maintained only loose connections with their American counterparts.[84]

Against a backdrop of an improved economy, record profits, and huge organizing breakthroughs in the United States, Canadian workers became more convinced of their own collective power. In 1937, the national strike rate jumped by 78 per cent as a wave of walkouts spread across Ontario and British Columbia.[85] "A general atmosphere of unrest exists throughout the industrial areas of the country," a Montreal manufacturer complained.[86] The CIO organizers, whom Tom Moore, the past president of the TLC, confessed to US officials were "abler and better trained" than their opposite numbers in the craft unions, took full advantage of the situation.[87] Despite the qualified success of the General Motors strike, activists began to distribute handbills throughout Southern Ontario that celebrated, if not glorified, what the auto workers had accomplished. Given the magnetic appeal of the CIO name, a lot of their efforts involved brand recognition. With messages like "the CIO has opened the doors for all Canadian workers to organize and better their wages and conditions by collective bargaining," wage-earners flocked to the new industrial unions, eager to improve their own standing in the workplace.[88]

Between 1935 and 1938, the union membership rate in Canada swelled by nearly 34 per cent, reaching its highest peak in over fifteen years.[89] The new members were predominately white male workers. Although most union records failed to distinguish between the sex and race of their members, well-entrenched gender and racial barriers limited the number of women workers and workers of colour employed in the CIO-targeted, mass production industries.[90] As Pamela Sugiman writes in her study of Southern Ontario, "most blacks understood that auto employment was unattainable to them."[91] To be clear, marginalized workers still demonstrated solidarity and militancy. In 1937, for example, several thousand female dressmakers went out on strike in Montreal.[92] But barriers to membership also existed within the unions themselves. According to historians Ruth Frager and Carmela Patrias, "the male culture of the labour movement tended to serve as a significant impediment to women's full participation in unions."[93] More variation did exist in the ethnic backgrounds of the new members; both native-born and immigrant workers joined the organizing drives.[94] And, despite the membership limitations, the ranks of organized labour still expanded rapidly, capturing headlines. In April 1937, a *Financial Post* survey discovered the CIO had gained footholds in five major industries.[95] According to Tom McGuire of the International Union of Mine, Mill, and Smelter Workers (Mine Mill), "Workers everywhere wanted some medium of expression and security."[96]

Looking back, it is perhaps difficult to understand why workers would join the fledgling unions in the midst of the Great Depression – even with the vigorous waving of the CIO banner. They not only risked losing their jobs because of employer reprisals, but also faced the very real possibility that they would not find other work any time soon because of the economic conditions. The prices for consumer goods fell faster than wages in the 1930s, so people fortunate enough to remain employed actually experienced increases in their standards of living.[97] But unemployment was a grim prospect. Thanks to low wages, not to mention bank failures, few wage-earners had personal savings to draw on during hard times. Direct relief from government agencies and voluntary aid from private charities were also limited. In short, losing a job meant poverty and suffering. It meant no longer being able to pay for food, clothing, shelter, and medical services. It meant children having to help with the economic survival of the family. It meant leaving the security and comfort of the home to try and find work in distant lumber and mining camps. Rather than gamble on the uncertain benefits of union membership, the more prudent or rational decision would have been to endure workplace conditions. Many workers agreed. "Work was so hard to get," a textile mill employee later admitted, "you just 'took it' and you didn't say anything."[98]

Yet, there were several reasons why many women and men put their jobs on the line and became union members in the midst of the Great Depression. In many parts of Canada, wage rates fell well below what even the federal government considered a subsistence income for a family of five. With the cost of living increasing slightly towards the end of the decade, the buying power of working-class families was declining.[99] And wage-earners experienced a lot of day-to-day uncertainty because of fluctuating rates and hours. "You might arrive at the shop at 8 a.m. only to be sent home at 8:15, being told there isn't any work today," a Canadian General Electric employee recalled. "On the other hand you might work twelve or more hours, including Saturday and Sunday at regular rates."[100] Perhaps even worse, it was difficult to maintain a sense of dignity and self-worth when supervisors and managers had the authority to hire and fire at will. To stay on the good side of lower management, employees were obliged to behave obsequiously. For women, efforts to curry favour or at least not to fall into disfavour had sexual implications. Fifty-five years later, a female worker from Peterborough, Ontario, still remembered "an assistant boss who wouldn't take his hand off the girls."[101] Meanwhile, outside the workplace, well-publicized relief strikes were setting a precedent for collective action. In search of assistance and justice, thousands of working-class people had joined unemployment organizations in cities and large towns across the country. Often their anger and frustration flowed over into the streets as they protested inadequate relief,

1.3 General Motors strike, Oshawa, 1937. Nearly five hundred war veterans with medals on their coats line up at Memorial Park to protest the use of replacement workers. Despite Mitchell Hepburn's claims of foreign subversion, the strikers believed unions were an extension of Canadian democracy.

Source: Walter Reuther Library, Archives of Labor and Urban Affairs, Wayne State University, Image 11435.

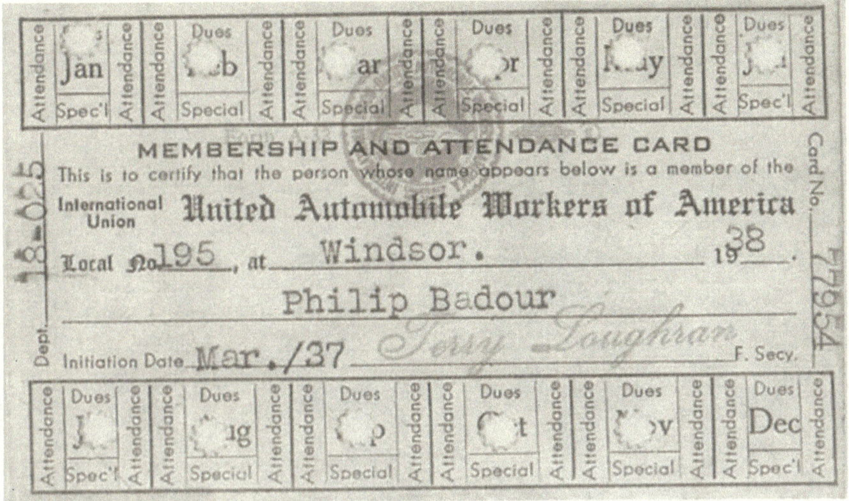

MEMBERSHIP AND ATTENDANCE CARD

This is to certify that the person whose name appears below is a member of the

International Union United Automobile Workers of America

Local No. 195, at Windsor. 1938.

Philip Badour

Initiation Date Mar./37 Terry Loughran F. Secy.

Dept. 18-025

Card No. 77954

Jan | Dec | Dues | Attendance | Special | Spec'l

1.4 United Automobile Workers (UAW) membership card, Local 195, Windsor, 1938. Note how holes were once punched for dues paid. An "air conditioned" card was when a worker paid twelve months in advance. After the war, the Rand formula and check-off provisions ended this practice.

Source: Unifor, Local 195, Windsor, Ontario.

food, and housing. In Alberta, alone, more than thirty relief strikes took place during the decade.[102]

As many historians have emphasized in recent years, the ranks of organized labour also swelled because the work experiences of wage-earners coexisted and interacted with idealized notions of gender, race, and other social relations. In her study of unemployment in the Great Depression, for example, Lara Campbell writes that "men were not 'just workers' but were also family men who laboured because of their responsibilities as husbands, fathers, and sons."[103] Besides trying to fulfill their roles as family breadwinners and providers, male workers responded to widely accepted perceptions of manliness as aggressive, strong, tough, and heroic, not to mention heterosexual – a perception engrained at home, in school, and on the streets.[104] There was nothing fixed, unified, or predictable about the meaning of working-class manhood. What it meant to act like a "man" depended on what an individual was personally thinking or doing at a particular point in time.

1.5 Léa Roback and the International Ladies' Garment Workers' Union (ILGWU), Local 262, Montreal, 1937. Female organizers, like Rose Pesotta and Léa Roback (with flowers), played a major role in winning recognition for Montreal garment workers, including orchestrating a strike of five thousand *midinettes* (dressmakers) in 1937. Afterwards, however, the male leadership of the ILGWU local limited the contributions of the predominately female membership.

Source: Léa Roback Fonds, Jewish Public Library Archives, PRO 14898

Still, a fairly narrow, highly constructed expectation of manliness did push many male workers to join unions. By becoming union members, they could act boldly and proudly, if not nobly, as "men" to confront degrading conditions in the workplace and satisfy the domestic needs of their families – to demonstrate their manliness.

Gender ideals also influenced the actions of women workers, both inhibiting and encouraging their embrace of unionism. Like with masculinity, notions of femininity were contingent, and they varied according to experience and identity. A Jewish immigrant working in the garment industry had a different understanding of what it meant to be a "woman" than a French-Canadian mill worker or an Anglo-Celtic assembly line worker. Along these lines, some women workers refused to support unions because they subscribed to middle-class notions of womanhood, preferring accommodation and loyalty to resistance and confrontation. Paternalistic managers and negative press contributed to their belief that unionism lay outside the realm of female propriety. Yet, as Joan Sangster discusses in her study of women workers in Peterborough, Ontario, "the language of respect and mutual obligation which had long justified paternalism could be appropriated, used as a rationale for women's rebellion against injustice."[105] Respectability certainly seemed key to a female strike leader in 1937, when she explained what a union meant: "You won't have to be good looking to get a break. You won't have to listen to some of that awful language we hear in the mill."[106] As mentioned earlier, what many women workers discovered was that union halls with their pub-like settings were just as gendered as workplaces. Often treated as intruders and excluded from leadership roles, female union members found themselves accommodating and contesting expectations about what constituted female and male space.[107]

Despite all the collective action, however, the flurry of organizing eventually fell flat. Union organizers soon realized that Hepburn's boast about quashing the CIO was not hyperbole. By July 1939, the Canadian CIO had signed up less than 5 per cent of its potential membership.[108] Union organizing had stalled for several different reasons. First, some of the blame lay with the "Roosevelt Recession," which hit Canada with a delayed but hefty punch between July 1937 and October 1938. A 24 per cent drop in industrial production underscored the precariousness of the economic recovery. As the unemployment rate rose from 12.5 to 15.1 per cent, union membership levels plummeted.[109] Second, with only minimal financial support from the United States, the newly formed industrial unions lacked the funds to sustain organizing campaigns and strike funds. During the General Motors strike, for example, the Canadians received a lot of empty promises, but not "one cent" of financial aid from the United States. George MacEachern of the Steel Workers' Organizing Committee (SWOC) in Sydney, Nova Scotia, admitted: "We were actually timid about going on strike because the international office had no funds … to send down here."[110] Third, and perhaps most importantly, the existing framework of labour laws did little to restrain hostile employers or, for that matter, crusading premiers. Although many workers wanted unions, they didn't want to lose their jobs or be put on an industry-wide "blacklist" for becoming members. "The main thing that had to be beaten was fear," Ray Stevenson of Mine Mill remembered, "fear of reprisal by the company, fear of being fired, fear of not being able to provide for your family."[111] Even with large memberships, unions found it extremely difficult to secure recognition or meaningful contracts. At best, the IDIA, where it did still apply following the 1925 *Snider* decision, provided the more established unions with a way to combat wage and workplace issues without having to resort to costly economic action. For more nascent unions, the national labour policy was next to useless. Intransigent employers could simply ignore the recommendations of the conciliation officers or conciliation boards; there was nothing the government could do to stop them. Without any legal recourse, workers faced the unsavoury choice of either capitulating or risking everything to go out on strike.

Labour leaders in Canada had little control over macroeconomic conditions and little influence over funding decisions made in American headquarters. But they could demand improved labour legislation at home. For many, though, this course of action involved a shift in mindset. Earlier in the decade, more radical labour leaders had denounced labour law reform as delusional "legalism" that co-opted workers.[112] How could workers wrest concessions from employers if contractual language limited their militancy and collective power? How was real social and political change going to take place if legislative bodies defined goals and behaviour? As the gains of the CIO unions proved incomplete, however, some activists began to realize that organizing workers and encouraging them to take a stand were not the same as obtaining union recognition and engaging in collective bargaining. In the late 1930s, John Stanton, a labour lawyer from British Columbia, noted that even left-leaning labour leaders began to agitate for "Wagner-style labour laws ... turning their backs, to some extent at least, on bare knuckle tactics."[113] As most of the CIO unions now recognized, it was one thing to join a picket line and quite another to win lasting concessions. Employers were too powerful and less skilled workers too vulnerable to rely solely on economic action. Improved working conditions and higher wages demanded government intervention; laws were needed to limit the arbitrary power of management and ensure negotiations for better conditions and wages.

At the TLC's 1936 convention, delegates from the CIO affiliates put forward a resolution to demand Wagner-like legislation from the federal government. For many convention attendees, however, the call for a compulsory collective bargaining law still remained an anathema. The international craft unions in the TLC were not inexorably opposed to government intervention. On the whole, they supported the operation of conciliation policies like the IDIA.[114] But the Canadian representatives of the American-based craft affiliates drew an impassable line at more forceful legislation. Many adhered to traditional notions of "voluntarism." Rather than submit their unions to the anti-labour biases of politicians and judges, they wanted industrial relations to remain in the private sphere, free of governmental interference. The only kind of labour legislation that they readily endorsed, like immigration restrictions or picketing protection, enhanced their ability to control the job markets and assert economic power. The leaders of the more established unions also worried about the spread of industrial unionism. With production techniques becoming increasingly mechanized, craft unions, like the Brotherhood of Carpenters and Joiners, had begun to organize selective pockets of less skilled workers. The TLC also granted temporary charters to federal labour unions of skilled and less skilled workers until the appropriate craft unions divided the workers up among themselves. But the CIO unions were much more effective at organizing all the workers in an industry regardless of skill levels. Overlapping and undermining the jurisdictional traditions or "property rights" of the craft unions, they were changing the rules of industrial relations.[115]

Not all the TLC delegates rejected the CIO resolution for Wagner-like legislation. Broad-minded craft unionists like J.W. Buckley, the secretary of the Toronto District Labour Council, wanted to steer a middle course between the demands of the craft and industrial unions. Patrick (Paddy) Draper, who, after many years as the TLC's secretary-treasurer, had succeeded Tom Moore as president in 1935, was also not willing to dismiss the CIO's demand. Although a member of an international union himself, he was an ardent nationalist who believed that the

Canadian labour movement should remain as unified as possible.[116] Despite the grumblings of more conservative delegates and clearly aware of the constitutional constraints, the TLC's executive drafted a model bill, more formally known as the "Freedom of Trade Union Association Act," to be submitted to the provincial governments. In contrast to existing labour policies, it guaranteed the collective rights of workers and levied criminal penalties for violations. But the model bill stopped short of forcing employer compliance or establishing administrative machinery; it lacked the teeth of a Wagner Act. Against the backdrop of the 1937 strike wave in Canada, the TLC's lobbying efforts met with success. Seven of the nine provinces decided to enact legislation along similar lines to the model bill. The only holdouts were Prince Edward Island, which had limited industry, and Ontario, where manufacturing was concentrated and Hepburn was premier. Acts in British Columbia, Nova Scotia, and Alberta actually provided for compulsory collective bargaining.[117]

The new provincial statutes were a departure from the conciliatory approach of previous labour laws. Thanks to the model bill's inadequate scope, however, they proved problematic. In lieu of independent administrative machinery, the more progressive statutes relied on the criminal courts to compel employer behaviour. This process meant trade unions had to incur legal expenses and submit to judicial biases. In 1938, one judge summarily dismissed charges brought against a large smelter in Trail, British Columbia, stating that the union's organizing efforts were like "a crown of thorns brought down on the brow of labour."[118] Moreover, none of the statutes held employers accountable for refusing to bargain collectively or for coercing union members. Instead, most of the provincial labour laws defined managerial prerogatives or authority very broadly and imposed penalties on employees who attempted to or succeeded in making fellow workers join a union against their will. Finally, only Saskatchewan distinguished between employer-influenced or company unions and bona fide unions. Taken together, these provincial laws were more forceful than the IDIA. But workers in Canada still lost more than 80 per cent of their recognition disputes between 1938 and 1939.[119]

Deep organizational and ideological fissures in the labour movement prevented further legislative gains. Despite increasing pressure from the American Federation of Labor in the United States, which suspended its CIO unions in September 1936 and expelled them a year later, the TLC initially refused to cast out its CIO affiliates. As late as the 1938 convention, Paddy Draper managed to convert forty-five resolutions on the question of the CIO into a call for unity that passed 526 to 18.[120] That same year, the CIO leaders even persuaded the TLC executive to amend the model bill so that it outlawed employer-dominated unions and included compulsory collective bargaining and the establishment of an administrative tribunal for determining certification and bargaining units.[121] But it was a pyrrhic victory. Most of the TLC's provincial executive committees failed to pursue the amendments with their respective governments. Resenting the left-leaning politics and more aggressive tactics of the CIO unions, many labour leaders in the craft unions were just waiting for the right opportunity to part ways. When a terminal illness forced Draper to resign in December 1938, tensions within the labour organization came to a head, and the more traditional craft unions prevailed. In January 1939, the TLC executive suspended the CIO unions.[122]

These actions did not enjoy widespread support among some of the craft union locals. As late as the spring of 1939, CIO leaders remained confident that "the rank and file of the AFL [American Federation of Labor] in Canada [would] defeat the effort" to oust their unions.[123] At the September convention, however, acting TLC president, R.J. Tallon, warned delegates that the executive officers of the international unions in the United States had threatened to withhold monies and to suspend their charters if the CIO unions remained in the congress. When the resolution to expel the CIO unions was subject to a rare public vote, the delegates felt compelled to cast ballots in favour or to not participate at all.[124] The motion passed by a large majority, and seven unions with a combined membership of 22,234 workers were turned out: the United Mine Workers, the Amalgamated Clothing Workers, the International Fur Workers, the International Union of Quarry Workers, the United Automobile Workers, the Steel Workers' Organizing Committee, and the Mine, Mill, and Smelter Workers. They soon joined forces with other CIO unions, like the United Electrical Workers and the International Woodworkers of America, which had remained outside the TLC.[125]

Left to their own devices, the CIO unions found that they lacked substantive political clout. Besides organizing setbacks, a serious ideological division made it difficult for them to band together as an internally cohesive and strategically coordinated movement. On the one hand, most of the formal appointments made by the US executive office – like Silby Barrett, the director for Central Canada and subregional director for the Steel Workers' Organizing Committee; or Charlie Millard, the CIO representative in Ontario, who had emerged as a strong-willed labour leader during the Oshawa General Motors strike – were social democrats. With forceful but pragmatic outlooks, they worried whether their more confrontational communist brethren recognized the realities of power and the costs of hardline positions. While acknowledging the competence of radical unionists, the social democrats in the CIO believed, in the words of one of Millard's young lieutenants, Murray Cotterill, that "it was hard enough to promote unionism without trying to carry Joe Stalin on your shoulders all the time."[126] On the other hand, the communist organizers, who had built the CIO unions from the bottom up, clearly resented the interference of the more cautious, reform-oriented leaders who placed a heavier emphasis on building bureaucratic structures and corralling worker militancy. The two factions tried to keep overt disagreements to a minimum, but considerable tension was evident. When Millard was appointed, for example, left-leaning organizers recognized that "Labour unity was more important than one person." At the same time, they hoped that if they "gave him enough rope he would hang himself."[127]

Several other labour organizations did exist in Canada, but they lacked either the will or the influence to pursue a Wagner-like act. The highly organized, international railway brotherhoods of firemen, engineers, trainmen, conductors, and brakemen, which remained independent of the TLC, already enjoyed well-established bargaining relations with employers. Heralded by the media and state officials as the "aristocracy of labour" and making up 6 to 7 per cent of the organized labour force, the running trades were mainly concerned with recouping a 15 per cent wage cut and winning the industry-wide application of the IDIA.[128] The Quebec-based Confédération des travailleurs catholiques du Canada (CTCC), which represented another 9 to 13 per cent of the labour movement, had a much different agenda. Created in 1921 as a church-driven response to international unionism, the CTCC sought to protect the cultural identity and traditional rural values of French-Canadian workers and to realize the corporatist ideal of joint committees where employers and workers looked after the general interests of one or more industries. Catholic unions did engage in economic action, but only as a last resort. In August 1937, for example, the Catholic Federation of Textile Employees conducted the largest strike of the decade when 9,000 Dominion Textile workers turned out in six different municipalities over the issues of recognition and collective bargaining, as well as wages and working conditions. Mainly focused on legislative developments at the provincial level, however, the CTCC sought broader corporatist goals that reduced class conflict. With a flexible institutional structure that encouraged organizing along craft and industrial lines, it also treated international unions as institutional rivals. There was no way the Quebec labour organization was going to pursue or support a Wagner-like act that helped other unions grow and prosper at its expense. As President Alfred Charpentier declared in 1939, the international unions "have joined hands in the destruction of the Confédération des travailleurs catholiques du Canada … But the CTCC was born to live and it will live!"[129]

Another organization, the All-Canadian Congress of Labour (ACCL), actually shared much in common with the CIO unions. Formed in 1927, when the powerful Canadian Brotherhood of Railway Employees (CBRE) joined forces with other, much smaller national unions, the ACCL made up nearly 20 per cent of the labour movement in 1935.[130] Like the CIO, its members were organized along industrial lines, often pirating TLC affiliates. Since the early 1930s, the ACCL leadership had also pushed for federal labour policies that "protect the workers' rights to organize in the manner of their choosing [and] enhance their power to bargain."[131] But the ACCL's unrelenting demands for the "Canadianization" of organized labour and the economy at large made collaborative demands with the CIO unions next to impossible – at least in the 1930s. As Norman Dowd, a leading ACCL official, proclaimed, the international unions were "an obstacle to national culture and national unity ... and ... should be broken as soon as possible."[132] The ACCL also found it difficult to influence the policy decisions of either the Conservative or the Liberal governments in the 1930s. Public officials seemed to agree with Tom Moore of the TLC that the congress was "made up of a good number of disgruntled labour leaders who had felt they had not gotten the recognition due to them under the international unions."[133] A bitter feud between two leading factions in the ACCL didn't help. In 1936, W.T. Burford, the ACCL's conservative secretary-treasurer, who belonged to a small radio and telegraph operators union in British Columbia, accused the much more dominant CBRE of pandering to communists. Within a month, Burford and ACCL president Aaron R. Mosher, who not coincidently was also the CBRE president, were contesting each other's authority in the courts. Finally, in late October, Burford led the dissenters into a reconstituted Canadian Federation of Labour (CFL). The CFL would eventually lose most of its members, becoming little more than a front for employer-dominated labour organizations.[134] And the membership base of the ACCL would soon shrink to less than 8 per cent of the labour movement.[135]

On the eve of World War II, the Canadian labour movement lacked the collective will and power to wage an effective campaign for far-reaching labour laws. Despite the limited jurisdiction and problematic application of existing policies like the IDIA, the well-entrenched craft unions of the TLC believed they had nothing to gain and much to lose by advocating for greater government intervention. Although the TLC's model bill did result in new provincial laws, the statutes offered few assurances that employers would sit down and negotiate with unions at the bargaining table. They had symbolic importance as statements of rights. But they did not come close to emulating a Wagner-like act. And, whether inside or outside the TLC, the CIO unions lacked the organizational muscle and ideological unity to sway policymakers. They had to continue to rely on the courage and determination of their organizers and workers to win greater security and dignity in the workplace. As the General Motors settlement revealed, victories usually proved incomplete. Meanwhile, the railway brotherhoods and the CTCC pursued legislative agendas that ignored or bypassed the issue of collective bargaining, while the ACCL proved too weak and divided to influence policymakers. With numerous internecine differences, not to mention unstable membership levels, the labour movement was at cross purposes when it came to labour legislation in the late 1930s.

The Employers

Sitting at his desk, G. Blair Gordon, the thirty-eight-year-old managing director of the Dominion Textile Company, which sold over 50 per cent of the cotton yarn and cloth in Canada, angrily reread the letter. The scion of a powerful Montreal family and reputedly the best polo player in the city, he did not like to be told how to run his business. Yet, here was the labour minister, Norman Rogers, urging him to bargain collectively with the Catholic Federation of Textile Employees. Gordon immediately dictated a response. He explained that his company had signed a one-year agreement with the federation following a large strike of Dominion Textile workers in 1937. Now that the contract had expired, he was unwilling to enter into new negotiations with the union. There were two reasons why. First, given the Great Depression, the industry remained too fragile for Dominion Textile to commit to fixed, much less improved, wages and hours. "When conditions and prospects have become more stabilized," offered Gordon, "we can then consider further collective bargaining with our employees." Second, the federation had used coercive tactics to sign up workers during the strike. As the courts subsequently agreed, it was a "campaign of intimidation by a militant minority of Catholic union members and 'sympathizers,' the latter including hired thugs." The company would not contribute to the "debasement" of collective bargaining by entering into negotiations with these "self-seekers who have little to lose in the long run and much to gain in the short term." This position was not "an arbitrary stand," he insisted, but a reflection of "the real situation." Although not opposed to the idea of collective bargaining, Gordon would decide when and with whom: Dominion Textile would engage in collective bargaining at its own discretion.[136]

Gordon's letter to Rogers typified corporate attitudes towards union organizing and collective bargaining in the late 1930s. Most employers in Canada abhorred unions. As the textile baron indicated, much of the animosity was economically motivated. Of all the advanced industrialized countries in the world, only the United States had encountered a greater decline in industrial output than Canada.[137] Although the *Toronto Globe* (shortly before its merger with the *Mail and Empire*) reported midway through the decade that "the records of increased physical volume of production ... provide inescapable support for optimism," few industrialists believed that they could afford the inflated costs associated with organized labour.[138] "There seems very little purpose in running this steel mill at all if we must raise the wages of the men while the Company is losing money," protested Sir James Dunn, president of Algoma Steel Corporation in Sault Ste Marie, Ontario.[139] Indeed, the intensified organizing activities of the CIO unions prompted managers of US branch plants, which produced over 25 per cent of the goods and employed nearly 20 per cent of the workers in Canada, to wonder if escalating wage rates might erase the cost advantage of manufacturing north of the border.[140]

Besides more material concerns, employers were extremely protective of their managerial prerogatives. Given the dictates of the marketplace, they believed that a profit-oriented firm required a hierarchical structure where the manager acted as the sole legitimate authority. This axiom was especially true in mass production industries where large, unskilled labour markets prevailed. The survival of an enterprise demanded that its employees defer to the unilateral decisions of management. How else could employers fulfill their primary responsibility of operating an efficient and profitable business? At Empire Cotton Mills in Welland, Ontario, for example, the management felt no compunction about decreasing wages until workers learned how to operate new machines at a faster pace. "It is really a case where they are being paid for going to school," a spokesperson explained to the local newspaper.[141] Uncertain where trade unions would draw the line in their demands, especially the more aggressive CIO unions, most employers refused to concede voluntarily, even to a partial degree, their right to manage. Whether it was determining wages and working conditions or defining the terms and conditions of collective bargaining, corporate decision-making must prevail. As Gordon made clear, he wouldn't give any "heed to the suggestions of irresponsible parties that they should have a hand in shaping the labour policies of the Management of the Company."[142]

In the mid-1930s, Canadian employers appeared relatively satisfied with the status of federal labour legislation. After all, the IDIA did not apply to most of the industrial workforce. And, when it did, nothing compelled management to recognize unions, engage in collective bargaining, or limit union discrimination. If anything, the IDIA seemed a useful tool for stalling and deflecting union drives. Any suggestion of more forceful measures, however, raised a loud outcry. After witnessing developments in the United States, for example, many Canadian executives denounced the 1933 passage of the National Industrial Recovery Act (NIRA), which required participating firms to guarantee workers minimum wages, maximum hours, and, most controversially, the right to collective representation.[143] There were exceptions. A number of employers in industries like construction and garment manufacturing, where low barriers to entry resulted in widely fluctuating labour costs, did support the passage of industrial standards acts in Ontario (1935), Alberta (1935), Nova Scotia (1936), Saskatchewan (1937), and New Brunswick (1939). Loosely based on the NIRA, these provincial statutes allowed government-supervised joint conferences of employers and employees to draft binding, industry-wide schedules of wages and hours. Importantly, however, the industrial standards acts stopped short of recognizing the right of workers to organize and bargain collectively.[144] As the Canadian Manufacturers' Association (CMA) declared in 1935: "[T]he great majority of employers would not approve of any interference with, or derogation from, the right to deal directly with their own employees."[145]

Willing to utilize political connections and flex economic muscle whenever necessary, individual employers, like G. Blair Gordon, regularly shared their anti-union views with high-ranking politicians. More

1.6 G. Blair Gordon, Dominion Textile

Source: *Winnipeg Tribune*, 8 June 1945, 12, Library and Archives Canada, Amicus No. 3831471.

reactive than proactive, they tended to make contact in the midst of a crisis. On behalf of mining interests, for example, George McCullagh, the president and chief editor of the newly created *Globe and Mail*, wined and dined Ian Mackenzie, the minister of national defence, to win support for General Motors during the 1937 strike.[146] These corporate appeals did sway cabinet members who already felt little empathy for the collective rights of workers. But they failed to influence the people most responsible for industrial relations in the government. Norman Rogers, the minister of labour, had little patience for belligerent anti-union attitudes. Convinced that collective bargaining was the key to industrial peace, he even threatened to resign his position when colleagues like Jimmy Gardiner, the minister of agriculture, began to question the federal government's tolerance of the CIO in Canada.[147] And Mackenzie King, while always susceptible to political pressures, condemned the unreasonable stances of employers, especially when

1.7 J. Stanley McLean, Canada Packers

Source: *Winnipeg Tribune*, 6 July 1938, 3, Library and Archives Canada, Amicus No. 382147.

1.8 R.J. Magor, National Steel Car Corporation

Source: *Toronto Daily Star*, 4 July 1942, 12, Library and Archives Canada, Amicus No. 7791836.

1.9 Harold Crabtree, Howard Smith Paper Mills

Source: *Winnipeg Tribune*, 11 June 1941, 17, Library and Archives Canada, Amicus No. 3821471.

they involved the exploitation of workers. With the Rockefellers as close friends, he certainly did not have an aversion to wealth and status. He was also a strong supporter of private enterprise and the pursuit of profit as an economic system. Much like his distaste for hardline labour leaders, however, King could not countenance truculent employers who refused to engage in negotiation and compromise. He considered their actions both immoral and dangerous. For a more humane and orderly society, he told King Edward VIII during a visit to London in 1936, management "would have to learn to share control or else would lose control altogether."[148]

Despite all their posturing, though, business leaders in Canada actually exerted little real influence over labour legislation. Or, to put it a bit differently, their opposition did not prevent the passage of a Wagner-like act in Canada. The deaf ears of King and Rogers explained

1.10 Battle of Ballantyne Pier, Vancouver, 1935. Confronted with a communist-led recognition campaign on the Vancouver waterfront, the BC Shipping Federation not only organized other employers in an anti-union crusade, but also arranged for several hundred armed officers from the city police force, BC provincial police, and RCMP to attack a defiant, but peaceful, parade of one thousand longshoremen. The longshoremen would not win union recognition for another ten years.

Source: Major James Skitt Matthews, City of Vancouver Archives, CVA 371-1127.

some of the corporate ineffectiveness. But another important factor was ambivalence. Although business organizations flourished during the Great Depression, employers preferred to deal with unions in their own ways and on their own terms at the moment of a crisis. Instead of implementing well-developed union avoidance schemes or participating in strategic lobbying efforts, they treated labour relations as a secondary corporate function and used ad hoc measures to thwart unionism. To borrow a phrase from industrial relations scholar Sanford Jacoby, it was "management by putting out fires."[149] This approach hadn't always been the case. After a series of general strikes in 1919, not to mention the revolutions in Russia and Germany, nervous employers had initiated a wide range of farsighted anti-union plans. Personnel departments also became more prevalent.[150] With the subsequent decline of organized labour in the 1920s and the tremendous setbacks of the Depression, however, firms began to overlook labour issues while they focused on stabilizing prices and/or finding new markets.[151] As war in Europe became more of an imminent reality, especially with the German invasion of Czechoslovakia in 1938, rearmament became the overriding concern. Given the limited scale and scope of the existing labour legislation, not to mention the abundant supply of unemployed workers, few employers were willing to spend the time, energy, and finances on industrial relations.[152]

The handful of companies that did take a proactive approach usually tried to ward off unions with long-term employment policies to secure the loyalty of their workers. The leading spokesperson for this more benevolent strategy, J. Stanley McLean, the president of Canada Packers, the huge meatpacking enterprise, explained that solutions to the labour problem "will not derive from an atmosphere of recrimination and strife, but of co-operation based on a genuine sense of partnership."[153] Along these lines, Canada Packers and a small number of diverse companies like Westclox (clocks), Penmans' (textiles), Campbell Soup (food products), John Labatt (beer), and the Dominion Foundries and Steel Company or Dofasco (steel) offered workers various profit-sharing, pension, and insurance schemes, as well as less expensive benefits like recreational activities and food facilities. They also attempted to check the arbitrary powers of their foremen and supervisors. Motivated by a strong dose of paternalism, these "progressive" employers considered it a moral imperative to look out for the best interests of their workers.[154] As one Ontario businessman claimed in 1937: "We have done everything we reasonably could do for our employees. We look on them as our friends."[155] They were also influenced by modern personnel management techniques that emphasized production increases through non-wage incentives.[156] In return for more humane capitalist practices, though, these employers expected loyalty and discipline from their workers, not unionism; they remained ardently opposed to organized labour. In 1936 and 1937, for example, Dofasco purged several union organizers from its payroll. The company also threatened to end its profit-sharing scheme if workers joined a union.[157] Although these benevolent efforts emphasized mutual interest over class struggle, they also reaffirmed uneven power relations and managerial prerogatives.

No single variable, like the type of industry or the size of a firm, determined how an employer responded to the threat of unions. A number of companies, like Algoma Steel, Canada Steamship Lines, BF Goodrich, and the women's garment manufacturers of Winnipeg, put up little resistance when confronted with recognition drives. Some believed that organized labour might help to limit price competition and/or stabilize industrial relations. Others simply wanted to avoid lengthy and costly disputes (though, like BF Goodrich, they often stopped short of bona fide recognition).[158] No hard and fast rules explain why these particular enterprises chose less confrontational approaches. Nor can any causal generalizations be made about more belligerent employer behaviour. In contrast to Algoma Steel, one of the smallest firms in the steel industry, the much larger Dofasco of Hamilton implemented its welfare plan while, literally next door, the Steel Company of Canada (Stelco) engaged in much more confrontational tactics.[159] Unlike Canada Steamship Lines, the largest carrier on the Great Lakes, most other shipping companies, both large and small, tried to force their seamen to join a CFL affiliate that was little more than a corporate front.[160] And, in contrast to BF Goodrich, J.A. Martin, the general manager of the Dominion Rubber Company in Kitchener, Ontario, threatened to move his plant out of the city and even out of the province when confronted with a recognition strike.[161] Rather than structural factors, it seems that individual management styles and the particular conditions at hand determined employer behaviour.

More combative anti-union responses ran a fairly limited gamut. At the first sign of trouble, most managers simply fired the ringleaders and union sympathizers, adding their names to a "blacklist" or roll of undesirables that circulated around the industry or community. "I was getting nowhere," remembered C.S. Jackson of the United Electrical Workers. "A group would get started and bingo – the leadership was fired or intimidated."[162] In Kirkland Lake, Ontario, the Lakeshore Gold Mine terminated 270 workers after discovering a single union application card.[163] Two sawmills in Port Alberni, British Columbia, owned by the rival lumber conglomerates of H.R. MacMillan Export and Bloedel, Stewart & Welch, jointly fired seventy-five workers who had just become members of the International Woodworkers of America.[164] The president of the Monarch Knitting Company fired the shop committee of an ACCL union and threatened to close down the plant if union activities continued.[165] And the Consumer Gas Company in Toronto dismissed several employees for their association with an ACCL union, while obliging their remaining workers to sign "yellow dog" contracts that stated they would agree, under penalty of termination, not to join a union.[166] What's more, company spies were often used to expose union agitators, forcing labour organizers to engage in clandestine activities that protected the identities of members, yet hampered union growth.[167] TLC president Paddy Draper, who according to the *Ottawa Citizen* was not someone "to make such accusations against employers," charged that Corporations Auxiliary, a US-based firm under congressional investigation, had planted labour spies in the mining towns of Northern Ontario. Their findings led to the dismissal of forty-seven Mine Mill members in just one week.[168]

Given the elimination of many personnel departments in the 1930s, companies usually relied on the hiring and firing practices of their on-site foremen and labour supervisors to defeat organizing drives before they gained momentum. As mentioned earlier, these low-ranking but influential taskmasters ruled over the interwar workplaces with what historian Peter McInnis calls "arbitrary tyranny," meting out discipline and favouritism at will.[169] Often they cared more about maintaining the flow of production than looking out for the well-being of the workers. "They treated you like their disposables," a steel mill employee recalled, adding that complaints were met with the standard retort: "If you don't like it you know what to do ... There's the gate."[170] At Ford Canada in Windsor, Ontario, foremen were so consumed with production demands that they timed bathroom breaks, peering over the specially designed, half-sized doors of toilet stalls to identify lingerers. Spending all of their time on the floor or in the camps and mines, the foremen and supervisors could realize fairly early on when workers were considering a union drive. Often, on their own initiative, they launched counter campaigns of thinly veiled threats to explain the "downsides" of unionism and especially strikes. At one factory, for example, workers "were dragged from the line … to look at the unemployed lined up at the gates."[171] Although usually promoted from among the ranks of the workers themselves, these "walking bosses" had little tolerance for collective action, perhaps apprehensive about what a union presence would mean for their own positions. With managers reluctant to undermine their authority and generally supportive of such actions, the foremen and supervisors provided an effective front-line defence against labour activism.[172]

Most employers – including, ironically, the executives of foreign-owned subsidiaries – liked to vilify union organizers, especially those from the CIO, as "outsiders" as soon as they appeared at the factory gates.[173] These xenophobic taunts spoke to the very real concerns that a large number of native-born Canadians, inside and outside the workplace, had about cultural dilution. With English-speaking Canadians worried about threats to their Anglo-Celtic identity and French-speaking Canadians worried about threats to their Catholic values, corporate efforts to deride unionism as a foreign blight proved effective. They usually involved blatant prejudice and discrimination. Since many native-born Canadians belittled immigrants as culturally, morally, and politically deficient, companies liked to highlight the ethnic backgrounds of union organizers whenever possible. In British Columbia, for example, the managing director of Pioneer Gold Mines, Dr Howard T. James, created such a furore about non-Anglo interlopers that local labour activists felt obliged to point out that, except for one individual with Norwegian background, they were all of "good old English and Scotch-Canadian stock."[174] Playing to the rampant anti-Semitism in the country, employers also liked to point out the Jewish backgrounds of union organizers. An employee at a garment factory in Toronto remembered how managers "would try to bring in the racial question, about the Jewish people, telling us that we should not belong to a union at all that was controlled by Jews."[175] Whether accurate or not, employers also liked to brand union organizers, especially CIO organizers, as revolutionary communists or, in other words, the purveyors of non-Canadian ideas and activities. As Ross McMaster, the Stelco president, insisted: "Their aim is to ... threaten not only the stability of labour relations, but political institutions as well."[176] Finally, much was made of the tenuous links between the Canadian CIO and their presumably powerful and lawless counterparts in the United States. "We in Minto," one coal operator proclaimed during a recognition strike, "are fighting for the whole of New Brunswick in opposing the first entrance of the CIO and the dictatorship of John L. Lewis and his henchmen."[177] Already convinced by newspapers and movies that the United States was a land of vice and crime, this connection was not much of a stretch for most morally righteous Canadians.[178]

Many employers also resurrected a popular anti-union technique of the 1920s called representation plans, industrial works councils, plant committees, or the more damning label of company unions. As an industrial relations advisor to the Rockefeller family, Mackenzie King had originally devised the strategy to ensure continuous production, not to thwart unionism. He viewed his employee representation scheme as a midway point on the organizational continuum. Rather than let highly charged union recognition disputes paralyze the production process, why not arrange to have worker and management representatives meet periodically to discuss company policies and workplace grievances? Once the channels of communication opened up and mutual trust was established, the union question could be revisited. What King hadn't anticipated was that corporations would use his plan to sidetrack and avert union drives. In the late 1930s, most arrangements represented quick fixes, hammered together in response to a pending or ongoing union campaign and adorned with a great deal of fanfare about shared decision-making; they were reactive, not proactive.[179] Two months after writing to Norman Rogers, for example, G. Blair Gordon created works councils at several Dominion Textile mills in order to "promote harmony and accord between employer and employee."[180] To be sure, the plant committees did not always work as planned. George MacEachern, a SWOC organizer, remembered that labour activists sometimes used "the company-sponsored plant council to build a real union. You were given a great deal of freedom if you were on the council."[181] Still, beneath the pretense of industrial democracy, employers usually dominated the proceedings. Although Frank M. Morton, the vice-president of International Harvester in Hamilton, likened what went on in the meetings to "collective bargaining," managerial prerogatives usually remained intact, and workers lacked the collective strength of organized labour. A popular business journal revealed the true motive of these works councils when it regaled Selwyn G. Blaylock, the president of Consolidated Mining and Smelting Company of Canada and creator of the "Blaylock System of Workmen's Co-operation Committees," as "[a] 'monarch' who has ruled his empire so wisely and so well, that, of their own accord, his employees have gradually forgotten the unions which flourished before his reign and whose labour relations are considered by many as a textbook example."[182]

To help snuff out more tenacious organizing drives and strikes, hostile employers almost routinely called upon local and provincial government officials for police protection. When municipal officials proved reluctant to comply with corporate demands, they discovered how powerful employers could make it extremely difficult for them.

During the Dominion Textile strike of 1937, for example, G. Blair Gordon publicly lambasted the mayor of Drummondville, Quebec, when he hesitated to take a hard line against picketers.[183] By involving law enforcement agencies, these companies hoped to stigmatize the unions as dangerous, if not anarchistic, and to convince strikers that they were fighting losing battles. Two factors helped employers realize these objectives. First, the police often seemed to instigate or tacitly support violence against strikers. In 1935, for example, hundreds of police on foot and horseback attacked approximately 1,000 striking longshoremen in Vancouver with clubs and tear gas, while other police provided cover with machine guns.[184] In 1937, several hundred vigilantes armed with blunt objects stormed sit-down strikers in the Holmes Foundry near Sarnia, Ontario, while the Ontario Provincial Police observed from a distance and then promptly arrested the strikers when they staggered out of the plant.[185] Second, by escorting strikebreakers into a workplace and safeguarding the passage of loaded trucks and rail cars, the police often incited violent reactions from strikers that inevitably tarnished a union's reputation in the community. Well aware that General Motors in Oshawa would try to provoke retaliation, Hugh Thompson, the UAW representative, told strikers that "as long as you maintain discipline you have the public on your side."[186]

Resistant employers could also rely on another branch of the state, the common-law courts, to counter the collective efforts of workers. Confused policymaking was to blame for the often pivotal roles of judges in labour disputes. In 1872, the federal government of John A. Macdonald had passed the Trade Unions Act to exclude registered unions from prosecution for criminal conspiracy in restraint of trade and the Criminal Law Amendments Act to restrict strike actions like "molesting, obstructing, watching, and besetting." Although both laws legitimized, at least ostensibly, the existence of unions, the legal boundaries for strike activities lacked clear definition. After all, what does "watching and besetting" involve?[187] A few years later, the labour movement managed to have provisions for peaceful picketing included in the Criminal Code, but once again the terms of conduct remained vague. The government left the determination of what constituted appropriate behaviour in labour disputes to judge-made common law.[188] By the late 1930s, employers only needed to prove a strike constituted a legal "nuisance" to obtain an injunction that made it illegal to continue the economic action. If the strikers failed to abide by the injunctions, they faced contempt of court proceedings, jail time, and financial penalties.

And it was not difficult for employers to win injunctions. Many judges were uninformed about labour relations, acquainted socially with top managers, and predisposed to conformity. They often defined the legal doctrine of "nuisance" as simply an act that hurt a firm's business, not one that was clearly wrongful in character. What's more, in granting injunctions, the judges only had to rely upon the affidavit evidence or sworn testimony of the employer; the unions had no opportunity to make counterarguments. Writing in 1936, Toronto labour lawyer J.L. Cohen observed that injunctions "effectively turn the scales in an industrial dispute [especially] at the critical moment of a strike."[189]

With individual employers fairly confident that they could handle unions on their own, business associations rarely pursued labour policy concerns during the late 1930s. Some resource-oriented organizations, like the British Columbia Loggers' Association, did keep a close eye on legislative developments. But most business groups maintained small memberships that focused almost exclusively on reducing competition in a particular industry.[190] Even the Canadian Chamber of Commerce, which represented a much broader membership and considered more general business problems, seemed to pay little attention to labour relations, perhaps because it was dominated by capital-intensive firms like banks and investment brokerages.[191] The Canadian Manufacturers' Association (CMA) was the only national business association in Canada to take an active interest in labour policy. Since its inception in 1900, the association had spent a great deal of time and energy trying to contain industrial unrest and derail labour policy. Beginning in 1917, an Industrial Relations Committee had met regularly to consider labour conditions and make policy recommendations. During the 1920s, for example, it encouraged members to introduce works councils while denouncing proposed legislation that "constituted an unwarranted interference with an employer's management of his own business."[192]

Like individual business leaders, however, the CMA found it difficult to influence policymakers. In the late 1930s, for example, it failed to prevent seven of the nine provinces from enacting the new labour laws that were based on the TLC's model bill. Although the association launched a series of counteroffensives in provincial legislatures, it quickly realized that it was waging a losing battle – except in Ontario, where Mitchell Hepburn controlled sixty-four of the ninety seats in the legislature.[193] The CMA tried to arrange for amendments that made the trade unions legally accountable for breach of contract and required to file copies of their constitutions, officer lists, and financial statements with government authorities. But it met with only mixed success. Although five of the seven statutes did include filing requirements, only Quebec held the unions liable for damages. In an overreaction to the toothless provincial laws, the Industrial Relations Committee lamented that the statutes signaled an end to the private ordering of industrial relations in Canada.[194]

The provincial statutes revealed two problems with the CMA's lobbying efforts. First, given the ambivalent attitude of employers to industrial relations, the business association usually played a game of policy catch-up. Rather than implement a long-term strategy to block unwanted bills, it had to confine lobbying activities to responding after the fact to legislative initiatives and government inquiries.[195] Second, the CMA lacked a broad consensus in the business community. While the membership included 75 to 80 per cent of those firms eligible to join in the country, it excluded employers that were not solely engaged in manufacturing, like vertically integrated and/or natural resource enterprises.[196] The membership restrictions were not uncommon. Thanks to the particular pattern of industrial development in Canada, the business community was highly fragmented, making cooperation across economic sectors, if not industries and firms, extremely difficult.[197] Even though employers throughout the country shared a firm, if not fervent, opposition to unionism, they lacked the collective capacity to sway labour policy outcomes. In early 1939, the Industrial Relations Committee seemed to admit as much when it urged members to forgo government interactions and instead convince workers on the shop floor that it was better to "get justice by dealing with their employers directly, rather than by fighting their employers, or supporting compulsory legislation regulating labour conditions."[198]

Other Groups

Bora Laskin, the future chief justice of the Supreme Court of Canada, walked up to the podium at the lakeside resort and launched into his lecture. It had been quite a year. Returning to Toronto in June 1937 with a LLM from Harvard University, he had tried repeatedly to obtain a position in an influential law firm or academic department. Confronted with anti-Semitism at every turn, the only permanent work he had found was with the *Canadian Abridgement* project, writing countless case summaries for a digest on Canadian common law. Understandably frustrated, Laskin decided to use his spare time to educate others about labour legislation, building on two articles he had written at Harvard on picketing and injunctions. Over the next several months, he taught evening classes at the Workers' Educational Association (WEA); gave a talk to the Labour Research Institute about the need for a Wagner Act in Canada; wrote a number of reports about existing labour policies for the Industrial Law Research Council; completed a short book on trade unionism for the WEA; and presented four lectures about the legal status of trade unions on CBC Radio. Now, in August 1938, he found himself speaking as a labour law "expert" at the highly regarded Lake Couchiching conference of the Canadian Institute on Economics and Politics near Orillia, Ontario. Although not tall, the twenty-five-year-old Laskin cut an imposing figure with his thick athletic build, wavy hair, and penetrating eyes.[199] Looking out over the audience, he offered two key reasons why Canada needed compulsory labour legislation. First, the common law was inadequate for "new social forces" like labour relations. Not only did it rely on "essentially individualistic notions" that devalued collective rights, but also judges had "neither the qualifications nor the facilities ... to deal adequately with the questions involved." Second, the recent passages of the TLC-inspired provincial statutes, while a "marked advance," were not enough, because they fell short of compelling behaviour. Thanks to their inadequate provisions, collective bargaining disputes were "still dumped into the laps of magistrates." What was needed was a Wagner-like act, which created the administrative machinery to promote and enforce proper conduct. "[A]ssuming that collective bargaining is a desirable method of ensuring industrial peace," he argued, "there should be some legislative guarantee of its effective operation."[200]

To borrow from Shakespeare, many Canadians would have found Laskin's call for a Canadian Wagner Act "wondrous strange." In the late 1930s, few people understood why unions, especially the more confrontational CIO unions, needed legislative protection. The escalating strike rate didn't help. With newspaper editors claiming that "outside professional trouble-makers with political ambitions" had commandeered the labour movement, many middle-class Canadians feared that the strike violence in the United States, like most recently at Republic Steel in Chicago, would spread north of the border.[201] But Laskin's audience at the Lake Couchiching conference, a place where academics, civil servants, journalists, and other well-informed participants gathered for two weeks every summer to debate the weighty issues of the day, probably responded favourably. Indeed, for the past year or so, a modest number of well-educated, politically concerned citizens had begun to turn their attention to industrial relations. Mainly from privileged backgrounds and the larger cities, few had direct ties to the labour movement and most rejected radical politics. If anything, they had been ambivalent about labour issues just a few years earlier. Shaken by the vagaries of the Great Depression and the continued unrest of the workers, however, they now recognized that the employment relationship between workers and employers had a wide-ranging impact on the public good. "Industrial relations are a part of life," argued W.A. Mackintosh of Queen's University, "an important and even critical phase of modern life."[202] Although more a collection of disparate forces than a cohesive bloc, they connected a strong economy and stable social order to a more fair and just balance of power in the workplace. And, unlike earlier generations of Canadians, these well-connected, outspoken reformers believed that Ottawa had both the responsibility and the expertise to regulate the activities of workers and employers.

Bora Laskin, himself, belonged to a small but energetic segment of the legal profession that believed comprehensive labour legislation was the key to industrial peace and business efficiency. Often working under the auspices of the WEA, several law professors at the University of Toronto taught courses at night school and wrote papers to convince both labour leaders and politicians that government regulation was the answer to the current labour strife.[203] As Jacob Finkelman, who created the first labour law course at the University of Toronto, explained: "The social utility of trade unions in the modern industrial community has become almost axiomatic."[204] Meanwhile, far removed from the hallowed halls of academe, labour lawyers, like J.L. Cohen in Central Canada and John Stanton in British Columbia, were making passionate, articulate pleas for policy reform in the courts and the press, as well as in some union headquarters. As legal advisors to the labour movement, they understood, perhaps better than anyone, the inadequacies of the existing legislative framework. Poorly paid and practicing a relatively new branch of law, they lacked the prestige and status of most other lawyers. Yet, unhampered by the formal codes of the profession and brimming over with conviction, they proved willing to voice their opinions to anyone who would listen.[205]

Justice William Turgeon of the Saskatchewan Court of Appeals was also calling for compulsory legislation. In January 1936, when G. Blair Gordon of Dominion Textile abruptly shut down one of his mills to punctuate demands for higher tariff rates, the King cabinet had appointed Turgeon to be chair of a royal commission that delved into the operations of the entire textile industry. During months of public hearings, the justice was shocked to learn about the industry's appalling working conditions and inferior wage rates, as well as the vehemently anti-union sentiments of mill operators. In his final report to the King cabinet in January 1938, he used strong language to convey his dismay. By ignoring or opposing the collective rights of their workers, the employers were "short-sighted" and acting "contrary to their own interests." Given that the mills regularly colluded to win high tariff rates, it was unreasonable that they "deny to their workers the same right of organization." Furthermore, "legislation appears necessary for those employers who continue to refuse to recognize trade unions."[206] Mackenzie King buried the report. He had established the Textile Commission to teach Gordon a lesson and to defer further discussion of the tariff question, not to serve as a legislative catalyst. Still, Turgeon's remarks made an impact. "The comment on employee relations," one business paper reported, "is by far the most complete section of the report and apparently one with which the commissioner has sympathetic leanings."[207]

Besides legal minds, religious leaders, mainly associated with the United Church of Canada, preached the virtues of organizing and collective bargaining. "Pray by all means, but do not stop there," Reverend John T. Stapleton of Hamilton's Grace United Church urged his congregation of Dofasco employees. "I advise workers to take action and form themselves into strong industrial unions."[208] According to Reverend John Coburn, who served on the Evangelism and Social Service staff of the United Church: "The right of collective bargaining ... is now conceded by all well-informed and socially-minded people ... [L]abour must be effectively organized ... and become a mighty force in creating a new and more equitable social order."[209] Often inspired by a philosophy of Christian socialism, though allegedly apolitical, these clergymen felt that a strong labour movement would help to overcome the immorality of unrestrained capitalism. Many belonged to the Fellowship for a Christian Social Order, a theological think tank of over 250 clergy and laity that, according to its mandate, sought to build "a new society in which all exploitation of man by man and all barriers to the abundant life which are created by private ownership of property shall be done away."[210] Although often at odds with the church hierarchy and eventually victim to ideological divisions, they were prolific writers, and their articles reached a wide audience.[211]

More indirectly, prominent liberals and left-leaning intellectuals were translating their civil liberties concerns into support for the labour movement. Led by people like R.L. Calder, the former Crown prosecutor of Montreal, or F.R. Scott, a McGill law professor, they were reacting to the 1937 passage of the "Padlock Law" in Quebec.[212] Following Mackenzie King's repeal of the repressive sections of the Criminal Code and Immigration Act, Premier Duplessis had decided to make it illegal for any house or hall "to propagate communism or bolshevism."[213] Since no definition of communism was actually offered in the act, the premier took it upon himself to close down all operations that hinted of subversive behaviour – especially unions. In January 1938, for example, the police raided the homes of every Steel Workers' Organizing Committee member in the province.[214] As one member of the Canadian Seamen's Union recalled, the Padlock Law "was used against any social or labour organization regardless of whether it was communist or not."[215] Across the country, influential citizens, who feared that Duplessis's abuse of legislative powers mirrored the rise of fascism in Europe, expressed their disgust with the assault on democratic rights. The Civil Liberties Committee, later known as the Canadian Civil Liberties Union, formed and quickly began a campaign to convince Ottawa to repeal the draconian measure.[216] These defenders of civil liberties were more concerned about protecting individual freedoms than assuring the rights of labour. But they did argue that a true democracy had to condone the collective actions of workers. Although sometimes manipulated by a communist agenda, their message was broadly received. At one event in Toronto, 350 "leading men and women" attended a twelve-hour conference on the Padlock Law.[217]

At the same time, the Co-operative Commonwealth Federation (CCF), Canada's fledgling social democratic party, the self-professed voice of labour in Parliament, was becoming more influential in mainstream politics. Formed in 1932 as an odd alliance of intellectuals, farmers, and labourites, it initially lacked much political power, winning only 7 of the 119 seats it contested in the 1935 election.[218] Despite the union backgrounds of several CCF members of Parliament (MPs) and the staunch support of many labour leaders, the party also found it challenging to establish solid relations with organized labour. Internecine differences were a big part of the problem. Rural members saw themselves at cross purposes with wage labour. And academics from Central Canada routinely denigrated the pragmatic, short-term objectives of union executives. As David Lewis, the CCF's part-time national secretary, acknowledged in 1937: "The situation is terribly bad. The Movement is at a low ebb."[219] Yet, towards the end of the decade, the CCF began to make inroads with the labour movement and to gain political traction.[220] Thanks to the efforts of Lewis, who became a full-time officer in 1938, resolutions were passed at party conventions that pledged the CCF's commitment to "do everything possible to assist and promote the interests of workers in the inevitable conflicts which are bound to arise."[221] This commitment included pushing for more comprehensive labour legislation at the provincial and federal levels of government. The national secretary also distributed leaflets that clearly stated the CCF's support for unionism to all the labour organizations in the country. In the summer of 1938, his hard work paid off when District 26 of the United Mine Workers in Cape Breton, Nova Scotia, voted, in an unprecedented move, to affiliate with the social democratic party, injecting it with much-needed funds. The centralization efforts of Lewis and Major Coldwell, a Saskatchewan MP and the CCF's national chair, also went a long way towards strengthening the party's organizational structure and fund-raising capabilities.[222]

The CCF tried to translate its newfound influence into labour policy gains. Beginning in 1937, J.S. Woodsworth, the party's highly respected leader, introduced private member's bills into the House of Commons that called for the penalization of union discrimination under the Criminal Code. Much like Léon Gouin before the Rowell-Sirois Commission, he insisted that a Criminal Code amendment circumvented constitutional impediments to guaranteeing a worker's freedom of association. He also argued that employees had the same right to organize into unions as employers had to organize through incorporation. At least initially, his innovative policy submissions fell flat. Both Ernest Lapointe and Norman Rogers quickly repudiated Woodsworth's measures. While Lapointe asserted that labour legislation was a provincial matter, Rogers (no doubt under King's direction) claimed that the conciliatory procedures of the IDIA were more than adequate, and that the federal government preferred to appeal to principles.[223]

Then, in spring 1939, there appeared to be a breakthrough. Faced with the growing appeal of the labour movement, an increasingly confident CCF, and an impending election, the prime minister decided to take action. When Woodsworth reintroduced his measure for the third time, Ernest Lapointe responded with a government bill that protected freedom of association. Despite loud objections from the Conservative

Party, the amendment took effect on 1 August as section 502A of the Criminal Code.[224] The CCF appeared to have won a major victory for the labour movement. Or had it? Not according to Lapointe. As the justice minister assured Ross McMaster of Stelco: "I, with my law officers, changed and altered the Bill of Mr. Woodsworth so that its dangerous features [were] eliminated and that it [will remain] within the jurisdiction of the Parliament of Canada."[225] Indeed, section 502A was a watered-down facsimile of Woodsworth's bill. It applied only in those provinces where similar legislation already existed; in Ontario, where union discrimination remained legal, the amendment was inapplicable. The prosecution also had to prove that an employer had no other reason besides "the sole reason" of union membership for dismissing an employee and that an employer had issued a threat "to compel" an employee not to join a union. Ambiguous justifications and milder forms of dissuasion proved easy to defend. Finally, section 502A only protected employees against reprisals for union membership. More aggressive union activities, like organizing, were still subject to discrimination. As labour lawyer J.L. Cohen remarked: "The protection afforded is illusory."[226]

That was it for federal labour policy in the late 1930s. Despite the slow swelling of popular support and the long wave of strikes, Mackenzie King refused to consider or allow any other labour policy innovations in Canada, certainly not a Wagner-like act. Although adamantly opposed to unions, the business community had little to do with his inaction. Regardless of their economic power, employers were too individualistic and shortsighted to exert much influence over policymaking. Perhaps a stronger, more cohesive labour movement could have pushed the prime minister in the right direction. With numerous internal differences and unstable membership levels, however, the labour movement lacked the collective will and organizational clout to pursue innovative labour legislation. The only real policy achievement for the unions – the adoption of the TLC's model bill in seven of nine provinces – failed to curtail union discrimination and ensure collective bargaining.

Still, given the prime minister's well-entrenched principles, it seems unlikely that even a more unified and determined labour movement would have won a compulsory collective bargaining policy. Although King supported collective action, at least to improve wages and working conditions, he deplored the idea of legislation that skewed the labour-capital equation and threatened the unity of the country. As he explained to Liberal Party stalwarts: "Liberalism always places the general good before the particular interest, be it of class, or race, or creed." Otherwise, there would be "tendencies to division and cleavage in our land."[227] Adhering to this key principle, the prime minister was only willing to use compulsion to promote investigation and conciliation, not to encourage union growth and industrial justice. He seemed unable to understand how the status quo actually favoured employers. Nothing held them accountable for anti-union behaviour; nothing forced them to sit down at the negotiating table. Instead, when confronted with demands for new policies, King took convenient refuge in the constitution. The one innovation he did commit to, section 502A of the Criminal Code, proved to be little more than a legislative placebo. In the area of labour policy, at least, he continued to rely on convictions formed decades earlier. "My place so far as being a leader [is] concerned," the prime minister affirmed to the Liberal Party caucus in January 1939, "[is] secured not in anything that might take place in the future, but what [has] taken place in the past."[228]

Chapter Two

The Breastplate of Righteousness, Fall 1939–Fall 1941

In the mid-afternoon of 10 June 1940, Mackenzie King strode uneasily up the walkway to the home of Norman Rogers, the minister of national defence. In a few minutes time, he would feel strangely jubilant. Right now, however, he was in very low spirits. Finding the front veranda door stuck, the prime minister made his way around the side of the house to the back entrance. That door was locked, so he began calling through open windows. Rogers's wife, Frances, woke from her nap and let him in. After sitting down together on a couch in the small living room, King turned towards Frances and gently explained the reason for his visit: Norman's plane had crashed the night before on the way to Toronto. "Surely, he is not gone," Frances replied in disbelief. "Not from your side," said King. "He is here with both of us right now." At that moment, J.L. Ralston, the minister of finance, arrived at the house and confirmed there were no survivors. Badly shaken, the prime minister walked into Rogers's study to collect his thoughts. It felt like his mind had a quality of "deadness" to it. In the background, he heard Frances choke: "Norman was all my life to me."[1]

That morning at his Kingsmere estate in the Gatineau Hills, King had observed a crow – what he believed to be a "sign of death" – near the pheasant's enclosure. He initially assumed the crow symbolized the general deterioration of conditions in Europe. Italy's declaration of war against Great Britain and France was imminent; the Germans were quickly converging on Paris. With only Great Britain and the British Commonwealth left to fight Hitler and Mussolini, it seemed to King that "the whole world was in doubt." The prime minister now realized the crow had signaled a more personal loss. Rogers's death was a very heavy blow. A Rhodes Scholar and history professor, who had served as King's private secretary in the 1920s and labour minister in the late 1930s, Rogers had been "a close friend" and one of "the best men in the administration." Much like a protégé, he had shared the same progressive ideals as the prime minister. He had also understood – though not necessarily supported – the reasons for King's evasive approach to policy innovations.[2] His death would make it much more difficult to deal with the conservative forces in the cabinet. And to make matters even worse, the prime minister's deep grief was compounded by guilt. He had pushed a reluctant Rogers to make the trip to Toronto the night before.[3]

As the prime minister stood in Rogers's study, his eyes fell upon an open Bible on the desk. Always in search of religious guidance and inspiration, he looked more closely to identify the passage. It was from the sixth chapter of Ephesians: "Stand therefore having your loins girt about with truth, and having on the breastplate of righteousness." As both a devout Christian and a spiritualist, King firmly believed in the power of coincidence – that unexpected events may provide meaningful insights. Moreover, given his conceit and strong ideals, he often looked to the supernatural for self-validation. The Bible passage seemed a clear message to remain true to his political beliefs – to continue to stand fast in the face of adversity. This stance was no easy task in the best of times, but it had been especially challenging in the past year. With the onset of war in September 1939, the prime minister's policymaking authority was greatly enhanced. The War Measures Act allowed the federal executive to rule virtually by decree, passing orders in council that stood as law until the return of peace. All constitutional constraints to sweeping change had been removed. But King had continued to adhere to his own particular brand of liberalism: moving forward slowly and cautiously by achieving consensus, and using moral force, not compulsion, to reconcile differences and identify a common ground. As King stood in Rogers's office, he took great comfort in the Bible passage. In the midst of his deep sadness, this message from beyond offered clarity and reassurance. With a renewed sense of purpose, he resolved to carry on with his convictions, wearing "the breastplate of righteousness" to deflect both political detractors and policy temptations.[4]

More of the Same

Several months earlier, the federal government's role in wartime industrial relations had begun inauspiciously. On 19 September 1939, nine days after Canada declared war against Germany, the prime minister announced his decision to move Norman Rogers to the national defence portfolio and appoint Norman McLarty, the postmaster general, as the new minister of labour.[5] McLarty was hardly an inspired choice. A corporate lawyer from Windsor, Ontario, who had married into money, enjoyed hobnobbing in high society, and counted several auto executives as close friends, the new labour minister even doubted his own ability to serve effectively in the position.[6] Intending to keep a close eye on labour matters, however, King chose McLarty for his personality, not his industrial relations expertise. Affable, slow moving, and conciliatory, McLarty's primary responsibilities were to maintain the status quo and keep King informed about new developments. According to one labour official, talking to McLarty "was like trying to take fingerprints in a dish of thin mud. There's no resistance when you put your fingers in and no impression when you take your fingers out."[7] As the war progressed, most observers agreed that King had badly miscalculated. McLarty's incompetence, not to mention his fondness for public drinking sprees, became serious liabilities that helped to debilitate Canadian industrial relations.

But this breakdown was still a year away. One month into the war, the leaders of four of the five main labour organizations met with the prime minister to express their qualified support for no-strike deals with the federal government. (Although absent from this round of meetings, the railway brotherhoods had promised to back the war effort earlier in the month.) The conditions were wide ranging. The Trades and Labour Congress (TLC), which represented nearly half of the union members in the country, told King that it would commit to a no-strike pledge if the government appointed labour men to wartime boards and agencies; extended the Industrial Disputes Investigation Act (IDIA) to all industries; and issued a "declaration of policy" that recognized the right to organize into unions, negotiate agreements through collection bargaining, and implement union shop agreements (all employees join the union and pay union dues).[8] Fearing a repeat of the Great War, when many union activities were prohibited, the TLC preferred to rely on its economic power, not a heavy-handed government, to make tangible gains. In a separate meeting, the Confédération des travailleurs catholiques du Canada (CTCC) explained that it opposed Canada's entry into the war on behalf of Great Britain, but would cooperate if labour and business were treated as equal partners. And, somewhat expediently, the All-Canadian Congress of Labour (ACCL), which had just experienced a 15 per cent drop in membership, offered its support for the war effort if the Liberal administration agreed to curtail belligerent employers.[9] Delighted that the three labour organizations emphasized cooperation over conflict and persuasion over compulsion, the prime minister promised to follow through on his end. Linking the proposals to his own past efforts to promote industrial harmony, he noted rather immodestly: "It was not often given to a man to seeing in his own lifetime the fruit of his labour."[10]

Later, in November, the delegates from the fourth labour organization, the Canadian Committee for Industrial Organization, received a much cooler reception. Formed just a few weeks earlier, the Canadian committee was mainly composed of unions that maintained loose ties with the Congress of Industrial Organizations (CIO) in the United States.[11] There were two groups: (1) CIO unions recently expelled from the TLC in September; and (2) CIO unions, like the United Electrical Workers (UE), which had remained independent of the TLC.[12] With an 18 per cent drop in overall membership in the past year, the Canadian committee planned to launch a far-reaching drive in the manufacturing and natural resources sectors to swell the ranks of their affiliates.[13] Communist organizers led the charge. Dick Steele of the Steel Workers' Organizing Committee (SWOC), who had just led out 600 workers at a General Steel Wares plant in Toronto, called for "a crusade to bring industrial democracy into every Canadian plant."[14] And, given the Nazi-Soviet Non-Aggression Pact of August 1939, radical unionists lacked any compunction about interrupting war production; they would do what was needed to win concessions for workers.[15] No surprise, then, that in the meeting with government officials, the delegates from the Canadian committee set a high price for a no-strike pledge: nothing less than compulsory collective bargaining along the lines of the Wagner Act in the United States. Mackenzie King, who disliked the hard-nosed, defiant attitudes of these particular industrial unionists, was conspicuously absent. On his behalf, McLarty flatly rejected the proposal and warned the CIO unions to be prudent in calling strikes. There would be no Wagner-like act in Canada.[16]

As a good faith gesture to the more mainstream TLC, the King cabinet immediately extended the coverage of the IDIA to all war production or about 85 per cent of the industries in the country.[17] Thanks to the 1925 *Snider* decision of the British Privy Council, which gave the provinces jurisdiction over industrial relations, Order in Council PC 3495 was the first truly national labour policy in decades. Given the limited scope of the IDIA in the 1930s, however, only a handful of labour leaders knew

2.1 Tom Moore, TLC

Source: *Winnipeg Tribune*, 1 October 1940, 2, Library and Archives Canada, Amicus No. 3821471.

2.2 Alfred Charpentier, CTCC

Source: Archives de la Confédération des syndicats nationaux, no. 2865.

2.3 Percy Bengough, TLC

Source: Don Coltman, Steffens-Colmer Studios Ltd., City of Vancouver Archives, CVA 586-883.

2.4 Patrick Conroy, UMW and CCL; Aaron Mosher, ACCL and CCL; Charles Millard, CIO and CCL

Source: Credit: *Toronto Daily Star*, 23 September 1946, 2, Library and Archives Canada, Amicus No. 7791836.

how it worked.[18] It was not long before there was widespread complaining. First, organizers disliked the strike vote requirement before workers could even make a conciliation board application. Moderates worried that the votes made negative impressions on the general public and predisposed workers to strikes. More ambitious organizers disliked how the votes allowed employers to intimidate workers and prevent the appointment of a conciliation board or to challenge results as a delay tactic.[19] Second, labour leaders discovered that the entire conciliation process took months to play out. Perhaps obviously, these lengthy proceedings eroded union support. Workers became discouraged and impatient, not to mention vulnerable to threats and bribes. As the Toronto District Labour Council criticized: "During the interval ... the very existence of the organization is endangered."[20] Finally, and most importantly, the conciliation boards lacked real power. Companies were compelled to participate in the hearings of conciliation boards, but not to abide by their findings. For union organizers, in particular, this made the IDIA next to useless. The Teck-Hughes Gold Mine in Kirkland Lake, Ontario, not only rejected a conciliation board's recommendation to recognize the union, but also fired over thirty union members. As a University of Toronto professor deplored: "The company ... ignored the findings of the board. The government did nothing."[21]

By early 1940, it was clear employers were having their way with unions across the country. One hundred miles south of Halifax, the Lockeport Cold Storage Company closed down its fish-handling plants for nearly two months to defeat a union drive.[22] In response to recognition demands, Pioneer Gold Mines in British Columbia evicted miners from company-owned bunkhouses and homes.[23] And, in what the Department of Labour called "the most important dispute of the year," a recognition strike of 2,000 workers at an artificial silk factory in Drummondville, Quebec, ended in an employer-controlled union.[24] A large part of the problem was that organized labour lacked the economic leverage to wrest concessions from employers. During the "phony war" of limited engagements by the Allies between September 1939 and May 1940, the British decided to hold back on war orders, and Ottawa spent only 0.5 per cent of its total war expenditures. Production levels remained down, and the unemployment rate continued to hover between 9 and 11 per cent.[25] But the unions also blamed the IDIA for their troubles. Several regional TLC federations began to echo the demands of CIO unions for a collective bargaining law. Away from the TLC's national office in Ottawa, voluntarist or non-legislative strategies, not to mention organizational rivalries, apparently had much less resonance. As a local TLC group asserted, the federal government must "use its emergency powers to make it COMPULSORY that all employers enjoying the benefits of government contracts be required to bargain collectively with the freely chosen organization of their employees."[26]

On 13 June 1940, Mackenzie King met with a joint representation of labour officials in his rather dingy office in the east block of the parliament buildings.[27] At first, he had paid little attention to the criticism about the IDIA. He was preoccupied with a federal election in March 1940 (the Liberals won a large majority) and the German *blitzkrieg* in April and May. Labour issues were not a priority, especially demands for more forceful legislation. In early June, however, W.J. Turnbull, the well-informed principal secretary of the Prime Minister's Office, recognized that wartime labour relations were imploding, and convinced King to address the policy concerns of the labour leaders.[28] The eleven o'clock conference took place three days after the death of Norman Rogers. Although dull and overcast outside, King had woken up in the morning still revitalized by the prophetic words in the Bible about the "breastplate of righteousness." It was good that he could draw strength from the verse, because it was a very heated meeting. By now, German advances had finally resulted in war contracts multiplying and the labour market tightening. For the first time in a long while, the labour movement enjoyed some semblance of power, and the labour force appeared primed for collective action. More workers had walked off their jobs in April 1940 than in nearly any other month in the previous ten years.[29]

After a brief tribute to Rogers, the normally diplomatic Tom Moore of the TLC got right to the point: the government was to blame for the recent rash of strikes. It had broken its promise to treat labour as an equal partner in the war effort. Since employers lacked any qualms about ignoring the collective demands of workers, unions had no choice but to lead their members out on strike. King was caught completely off guard by Moore's cutting tone and the rare display of labour solidarity. Privately wondering why Norman McLarty hadn't kept him better informed, he managed to respond that not all employers were alike and that compulsory legislation was misguided. But the prime minister was on the defensive throughout the meeting. Not only did the labour leaders from the different organizations speak "out from the shoulder quite critically," but they were also unified in their enmity towards the government. It was a big change from the previous fall. In the end,

King promised that something would be done right away to protect the rights of workers.[30]

Following the conference, King took steps "to see that Labour got its recognition in connection with the war effort."[31] Since he continued to wear his "breastplate of righteousness," however, these new developments reinforced rather than shifted the status quo. His first decision was to replace the hapless McLarty with Tom Moore, the TLC president, over the strenuous objections of cabinet colleagues. It made perfect sense, because the sixty-two-year-old labour leader was highly regarded in traditional labour circles, shared many of King's views about compulsion, and was politically moderate. Unfortunately for the prime minister, Moore was also "pulling things together" in the TLC after the CIO-lenient presidency of Paddy Draper. Refusing the position, the labour leader explained he could do a better job of keeping workers in line by remaining outside the government. When Moore agreed to serve as a confidential advisor, King decided to stick with McLarty for the time being.[32]

Next, the prime minister arranged for the passage of PC 2686, which established the National Labour Supply Council (NLSC) to advise the government on industrial relations problems. As a bipartite agency with an equal number of labour and business representatives, the NLSC appeared to recognize organized labour as a full partner in the war effort. Importantly, though, King stacked the NLSC so that it reflected the views of more traditional labour organizations. The CIO unions, the most aggressive proponents of a collective bargaining policy, were not offered a permanent board seat.[33] The NLSC also lacked much tangible authority. The agency was only allowed to provide advice on issues referred to it by the labour minister. Requests for more proactive and expansive powers fell on deaf ears. Within less than a year, even the most willing labour statesman, like A.R. Mosher of the ACCL, had to admit that the NLSC was ineffective and powerless.[34] J.L. Cohen, the pre-eminent labour lawyer of the wartime period, dismissed it as "much like a roof without a building."[35]

The final development was the passage of Order in Council PC 2685 or the Declaration of Principles for Wartime Regulation of Labour Conditions, which outlined the government's position on wartime industrial relations. Although King personally drew up the list of ten principles in the order, PC 2685 was not a foregone conclusion. He experienced "a rather embarrassing time" convincing members of his cabinet to support it.[36] His colleagues had balked because two of the ten principles dealt directly with collective rights, stating that workers "should be free to organize into trade unions" and "should be free to negotiate with employers ... with a view to the conclusion of a collective agreement." Much to the delight of the CIO leaders, as well as many local TLC and ACCL affiliates, the order appeared to sanction widespread organizing. SWOC began distributing leaflets with the message: "Join now! Your Government expects YOU to organize. Union Membership is not only a Personal Advantage ... It is now a National Duty."[37] Joseph Mackenzie of the United Rubber Workers wrote to a local in Kitchener, Ontario: "This [policy] really puts a club in our hands."[38] But the labour movement was badly mistaken. As Norman McLarty explained to a concerned Ernest Lapointe, the minister of justice, PC 2685 "merely endorsed the soundness of the principle of employers and employees bargaining collectively."[39] By carefully inserting the qualifier "should" at various points in the text of the order, King had made sure that his wartime labour policy relied on nothing more than moral force to entice the cooperation of employers. "The maggot was in the apple of PC 2685," remarked J.L. Cohen, "before labour commenced to taste of its fruit."[40]

King's initiatives appeased the TLC leadership. In a radio broadcast, Tom Moore applauded PC 2685 because it was a form of "voluntary co-operation" that encouraged "the democratic procedure of recognizing equality or partnership between employer and employee in industrial activities."[41] For more fledgling unions, however, King's ameliorative efforts were next to useless. In fall 1940, the conditions should have been ripe for organizing. After France surrendered to the Germans in June, companies found themselves swamped with orders to produce munitions and supplies for British and Canadian forces. As the Dominion Bureau of Statistics announced, there was an "unprecedented expansion in industrial employment."[42] The capital investment rate in manufacturing quadrupled, and the unemployment rate was cut in half.[43] In dire need of workers, manufacturers even began to use wage enticements to "poach" skilled workers from one another.[44] After many lean years, the last thing employers wanted was work stoppages. Another positive development for unskilled workers was the merger of the Canadian Committee for Industrial Organization and the ACCL into the Canadian Congress of Labour (CCL). Given the more moderate politics of the ACCL, the social democratic leadership of the Canadian committee hoped to limit the influence of communist organizers in the CIO unions and gain more respect from the government. And the ACCL unions, though hostile to international labour organizations, needed to tap into the vitality and resolve of the CIO unions to stay relevant.[45]

Despite the increase in bargaining power and the decrease in organizational rivalry, however, total union membership grew by less than 1 per cent between the fall of 1939 and the end of 1940.[46] Why? The answer was simple: lackluster labour laws. Just like before the war, the prime minister only permitted the use of compulsion to investigate and conciliate conflicts, not to protect collective rights. He continued to avoid what he considered to be one-sided policies that might provoke backlash and destabilize the economy. Left to their own devices, employers could still go to great lengths to defeat organizing drives. Although Tom Moore and the TLC leadership expressed more satisfaction with the wartime labour policies after the June meeting, many labour officials, whether in local craft unions or on the CCL executive council, began to demand legislation like the Wagner Act in the United States.[47] They agreed with Patrick Conroy of the United Mine Workers (UMW) that PC 2685 "[was] a joke. The Government asked for the cooperation of organized labour and gave it a piece of paper."[48]

Incongruities

At the same time, other government departments and agencies began to implement wartime policies that circumscribed union activities. It seemed clear to many members of the labour movement that duplicity was at work. On the one hand, the almost chimerical and definitely paternalistic prime minister insisted that the government remain "neutral" in industrial relations, convinced that forceful labour policies would cause more harm than good. "Labour's hard-won liberties must be maintained," he had said at the contentious June meeting. "However, it [is] far better not to proceed by coercion."[49] But all his rhetoric about impartiality ignored how the current legislative framework clearly favoured employers over workers. As the single source of authority in the workplace, managers could still operate at will, making unilateral decisions as they saw fit. On the other hand, the prime minister appeared to have no compunctions about letting cabinet ministers and civil servants use their wartime authority to compel and check union behaviour. Their actions made all the prime minister's talk about the dangers of forceful labour laws seem not only shallow, but also opportunistic. Why the Janus-faced behaviour? In part, it reflected King's managerial style as prime minister. Aside from the Labour Department, he rarely interfered with the ministerial prerogatives of his colleagues. Even if King personally disliked the measures, he did little to prevent their implementation.[50] Also, as far as he was concerned, labour policies that dealt more narrowly with industrial relations and labour policies that addressed broader issues of national security and economic stability were two different entities. He restricted his expertise to the former and let his colleagues deal with the latter. Of course, it was a specious distinction to many labour leaders. As legal scholars Judy Fudge and Eric Tucker write: "This inequality in the exercise of state compulsion proved to be the crux of labour's discontent with the federal government's labour policies."[51]

The suspension of civil liberties was a case in point. In September 1939, King had sanctioned PC 2483 or the Defence of Canada Regulations. High-ranking officials in the Justice Department and the Royal Canadian Mounted Police (RCMP) secretly drafted the policy to ensure the internal security of the country.[52] Although most of the sixty-four regulations were fairly innocuous, a few imposed severe constraints on what people could say or do during wartime. Overzealous politicians and law officers decided to use these particular directives to combat a wide range of union activities. In December 1939, for example, the attorney general of Ontario ordered the arrest of Charlie Millard and a raid on his office because the CIO leader publicly questioned fighting for democracy abroad "while there was Hitlerism right here in Canada."[53] And the police in Windsor, Ontario, arrested forty-six picketers at a Chrysler plant because regulation six of PC 2483 prohibited loitering at war production sites. Both these actions resulted in loud outcries, including a formal complaint by Philip Murray, the CIO president in the United States. Charlie Millard was quickly released, but a Windsor magistrate decided to fine the Chrysler workers. In response to public pressure, Norman McLarty did arrange for a special IDIA commission to conduct an inquiry. Given the labour minister's links to the auto industry, though, it was little more than a kangaroo court. Commissioner William H. Furlong called the employees' version of what happened "unreasonable beyond belief" and cleared Chrysler of any wrongdoing.[54]

To curtail further abuses, the King cabinet amended PC 2483 to allow "good faith" criticisms of the government and peaceful picketing.[55] Besides this one concession, however, the federal government continued to use the Defence of Canada Regulations to influence wartime industrial relations. Applying regulations twenty-one and twenty-two,

Ernest Lapointe, the justice minister, arrested and interned over forty communist labour leaders because their actions were considered detrimental to national security.[56] For the most part, he used the extremely problematic intelligence gathering efforts of the RCMP to make his internment decisions.[57] Arrested without charges, the internees were sent to Camp Petawawa in the Ottawa River Valley where they shared a hut and laboured in work gangs. Fascist sympathizers and political prisoners of other nationalities lived in adjacent quarters. There were strict restrictions on outside news and visitors – including lawyers. Internees could ask for the particulars of their arrest and appeal to an advisory committee for release. But even these paltry rights were limited: it took a long time for prisoners to find out why they were detained; the onus was on the accused to prove why the justice minister was in error; and the justice minister could override the recommendations of the advisory committee.[58]

Ernest Lapointe insisted the internees were imprisoned for past and/or present communist activities since Canada, unlike other Allied countries, had just outlawed the Communist Party.[59] And it was true that most of these interned labour leaders did have communist backgrounds. But J.L. Cohen, who represented several of the internees, strenuously disagreed with Lapointe. "[T]rade union and labour events are not only coincidental," he argued, "but even ... associated with these arrests and detentions."[60] He was right. The government had much more than a passing interest in the union activities of the internees. Pat Sullivan, the president of the Canadian Seamen's Union (CSU), was interned in the midst of a heated dispute with several Great Lakes shipping companies. Later the advisory committee grilled him on a wide range of union actions and even provided a list of charges that dealt exclusively with the CSU. It refused to explain how the charges justified Sullivan's continued detention.[61] Similarly, C.S. Jackson of the United Electrical Workers (UE) was interned while leading a pivotal organizing campaign against Canadian Westinghouse in Hamilton and an illegal strike against Canadian General Electric in Toronto. With Justice Department and RCMP officials in attendance, the chair of the advisory committee went on a "fishing expedition" to find out information about UE organizing activities. He even demanded that Jackson show him "any legislative enactment that imposes a legal obligation upon employers to enter into conference with their employees." To use Cohen's words, the government's actions were a "violation of the lawful liberties of a labour organizer – or indeed of any citizen."[62]

2.5 Internment camp, Petawawa, Ontario. Living in a hut adjacent to fascist sympathizers, German prisoners of war, and Italian Canadians, communist labour leaders wore prison uniforms, ate army food, and laboured in work gangs. The coincidental timing of their arrests did not go unnoticed in the labour movement. After protesting conditions, the left-wing internees were eventually transferred to an empty jail in Hull, Quebec. None were released until late 1941.

Source: National Film Board of Canada, Still Photography Division, Library and Archives Canada, PA-188744.

At first, more mainstream unionists like Tom Moore of the TLC expressed support for the internments.[63] Not only did these old-school unionists back the government's campaign against wartime subversives, but they were also happy to get rid of radical unionists who continually questioned, if not obstructed, the top-down decision-making of their organizations. A month before Jackson's arrest, other CCL leaders had suspended his participation on the executive council because of "irresponsible" behaviour, like attacking the leadership for power mongering and creating shop steward councils that cut across

2.6 Protest pamphlet

Source: Committee for the Release of Labour Prisoners, Memorial University Archives, Special Collections, No. 817837.

2.7 Pat Sullivan, CSU and TLC; C.S. Jackson, UE and CCL. Over forty communist labour leaders, including Sullivan and Jackson, were arrested and interned because their actions were considered detrimental to national security.

Source: *Winnipeg Tribune*, 8 September 1948, 7, Library and Archives Canada, Amicus No. 3821471.

industries and labour organizations.[64] Norman Dowd of the CCL actually believed the government should have interned Jackson earlier in the war.[65] Still, the timing of the arrests, the ambiguous charges, and the broad-ranging interrogations did generate a great deal of resentment, even in the more conservative wing of the labour movement. Convinced that the government was using its coercive powers to repress unions, many locals began to demand fair trials and/or clemency for the internees.[66] Eventually, even Dowd began to criticize the government for "the practice of arresting Labour leaders in the midst of Labour disputes."[67]

Thanks in large part to the efforts of J.L. Cohen, a wide array of civil rights groups, newspaper editors, and politicians raised objections.[68] Within the Prime Minister's Office, a staff member actually lamented how "the police are attending and reporting on often completely harmless meetings, and spying on the daily activities of peaceful and law-abiding citizens."[69] But Mackenzie King made no effort to stop the internments. Privately, he expressed misgivings about repressing civil liberties – even with communists.[70] Curbing the arrests, however, would have alienated Ernest Lapointe. The justice minister was a devout Roman Catholic from rural Quebec, who considered communism to be an atheistic threat to traditional French-Canadian values, not to mention all Christian civilization. Although the prime minister was surprised "at how fearful Lapointe is in these matters, and how reactionary he is prepared to become during the war period," he was willing to grant his justice minister considerable leeway.[71] Lapointe not only was King's closest, most trusted associate, but he also played a critical role in reassuring French Canadians that their cultural and economic interests were being looked after in Ottawa. At the start of the war, he had personally orchestrated the defeat of the powerful premier of Quebec, Maurice Duplessis, an outspoken critic of King and his war powers. It was an impressive feat since most French Canadians opposed Canada's entry into the war and feared the possibility of conscription or a draft. So, as far as King was concerned, the coercion of a few radical unionists was a small price to pay for Lapointe's contributions to national unity.[72] Although Canadian communists did an about face and became ardent supporters of the war effort when Germany invaded the USSR in June 1941, Ottawa continued to intern radical labour leaders until a few months after Lapointe's untimely death that winter.[73]

Besides the suspension of civil liberties, King also agreed to wage controls. Once again, these restrictions were not his idea, but the handiwork of a cadre of high-ranking civil servants called the Interdepartmental Committee on Labour Co-ordination (ICLC). Created in October 1940 to unify the responses of different government branches to the shrinking labour supply, the ICLC soon began to advise the prime minister on a wide range of labour matters. The credentials of the members were impressive.[74] Several people on the committee were academically trained economists whose research interests included the employment relationship. Bryce M. Stewart, the ICLC chair and newly hired deputy minister of labour, had followed in the footsteps of Mackenzie King. After working in the Labour Department during the Great War as a statistician and editor of the *Labour Gazette*, he moved to the United States in 1922 and earned a PhD in economics from Columbia University. During the 1930s, Stewart became nationally recognized in the United States as a leading authority on unemployment insurance. He was also employed as research director at the Rockefeller-funded Industrial Relations Counselors, Inc. (IRC) in New York City, which promoted the "progressive" industrial relations philosophy of Mackenzie King. Another important ICLC member was W.A. Mackintosh from the Finance Department. The former head of the Department of Commerce and Administration at Queen's University and currently the vice-chair of the powerful Economic Advisory Committee, Mackintosh's area of expertise was applied economics. Collaborating with Stewart in 1937, he had established the study of industrial relations at Queen's University, describing it as a "critical phase of modern life." Other notable ICLC personalities included James C. Cameron, the director of the new Industrial Relations Section at Queen's and a former economist at Canada Packers, a firm renowned for its advanced human resource practices. There was also W.J. Couper, an economics scholar on loan from the International Labour Organization, who had collaborated with Stewart on unemployment questions in the 1930s. He later left Ottawa to join the IRC.[75]

Neither employers nor union officials, these like-minded thinkers believed that innovative policymaking and improved managerial practices could solve all labour problems. They had their work cut out for them. "Industrial relations in Canada," Bryce Stewart confided to an American colleague, "both as regards governmental and company policy is much more in the formative stage."[76] With close connections to many other influential civil servants in Ottawa, this second generation of industrial relations experts enjoyed considerable bureaucratic autonomy, believed it was the government's responsibility to manage the economy, and supported the collective organization of workers – though not necessarily into unions. Although King remained leery of activist civil servants, especially those associated with Queen's University, he appreciated the knowledge and ability of the ICLC members.[77] After all, much of their work reflected what he, himself, had promulgated as an industrial relations visionary many years earlier. Given the ineptitude of his labour minister and what one newspaper editor described as the "somnolence" of the Labour Department, it was really not surprising that the prime minister allowed the ICLC considerable latitude.[78] In fact, the creation of the committee usurped what modest authority McLarty enjoyed and ensured the National Labour Supply Council would have no real policymaking influence. After spring 1942, the ICLC would focus almost exclusively on manpower questions. As Bryce Stewart later conceded, however, until then "recommendations on war labour policy and its administration derived from this committee."[79]

There were both practical and altruistic reasons for the wage controls. Since the fall of France in June 1940, the accelerated war production and tightening labour market had pushed up wages in most industries. Average yearly earnings in manufacturing, which included overtime work, had surged by nearly 12 per cent since 1939.[80] The responsibility for mobilizing and coordinating war production lay with officials in the Department of Munitions and Supply (DMS), and they worried about the transfer of the increased wage costs to the government. They also blamed union organizing for the inflation. Headed by C.D. Howe, the DMS was staffed by "dollar-a-year men," or corporate executives who supposedly volunteered their services to the government but usually continued to receive full compensation from their companies.[81] Besides allocating essential resources through a board of controllers and building Crown corporations or government-owned facilities, the DMS awarded millions of dollars of war contracts to established businesses. Under pressure to become more cost conscious, C.D. Howe and H.B. Chase, the director of labour relations for the DMS, explained to the ICLC that (1) war contractors were being forced to raise wages and, subsequently, prices to outflank or even accommodate "irresponsible" organizing campaigns; and (2) the wage recommendations of conciliation boards were inconsistent and inflationary. For the sake of the war effort, there needed to be a wage ceiling.[82]

Most of the ICLC members took a longer view of the situation. During the Great War, inflation had spiraled out of control. An extremely severe recession followed in the early 1920s where, on average, workers lost 20 per cent of their incomes.[83] Having worked during the Great Depression in both Canada and the United States to soften the blows of mass unemployment, the ICLC members were already predisposed to providing wage-earners with income security. With another economic crisis looming, they recognized something had to be done to prevent a repeat of history. True, wage controls would be unpopular. As Stewart argued, however: "[T]he only alternative is to stand idly by while uncontrollable changes in wages and prices impose unpredictable sacrifices on all classes, but put the heaviest burden on those not fortunate enough to occupy strategic positions in the economy."[84] This reasoning is not to say that fiscal constraints were not an important concern. They were. But what really mattered to the forward-thinking ICLC members were the living standards of workers and their families. Linking runaway inflation to human suffering and deteriorating industrial relations, they wanted to elude "random shifts in economic welfare" and insure "the health, the morale, and the productivity of our labour force."[85] Although Mackenzie King worried about the political ramifications of wage controls, he essentially agreed. Earlier in the year, he had also consented to the passage of the Unemployment Insurance Act to ease the shock of demobilization.[86] With ordinary Canadians sacrificing so much for the war effort, he loathed leaving their incomes to the vagaries of market forces. In December 1940, when the ICLC introduced PC 7440 or the Wartime Wage Policy, he dubbed the order a "far-reaching one so far as workers are concerned."[87]

What King really liked about PC 7440 was that it was more of an exhortation than a decree. Rather than subject wage regulations to political fallout, the ICLC had rejected an outright freeze, like the DMS wanted, for a more gradualist approach.[88] The order instructed conciliation boards to keep their non-binding wage recommendations below the highest level paid by an employer between 1926 and 1940. The labour minister and later a justice from the Supreme Court of Ontario were given the authority to review and possibly modify the wage recommendations of the boards. King also liked that PC 7440 reaffirmed the principles laid out in PC 2685 – though he probably had misgivings about its use of more assertive language. Unlike PC 2685, the wage order stated: "All agreements negotiated during the war period shall conform to the principles." By using the phrase "shall conform," which suggests a binding obligation, the ICLC made clear that a joint determination of the employment relationship was preferable to autocratic managerial practices. It was a simple, but groundbreaking, equation: improved conditions for workers equalled continuous wartime production and a healthy economy. "Good industrial relations are especially important in war-time," noted Bryce Stewart. "The aspirations of workers to the right of association and to enter into collective agreements will [make] for fuller co-operation between employers and employed."[89]

The country's labour leaders doubted whether wage increases had much impact on inflation and disliked removing wages from the realm of collective bargaining. Although initially willing to take a "wait and see" attitude, they soon denounced PC 7440 as misguided and intrusive.[90] There were two main problems. First, the government became increasingly rigid about wage rates, refusing to consider the particular conditions of a case. The flashpoint for organized labour was a SWOC strike at Peck Rolling Mills in Montreal. In April 1941, the three members of a conciliation board had unanimously advised management to recognize the union, but were divided over whether to increase wages, which were relatively low for the steel industry. The chair and employer representative rejected increases because the present rates were comparable to those paid in other Montreal firms and higher than 1926–9 levels. In a forceful minority report, labour lawyer J.L. Cohen, the employees' representative, reminded his colleagues that PC 7440 was not a mandate and called for substantial increases to the subpar wages of the workers. When McLarty supported the majority decision, 324 Peck workers turned out for a strike.[91] Despite the protests of CCL leaders, the government refused to overturn the board's decision. Bryce Stewart admitted to the US ambassador that the wages were "indefensibly low." But he disliked how SWOC's larger goal was to establish a uniform wage rate in the whole steel industry. By encouraging Peck workers to demand the same wages paid at larger mills, like Stelco in Hamilton, the union was trying "to get labour to react along more radical lines."[92] In the end, the government did agree to raise the minimum wage for Peck workers by five cents an hour and to clarify PC 7440 so that conciliation boards had a bit more flexibility in alleviating poor wages. Satisfied that their demands had been partially met and extremely low on strike funds, the strikers, minus twenty blacklisted union members, returned to work in early June. For many labour leaders, however, the Peck strike revealed the danger of letting the government, not free collective bargaining, define wage rates.[93]

The second problem with PC 7440 was that the principles articulated in PC 2685 were still not enforced. Given the improved economic conditions and the belief that PC 7440 had added teeth to PC 2685, many industrial unions had launched organizing drives in spring 1941.[94] The CCL's community drive in Kitchener, Ontario, was one of the most ambitious. In March, Arthur Williams of the CCL, along with several union organizers, began making contacts in Kitchener's heavy manufacturing, leather products, and meatpacking plants. By clearly explaining the widespread benefits of unionism, like the impact of wage gains on the local economy, they established cordial relationships with municipal politicians and police officers. Rather creatively, the organizers also arranged for a series of radio skits about a fictitious working-class family that had struggled to make ends meet until a union came to town. After the broadcasts played for a week, Williams reported they were "getting more requests from workers desiring to be organized than we [can] handle."[95] Spontaneous strikes broke out as workers released their pent-up frustrations with employers and demonstrated their impatience with the conciliation process.[96] Committed to responsible unionism, the organizers convinced the strikers to return to work and await the outcomes of hastily appointed conciliation boards. But the results were devastating. Although government-supervised plant votes confirmed the desire of Kitchener workers for representation, employers refused to accept the results, and the Labour Department did nothing. The CCL failed to win recognition in any of the war production plants in the city.[97] "The unions thought 7440 gave them the legal right to insist on union recognition and collective bargaining," noted political economist Eugene Forsey. "They went ahead on that understanding, and then King double-crossed them."[98]

During the fall of 1941, the labour movement became increasingly critical of PC 7440. At the TLC's annual convention in September, delegates condemned McLarty's interference with the wage recommendations of conciliation boards and urged a more flexible interpretation of the wage guidelines. About the same time, the CCL convention called on the government to abolish the order.[99] The most damning and influential denunciation actually came from J.L. Cohen. Deeply committed to increasing the economic and political power of workers, the forty-four-year-old labour lawyer had served as the employee representative on many key conciliation boards, defended most of the interned labour leaders, acted as counsel to numerous strikers brought up on charges, and even written the CCL's constitution and by-laws. Although other lawyers, like John Stanton on the West Coast, made valuable contributions, Cohen's reputation as the premier legal advisor to the labour movement was indisputable. During the Peck strike, SWOC had hired him to write a pamphlet that explained the inadequacies of the existing labour policies and the importance of union representation. Published in September 1941, *Collective Bargaining in Canada* caught the attention of many people outside the labour movement.[100] B.K. Sandwell, the editor of *Saturday Night* magazine, decreed: "It should be in the hands of every Canadian who has anything to do with the relations between labour and employers."[101] The pamphlet even made the rounds of the Prime Minister's Office, though it was probably not well received.[102] Scorning the government's supposedly neutral position in industrial relations, Cohen revealed in a series of convincing examples how "vigilance as to the wage policy of PC 7440 [was] paralleled by indulgence as to the trade union and collective bargaining principles of PC 2685." What was his solution? Abolish PC 7440 and "replace it with a national wage policy democratically arrived at by the process of collective bargaining."[103]

A month later, in October, the government did decide to replace PC 7440, but with a mandatory wage freeze. Not exactly what Cohen had called for. As a Labour Department document later revealed, McLarty's bungled administration of PC 7440 had rendered it ineffective. Rather than ensuring the consistent application of the order, he had taken a piecemeal approach to reviewing wage recommendations, allowing "expediency alone" to dictate his actions.[104] With inflation unabated, officials in the Bank of Canada and the Finance Department pushed for a total freeze on wages as well as prices.[105] Passed into law as PC 8253, the wage ceiling was fixed at mid-November rates, and financial penalties were levied for unauthorized increases. The new order also created a two-tier system of tripartite national and regional war labour boards to administer the wage controls. More informed than consulted about PC 8253, labour leaders in both the TLC and CCL were incensed that the government had removed wages – one of the main incentives for workers to join unions – from the bargaining table.[106]

As the authors of PC 8253, the ICLC members regretted placing restrictions on collective bargaining and agreed that PC 2685 needed to be stronger. Convinced that negotiations between employers and employees were mutually beneficial, their solution was to give the new National War Labour Board (NWLB) the authority to develop "a code of labour policy." Rather than have the government force employers to bargain collectively with their workers and risk a massive wave of resistance, the ICLC believed that members of the business community and the labour movement should jointly define the rules for wartime industrial relations.[107] It was an inspired bit of policymaking that would have important ramifications for the future. Right at that moment, however, its significance eluded organized labour. Given the limited influence of the National Labour Supply Council, labour leaders dismissed the NWLB as yet another ankle-deep gesture.[108] Frustrated, if not angered, by the inconsistencies in the wartime labour policies, many agreed with Sol Spivak of the Amalgamated Clothing Workers that "the Government is doing everything possible to keep labour from organizing."[109]

Fine-tuning

Throughout the spring and summer of 1941, as the government repressed civil liberties and wrestled with wage policies, the strike rate jumped by nearly 60 per cent. The number of workdays lost because of strikes almost doubled. Emboldened by improved economic conditions, inspired by aggressive organizing campaigns, and angered by resistant, if not truculent, employers, more and more workers were taking matters into their own hands and walking off their jobs. Half of the disputes took place in the less skilled manufacturing sector, most were of short duration, and many were illegal because they disregarded the conciliation process of the IDIA.[110] Although wage disagreements often sparked the disputes, the *Financial Post* reported that "the crux of the present disturbed situation, in fact, is ... the fundamental question of unionization."[111] Bryce Stewart blamed the strikes on the "evangelistic methods" of union organizers who had convinced workers they had everything to gain and nothing to lose by demanding impossible concessions from management.[112] Many labour leaders actually worried that the strike wave would irreparably damage the reputation of their unions as responsible partners in the war effort. They called on the government to enforce the PC 2685 principles and erase employer belligerency as a trigger. "We are reaching a danger point across Canada," Tom Moore warned King, "unless steps are taken to treat labour differently than it has been treated in the last eighteen months."[113]

Throughout 1941, however, the prime minister refused to deviate from labour policies that emphasized investigation and conciliation. When the historical record is considered in its entirety, it seems clear that this lack of innovation was not simply due to political expediency. It was his "breastplate of righteousness" that mainly repelled demands for change. Oblivious to the labour movement's charges of duplicity, he would not consider forcing employers to recognize and bargain with unions. When it came to the more immediate field of industrial relations, the prime minister continued to believe his government should remain an "impartial umpire," encouraging negotiation and compromise between employers and employees, not taking sides or determining outcomes. How could he justify such limited intervention? After careful coaching from King, McLarty offered the following explanation in the House of Commons:

> If you enter into the field of compulsion on the one side, you have to enter it on the other, and then you stir up inevitable difficulty. One trouble leads to another. [114]

Besides the prime minister's deep-rooted concern about employer backlash, he also remained convinced that compulsion was a slippery slope for workers. Although it may prove beneficial in the short run, the long run advantages were exceedingly questionable. For example, compulsory collective bargaining might lead to compulsory arbitration where workers would be forced to accept the awards of arbitrators – probably arbitrators with business sympathies. What King failed to recognize was that his argument was both outdated and moot. It ignored not only the realities of power in the less skilled workplace, but also the reality that compulsion in the form of wage controls was already a fact of life for most workers.

King's political principles were not the only deterrent to labour policy innovations. Extenuating circumstances also played a role. The exigencies of the war effort made it difficult for King to devote his full attention to industrial relations. In early 1941, for example, he was absorbed with sustaining Canada's military contribution, preventing diplomatic rifts between Great Britain and France, hosting the Dominion-Provincial Conference on the Rowell-Sirois Report, and negotiating the use of the St Lawrence Seaway. With Franklin D. Roosevelt, the US president, he also drafted a mutual defence purchasing pact called the Hyde Park Agreement.[115] Another mitigating factor was that most of the cabinet actually wanted more stringent restrictions placed on the labour movement. In late May and early June, King found himself in constant battle with C.D. Howe; J.L. Ralston, Rogers's replacement as minister of national defence; J.L. Ilsley, the new finance minister; and Angus MacDonald, the minister of national defence for naval services. Influenced by the exaggerated reports of the RCMP, his colleagues were intent on using the government's emergency powers "to crush out the CIO forms of organization." King had to insist repeatedly that autocratic policies had no place in "the art of government" and that "if Labour lost faith in the government it might slip away altogether in the forces of revolution."[116]

At one point, C.D. Howe even threatened to resign if he wasn't given the power to curtail illegal strikes in crucial war industries. The minister of munitions and supply was not opposed to "responsible unionism" that emphasized negotiation and accommodation. He had even thought of extending an invitation to William Green, the president of the American Federation of Labor, to come to Canada and preach the virtues of industrial stability to Canadian workers.[117] What mattered to Howe above all else, however, was continuous war production. In July 1941, he flew into a rage when 4,500 workers at the Aluminum Company of Canada in Arvida, Quebec, went on strike. Howe was convinced that the strike was a deliberate act of sabotage by "enemy aliens" (by which he meant left-leaning union organizers from the United States), because the Arvida compound provided most of the aluminum for British airplanes. When King rejected his request to send in federal troops, the DMS minister formally submitted his resignation. The prime minister immediately opened negotiations with the strikers and arranged for the provincial police to safeguard plant property. He discovered that much of the problem had to do with the government sending in a conciliator who only spoke English. But Howe was hardly assuaged. He refused to withdraw his resignation unless he was given the authority to use the army in future strikes.[118] King believed that it was "the old story of a man with great power wanting to get things his own way."[119] Still, he acquiesced, afraid to lose Howe's valuable organizational and administrative skills. It was an extraordinary incident that highlighted, once again, the government's selective use of compulsion and, especially, what King was up against in the cabinet when it came to workers' rights. "The rumours of sabotage, foreign agitators, and subversive ideas," a royal commission later reported, "[were] not justified."[120]

An additional problem for King was the increasing ineffectiveness of Norman McLarty. In early June, King had to stop his minister from reading a reactionary statement about strikes in Parliament that "lacked altogether the proper method of approach." When McLarty responded that he was extremely fatigued, so much so that the mere mention of a strike put him over the edge, King replied sharply that his real problem was alcohol. Drinking even a little bit "changed his character and gave him a false sense of his own strength," making it difficult to use good judgment in dealing with labour conflicts. King also shared that several cabinet members were worried about McLarty's drinking. Indeed "it was an embarrassment to us all." Given that the country was "in the beginning of what might come to be continuous industrial unrest," the prime minister warned McLarty to either get his act together or resign. Reluctant to disrupt government in the middle of a war, the prime minister hoped that his sermon had the desired effect. He knew, though, that McLarty would have to be replaced sometime in the near future.[121] More a liability than an asset, his labour minister could not be relied on for support or wise counsel. King, alone, would have to advocate for workers' rights in the cabinet – an uphill battle.

Fortunately for the prime minister, Bryce Stewart and the ICLC were prepared to act as watchdogs. Sharing many of the same industrial relations principles as King, these experts believed that they needed to tighten up, not discard, existing labour policies. Certainly the rising strike rate was regrettable. As Stewart noted, though, Canada was having "less trouble" with disputes than other countries. Something must be working right.[122] Rather than a complete policy overhaul, all that was required was some fine-tuning. The ICLC identified three areas that needed attention. The first had to do with the loopholes in section 502A of the Criminal Code. Although passed into law shortly before the war to outlaw union discrimination, section 502A only protected employees against reprisals for union membership, not for more aggressive activities like organizing. Even then, the prosecution had to prove clear intent on the part of the employer.[123] Stewart believed that this ineffective safeguard for freedom of association had "given rise to smoldering resentment in labour circles."[124] The previous month, for example, J.L. Cohen had brought charges against a foreman at the munitions-producing National Steel Car Corporation (NASCO) in Hamilton, Ontario, who had harassed workers for supporting a SWOC drive. Despite the testimonies of numerous witnesses, the judge ruled, rather reluctantly, that he could not find "any real intent to compel by threats any person to abstain from joining the union."[125] With outcomes like this, it was not surprising that many workers opted to go on strike to protest anti-union tactics rather than waste time in the courts.

The second area of focus for the ICLC was the conciliation process. Although the number of applications for conciliation boards had more than doubled in the last year, the conciliation branch of the Department of Labour (DOL) remained woefully understaffed with just eight officers. The time gap between an application for a conciliation board and the final report had become even more pronounced.[126] After gathering their courage to challenge employers, workers were told to keep their emotions in check for weeks on end, not even to take action if friends fell victim to unfair labour practices. It was asking too much. The rash of wildcat strikes in the spring and summer of 1941 largely reflected the severe delays in the conciliation process. Reluctant to dampen the enthusiasm of new union members and putting their faith in the power of collective action, more militant organizers encouraged or at least did little to prevent these illegal strikes. In April 1941, for example, Alex Welch of the Canadian Hosiery Workers decided to call a strike of the mostly female workforce at Schofield Woollen Mill in Oshawa, Ontario, a major producer of men's underwear, rather than get bogged down with the conciliation process.[127] Even the TLC complained to the prime minister that the inefficient operation of the IDIA "causes trouble instead of preventing it."[128] This frustration was not limited to the labour movement. Up to this point in the war, employers had remained fairly mute about labour policy. They were satisfied with the conciliation process because the outcomes were so benign and the delays dampened the enthusiasm of workers. They could also continue to rely on private reprisals to thwart unionism. But now wildcat strikes were becoming a real problem. Fed up with the way McLarty "has dilly dallied," the business community demanded immediate action to enforce the IDIA.[129]

The final problem for the ICLC was the question of union recognition. Even if the ICLC figured out a way to make the conciliation process work more effectively, it was next to impossible for conciliators or conciliation boards to facilitate compromises in recognition disputes. An employer either recognized a union or didn't – there was no middle ground. The sequence of events usually worked like this: workers would go out on strike illegally before applying for a conciliation board; DOL conciliators would convince them to return to work and apply for a conciliation board; the conciliation board would meet and recommend union recognition; the employer would reject the recommendation of the conciliation board to recognize the union; the workers would go out on strike once again. The lack of clear-cut direction in the IDIA and PC 2685 infuriated local union leaders. Take the CCL's Kitchener drive, for example. In May 1941, a federal conciliation officer convinced meatpacking workers at Dumart's Ltd. to stop their illegal strike and apply for a conciliation board. When the employer rejected the board's recommendation to recognize the union, the workers walked off their jobs once again.[130] Desperate to move forward, the local president bypassed his union executive and sent a telegram to King: "Urge that you request Dumart Mgt. to enable workers to go back by granting genuine CB."[131] But the government took no further action, and the strike dragged on. "In retrospect," a DOL report later admitted, "it does seem that a great many needless disputes occurred and were incapable of solution during the early ... war days, for want of clear expression of the right to organize and bargain collectively."[132]

The ICLC's efforts to improve wartime industrial relations began slowly and hesitantly. In February 1941, Bryce Stewart initiated a discussion about union discrimination with McLarty and the National Labour Supply Council.[133] Over the next two months, ideas flew back and forth about appropriate actions.[134] J.L. Cohen – through the CCL representatives on the NLSC – proposed the most far-reaching scheme, calling for the creation of a tripartite Labour Policy Enforcement Board. The board would have the power to investigate and levy penalties for violations of PC 2685.[135] Patrick Conroy, the new secretary-treasurer of the CCL, hailed the proposal as "a step in the right direction to the kind of machinery found in the Wagner Act."[136] But other NLSC members objected to the "threat of compulsion" in the board's operation. Instead, they called for a plan that emphasized mutual communication and economic context. The NLSC also considered the impact of employer penalties on the war effort.[137] Much debate ensued as amended proposals made the rounds. The moderates had the edge, especially after A.R. Mosher, the CCL president, resigned his NLSC seat to protest the stricter enforcement of wage controls. By late April, the ICLC had yet to make a recommendation to the King cabinet. Despite the escalating strike rate, the policymakers wanted to win the approval of all players in organized labour and the business community before moving forward on such a controversial issue.[138]

Ongoing developments at NASCO in Hamilton changed everything. In early February 1941, while J.L. Cohen pressed charges against the company for union discrimination, the workers had applied for a conciliation board to resolve the issue of union recognition. True to form, management dismissed the local president. When the conciliation board issued an interim report that urged reinstatement and a plant-wide representation vote, the notoriously anti-union company president, R.J. Magor, who was highly regarded in the business community, refused to comply.[139] In response, over 2,000 workers went out on strike. With NASCO involved in critical war work and sympathy strikes threatening to break out in steel plants across the country, Magor's belligerency caught the attention of Mackenzie King. He could not believe that these minor issues, especially the question of reinstatement, were about to paralyze war production. In private, he fumed about employers who "are not willing to make concessions to anyone in the ranks of labour who has the courage to speak out."[140] At the prime minister's direction, McLarty urged Magor to rehire the local president. Magor bluntly refused. The King cabinet then made the extraordinary decision of appointing Ernest Brunning, the Department of Munitions and Supply official who oversaw the country's steel production, as controller of the NASCO plant. Taking charge of daily operations, Brunning was given the same power to manage and carry on the business as a board of directors. It was an incredible flexing of muscles by the government. "[T]he company was given every opportunity to reinstate the man ... [even] told that they might divest themselves of embarrassment in the matter by placing the blame ... on the Government," Bryce Stewart explained. "The continuous operation of the plant was so vitally important that immediate action seemed necessary."[141] The strike ended, all the dismissed workers were reinstated, and SWOC won a three-to-one majority in a government-supervised recognition vote.[142]

Employers across the country expressed outrage at the government's action. But King barely flinched. Given his limited tolerance for obdurate stances, whether by labour leaders or employers, he took a very firm position on the takeover in a meeting with a delegation of business representatives, which included Magor and Harold Crabtree, the hard-nosed pulp and paper baron and current president of the Canadian Manufacturer's Association. After listening to a lengthy diatribe about "appeasing" the labour movement and the "evils" of the CIO, the prime minister responded with two points.[143] First, he assured his visitors that the NASCO takeover was consistent with his liberal philosophy of promoting cooperation and preventing large-scale unrest. To prevent a possible "revolution," the government was sending a strong message to the business community to be less arbitrary and more reasonable in its approach to industrial relations; it was counterbalancing that "certain blindness in human beings, which cause[s] them to see only one side of the question they [are] interested in." The takeover was about the public good, not about taking sides. Second, King made it clear that the business community was answerable to Ottawa, not the other way round.

Especially in a time of war, "there could only be one final authority and that was the government." It was strong language – certainly not what the businessmen expected to hear. But the prime minister wanted to make sure that the delegation, which he later called "as reactionary a group as I have ever met," understood his views on compulsion.[144] When it came to routine conflicts, the government would ensure negotiations, but not impose solutions. When it came to extreme behaviour by either workers or employers, the government would do what was necessary to restore order and stability.

The NASCO incident made it clear that policy reform was needed immediately. All sides agreed that crisis conditions prevailed in Canadian industrial relations. The business community called for "a more decisive, firmly administered Government policy on wartime labour problems."[145] Labour leaders blamed the lackluster enforcement of the IDIA and PC 2685 for the rising strike rate.[146] As a first step, the government began to crack down on illegal strikes.[147] McLarty appointed a royal commission to investigate the culpability of the organizers and workers in the Schofield Woollen dispute. In late May, the commission recommended that both the local president and Alex Welch, the secretary-treasurer of the Canadian Hosiery Workers, be prosecuted for only half-heartedly attempting to persuade workers to participate in the conciliation process.[148] At the same time, McLarty pressed charges against C.S. Jackson, the UE president, and fourteen shop stewards when they blatantly ignored his warning to abide by the IDIA and, instead, organized a "holiday" of 700 workers at two Canadian General Electric plants in Toronto. Jackson, who "coincidentally" was interned a few days later, argued in court that a "holiday" was not the same as a strike because it lacked demands or pickets. But the judge found the union activists guilty of contravening the law and fined them twenty dollars a person for each day of the strike.[149]

Besides trying to enforce participation in the conciliation process, the ICLC took three steps to improve the effectiveness of the IDIA. Unlike the earlier, consensus-building effort with the National Labour Supply Council, these initiatives were quickly and unilaterally drafted – though subject to the final approval of Mackenzie King.[150] First, in early June 1941, the King cabinet passed PC 4020, which created a three-member Industrial Disputes Inquiry Commission (IDIC) to conduct, at the labour minister's request, preliminary investigations into existing or impending strikes. On the basis of its inquiry, the IDIC would recommend whether or not to appoint a conciliation board. Although another step had been added to the IDIA, PC 4020 was actually supposed to streamline the practice of conciliation. "We hope by that process," Stewart clarified, "and by the mediation that a board of that sort can undertake, to be able to dispose of most disputes shortly after they appear on the horizon."[151] To dampen enthusiasm for strikes, PC 4020 also eliminated the controversial strike vote requirement for a conciliation board application. Second, a week after the passage of PC 4020, the government amended the IDIA to prevent someone who had recently worked as either a labour or corporate lawyer from sitting on conciliation boards. The idea was to preserve and/or restore the standing of the boards as impartial fact-finding bodies. It was also an effort to encourage more unanimous reports. Third, in early July 1941, the King cabinet passed PC 4844 (which became section 5 of PC 4020) to give the IDIC the power to investigate and resolve union discrimination charges. Once the IDIC determined that a discharge was unjustified, it could try to convince employers to hire back workers. In the worst-case scenario, the IDIC could also advise the labour minister to order a reinstatement.[152]

Mackenzie King's imprint on this flurry of activity was very evident. When colleagues tried to impose stricter restrictions on organized labour, he blocked their efforts to preserve the "impartiality" of the government. At the same time, he made sure that none of the new orders were significant policymaking departures. The goal was to tighten up the conciliation process, not to introduce new ways of doing things. Under King's watchful eye, in other words, the ICLC crafted orders that improved the conditions for investigation and conciliation without seriously impugning what he considered to be the neutral role of the government. Even PC 4844, which the Department of Labour later claimed was the "first step" away from the principle of evenhandedness because employers could be pressured to rehire workers, supported the status quo in practice.[153] In nearly half of the clear-cut cases of union discrimination considered in 1941 (seventeen of forty cases), the IDIC was not able to use its powers of persuasion to get workers rehired. Nor did the labour minister order any reinstatements. The ambiguous powers of PC 4844 made it a far cry from a "Labour Policy Enforcement Board."[154]

The response of the labour movement was mixed. Clearly the government's effort to address union discrimination was welcomed.[155] Most labour leaders also expressed limited support for the actions taken against radical unionists who evaded the conciliation process; as mentioned earlier, they worried how this kind of "irresponsible" union behaviour would stigmatize the labour movement. But there was considerable disagreement about PC 4020 and the IDIA amendment. The more established craft unions in the TLC largely supported these initiatives; King had actually asked for Tom Moore's views before agreeing to the idea of the IDIC.[156] Convinced the IDIC would further delay the conciliation process and exhaust the patience of workers, the CCL leadership emphatically disagreed.[157] It also recognized the IDIA amendment as a barely concealed effort to restrict the activities of the omnipresent J.L. Cohen.[158] Since the onset of war, the intensely driven labour lawyer had sat on twelve conciliation boards. Although eight of the boards produced unanimous reports, the ICLC believed that Cohen's strong views on collective bargaining rights hampered the conciliation process.[159] As Norman Dowd of the CCL remarked, however, Cohen was one of the few labour representatives who "[was] capable of fighting against the prejudices of the other members of the Board."[160] Many TLC locals agreed. In fact, his participation in the conciliation process probably encouraged more nascent unions to abide by the IDIA. Perhaps for this reason, the amendment was later repealed.[161]

Plant Committees

The question of union recognition remained. It was all well and good to improve the effectiveness of the conciliation process. But what was the point if compromise was next to impossible? The solution was obvious to the prime minister and the ICLC members with industrial relations expertise: the government needed to become more intentional about promoting non-union plant committees. Also known as employee representation plans, plant committees were initiated by employers and involved an equal number of management and employee delegates who met on a regular basis to discuss matters of mutual concern. King had originally conceived of the idea twenty-five years earlier to provide "a guarantee of fair play" in the Colorado mining camps of the Rockefellers.[162] Although similar kinds of non-adversarial, company-driven plans had existed before, King's approach was unique because the workers enjoyed a relatively fair amount of influence. They won collective representation and long-term advances in wages, job security, and self-respect. There was also a non-reprisal feature for union membership. The joint committee was attractive to employers because they avoided the adversarial demands and economic costs associated with union recognition. The public good, as a whole, benefited.[163] As the former research director at the Rockefeller-funded Industrial Relations

Counselors, Inc., Bryce Stewart of the ICLC was quite familiar with plant committee schemes. During the 1920s, his firm had encouraged numerous clients, including Dofasco and several US subsidiaries in Canada, to implement them because they undercut the proclivity for "class struggle and strife" by emphasizing cooperation and mutual gain.[164] Although most plant committees in Canada folded during the Great Depression, when many employers decreased wages unilaterally, Stewart believed that war production necessitated the scheme's resurrection. With the strike rate surging, he worried that the new generation of labour leaders in the industrial unions was "raw and uncouth" and wanted "to rectify things drastically."[165] Wouldn't the interests of workers, not to mention the country, be better served if strikes were avoided? Stewart warned the Canadian Manufacturers Association that "certain kinds of protection for labour must inevitably be developed" in the modern era. Rather than deal with confrontational unions, however, it made far more sense for employers to be proactive and establish plant committees.[166]

Historically, employers had often created plant committees in response to union organizing and labour unrest. So did the government promote them as union avoidance strategies? Yes and no. Both King and Stewart agreed that a plant committee, which recognized the common interests of workers and management, was far superior to a combative labour organization. What mattered above all else was not union recognition, but establishing the conditions for negotiation and problem solving – for industrial peace and improved working conditions. It was only in the absence of conflict and acrimony that grievances could be resolved and material improvements realized. Although plant committees were the products of managerial reform, all parties benefited because the committees cleared away misunderstandings, encouraged collaboration, and heightened productivity; reason and intelligence, order and stability prevailed.[167] Yet King and Stewart also acknowledged the desirability of bona fide unions. Workers needed the industry-wide strength and financial support of national or international unions to become real industrial citizens. Although a plant committee may enjoy some authority, it was authority given to it by the employer. It lacked the collective, independent power of a union.[168] Since employers hired consultants and belonged to associations, Stewart wrote in a 1941 article, "employees ... are entitled also to outside assistance."[169] But there was an important caveat. Responsible, moderate labour leaders – leaders like Tom Moore who avoided hardline positions – needed to be in charge of these unions. The only legitimate labour organization, in other words, was one that eschewed conflict and hostility for open-mindedness, negotiation, a method to remove the cause for the dispute as stated in the application by the Kirkland Lake Mine and Mill Workers Union No. 240 under date of July 17, 1941, for the establishment of a Board of Conciliation and Investigation, the Commission would have been disposed to recommend that the establishment of a Board would not be justified.

The mining companies having undertaken to negotiate signed agreements to govern rates of pay and working conditions of their employees with committees of employees chosen by the employees themselves, it is the opinion of the Commission that upon the election of committees as provided for, negotiations between such committee of employees and the companies should be proceeded with, such action being within the spirit and intent of Clause 7 of Order in Council P. C. 2685. If the Kirkland Lake Mine and Mill Workers Union No. 240 have the membership they claim in each of the mines the Union should be able to elect the committees to represent the employees. If after the election of committees of employees and following negotiations between such committees and the companies there remain any questions in dispute, such specific questions, if desired and justified, could then be matters for reference to a Board of Conciliation and Investigation.

However, it developed in the discussions with the representatives of the employees that as a result of a visit of the Chief Conciliation Officer, Mr. M. S. Campbell, to Kirkland Lake on June 21-22, 1941, they had understood from Mr. Campbell that he would recommend the establishment of a Board of Conciliation and Investigation. There was evidently some uncertainty on the part of the employees about this understanding, and under date of July 8, 1941, Mr. R. H. Carlin, Secretary, Kirkland Lake Mine and Mill Workers Union, addressed a telegram to the Minister of Labour, reading as follows:

"Conciliation Officer Campbell advised negotiating committee he would recommend Conciliation Board without strike vote. Would you kindly confirm this to expedite matters."

In reply to this message, Mr. Gerald H. Brown, Assistant Deputy Minister of Labour, addressed on July 9, 1941, to Mr. R. H. Carlin, a telegram reading as follows:

"Reference night letter to Minister would advise your understanding correct. Mr. Campbell recommends establishment of Board without strike vote. Board application forms being mailed tonight and presume application will be received in due course."

The conditions as they existed at the time Mr. Campbell visited Kirkland Lake have been materially changed by the undertaking of the mining companies to the Industrial Disputes Inquiry Commission. However, it appears to the Commission, notwithstanding the facts as they have been developed as a result of its inquiry, that in view of the statement of the Chief Conciliation Officer to the

2.8 Report #19 of the Industrial Disputes Inquiry Committee (IDIC), Kirkland Lake Gold Mines, August 1941. As the IDIC made clear in its Kirkland Lake report, the wartime government actively supported plant or employee committees as alternatives to bona-fide unions. In response, many employers began to encourage these less invasive set-ups when confronted with organizing campaigns. Some, like Stelco and Ford Canada, paid for large newspaper advertisements to convince workers to support their non-union schemes in representation votes (see figures 2.9 and 2.10).

Source: Library and Archives Canada, Report #19 of the Industrial Disputes Inquiry Committee, 12 August 1941, RG 27, V.637, File 188.

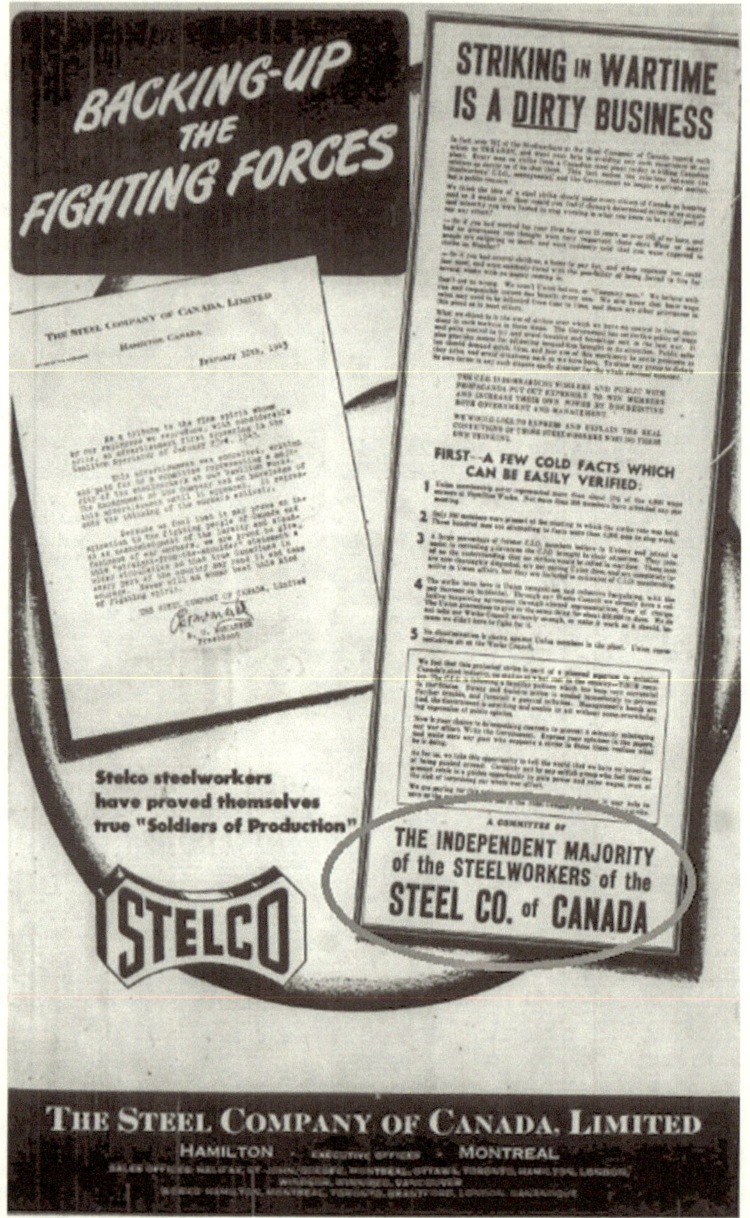

2.9 "Striking in Wartime Is a Dirty Business," Stelco newspaper advertisement, February 1943

Source: *Toronto Daily Star*, 13 February 1943, 5, Library and Archives Canada, Amicus No. 7791836.

FORD OF CANADA AND THE C.I.O.

Today Ford Employees Vote on a Matter of National Importance

TODAY in Windsor, Ontario, nearly 12,000 Ford employees are casting their votes to decide whether the U.A.W.-C.I.O. shall be their sole and exclusive representative in their dealings with this Company, or whether the employees shall form their own organization and elect their own representatives from among themselves, to deal directly with the Company.

The result of this vote, which is being conducted by the Dominion Department of Labour, is of vital importance to you as a Canadian citizen.

At the present time the Empire faces the greatest crisis in its history. The great Ford plant at Windsor is one of its most valuable assets because it is the greatest single source of mechanical transport for Empire armies.

For the past two years the production of this plant has continued without a break. Through the whole-hearted co-operation of its thousands of loyal Canadian employees the Company has been able to produce more than 112,000 military vehicles. During this time the Company and its employees have continued to work together in peace and harmony, united in a single objective—to help win this war.

Now outside influences are being brought to bear. These influences may interfere with the steady production of the plant.

Official statistics show that of all the time lost through strikes in the first six months of this year, 86.9 per cent has occurred where the C.I.O. is involved; this in spite of the fact that the C.I.O. represented only 1.4 per cent of workers in Canada.

This Company is keenly aware of its responsibility to Labour. It offers to negotiate a collective bargaining agreement with a committee elected from among, and by the employees themselves. It has offered to negotiate with such a committee, matters affecting adjustments in rates of pay (subject to government regulations), seniority rules, grievance procedure, medical, surgical and hospitalization plans and other matters affecting their employment with the Company.

The U.A.W.-C.I.O. has advanced no proposals to the Company regarding benefits it hopes to obtain for the employees. It simply—as an outside organization—demands that the Company recognize it as the sole representative of the employees.

Today the employees of this Company are making a vital decision regarding the future of the Company's operations. They are deciding whether or not the operations of this great war industry shall be controlled in Canada by Canadians. The results of this vote may have far-reaching implications affecting the successful prosecution of the war.

FORD MOTOR COMPANY OF CANADA, LIMITED

The British Empire's largest single source of military vehicles

2.10 "Ford Canada and the CIO," Ford newspaper advertisement, November 1941

Source: *Winnipeg Tribune*, 3 November 1941, 15, Library and Archives Canada, Amicus No. 3821471.

and compromise. In the absence of this ideal, a plant committee was the preferred form of collective representation. King claimed that plant committees were like midway points on a continuum with individual workers on one end and responsible unions on the other.[170] They could serve as springboards for unionism once workers learned the benefits of cooperation and management learned the benefits of collective representation. A plant committee "was not intended to be a substitute for unionism, but rather a means to leading up to it where circumstances justified such a course."[171]

Many detractors dismissed government-sanctioned plant committees as company unions or, to paraphrase industrial relations scholar Bruce Kaufman, the "toothless creatures of management domination."[172] To be sure, they were management driven. It was the employer who established and terminated a plant committee. It was the employer who determined the scale and scope of a plant committee – what issues were open for discussion and what actions would be implemented. It was the employer who often pushed a plant committee scheme on workers during a union drive to remain in control. "If there are matters to be improved now because of changing conditions," one shoe manufacturer wrote to his workforce, "how about forming your own Shop Committee to work for you?"[173] Still, the Labour Department mandated three redeeming features to distinguish plant committees from company unions.[174] First, workers must remain free to form and belong to unions – their collective rights must be acknowledged. Although used as anti-union devices, plant committees did not preclude the presence of unions. Second, employee representatives on the plant committee had to be elected by a majority of workers in a secret ballot; the company could not interfere in any way with the voting process. This procedure meant that union members often held seats on plant committees. "There's nothing that keeps a union from controlling plant committees," explained Stewart.[175] Third, the employer had to negotiate and sign a collective agreement with the committee, ensuring consistency and commitment. When the Packinghouse Workers Organizing Committee began to organize six Canada Packers plants in Toronto, for example, the government refused to recognize the firm's existing employee representation plan as a legitimate entity because it lacked a "contract basis."[176] In sum, government-sanctioned plant committees involved some semblance of power sharing between management and employees. For unorganized workers, who held out little chance of winning union recognition, this kind of collective representation was better than nothing. It offered a number of opportunities to curb arbitrary managerial behaviour and win benefits. For unions that found it difficult to organize a workplace, plant committees could be used as jumping off points to recognition. As George Burt of the United Auto Workers acknowledged, it sometimes made sense for members to join plant committees and gain shop floor power rather than "stick their necks out" and face employer recriminations.[177]

During the summer of 1941, the government began to actively promote plant committees as the solution to recognition disputes. "[E]mployers would be well-advised," Stewart privately counselled the Canadian Manufacturers Association, "to organize some kind of shop committee or works council representing the employees, and enter into a collective agreement with them."[178] Once again making headlines, the NASCO dispute in Hamilton became the model for wartime industrial relations. Despite the government takeover, workers had not fared well. Although SWOC won a DOL-supervised recognition vote at NASCO, Ernest Brunning, the government-appointed controller, refused to meet with the union. Normally the president of Consumer's Glass in Montreal, he harboured well-entrenched anti-union biases.[179] As Mackenzie King acknowledged, dollar-a-year men in the DMS as a whole carried "into their relations with the government prejudices which they, themselves, had against dealing with Unions."[180] But this union avoidance was not just Brunning's initiative. High-ranking DMS officials had given him direct orders to avoid negotiating a collective bargaining contract on behalf of the employer. They felt strongly that the question of collective representation remained a managerial prerogative; it lay outside the scope of the takeover. Instead of the union leadership, Brunning met with an informal group of employees to discuss wages and working conditions. On 28 July when NASCO workers learned about the meeting, the strike resumed.[181] An incensed Charlie Millard, who now headed SWOC, wrote McLarty:

> The refusal to sign an agreement with the organization chosen by the employees, chosen in a ballot conducted by your own Department ... is a complete denial of the principle of Collective Bargaining which the government claims to favour and support.[182]

Over C.D. Howe's strenuous objections, King had his office schedule a meeting with strike leaders for 31 July. On the day of the conference, he was utterly exhausted, "so much so that [he] experienced almost physical pain." Extremely upset with Brunning's "arbitrary and bad judgment," however, he decided to obey his "voice of conscience" and meet with the delegation in the late afternoon. The workers were "hard-looking customers," though King admitted they had to be to fight for their collective rights. Speaking quietly, but purposefully, he explained how the government did not take sides, but looked after the public good. He promised that his administration would stand behind PC 2685 if the NASCO employees returned to their jobs. The strike leaders responded favourably, asking to meet that evening with officials from the DOL and DMS to discuss demands. Shaking hands on the way out, one of the men remarked to the prime minister that he had "done a great thing in saving this situation from becoming more dangerous."[183] The next day SWOC ended the strike in anticipation of a contract, and the DMS replaced the now despised Brunning with a new controller.[184] But the strike leaders had been badly and rather deceitfully misled. What the prime minister had failed to explain was that he defined collective representation very broadly. Within twenty-four hours, the new controller had established a plant committee at NASCO. When Millard complained bitterly to McLarty, he learned that the government recognized SWOC – just not for the sake of collective bargaining.[185]

The new Industrial Disputes Inquiry Commission (IDIC) also pushed plant committees as a solution to recognition disputes. Since its inception in June 1941, the IDIC had significantly reduced the workload of the conciliation boards, disposing of 45 per cent of applications involving war industries and bringing about settlements in nearly half of its investigations.[186] The three members of the IDIC shared a low tolerance for the recognition demands of workers, especially when more militant unions were involved. George Hodge, the personnel manager for Canadian Pacific Railway, gained most of his industrial relations experience working with the well-established railway brotherhoods. A strong advocate of industry-wide councils, where groups of companies and unions discuss industry conditions, he believed that only "reasonable and fair-minded men" could resolve differences between employers and workers.[187] Gilbert Jackson was a financial consultant with an academic background. As president of Sentinel Securities of Canada, he was considered by the Canadian Manufacturers' Association to be pro-business. Indeed, he tried to use his influence in the government to defeat the union organizing campaign of the Packinghouse Workers at Canada Packers.[188] Humphrey Mitchell, the IDIC chair, was a British-born electrician from Hamilton who had held many leadership positions in the Ontario TLC and sat in the House of Commons from 1931 to 1935 as an Independent Labour member. Since losing his seat in Parliament, he had received several appointments to government agencies and panels in the King administration, most recently as secretary of the Labour Co-ordination Committee and the National Labour Supply Council. Much like King and Stewart, Mitchell was more interested in developing mutually beneficial industrial relations than usurping the power of employers. According to the *Financial Post*, he was someone who "loathes extremist views either of left or right ... He talks labour's language, yet can be depended upon to give the boss a fair deal." Certainly, Mitchell disliked the idea of aggressive unionism during a national crisis. As he warned rather pointedly: "Anyone who thinks the war is a bloody Christmas tree has another thing coming."[189]

After some initial success promoting plant committees, the IDIC gained considerable notoriety when it attempted to pursue a similar agenda in a recognition dispute between the International Union of Mine, Mill, and Smelter Workers (Mine Mill) and twelve gold mine operators in Kirkland Lake, Ontario.[190] After the Teck-Hughes debacle a year earlier, the miners had regrouped and, with some limited assistance from the CCL, initiated a new organizing campaign. Although a federal conciliation officer promised the appointment of a conciliation board when the operators refused to recognize the union, it was the IDIC that arrived in town in early August 1941 to conduct an investigation. Upon hearing both sides of the conflict, the commission recommended that each of the mines agree to enter into a one-year contract with an employee committee. All employee representatives would be elected by secret ballot in a DOL-supervised vote. Deprived of union recognition and a collective agreement, the gold miners rejected the proposal as "contrary to the principles of the labour movement." The mine operators accepted the recommendation, however, because they recognized that plant committees were far preferable to Mine Mill. The IDIC commended them for agreeing "to go as far as is required under the provisions of Order in Council PC 2685." When plant committees were established at each mine, the IDIC declared the case closed. The miners, however, were far from defeated. In a few months, the Kirkland Lake dispute would erupt into one of the pivotal strikes of the war.[191]

Soon to become the CCL's research director, Eugene Forsey observed that the government's plant committee scheme was like "a red flag to a bull to every union."[192] Labour leaders across the country expressed outrage. Yet, by endorsing plant committees, the government insisted it was simply trying to define a middle ground, not to deny workers their collective rights. "Our endeavour," Humphrey Mitchell explained, "is to get [the employer] to go as far as possible towards establishing a collective bargaining relationship with representative employees."[193] This rationale for what became known as "the Kirkland Lake formula" was lost on the labour movement. Throughout the summer and fall of 1941, labour leaders repeatedly skewered the King administration for violating the principles of PC 2685 and departing from its much-heralded position of impartiality. Even the moderate TLC believed that government-sanctioned plant committees were "nothing more or less than a policy of 'company unions.'"[194] Most labour leaders agreed with J.L. Cohen that a plant committee "was really an intimidation of the worker, because it reminds him ... that the employer is in complete control, not only of the company side of the bargaining process, but also of the workers' side."[195]

As if the plant committee scheme was not enough, the government further angered the labour movement when it passed PC 7307 in September 1941. A late and rather desperate effort to enhance the conciliation process, the new order made it illegal for workers to strike after the release of a conciliation board report until a majority of the workers cast favourable ballots in a DOL-supervised vote. The affected employees had to request the vote. Fines and prison sentences enforced the strike ban.[196] A direct response to a protracted strike of 4,000 auto workers at McKinnon Industries in St Catharines, Ontario, the order was drafted, according to McLarty, "to prevent the calling of strikes by snap decisions of minority groups."[197] Policymakers assumed that workers would act "reasonably" if given the chance to vote on strike action – their desire to support the war effort would prevail over their economic concerns. As the DOL later admitted, though, PC 7307 was "based upon a faulty premise and psychology."[198] Between 1941 and 1944, workers voted against strike action only five times. All but one of the anti-strike instances took place within a few months of the order's passage.[199] Although Tom Moore helped to draft PC 7307, it mainly incited the wrath of organized labour.[200] Most labour leaders agreed with the normally moderate Norman Dowd of the CCL that "the government has demonstrated once again its inability or unwillingness to understand the purpose and function of the Labour movement."[201]

For the first two years of the war, Mackenzie King donned his "breastplate of righteousness" to spurn pleas from labour, business, and even his own colleagues for labour policy reforms. When hampered by an incompetent labour minister and preoccupied with developments overseas, he depended on the ICLC, whose members also believed in the sanctity of cooperation and compromise, to reinforce his conciliatory approach to industrial relations. Far removed from the realities of the workplace, the prime minister and his industrial relations experts failed to recognize how their commitment to the status quo perpetuated power inequities in the employment relationship. "Even an attempt to occupy a neutral position," Cohen tried to explain, "implies an attitude, and so constitutes an influence, on the whole process of recognition and acceptance of ... trade unions."[202] Genuinely concerned about the plight of working people, but burdened with the blind arrogance that often accompanies formal education and authority, the government officials also didn't understand how the imposition of wage controls, the incarceration of radical unionists, and the rejection of a compulsory collective bargaining policy could be perceived as inconsistent, if not duplicitous, policymaking.

By the fall of 1941, a large number of labour leaders demanded a complete overhaul of the wartime labour policies. At both the TLC and CCL conventions, delegates moved for the passage of a Wagner-like act that forced employers to recognize and bargain with unions. While more conservative voices called for patience and diplomacy, many others urged an all-out fight to win favourable policy outcomes.[203] As Patrick Conroy of the CCL wrote to a colleague:

> The only action left for us is to arouse the whole trade union movement to bring about a definite and concrete policy on the part of the Government that will give true protection to workers seeking fair wage adjustments and recognition of their unions.[204]

In the months ahead, this sweeping call to arms would bring Canadian industrial relations to a critical juncture. Thanks to an escalating strike rate and an effective promotional campaign by the CCL, people from all walks of life would begin to recognize the benefits of compulsory collective bargaining – to associate it with the public good. Although Mackenzie King continued to remain true to his principles, his "breastplate of righteousness" would be put to the test, like never before.

Chapter Three

The Task That Lies Ahead, Fall 1941–Fall 1942

On the morning of 15 December 1941, Mackenzie King reached for his well-thumbed copy of *Industry and Humanity*, turned towards the back of the book, and proceeded to read aloud: "To democratize Industry, so that along with democracy in government there may be a true Industrial Democracy, is the task that lies ahead."[1] Humphrey Mitchell, the tall, burly chair of the Industrial Disputes Inquiry Commission (IDIC) who had just entered King's library on the third floor of Laurier House, listened intently. Closing the cover, the prime minister told Mitchell that even though he wrote the book twenty-five years ago, he still subscribed to those words. One of the main goals of his public life had always been to contribute "toward [the] improvement of labour's conditions." Given that, King continued, he wanted the IDIC chair to become his new minister of labour, replacing the hapless Norman McLarty. Wartime industrial relations were in a "critical situation," he explained. What was needed was a real "labour man" in the cabinet who would "watch labour's interests closely." Pleased to learn that Tom Moore of the Trades and Labour Congress (TLC) had recommended him, Mitchell agreed to join the government, though he stressed that it was from a sense of duty, not because he had political ambitions. After further discussion, King picked up another set of writings, this time by his grandfather, the outspoken reformer William Lyon Mackenzie, and shared a passage about working for the oppressed. When finished, he looked up from the book and said to Mitchell, "I want [you] to help me continue the struggle on labour's behalf against the monopolies of wealth, privilege, and power." With an English accent that traced back to his working-class upbringing in Sussex, Mitchell assured King that he was "a Liberal in the broad sense of the term … regarding the extreme right and extreme left as both the wrong attitudes." That was just what the prime minister wanted to hear. "[T]he more I talked with Mitchell," he later reflected, "the more I liked him and the more I became convinced that the right choice had been made."[2]

Even with the highly vaunted Mitchell in office, however, wartime industrial relations continued to deteriorate in 1942. When the unemployment rate dropped to below 3 per cent due to increased government expenditures, workers realized the balance of power had finally tipped in their favour.[3] One out of five dared to sign a union card, and the ranks of organized labour swelled. Thanks to corporate resistance, the strike rate also escalated dramatically, especially in the manufacturing sector.[4] Worried that the "Canadian labor problem" undermined the Allied war effort, Frances Perkins, the labor secretary in the United States, considered offering Canadian authorities some advice on stemming the unrest.[5] Meanwhile, more Canadians, inside and outside the labour movement, were demanding comprehensive labour policies that did a better job of protecting, if not advancing, the collective rights of workers. Their diverse calls lacked organizational unity and clear-cut leadership. They also involved different motives and convictions. Some people sought industrial stability and heightened productivity. Others expressed concerns about power relations and shop floor justice. Still, a growing number of Canadians shared a healthy contempt for the ineffectiveness of the existing wartime labour policies. "Until such time as Labour receives proper protection in the matter of collective bargaining," Pat Conroy of the Canadian Congress of Labour (CCL) warned Mitchell, "we are going to have a continuance of Labour trouble in this country."[6]

Before the year was over, a frustrated King was ready to dismiss the new labour minister for his "surprising lack of endeavour to have the cause of labour really advanced rather than antagonized."[7] Imperious in manner and not fully understanding the issues, Mitchell mainly succeeded in alienating labour leaders in both the craft and industrial unions. But was he solely to blame for the crisis conditions? What escaped the prime minister was that his own vision for Canadian industrial relations was increasingly at odds with the rest of the country. Despite growing public support for the pro-labour Co-operative Commonwealth Federation (CCF), the drafting of compulsory collective bargaining bills in two provinces, and the Conservative Party's surprising adoption of a collective bargaining plank, King continued to advocate an ostensibly impartial approach to industrial relations.

Clearly, the prime minister wanted improved conditions and greater influence for workers. He still believed that "to democratize industry" was "the task that lies ahead." But King also remained convinced that "the task" could only be accomplished through investigation and conciliation – by appeals to reason and efforts to compromise. Although many groups demanded legislative reform, he clung to his principles, confident that his conceptual framework for industrial relations was the right approach – certain that "the task" could be accomplished without a Wagner-like act. Rather than alienate employers and threaten the unity of the country, he continued, in effect, to perpetuate the inequities of the employment relationship.

The Campaign

During the late afternoon of 22 October 1941, the leaders of the CCL met with Norman McLarty (Mitchell's appointment was still several weeks away) to complain about the passage of PC 8253 or the wage freeze policy. What they were particularly angry about was not that PC 8253 had been imposed on them, but that the order – unlike PC 7440, the earlier wage policy – failed to affirm the principles of union recognition and collective bargaining. In no uncertain terms, the labour leaders called on the federal government to do something to protect the collective rights of workers. Their demands fell flat. "You suggest that we might go further and make ... a Wagner Act for Canada," responded McLarty. "The only difficulty is that the Wagner Act hasn't worked any too well in the United States ... This idea of compulsion in Labour matters has not been successful." Although the labour minister agreed that "the right of collective bargaining is a fundamental one," he refused to support "an arbitrary edict that unions must be recognized." Given the imposition of wage controls and the imprisonment of radical unionists, McLarty's answer deeply angered the CCL leaders. Convinced that policymaking had more to do with political expediency than professed principles, they told the labour minister that collective bargaining was going to become a rallying cry for workers in the factories, mines, and camps. With war production booming and the labour supply shrinking, unions would also use economic action to wrest concessions from the government. "Organized Labour will not provide cooperation," A.R. Mosher, the CCL president, promised, "unless the Government is prepared to apply the same compulsion to the employers in regard to Collective Bargaining as being put on workers in regard to wages."[8]

"Collective bargaining is vital!" exhorted Charlie Millard at a follow-up meeting of the CCL's executive committee.[9] Despite their ideological differences, everyone in the room agreed. Given Joseph Stalin's recent call for the defeat of fascism,[10] even the communists linked contractual relations to an enhanced war effort. Recently released from the internment camp, C.S. Jackson of the United Electrical Workers (UE) insisted: "Full production potentials are realized only where bona fide collective bargaining exists between management and organized labour."[11] More moderate CCL leaders also understood that the organizational survival of their unions was at stake, except they believed that collective bargaining, especially at the industry level, would lead to a general accommodation between labour and business, not a radical restructuring of society. In the words of Patrick Conroy, the CCL's secretary-treasurer, it would signal "that Labour has the equal part in industry ... thereby creating the basis of confidence between the two partners."[12] Since 1940, the congress had experienced phenomenal growth as its affiliates made inroads in numerous mass production industries.[13] Despite these promising developments, however, the unions had not cracked the country's leading companies. With many employers refusing recognition, much less negotiating and signing contracts, these fledgling labour organizations lacked permanency. The CCL leaders realized that less skilled workers were not going to continue to put their jobs on the line for illusive promises of higher wages and better working conditions, especially if the economy slumped again. With limited cash flows and formidable organizational barriers, they needed a Canadian Wagner Act to ensure their future.

In the late fall of 1941, a week after the meeting with McLarty, the CCL leadership decided to take a forceful stand on collective bargaining. The catalyst was the protracted dispute between gold miners and mine operators at Kirkland Lake, Ontario. Earlier, when the IDIC's plant committee solution failed to placate the recognition demands of the miners, Norman McLarty had, rather reluctantly, agreed to appoint a conciliation board to investigate the dispute.[14] During the board's hearings, the corporate lawyer abruptly withdrew, stating: "We are unalterably opposed to entering into any agreement with Local 240, which is affiliated with the CIO. We feel that it has not justified itself ... It has been nothing but a disturbing element."[15] On 15 October, the conciliation board unanimously recommended that the operators recognize and bargain with the International Union of Mine, Mill, and Smelter Workers (Mine Mill). But the mine operators refused to accept the conciliation report. Anticipating a strike, the CCL threw its full support behind the miners. Although A.R. Mosher, the CCL president, expressed reservations, most of the executive committee agreed that it was time to fight for the principle of collective bargaining.[16] On 8 November, despite some questionable revisions to the procedural rules of PC 7307, the recently passed strike vote requirement, eight of the twelve mines voted in favour of strike action. Ten days later, with the operators as obdurate as ever and mediation efforts at a standstill, the night shifts at the eight mines failed to report to work. Pat Conroy wrote to Allan Haywood, the CIO's director of organization, that Kirkland Lake had become "the battle-field [for] the question of collective bargaining for the entire Dominion."[17]

The striking miners received funding and encouragement from labour organizations and other sympathetic groups across the country. But the operators held the upper hand. Not only did the strike take place in the dead of winter in Northern Ontario, but the recent passage of the Lend-Lease Act, which allowed the transfer of war materials from the United States to Britain without payment, and the Hyde Park Agreement, which guaranteed a flow of US dollars into Canada, had dampened the demand for gold production (gold was no longer needed to buy equipment from the Americans).[18] Bryce Stewart, the deputy minister of labour, observed that "the gold mine operators don't have to worry. They can shut down the mines until after the war."[19] Despite repeated appeals, the federal government also refused to intervene on behalf of the miners. Mackenzie King claimed that the Department of Labour (DOL) had done everything within its power to prevent the strike and could do nothing more.[20] Pat Conroy warned the prime minister that "the Government's toleration of the anti-Labour attitude of the mine-operators has seriously disturbed the workers all over Canada."[21] Privately, King agreed, as did, surprisingly, most of the cabinet. Given his fear of backlash and the government's presumption of impartiality, however, King was not about to force the hand of the employers.[22] Meanwhile, at the behest of the operators, Mitchell Hepburn, the Ontario premier, sent in the provincial police to protect replacement workers and intimidate strikers. Obliged to end the strike in early February 1942, Reid Robinson, the international president of Mine Mill, wrote to Philip Murray, the CIO president: "In all my experience I have never encountered so much indifference on the part of governmental officials toward the rights of the workers."[23]

Unions representing over 100,000 workers, including some regional councils of the Trades and Labour Congress (TLC), had supported the gold miners.[24] Yet, this impressive display of economic power failed to trigger the policymaking process. "There is no point in denying that [the Kirkland Lake strike] has been a defeat for organized labour in this Dominion," a labour journalist wrote.[25] To make matters worse, the CCL's participation on government bodies was also proving fruitless. At the request of the TLC, the government or, more specifically, Bryce Stewart and the Interdepartmental Committee on Labour Co-ordination had disbanded the impotent National Labour Supply Council and created a smaller Consultative Committee on Labour Policy, which consisted of two separate groups of labour and business representatives.[26] With the CCL allowed only two seats on the eight-person labour panel, Pat Conroy held out few hopes that it would serve as a collective bargaining vehicle.[27] The congress was also underrepresented on the new National War Labour Board (NWLB), which PC 8253 or the wage freeze policy had created, with no seats on the executive and only one on the advisory body.[28] In late February, an angry CCL delegation presented a memorandum to King that listed in detail how the government had wronged labour since the beginning of the war. "As I looked into the faces of the men there," the prime minister later wrote in his diary, "they seemed to be those of men who ... were feeling the whole of society was against them. That they were full of grievances and full of suspicion, and not believing anything that was being told them."[29]

All was not lost. If nothing else, the Kirkland Lake strike had revealed the inadequacies of the wartime labour policies to a much wider audience. As one commentator noted: "The eyes of the general public [were] opened a little at least to the ranting hypocrisy of the federal government."[30] With few other options, the CCL launched a multifaceted campaign to draw on and cultivate this popular opinion – to improve its own public image and place compulsory collective bargaining on the national agenda. As Conroy wrote to Philip Murray in the United States: "The future organization of Canada lies with our own Congress in trying to wake up the people."[31] This plan meant convincing Canadians that unions were vital for order and stability or, conversely, that anti-union employers encouraged conflict and mayhem. The CCL also needed to persuade the country that compulsory collective bargaining was a reasonable demand in a democratic society. As the CCL's articulate secretary-treasurer told a radio audience, the rights of workers deserved recognition "both on the basis of morality and in the light of necessity."[32] Admittedly, the term "campaign" should be used loosely; the CCL's struggle to mould and shape public opinion was a makeshift, ad hoc process that evolved over time. Nothing suggests that the congress followed a grand plan or strategy. In the wake of the Kirkland Lake strike, however, it seems evident that CCL leaders were dedicated to mobilizing Canadians, especially wage-earners, around the issues of industrial unionism and collective bargaining. "The fight of the Kirkland Lake miners has not and will not be forgotten," the CCL's executive report promised.[33]

The CCL continued to sponsor community organizing drives. But now the emphasis was as much on generating publicity for collective bargaining as it was on organizing the unorganized. In March 1942, the congress and its affiliates targeted the industrial city of Hamilton, Ontario. The Amalgamated Clothing Workers were already well established there, and, for several weeks, the Steelworkers had conducted an "educational campaign" to lay the ground work.[34] When Charlie Millard claimed that the city was ripe for an "organizational blitz," the Electrical Workers, Packinghouse Workers, Rubber Workers, and the CCL decided to join the Steelworkers in a major assault.[35] Besides recruiting workers at anti-union strongholds like Stelco, the unions built on their previous experiences in Kitchener and used radio programming to win over workers and non-workers alike. From early April to early May, the CCL financed a nightly, fifteen-minute broadcast on a local station. The airtime allowed labour leaders to underscore the democratic rights of workers, the responsible motives of the labour movement, and the weaknesses in federal labour policy. In addition, a series of skits about the Higgins, a fictitious working-class family, revealed to listeners in accessible language and imagery how the anti-union sentiments of employers were not only unjust, but irrational and archaic.[36] Although the Hamilton drive failed to gather much organizational momentum and eventually collapsed in mid-May, Arthur Williams, the CCL's general organizer, called it a success from a publicity point of view. "This [radio] campaign being an experiment," he reported, "has shown a real difference between ... [corporate] statements of cooperation and actions."[37]

To further increase popular support for a Canadian Wagner Act, not to mention consolidate power and authority, the CCL leaders also attempted to eliminate strife and factionalism within their own ranks.[38] With the strike rate jumping by over 50 per cent between 1941 and 1942, CCL executives did not plan to endorse a no-strike pledge like their US counterparts.[39] "In the absence of legislation enforceable by government action," A.R. Mosher, the CCL president, stated, "the workers must fight [the] opposition with their own unaided strength."[40] Without some semblance of internal order and discipline, however, the CCL executive feared that compulsory collective bargaining would never be realized – that the country would not support its quest to become equal partners in industry. Along these lines, the leadership took questionable steps to repress the power brokering and shop floor militancy of the communist unions.[41] A particularly close eye was kept on the West Coast, where local radicals were trying to capture control of the extremely large and affluent Boilermakers and Iron Shipbuilders Union.[42] In addition, Conroy attempted to resolve jurisdictional disputes between the UE, United Automobile Workers (UAW), and United Steelworkers (SWOC became the USW in May 1942). As the CCL's secretary-treasurer warned the unions, "their fratricidal warfare" was "a source of jocular observations by those on the outside" that undermined the credibility of the congress.[43]

Convinced that displays of labour solidarity would impress the federal government and the general public, the CCL also attempted to join forces with the TLC. In late 1941, Mosher suggested to Tom Moore that they both participate in a legislative conference with Philip Murray of the CIO and William Green of the AFL. Although local and regional TLC unions supported the idea, Moore and other executives refused, accusing the CCL of inciting unnecessary strikes and trying to exploit the TLC's positive image.[44] In spring 1942, Conroy wrote to Moore three more times, but the TLC president still balked at having anything to do with the CCL.[45] "It is our opinion," the CCL's secretary-treasurer informed Allan Haywood of the CIO, "that Mr. Moore's efforts are directed not towards improving the position of Labour but in maintaining the temporary superiority in numbers of the American Federation of Labour in Canada."[46] Then, in early May, Moore suffered a debilitating stroke, and the TLC underwent a leadership change. The executive board appointed fifty-nine-year-old Percy Bengough as acting president. British-born Bengough was a machinist by trade, who had served for many years as a general organizer and business agent for the International Association of Machinists (IAM) in British Columbia and had held the post of TLC vice-president since the 1920s.[47] He proved much more open to collaborating on legislative demands with the CCL, at one point even visiting Mosher at his office to write up a joint statement to the government about pursuing a collective bargaining policy.

"On the whole," Conroy wrote to a West Coast colleague, "the situation between the two Congresses is considerably better than it has been for some time."[48] Meanwhile, regional TLC and CCL leaders in Ontario and British Columbia were meeting on a regular basis to discuss changes to provincial labour legislation.[49]

For active social democrats like Charlie Millard, another aspect of the "campaign" was strengthening ties between the CCL and the Co-operative Commonwealth Federation (CCF). As Murray Cotterill of the USW explained, "I am becoming more and more convinced that the only hope for labour and the country is an open drive to unseat the present administration ... war or no war."[50] Without question, the CCF was enjoying an unprecedented surge of popularity. In the provincial elections of 1941, the party had not only increased its number of seats in the Nova Scotia legislature, but had actually become the official opposition in British Columbia. Most recently, in the federal by-election of February 1942, a relatively unknown CCF candidate, J.W. Noseworthy, defeated former Conservative prime minister Arthur Meighen – the new leader of the opposition in the House of Commons – for the parliamentary riding of York South (Toronto). During 1942, over 100 local unions in Ontario also established formal relations with the CCF.[51] "The tragedy of Kirkland Lake," observed Norman Dowd, the CCL vice-president, "may be just enough to put over the idea of electing Labour representatives to legislature and parliament."[52] Patrick Conroy remained skeptical that the electorate, including most industrial workers, would abandon "the old line political parties." Rather than promote political attachments, he urged CCL affiliates "to proceed on a trade union basis."[53] With CCF members of Parliament calling repeatedly for labour law reforms, however, many union leaders agreed that this "political arm of labour" offered the best prospect for a collective bargaining policy.[54]

Despite the CCL's dismal lobbying record, it still continued to try and build support for compulsory collective bargaining within the government. Since Mackenzie King and the Department of Labour seemed to harbour deep-seated prejudices, the congress focused much of its energy on Elliot M. Little, the new director of the National Selective Service (NSS). Formed in March 1942 to address the labour supply problem (without consulting the labour movement), the NSS, which one newspaper editor called one of the most "important experiments in governmental regulation of the lives of men and women that Canada has yet experienced," mainly transferred workers from non-essential to essential war industries. It operated under the auspices of the Labour Department.[55] Normally the general manager of Anglo-Canadian Pulp and Paper Mills and president of Gaspesia Sulphite, Little was a former union member who held enlightened views about employer-employee relations. As he told a meeting of Canadian publishers: "I know that men do better work if they feel that they are working with you and not merely working for you."[56] Although the NSS director remained undecided about the question of compulsory collective bargaining, preferring instead to encourage plant committees, CCL leaders believed that he could be brought around to their point of view.[57] Throughout the summer of 1942, they tried to convince him that a successful selective service policy had "to be anchored to a genuine and positive collective bargaining programme."[58] As Conroy remarked to Millard: "We are counting upon him more than any other single individual in the Government to get actions along the lines of collective bargaining."[59] It was an unfortunate choice. Within a few months, Little had resigned his position, complaining with considerable justification that Humphrey Mitchell, the newly appointed labour minister, was interfering in NSS operations.[60]

In 1942, the number of workers affiliated with CCL unions grew by 60 per cent. The congress now represented nearly 35 per cent of the total union membership in Canada, an increase of nearly 8 per cent from the year before.[61] Despite these impressive gains, however, the leadership worried that the organizing success of its unions would be short lived without the passage of a Wagner-like act in Canada. When the Kirkland Lake strike failed to move government officials, the CCL leaders realized that they needed to garner public support for labour law reform. In what broadly resembled a campaign, they began to use a variety of methods to sell the country on the rights and benefits of industrial unionism and collective bargaining. There was a media component that used the relatively new medium of the radio; a bureaucratic component that emphasized internal unity and responsible unionism; and a political component that involved stronger ties to the CCF. Although the TLC maintained its distance during the presidency of Tom Moore, it eventually joined in the effort when Percy Bengough assumed office. With policy demands falling on deaf ears in the federal government, the CCL wanted to put collective bargaining on the national agenda – to use public pressure to force policymakers into action. What the labour leaders did not anticipate was how the hostile reactions of employers to the organizing surge would greatly contribute to the swaying of public opinion.

Intransigence

Most employers continued to fear that unionism would result in elevated labour costs and market share losses to unorganized competitors. They also remained obdurate about their managerial rights or prerogatives. After decades of paternalistic rule, they deeply resented haggling over the terms and conditions of the employment relationship – or anything else. Certainly, some firms acquiesced voluntarily to organizing drives and contract negotiations. They appreciated the organizational benefits of unionization, like regulated labour markets and rationalized job structures, and/or sought to avoid the destabilizing costs of production interruptions. As George W. Huggett, the president of Canadian Industries Limited, a large chemical manufacturer, warned colleagues, unions and collective bargaining "have become more and more accepted as a normal part of industrial life." Rather than invite further confrontation, managers should have "the good sense to get off the lid and let what [is] basically an employee right become established ... The future will hold for us what we make it hold – not by bucking the tide ... but by leadership, by the demonstration of sincerity of purpose, and by the proposal of constructive policies which will merit and win the approval of the public and labour."[62] B.M. Hallward, a Quebec-based pulp and paper mill operator, put it more succinctly: "We shall never get anywhere by objecting to unions."[63] As the Kirkland Lake gold mine operators demonstrated, however, the majority of employers still found it difficult to accept the prospect or reality of trade unionism and collective bargaining. "If industrialists in Canada preserve their present frame of mind," US state officials predicted in early 1942, "there are bound to be serious labor disturbances in the Dominion. Canadian industrialists, especially in Toronto, have preserved a strength and arrogance surprising to an American."[64]

The business community routinely denounced the more aggressive leaders of the industrial unions as corrupt power mongers who cared little for the well-being of workers or for the exigencies of war production. "Canadian workers are honest, intelligent, patriotic," the *Financial Post* reported. "But they are also human, and that means that they are easily swayed by an incorrect story when it is told to them by skillful demagogues and agitators."[65] According to Harold Crabtree of the Canadian Manufacturers' Association, who not only ruled over a pulp and paper empire in Eastern Canada but also served as the president of Allied War Supplies (a munitions-producing, government-owned corporation), the best industrial relations strategy was simply a no-holds-barred resistance to organization. Convinced that the average employer "is imbued with a keen sense of fairness to his working people [and] has their welfare at hearts," he urged "the elimination of a comparatively small number of labour agitators who are exercising a subversive influence."[66] Given these sentiments, it is not surprising to learn that there was widespread applause in the business community for the provocative actions of the Kirkland Lake gold mine operators. "The bulldozing tactics of the CIO can be licked," a business paper heralded, "and licked to a faretheewell. There is no need for anyone to cringe under the CIO's threats ... If the employer's course is right and sound, the CIO can be beaten."[67]

Still, most employers were reluctant to emulate the heavy-handed measures of the mine operators. Although just as adamant in their opposition to unions, they could not afford protracted workplace struggles, especially in the heavily capitalized mass production industries. Beginning in late 1941, many companies decided to follow the advice of the government and urge their workers to form and join non-union plant committees. Corporate lawyers, who had recently become "experts" in labour law, often spearheaded these schemes. For example, R.R. Evans of Hamilton played a key role in the plant committee setup at Canadian Westinghouse, while John B. Aylesworth of Windsor was instrumental in establishing plant committees at several auto parts companies in Southwestern Ontario.[68] By offering this benign form of representation at the first sign of a union threat, managers addressed the collective demands of their workers but also retained a considerable degree of control in the workplace. Certainly, to receive the blessing of the Department of Labour, the employers had to relinquish some authority. They could not interfere with the election of representatives, the committees usually had to win government-supervised plant votes, and contracts had to be negotiated and signed. By implementing plant committee schemes, however, the industrialists could often dilute the appeal of unions and isolate their workers from the labour movement. In Montreal's booming aircraft industry, Canada Car and Foundry used plant committees to defeat organizing drives at two separate facilities.[69] In Calgary, Alberta, Riverside Iron Works established an employee association that received the approval of a conciliation board.[70] And Atlas Steel in Welland, Ontario, put a serious crimp in a union drive when it converted an old company union into a plant committee.[71]

Just because a firm established a plant committee did not mean that it eschewed strong-arm tactics. It was common for lead hands and foremen to fire union members and/or bully workers into signing petitions and membership cards for non-union associations.[72] But employers also realized that they needed to appeal to the loyalty of their workers – what industrial relations scholar Sanford Jacoby refers to as their "enterprise consciousness."[73] They launched propaganda campaigns to denounce unions as unpatriotic, outside organizations that tore apart industrial communities with false expectations and unnecessary conflict. Similar to the late 1930s, managers continued to use nativist or ethnocentric language to drive home the point. When Joe Starr of the International Fur and Leather Workers Union began to organize the Davis Leather Company in Newmarket, Ontario, the company president urged his workers to support a plant committee rather than "twist in the fairy promises that are being made by some unknown Jew from Toronto."[74] The personnel director at Canada Packers in Toronto claimed incorrectly that union organizer and former employee Adam Borsk was not only a German immigrant (his parents were Polish immigrants) but also a Nazi sympathizer.[75] At the same time, employers portrayed themselves as the protectors of individual rights and democracy. With plant committees, they emphasized how workers could practice collective bargaining and not have to comply with mandatory union memberships, answer to autocratic labour bureaucrats, or abide by unreasonable international policies. Driving home these points, Wallace Campbell, the president of Ford Canada, wrote a letter to auto workers that was reprinted as a full-page newspaper advertisement:

> Thousands of Canadian employees in many leading plants throughout Canada have already been faced with this same issue – and have declined in favour of running their own affairs through direct negotiation with their employers. Canadians have always guarded their freedom to determine their rights and privileges. Let us not surrender these rights in Windsor.[76]

These corporate efforts to redefine the meaning and practice of collective bargaining were not always successful. US subsidiaries, whose parent companies had recently succumbed to the CIO, found it particularly difficult to secure the loyalties of Canadian workers. Given the recent victory of the United Automobile Workers (UAW) at the immense River Rouge complex in Dearborn, Michigan, 60 per cent of the workers at Ford Canada voted for union representation. Pressured by a jittery head office in Detroit, Wallace Campbell signed a contract in early January.[77] Later, in September, Chrysler Canada also reached an agreement with the UAW. Although management tried to rally support for a plant committee, the union won a representation vote by 2,856 to 707.[78] As well, Goodyear Tire and Rubber in Canada signed a contract with the United Rubber Workers at its large plant in New Toronto. Although Goodyear had a long history of thwarting union drives, its plant committee – recently evolved from a company union – lost a representation vote by 940 to 204.[79] Most of these agreements contained open-shop clauses – there was no automatic union membership or dues check-off. But they also represented path-breaking victories for the labour movement. As George Burt, the Canadian UAW director, recalled, "It gave such an impetus to the whole labour field in Canada to have Ford organized this way."[80]

Thanks to the federal government, though, plant committees proved to be an effective deterrent to unionism. Officials in the Department of Munitions and Supply (DMS) went to great lengths to ensure their success. In March 1942, D.D. Rosenberry, the assistant timber controller, informed organizers from the International Woodworkers that the logging companies in the Queen Charlotte Islands of British Columbia, which supplied most of the spruce for the airplane industry, would only negotiate with plant committees. Rosenberry even arranged for anti-union notices to be posted in the Queen Charlotte camps that warned loggers: "Possible Saboteurs Not All Japs."[81] A.W. Crawford, the director general of the Labour Relations Branch for the DMS, admitted to Pat Conroy: "Our only purpose was to promote conditions which would not interfere with the production of the war effort."[82] Despite union representation claims, the DOL also refused to invalidate contracts signed between employers and plant committees. In the fall of 1942, for example, Judge I.M. Macdonell, an IDIC commissioner (since the beginning of the year, individuals investigators had fulfilled the duties of the committee), rejected the UAW's bid for recognition at De Havilland Aircraft in Toronto because a one-year wage agreement already existed between the company and an employee association.[83] With the government's support, if not encouragement, employers proved remarkably adept at manipulating or revising the language of collective bargaining.

But the business community could not escape the increased scrutiny of the general public. Scarred by the Great Depression and turned upside down by the war, ordinary Canadians had become much more sympathetic to collective action. Although the country as a whole frowned upon the proliferation of strikes, a Gallup poll revealed that 63 per cent of the country supported the existence of trade unions.[84] "Certainly [people] do not want strikes," a commentator wrote, "but they are more inclined to look where the real responsibility lies."[85] Most importantly, many Canadians blamed the intransigent behaviour of employers for the unrest. With military production climbing from $513 million in 1939 to $2.5 billion in 1942, they found it hard to believe that employers were sharing in the sacrifices of the war.[86] Convinced that a more secure and better-paid labour force would increase productivity and enhance the war effort, a growing segment of the country supported the CCL's campaign to win a Canadian Wagner Act.

Public criticism of Mackenzie King's hapless labour policies also intensified. Although plant committees partially addressed the collective demands of workers, the general public seemed to agree with Charlie Millard "that this is the latest device to thwart the growing desire of the workers to organize in bona fide unions of their own choice and that the Government is in collusion with these anti-labour interests."[87] For three reasons, widespread demands for a compulsory collective bargaining policy began to gain traction. First, people argued that a compulsory collective bargaining policy would be a much-needed antidote for the ramped up industrial conflict. As the relatively low strike rate in the United States indicated, trade unions were capable of inspiring industrial order and stability. They could act responsibility and help to increase war production.[88] Second, it was difficult to ignore how the wartime state already regulated most of the Canadian economy. Given the recent imposition of wage and price controls, not to mention huge increases in income tax and efforts to limit job choice by the NSS, it made sense that the government should play a more assertive role in industrial relations.[89] Third, they stressed that it was inconsistent, if not abhorrent, for Canadians to be fighting for democracy abroad, when employers were ignoring the democratic rights of workers at home. For the sake of human decency, it was time to curb the arbitrary powers of management in the workplace. "[A] union is an absolute necessity to protect the interests of the worker; it is a right that everyone has," argued Thérèse Casgrain, president of the League for Women's Rights and wife of a former secretary of state. "[T]here is no reason why anyone should object ... [T]hat is what there should be in a well-organized society."[90]

Similar to the pre-war days, several religious organizations, led by people like J.R. Mutchmor and J.D. Coburn of the United Church's

Board of Evangelism and Social Services or Henry Somerville of the *Catholic Register*, proved extremely outspoken in their criticisms of employers and the Liberal administration. In a meeting with Humphrey Mitchell in early 1942, the Christian Labour Forum, a joint committee of Protestant church delegates and TLC leaders from Toronto, decried the spread of "company unions" and the government's failure to articulate a "clear-cut" collective bargaining policy.[91] In March, three presbyteries of the United Church of Canada urged the government to enforce the principle of collective bargaining and denounced the interference of employers in employee organizations.[92] In May, the Fellowship for a Christian Social Order called for the passage of a Canadian Wagner Act and spurred members "to do everything in their power to promote a better understanding of the aims and methods of the labour movement." A journalist that year reported: "There is a movement of some power afoot within the churches, and numbering influential members of the churches whose leavening power will be considerable."[93]

Perhaps surprisingly, some prominent members of the judiciary also became outspoken critics of the belligerent behaviour of employers and lackluster wartime labour policies. Prior to 1939, it seems unlikely that many of these legal minds paid attention to the employment relationship, and, given their privileged positions, they probably took the proprietary rights of management for granted. J.L. Cohen had observed that most of Ontario's judges had "little or no experience with or knowledge of labour matters" and also suffered from "unfavourable prejudices."[94] In serving the wartime government as IDIA investigators and conciliation board chairs, however, they had witnessed first-hand how employers went to unreasonable lengths to avoid unionism. Dismayed by the escalating strike rate, many became convinced that collective bargaining between unions and employers would restore the industrial order. As Justice M.B. Archibald of the Nova Scotia Supreme Court reported in his investigation of a coal-mining production in Minto, New Brunswick: "I am satisfied that the miners if permitted to organize and enjoy the benefits of collective bargaining ... would co-operate with the operators in producing the maximum amount of coal."[95] And, in early 1941, Justice C.P. McTague of the Ontario Supreme Court chaired a conciliation board that severely admonished Great Lakes shipping firms for refusing to recognize and negotiate with the Canadian Seamen's Union. The assertion in the final report that "labour can no longer be regarded ... merely as a commodity" became a standard reference for subsequent boards.[96] Later that year, McTague also chaired the Kirkland

Lake conciliation board, which questioned the validity of plant committee setups and the effectiveness of existing labour policies. Although written by Cohen, the Kirkland Lake board's report was unanimous.[97] Justices in other provinces were also challenging truculent employers. As the Appeals Court of British Columbia ruled in the Red Band Shingle Mill case, it was an "inherent right of employees" to belong to a trade union and to engage in collective bargaining.[98]

Most war producers remained impervious to the public recriminations. Like W.D. Black, the president of Otis-Fensom Elevators in Hamilton, they continued to boast that their union avoidance plans achieved "full co-operation between employers and employees in the manner best suited to individual concerns [and] maximum production."[99] Given the unyielding attitudes of employers and the inaction of the government, no one could predict that the groundswell of pro-union sentiments in the country would translate into a meaningful labour policy. By alienating popular opinion, however, anti-union employers were contributing to their own undoing. In earlier years, the public had viewed collective bargaining in narrow, class-specific terms. Now it was becoming a part of the political discourse or lexicon. Concerned about the war effort and influenced by the CCL's far-reaching campaign, an increasing number of people demanded that the government respond to the ongoing deterioration in industrial relations. "If [Mackenzie King] cares anything for his own reputation as a liberal statesman," a journalist observed in late 1941, "he will lose no time in reversing the present policy and ordering ... the law on collective bargaining."[100]

Respect and Dignity

Of course, the CCL's campaign for a compulsory collective bargaining policy struck the most resounding chord with the industrial labour force. As the widespread support for the Kirkland Lake strike suggested, large groups of workers in different parts of the country wanted to engage in a full-fledged fight for collective rights. Importantly, the unions were not foisting the idea of workplace contractualism on their members. In search of shop floor justice, wage-earners were ready, if not eager, to win a workplace rule of law. Practical goals like higher wages and shorter hours partially explained their collective determination. They also sought more intangible objectives like respect and self-worth. "This society of ours," Pat Conroy explained, "cannot claim that it represents all the things for which it stands, unless the men and women at the bottom of the social scale are raised to a position consistent with human dignity."[101] Unlike a few years earlier, union organizers now found they had little trouble convincing workers to put their jobs on the line for contractual relations. In fact, they faced the opposite problem of managing all the collective action. A much bolder, more defiant attitude could be found in the factories, around the camps, and in the mines. With labour in short supply and employers just as intransigent, a high number of relatively short and small strikes took place throughout 1942; many Canadians engaged in spontaneous, often illegal, walkouts and slowdowns to win union recognition and collective agreements.[102]

At first glance, the militancy of the wartime labour force might seem puzzling. Given the expansion of the war economy and the enlistment of 700,000 people into the armed forces, hundreds of thousands of people had joined the industrial labour force for the first time.[103] Long ignored by unions, enjoying relatively high wages, and worried about the permanency of their positions, especially for the long term, they would not seem prone to collective action. Why would they expose themselves to the risks and uncertainties of union membership? To understand the answer to this question, some background information is useful. Two overlapping demographic groups gained access to industrial jobs during the war. The first included "peripheral" workers of Southern European, Eastern European, African, and Asian descent. Although difficult to quantify in precise terms, they belonged to the 19 per cent of the population that was not Anglo-Celtic or French Canadian in origin.[104] As historian Carmela Patrias documents, employment discrimination remained prominent during the war. Labour-starved employers often proved reluctant to hire workers with "foreign-sounding" names or workers who belonged to visible minorities. Some questioned their loyalty to Canada; others thought them untrainable. Still others worried about the discriminatory attitudes of their existing workers. What's more, government administrators did little to curtail or check the xenophobia and racism. Although not universal, many NSS officers unofficially complied with corporate requests for "no aliens or no Jews" and relegated Canadians with Asian backgrounds to low-paying menial work. Still, thanks to the intervention of ethnically based organizations, minority activists, prominent English Canadians, and the Nationalities Branch of the Department of National War Services, not to mention the demands of the booming war economy, the barriers to industrial jobs did lower for many previously excluded groups.[105] For example, Ford in Windsor, Ontario, hired over fifty Chinese Canadians, and McKinnon

Industries in St Catharines, Ontario, actively recruited black male workers from Nova Scotia.[106] One company newspaper stated it was "proud of its coloured workers, working on inspection, assembling and filling benches in good comradeship with white workers."[107] A government report later estimated that workers without Anglo-Celtic and French-Canadian backgrounds comprised about 25 per cent of the industrial labour force during the war.[108]

Women were the second group of workers who secured higher paying industrial jobs for the first time. During the Depression years, when many people accused female wage-earners of taking employment away from men, women had made up roughly 17 per cent of the paid labour force.[109] By the end of 1942, however, women filled about one of every three jobs in Canada.[110] Driven more by economic necessity than patriotism, over 20 per cent of the paid female labour force was engaged in war work; female workers made up 26 per cent of the labour force in the manufacturing sector.[111] Many of these changes took place in 1942 when the National Selective Service (NSS) started to encourage women to transfer from non-essential industries like commercial laundries and domestic service to war production facilities. In a typically demeaning tone, Humphrey Mitchell explained that the NSS was asking the "girls making golden slippers and fancy handbags ... to take war jobs."[112] Initially, the NSS focused on the recruitment of single and then married but childless women. Then, as labour shortages persisted, the agency targeted married women with children. The proportion of married women in the paid female labour force increased from 9 or 10 per cent to 27 per cent.[113] The government also paid rural women to relocate to industrial centres and established daycare centres for the children of wage-earning mothers.[114] In 1942 alone, the NSS conscripted 75,000 women for employment in war industries. That total would rise to roughly 260,000 by October 1943.[115]

Government officials promised in bulletins and advertisements that most women workers would put down their tools and return to their homes in peacetime, refocusing their attention on the more conventional gendered goals of marriage and motherhood.[116] Indeed, they referred to women workers as "part-time" in government periodicals.[117] But the reality was much more complex and ambiguous. Certainly, many female wage-earners viewed themselves as temporary employees. As a General Motors worker recalled: "I knew that when [my husband] got out of the service, that I was going to quit work. I guess because I thought we were gonna have a family."[118] An informal

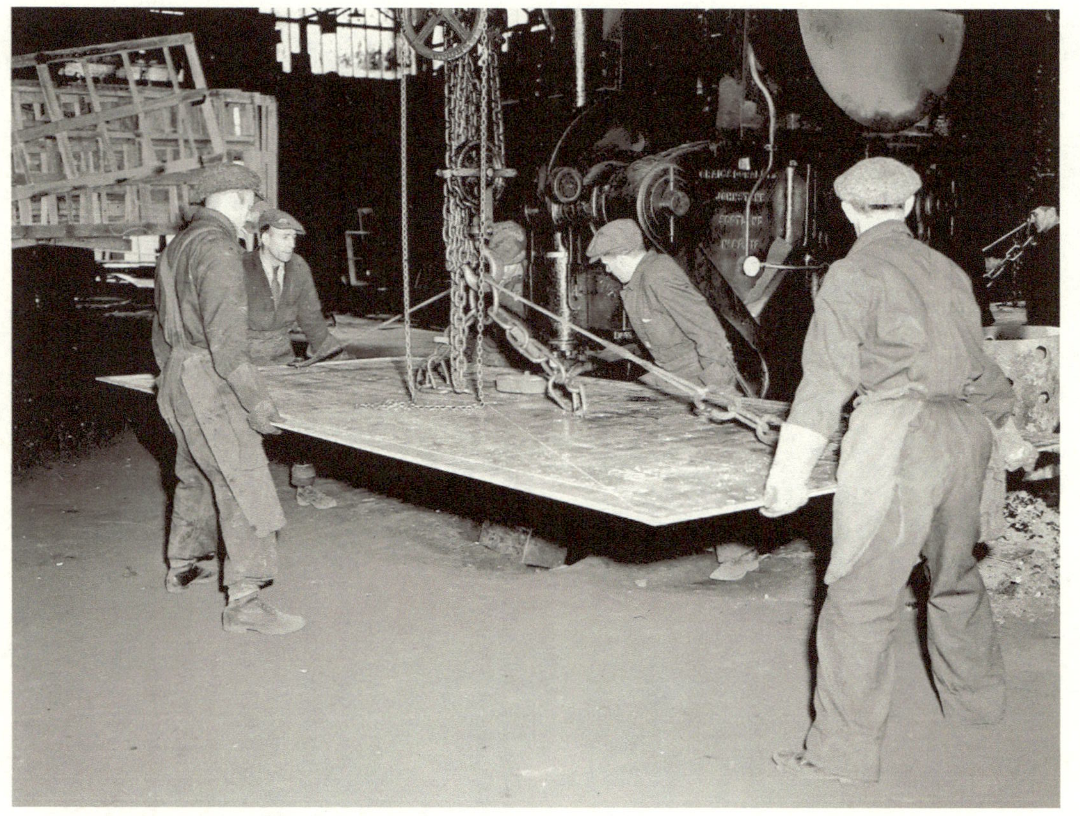

3.1 *Male Workers Holding Corvette Steel Plates for the Drilling of Rivet Holes*, unknown location, 1940

Source: National Film Board of Canada, Still Photography Division, Library and Archives Canada, e000760083.

3.2 *Female Shipyard Worker Driving a Rivet into Place,* Pictou, Nova Scotia, 1943

Source: National Film Board of Canada, Still Photography Division, Library and Archives Canada, e000761162.

government study suggested that roughly one-half of the female war workers planned to resume or enter the occupation of homemaking with the return of peacetime conditions.[119] Yet, at the same time, many women who were proud of their accomplishments and grateful for their wages wanted to hold onto their industrial jobs after the war. A more formal Labour Department survey discovered that 72 per cent of the female labour force wanted to stay employed.[120] This sentiment was especially true for women who had to remain in the labour force to support their families; it was far more appealing to stay in industrial work than to return to low-paying, traditionally female occupations. As a Toronto newspaper reported, 75 per cent of the women workers in the airplane industry hoped to continue with the same kind of work in peacetime.[121]

3.3 *Women Workers Producing Weapons at Small Arms Ltd.*, Long Branch, Ontario, 1942

Source: National Film Board of Canada, Still Photography Division, Library and Archives Canada, C-023699.

3.4 *Female and Male Workers Constructing a De Havilland Mosquito Airplane,* Downsview, Ontario, 1944

Source: Ronny Jaques, National Film Board of Canada, Still Photography Division, Library and Archives Canada, e000762773.

3.5 Simpson's catalogue cover, 1942. According to this cover illustration, women could engage in war work and still retain their femininity.

Source: E.A. Bollinger Fonds, Nova Scotia Archives, Acc. No. 1975-305, No. 571-1.

Without question, the wartime recruits to the industrial labour force gained a good deal of economic and emotional independence. Between 1942 and 1943, the consumer price index increased by only 3 percent, while, regardless of government controls, the average wage rate index jumped 9 per cent. In the manufacturing sector, the average wage rate was up by 11 per cent.[122] "Even with record taxes, Victory bond purchases, and war-related donations," historian Jeffrey Keshen writes, "Canadian households ... had far more available cash."[123] Granted, the government had imposed food rationing. With factories converted to war production, many consumer durable goods, like homes, cars, and electrical appliances, were also in short supply. As one worker recalled, though: "In the war, we lived good. Real good."[124] After working as bell hops, elevator operators, and general labourers, black male workers in Ontario's auto plants enjoyed a significant upturn in wages.[125] Even female wage-earners experienced an 11 per cent wage increase between 1942 and 1943.[126] In particular, the war provided more mobile, single women with unprecedented opportunities to escape the social and economic privations of traditionally female wage-work in the service sector or textile mills. Though still subject to sex inequalities, they seemed grateful for the autonomy that accompanied war production jobs – often in distant cities. "My God," reminisced a radio plant worker, "there were tens of thousands of us living a kind of life we'd never known before, money and good times and lots of men and, more than anything, I guess you could say freedom."[127] Another woman, who moved from Saskatchewan to work on airplanes at Canadian Car and Foundry in Fort William, Ontario, agreed: "[I]t was really, really a great thing ... I thought I was a millionaire."[128]

Despite their material gains and tenuous job security, however, many of these workers signed up to become union members. There were two main reasons why. First, national wage figures obscured regional, occupational, and sex disparities. According to the *Report on Social Security for Canada*, two-thirds of the male heads of urban households in Canada actually earned less than "a desirable minimum budget" of about $123/month.[129] Although wages on average had increased substantially, the booming war economies of Ontario and British Columbia had skewed the national figures upwards. Workers in the Maritime provinces made about 20 per cent less than their counterparts in Ontario, while workers in Quebec earned about 11.5 per cent less. Even within Ontario,

Hamilton workers earned weekly wages that were 30 per cent less than Windsor workers.[130] Wage controls and the National Selective Service had also trapped many male workers in "essential" war jobs with low pay scales. "It was a rotten system," remarked a flour mill worker, "frozen, making four bits an hour, and guys all around you in town making up to a buck an hour."[131] Moreover, within the same factories, mines, and lumber camps, non–Anglo-Celtic and non-white workers often found themselves relegated to the least desirable and lowest paying jobs, feeding furnaces, pouring iron, and pushing wheelbarrows.[132] Women engaged in war work experienced severe wage differentials, earning on average about 45 to 50 per cent of men's pay, mainly because employers argued that female workers lacked the strength of male workers and should be paid accordingly.[133] With husbands enlisted in the armed forces, married women found it particularly challenging to find decent paying jobs. Although essentially single parents, their wages continued to reflect their "dependent" or supplementary income status. Often unable to travel to higher paying places of employment with children in tow, they found it difficult to make ends meet.[134]

Second, all war workers, regardless of seniority, sought a more humane and fair work environment where they could be assured greater respect and dignity. They believed that a collective agreement with standardized rules and regulations would alleviate many of the uncertainties, insecurities, and degradations of the workplace. Few of these new union members were radical or revolutionary in intent. They didn't join the labour movement to challenge property rights and control the marketplace. What they did want was to be treated as full-fledged industrial citizens – as individuals with rights. "I'm in favor of labour unions all right," explained a Winnipeg munitions worker. "[W]hen you have something to say you can say it."[135] Informal bargaining between foremen or supervisors and workers had long been a way of life on the shop floor. Even in the mass production industries, where machines undermined functional autonomy, workers had found numerous ways to influence hiring, firing, promotion, and discipline practices. Without binding contracts, however, they were subject to the unpredictable, if not humiliating, whims and fancies of lower management. To avoid reprisals and curry favours, many workers felt obliged to bribe and otherwise wait on their foremen and supervisors. But now, with the onset of war and full employment conditions, they could join unions to try and curb the arbitrary powers of management – without retribution. A packinghouse worker from Alberta explained what a collective agreement meant:

> Nobody buys the boss any booze, nobody is going to date the boss to keep their job. You're humanized ... [Y]ou can walk in there, lift up your head and you can tell the foremen, O.K., I'm working too hard, or whatever. You can stand toe-to-toe to him and talk to him without fear of getting fired ... [A]n atmosphere [is created] where everybody is proud to be a human being and is, in most cases, treated like a human being.[136]

Shop floor quests for self-esteem, honour, and justice were not just motivated by the lived experience of wage-earning. The way people thought about race, ethnicity, and gender also mediated their collective action. As sociologist Pamela Sugiman notes in her study of black male auto workers, there were "many parallel, but separate working-class realities."[137] Given how idealized notions of race, ethnicity, and gender were (and are) overlapping, contingent, and inconstant, it can be very challenging to figure out why a particular individual decided to join or spurn a union at a particular point in time. Although two Eastern European Jewish women workers in Toronto's garment industry shared similar working-class backgrounds, they didn't necessarily have similar responses to the solicitations of organizers. Perhaps one was married to a scholar and considered unions to be disreputable, while the other was single and wanted to join because of her concerns about employment discrimination.[138] As most scholars now agree, however, it is still important to recognize how constructs of gender, race, and ethnicity affected the actions of workers during World War II. Women and men in the camps, mines, and factories acted together to gain more power and improved conditions because they were first and foremost wage-earners. But their understanding of what it meant to be female or male, black or white, Hungarian or Anglo-Celtic also informed and varied their working-class experiences. In 1942, for example, 250 young French-Canadian women went on strike at Banque Nationale in Montreal because they wanted not only to win union recognition but also to be paid the same amount as English Canadian employees. The other 2,200 female clerks on the island viewed their work experience through a different lens. Less concerned about discrimination and more about propriety and conformity, they signed yellow dog contracts.[139]

Angered and humiliated by their loss of status in the workplace and family during the Great Depression and perhaps embarrassed by their inability or reluctance to serve overseas, many male workers equated collective action with masculine redemption. As a labour organizer told B.M. Hallward, the pulp and paper mill operator: "A man wanted to be a MAN. A man wanted to be free to talk to whom he likes, to join what he likes and to consult whom he likes."[140] In contrast to artisans of previous generations, who controlled the scale, pace, and routine of production, the individual working man at the machine or on the assembly line found it difficult to assert or demonstrate his heterosexual "manliness" – those enduring and mythical qualities of strength, autonomy, purposefulness, and self-expression. With unions and contractual relations, however, he could defy unjust authority and address equity issues, gaining some measure of independence and worthiness. To borrow from the popular culture of the day, many male workers seemed to view their concerted activities – in the face of impersonal market forces and oppressive power relations – as analogous to the emasculated Clark Kent shedding his glasses and donning his cape to become the heroic, courageous Superman or to the ninety-pound victim of a sand-kicking bully transforming himself into the muscular, assertive Charles Atlas.[141]

Given the broader crisis in masculinity, some male workers also joined unions to address the feminization of the workplace and disruptions to traditional gender relations. How were they supposed to demonstrate their manhood as breadwinners when women were wearing pants and doing "men's" work? In response, labour leaders objected to the hiring of women, especially married women, while able-bodied men were still looking for work.[142] When the unemployment rate became negligible, they began to call for "equal pay for equal work," claiming that their unions were not opposed to the hiring of female workers per se, but to the dampening impact of low female wages on established male rates.[143] Government administrators and employers tried to alleviate concerns about gender failure by stressing the temporary, patriotic nature of female war work and reinforcing sexual stereotypes and hierarchies. The Department of Munitions and Supply (DMS) began a publicity campaign to alleviate anxieties about women in coveralls and new representations of the female body.[144] The Goodyear Tire and Rubber Company in New Toronto stressed how "the small hands of women are peculiarly adapted ... to delicate operations."[145] Advertisements assured women workers: "It's a reflection of the free democratic way of life that you have succeeded in keeping your femininity – even though you are doing a man's work!"[146] The company newspaper at

Canada Car and Foundry recognized the productive value of women workers, but also displayed them as front-page pinups to reinforce their feminine identities.[147] Sometimes, though, these efforts to placate concerns about women workers and the masculine workplace were insufficient. In November 1942, Ford Canada triggered a wildcat strike of over 9,000 male UAW members when it hired thirty-seven women for a stock department.[148] Similarly, in the shipyards of British Columbia, thousands of union men threatened to walk off the job to protest the addition of women welders and electricians to company payrolls.[149]

These kinds of patriarchal attitudes hindered the unionization of female wage-earners. Unwilling to expend scarce resources on what were assumed to be "temporary" workers, many labour leaders refrained from organizing women, especially those employed in the male-dominated sectors of the economy. As an official from the Cannery Workers in British Columbia explained, the union "would prefer to conduct negotiations only for the steady employees."[150] Unions that did attempt to organize female workers failed to consider how space was gendered differently for women. With children to care for, meals to cook, and laundry to clean, few wives and mothers could attend late night meetings at smoky, alcohol-infused union halls. It was a question of both time and respectability.[151] Moreover, female workers rarely obtained leadership positions in their unions. "If I was a man," Pearl Wedro of the International Fur Workers observed, "I think I would have been placed with the highest responsibility and having a chance ... [to] really make a full contribution. But that was not the case."[152] Or, as an aircraft worker recounted: "It was new for women to be active in the unions and a lot of them did what men told them to do. I remember being furious when I was working on a particular case, and this man said he might support me if I went to bed with him."[153]

Not surprisingly, many women workers decided to eschew collective action. Intimidated by masculine power constructs in the labour movement, responsive to the paternalism of employers, fearful of losing their jobs, and inculcated by familial and mass media missives, they identified more with the dominant gender norms of the day than with their roles and experiences as workers. The labour movement was regarded as a bastion of maleness, of roughness and aggressiveness – no place for a woman who equated femininity and moral propriety with acquiescence and dependence.[154] "That was men," one female auto worker remarked about the UAW. "It was men that were lookin' after all that."[155] This attitude did not mean these women workers were passive. Rather than participate in collective action, they opted to deal with untenable situations individually and non-confrontationally. "In the absence of central collective bargaining strategies and in the presence of a tight labour market," historian Jennifer Stephen writes, "[women] workers usually voted with their feet and left in search of jobs with better wages and working conditions."[156]

At the same time, these concerns about feminine respectability pushed more than 45,000 female wage-earners to join unions between 1941 and 1943. This number is a conservative estimate because many labour organizations failed to keep records about the sex of their members. As the Labour Department noted, the reported female membership was "undoubtedly far short of the actual number of women workers identified with organized labour."[157] These women signed union cards to win wage increases and better conditions; they identified as members of the working class. In the words of a female striker in St Catharines, Ontario, it was about being "able to live not merely exist."[158] But they also wanted to assert their presence on the shop floor as women. Just as men needed to establish their masculinity, these female workers needed to reaffirm their femininity. Often trained for male jobs and obliged to wear slacks or pants, they sought to reconcile the tough and rough image of the industrial workplace with conventional standards of "womanhood." Both the government and larger employers tried to "domesticize" war production facilities by establishing daycare facilities, emphasizing cleanliness and safety, piping in music, and making somewhat absurd housework analogies like comparing igniter cap assembly to cookie-making.[159] For example, at the General Engineering Company in Scarborough, Ontario, where women comprised over half of the nearly 4,000 workers, management awarded "Good Housekeeping" shields to the cleanest departments.[160] But many companies lacked the resources and/or the will to indulge the gender consciousness of their female wage-earners. Confronted with inadequate bathroom breaks and facilities, mandatory night shifts, inhuman speed-ups, and rampant sexual harassment, women workers turned to unionism and collective bargaining to preserve their moral respectability.[161] A female textile worker made this clear when she spoke to prospective unionists at another mill. As an audience member recalled:

> She told us her boss was a big man and a bully and he was very mean, almost vicious. She dreaded going to work in the morning. You women know how it is, she said. He would rub against me and turn and smirk. It

> was his way of making [us] feel like dirt. I'm in the union now. I know my rights and his place. I go into work cheerful and happy. I look him straight in the eye and he knows better than to put one finger on me ... I have my rights and my dignity and he must respect them ... You ask me what has the union done? The union made me strong.[162]

Besides class and gender-based concerns, both female and male workers joined unions because of their lived experiences as visible minorities and "foreigners." Racism and ethnocentrism were hardly absent in the labour movement. Although several unions, like the United Auto Workers, United Electrical Workers, and United Steelworkers, emphasized equal rights for all workers, white Anglo-Celtic shop stewards and local executives were products of their times.[163] Black workers in the auto plants often found their grievances ignored. Japanese Canadians were coldly received when the NSS relocated them to war plants in different parts of the country.[164] Workers with non–Anglo-Celtic or French-Canadian backgrounds recognized, however, that unions could work to get them reinstated, spearhead fights against prejudicial hiring practices, and win them better wages and job security. Especially by negotiating a collective agreement with legally binding rules and regulations, the labour movement offered the greatest hope for ending employment discrimination and achieving fair treatment. "Most black workers believed that the union contract could be used as a tool to protect their rights," writes Pamela Sugiman. "The collective agreement was a tool for the achievement of a better life, a measure of dignity, and equal opportunity at work."[165] The unions were far from perfect when it came to recognizing and addressing ethnic and racial differences in their memberships. They preferred to gloss over the lived experiences of racism. "Black, yellow, or brown, is but a colour of the skin. We are all workers," claimed a union paper.[166] But they did help make these workers feel less vulnerable and insecure. With managements mainly made up of white English Canadians, organized labour provided a solid line of defence against corporate discrimination. As a worker of Croatian descent explained, workers with immigrant backgrounds joined unions because "that would give them the chance for self-respect and decency [which] was more important to them than even the money."[167]

Given these sentiments, a growing number of new industrial workers proved willing to sign membership cards. Along with workers previously employed in manufacturing jobs, many also seemed to agree that it was the responsibility of the government to protect their collective rights. Clearly plant committee setups were not cutting it. Despite signed contracts, war workers still found themselves subject to the capricious actions of management. In May 1942, packinghouse workers at Dumart's Ltd. in Kitchener, Ontario, complained that the company's refusal to meet with a five-member plant committee "had the effect of nullifying the whole procedure laid down by the agreement for dealing with grievances."[168] To thwart unionism, corporate lawyers had also created the Niagara Institute of Industrial Relations to help establish and protect plant committees in the Welland-Niagara-St Catharines region of Ontario. According to C.S. Jackson of the United Electrical Workers, its members were "completely ignoring the fact that employees at any time had fundamental rights."[169] Frustrated and impatient, the labour force became more vocal in its demands for a Canadian Wagner Act. After all, the federal government was intervening in most other aspects of everyday life. Since the beginning of the war, Ottawa had frozen wages and prices, imposed rationing, regulated labour market conditions, and expanded income taxes. Encouraged by the CCL's policy campaign and cultural vehicles like the *National Labour Forum* radio series on the CBC, which regularly promoted compulsory collective bargaining, wage-earners believed they were productive members of society who deserved the protection of an activist state.[170]

In the words of Alf Ready, a union organizer at Canadian Westinghouse in Hamilton: "These were the reasons why political parties like the CCF took off."[171] Given the elusiveness of collective agreements, workers began to relinquish their traditional political ties for a third party that took their interests to heart. Eager to win converts, CCF leaders pressed the point:

> If we are to have a satisfactory and enthusiastic war effort, we have to safeguard the rights of the common people to determine through their organizations their own activities and their own way of life to a larger extent than we have in past days.[172]

In February 1942, the defeat of Arthur Meighen, the Conservative Party leader and former prime minister, in the York South by-election revealed in dramatic fashion the leftward shift of working-class voters.[173] Working people were not alone. Worried about the return of an unstable economy, more affluent citizens also desired a more interventionist government. In the summer, a public opinion poll found that nearly half of the English-speaking population agreed that government controls implemented during the war should be continued with the return of peace.[174] Still, according to Brooke Claxton, a Liberal Party backbencher, it was the government's "lousy" labour policies that were largely to blame for the CCF "coming up steadily right through the country."[175] R.K. Finlayson, a leading Conservative, agreed. "It seems to me," he wrote to a friend, "the CCF is making real gains ... in their attitude to labour."[176] In September 1942, public support for the social democratic party reached an unprecedented, 21 per cent – a two-fold increase since January.[177]

Adherence

After dealing with the Kirkland Lake strikers, who seemed "under the influence of the worst elements of the CIO," Mackenzie King remained almost oblivious to the mounting social and political pressures – at least for the first half of 1942.[178] The February by-elections had distracted him, not only because two new cabinet appointees, Humphrey Mitchell and Louis St Laurent, were vying for House seats but also because Arthur Meighen, his old political nemesis, might "have all Canada 'by the ears' in short time."[179] The prime minister was also busy containing the political fallout from the Hong Kong crisis and winning greater international respect for Canada's war contribution. Most of all, the conscription crisis or question of compulsory enlistment in the military consumed his time and energy. It was such a contentious issue that one of his ministers resigned and another nearly followed.[180] During this time, King left industrial relations matters in the hands of Humphrey Mitchell. At least initially, he expressed confidence in his new labour minister, "glad to have at my side one who can help at the Council table to voice in emphatic terms the views of labour and help to defend its rights."[181] Impressed with Mitchell's background as an electrician, a long-time secretary of the Hamilton Trades Council, and a former MP, as well as his willingness to "express an honest forthright opinion," the mainstream media applauded Mitchell's appointment as "a choice that could hardly be improved upon."[182] As one newspaper enthusiastically described, he was a "rugged individualist" and a "man of action" who was "eager to sally forth to hunt down and slay dragons when and where he finds them."[183]

During his time on the IDIC, Mitchell had revealed a real penchant for plant committees. But he also understood that the Liberal administration's reluctance to abide by its own principles was an extremely sore point with the labour movement.[184] One of his first actions as labour minister was to have the newly constituted National War Labour Board (NWLB), which he chaired, study the matter of collective bargaining in Crown or government-owned corporations. The Justice Department had previously ruled that the labour minister lacked the authority to interfere in the operation of these enterprises; they were the purview of C.D. Howe and the Department of Munitions and Supply.[185] Mitchell reasoned, however, that "the Government cannot consistently declare as in Order in Council PC 2685 that the right of collective bargaining should apply in industry and refuse to recognize any measure of collective bargaining in its own establishments."[186] As a first step, the NWLB asked J. Henry Richardson, an industrial relations professor from Leeds University who currently lectured at the University of Toronto, to compare Canada's labour laws to those in Great Britain and the United States. Upon completing his report in March 1942, Richardson recommended that the government let employees in the Crown corporations organize into unions and negotiate collective agreements. He also pushed for the creation of a tripartite board to oversee the certification of employee organizations.[187] It seemed like a very promising development to organized labour. Finally, there appeared to be some movement towards a Wagner-like act.[188]

But nothing happened. "We have appealed to the government on numerous occasions," Pat Conroy complained, "and when there is not outright hostility there is a sort of deathly silence, leading to an apparent planned inaction, both of which have a similar final effect."[189] There is no evidence that the prime minister told Mitchell to file away Richardson's recommendations. Given his aversion to compulsory collective bargaining, however, it seems likely that King found them problematic. C.D. Howe, the minister of munitions and supply, may have also had something to do with dissuading Mitchell. Intent on surpassing 1941's war production level by 250 per cent, the powerful minister had little patience for unions and exerted a considerable influence over his counterpart in the Labour Department. Even Mackenzie King noticed that "Mitchell is far too much in Howe's pocket."[190] What is clear is that the labour minister abruptly shifted his attention to other priorities in the spring of 1942. Declaring in the House of Commons that "if we win this war, it will be a miracle," he focused mainly on the distribution of workers to war essential jobs, the relocation of Japanese Canadians, and the resolution of wage questions, not to mention his election to office.[191] Though disappointed, the leaders of the industrial unions

3.6 Humphrey Mitchell
Source: Arthur Roy Fonds, Library and Archives Canada, PA-047324.

were not surprised. His previous work as IDIC chair, especially in the Kirkland Lake conflict, had made them question his credibility right from the beginning. "My experience with Mitchell," derided Charlie Millard, "makes it impossible for me to believe that he is anything but a crafty stooge for the manufacturers and politicians in power."[192] And, in truth, the British-born Mitchell, who arrived in Canada as a young adult, seemed more concerned about winning the war than protecting or advancing the collective rights of workers. In the early summer of 1942, Conroy complained that the labour minister was evading his demands for "a direct and forthwith discussion on the question of a proper and just collective bargaining policy."[193]

Within the ranks of the Labour Department, however, momentum was building for labour law reform. In May 1942, Margaret Mackintosh, the chief of the Legislative Branch, told an audience of federal and provincial labour officials that "the greatest production can only be got where there is goodwill, and goodwill is engendered through

3.7 Bryce Stewart

Source: Library and Archives Canada, *Labour Gazette*, 1950, 1333, Amicus No. 52993175.

3.8 M.M. "Kay" Maclean

Source: Library and Archives Canada, *Labour Gazette*, 1958, 473, Amicus No. 52993175.

3.9 Arthur MacNamara

Source: Library and Archives Canada, *Labour Gazette*, 1953, 410, Amicus No. 52993175.

3.10 Vincent MacDonald

Source: Vincent C. MacDonald Fonds, MS-2-171, Dalhousie University Archives.

3.11 Margaret Mackintosh. Unlike her male colleagues and despite her legislative contributions, professional images of Mackintosh are non-existent. The only woman to attend the 1943 Dominion-Provincial Conference on Labour, she barely made it into this official photograph. She is seated on the far right, holding her chin.

Source: *Ottawa Journal*, 10 November 1943, 7, Microfilm, Ottawa City Library, Main Branch.

mutual recognition and discussion on an equitable basis, a basis which trade unions and collective bargaining enable the workers to achieve." An authority on labour law and comparative labour history, Mackintosh added that "nothing steadies a union like collective bargaining and working under agreements. Nothing develops a militant and aggressive leadership like the refusal to deal with a union."[194] New recruits to the DOL, which had just been reorganized to accommodate its expanded responsibilities, also connected the passage of a collective bargaining policy to industrial peace and stability.[195] In early August, M.M. "Kay" Maclean, a CCL vice-president, joined the DOL as the director of the Industrial Relations Branch. Essentially, he was in charge of the government's conciliation services. An old-style business unionist, Maclean supported the persuasive mechanisms of the IDIA, worried about excessive legalism, and took a dim view of wartime strikes. No doubt the recent death of his son in the war hardened his opposition to shutdowns. But he also felt that a collective bargaining policy could foster orderly industrial relations and curtail corporate arrogance.[196] A few weeks later, the DOL also hired Vincent MacDonald, the dean of Dalhousie University's Law School, as acting assistant deputy minister of labour. A strong advocate of constitutional reform, he too believed that the federal government should play a more assertive role in industrial relations.[197]

As the strike rate escalated, two other developments added to this bureaucratic impetus.[198] First, an industrial relations subcommittee for the National Selective Service (NSS) informed the DOL that constitutional barriers to a Canadian Wagner Act were no longer in effect. By interfering in the lives of workers in both war and non-war industries, the NSS had inadvertently expanded the federal government's jurisdiction in industrial relations.[199] Second, at a mid-August meeting of the national and regional war labour boards, government officials from across the country expressed support for more forceful measures. Although the meeting was mainly called to focus on wage levels and selective service, Ontario's minister of labour, Peter Heenan, who was once active in the railway brotherhoods and had served as Mackenzie King's labour minister in the late 1920s, suggested that the regional war labour boards compel employers "to formally recognize any Trade Union, association of employees, or committee of employees which such Board may find to be the proper bargaining representations of any particular group of employees, and provide proper penalties for violations." The labour minister for Nova Scotia, L.D. Currie, a former coal miner, seconded the motion.[200] Importantly, the ministers were not giving the federal government the go-ahead to explore the possibility of a more comprehensive, national labour policy. But they were recognizing the inconsistencies in the existing orders. If the federal government had the authority to mandate wage freezes, why couldn't its agencies impose collective bargaining?

In late August, Humphrey Mitchell finally took action, summoning the labour panel of his consultative committee to discuss changes to PC 2685.[201] With Kay Maclean serving as a well-placed contact in the government, the CCL unions realized that the policy door was slightly ajar. They began to besiege the DOL with demands for action in the Crown or government-owned corporations. By setting an example for private industry, the UE argued, the government "would do more than any other single act to bring about a new and necessary high level in the morale of the production workers."[202] On 3 September, the CCL also orchestrated the public release of the NSS report on constitutional reform, pointing out how it reaffirmed the findings in Richardson's study.[203] A few days later, when Mitchell spoke at the CCL convention, delegates continually interrupted him with chants: "We need the Wagner Act."[204] On 19 September, CCL delegates met with Bryce Stewart, the deputy minister of the DOL, to request "an immediate clarification of the rights of workers in Government owned and operated plants." Perhaps recognizing the dangers of a failed promise, Stewart assured the labour leaders that a draft would be on Mitchell's desk by 21 September and implemented by the following week.[205]

A number of factors, like the NSS report, the urging of his own staff, and the rising strike rate, finally pushed Mitchell into action. He was especially impressed to learn that the TLC supported the CCL's demands for labour law reform. In late August, the more mainstream, craft-based congress had captured national headlines when convention delegates in Winnipeg passed a strongly worded resolution in favour of compulsory collective bargaining. Rather impulsively, R.C. McCutcheon of the Boilermakers and Helpers thundered: "We should tell the Dominion government ... to give us this legislation, which is in effect in the United States, Australia, and New Zealand, or we'll sabotage your war effort."[206] The business press expressed outrage at McCutcheon's threat, but the TLC's aggressive policy demand caught the attention of Humphrey Mitchell.[207] With Percy Bengough now acting as TLC president, the labour movement as a whole seemed a much more cohesive force. Jurisdictional and ideological divisions still existed between and within the major labour bodies. But the federal government could no longer dismiss calls for a Canadian Wagner Act as the rantings of upstart industrial unionists. In the words of W.J. Couper, a DOL official, "the Government would listen" if the TLC and CCL "got together and agreed on Collective Bargaining."[208]

In early October, after two meetings of Mitchell's Labour Consultative Committee, the DOL presented a very rough, secret draft of a collective bargaining policy to CCL and TLC leaders for comments. It went much further than labour leaders had anticipated. The proposed order amended PC 2685 by replacing the word "should" with "shall," prohibiting "company unions," establishing a five-member "Labour Policy Enforcement Board," and prescribing penalties for violations.[209] It also seemed to apply to all employers, not just Crown corporations. Not surprisingly, labour leaders were ecstatic. To be "in a position to take advantage of the Collective Bargaining legislation now under way," the CCL executive committee began to search for the funding to hire full-time directors of organization.[210] Demonstrating the new spirit of unity in the labour movement, Percy Bengough of the TLC and A.R. Mosher of the CCL worked together on "a confidential outline" that was sent back to the DOL.[211] In response, DOL officials assured them that a bill would be drawn up for policymakers at an early date. After years of frustrated demands, the industrial unions had finally achieved their goal of a Wagner-like act.[212]

Or not. Once again, Mitchell failed to follow through on either a Crown corporation or general collective bargaining proposal. Instead, he suddenly left Canada for a month-and-a-half-long trip to England. Even Mackenzie King was surprised, if not critical, of the timing of his departure.[213] When labour leaders complained about the delays with the promised policy, DOL officials told them that nothing could be done until Mitchell's return.[214] Extremely frustrated, C.S. Jackson of the United Electrical Workers observed that "the question has become a football to be tossed back and forth."[215] When Mitchell finally returned to Ottawa on 16 November, he continued to stall on the labour policies, refusing to meet with labour leaders or to provide explanation for the holdup.[216] Charlie Millard reported that the DOL would only state that "the representations of the [CCL] in respect to a Collective Bargaining Order are 'receiving consideration.'"[217]

What was going on? A big problem was that power struggles within the DOL had bogged down the policymaking process. In September, Bryce Stewart, the influential deputy minister of labour, had announced he would be returning to his position at Industrial Relations Counsellors, Inc. in two months' time. The deputy minister complained that he was "disgruntled and disaffected" with the intrusions of C.D. Howe's department, the ineffectiveness of the NSS, and the lackadaisical enforcement of the wage and price controls.[218] As mentioned earlier, in mid-November, E.M. Little, the NSS director and favourite of the labour movement, also resigned abruptly because of interference from Mitchell. In support of Little, the labour movement and some high-ranking civil servants urged King to fire his labour minister. But DOL officials and several cabinet ministers backed the minister.[219] As one staff member observed, "Elliot Little was an industrialist who simply did not know anything about how to work at Ottawa."[220] In the end, King decided to accept Little's resignation.[221] Arthur MacNamara, the newly appointed deputy minister of labour who enjoyed a reputation as an administrative troubleshooter, assumed the responsibilities of the NSS director. His services were badly needed. "Like the little Dutch boy who rushed to the hole in the dike and with one finger bravely held off the flood," a reporter wrote, "MacNamara bustled in to stave off the flood of criticism that ... threatened to engulf the entire Mackenzie King Government."[222]

The largest obstacle to change, however, was the prime minister. Despite all the new developments, he still refused to commit his government to "one-sided" intervention. In late August 1942, King had finally refocused his attention on industrial relations when the USW threatened a nationwide strike for a base wage of fifty-five cents an hour.[223] After personally appealing to the patriotism of Charlie Millard, the leader of the Steelworkers, King began to wonder for the first time about Mitchell's capacity to handle labour matters. As he wrote in his diary, the labour minister "is inclined simply to state that things can be done; will be done; must be done, without any real appreciation of what is involved."[224] Re-establishing his ties to organized labour, the prime minister attended the CCL convention at the Chateau Laurier in Ottawa, where he listened to Philip Murray, the CIO president, give a speech, visiting with him afterwards in his hotel room.[225] In October, King gave the keynote address at the American Federation of Labor (AFL) convention in Toronto, which was broadcast live across Canada and the United States. Much to his delight, he received a standing ovation from the delegates.[226] Yet, Brooke Claxton, the Liberal Party backbencher, noted that King still seemed oblivious to how "revolutionary changes are proceeding at a rapid pace."[227] Rather than acknowledge the realities of power in the workplace and the inadequacies of the existing labour laws, he continued to preach the virtues of investigation and conciliation. As he later admitted, his goal at the AFL conference had been "to say something which would really help to get recognition in the right place ... away from this worshiping of false gods."[228]

While the policymaking process bogged down in Ottawa, the provincial governments of Ontario and British Columbia responded more directly to the heightened pressures for new labour legislation. At the CCL convention, Peter Heenan had announced his intention to present a collective bargaining bill at the next session of the Ontario legislature. In surprising support, Mitchell Hepburn, the outspoken Ontario premier, explained that "it seems to be the only way to obtain industrial and labour peace which is so essential in these critical war years."[229] Why would the rabidly anti-labour premier agree to such a measure? According to George Drew, Ontario's Conservative leader, it was a "political stunt" to embarrass Mackenzie King. Anticipating the passage of a federal labour policy, Hepburn wanted to usurp King's efforts to win back the industrial vote, not to mention weaken support for the CCF.[230] As one journalist commented: "The much tooted Heenan collective-bargaining bill is an obvious Ontario Liberal sop."[231] It also seems likely that Hepburn wanted to bring his scandal-plagued career to a close on a positive note – to go down in history as an advocate for labour. The Ontario government secretly hired J.L. Cohen, the omnipresent labour lawyer, to draft the collective bargaining bill for anticipated passage in spring 1943.[232]

Meanwhile, in British Columbia, George Pearson, the labour minister in John Hart's coalition government of Liberals and Conservatives, had announced that "free bargaining cannot be properly achieved unless greater obligations are placed on the employers." A fairly progressive member of the Liberal Party who was sympathetic to the plight of the working people, Pearson claimed that the escalating strike rate necessitated amendments to the Industrial Conciliation and Arbitration (ICA) Act of 1937.[233] Rather than concerns for the working class, however, his declaration largely reflected the growing popularity of the CCF in the provincial House. During the spring, CCF legislators had organized a series of meetings with CCL and TLC representatives to discuss amendments to the ICA Act.[234] In the fall, CCF leader A.J. Turner received considerable publicity when he called for the end of "old fashioned anti-labour" attitudes.[235] Pearson realized that policy changes were needed to undercut the CCF's support in labour circles.

The original ICA Act made provisions for collective bargaining, but lacked the proper administrative machinery to determine bargaining units and failed to compel employers to sign contractual agreements with unions.[236] As well, a controversial 1938 amendment that blatantly targeted CIO affiliates denied bargaining rights to unions formed after 7 December 1938.[237] Alan Wright, a SWOC organizer, stated that the ICA Act "is enough to give a man babies."[238] In January 1943, after the TLC and CCL submitted their first joint memorandum to the provincial cabinet, Pearson began to make revisions.[239]

Besides the provinces, another startling development was the Conservative Party's embrace of compulsory collective bargaining. Deeply concerned about the rise of the CCF and convinced that Liberal hegemony or supremacy was waning, a cohort of relatively young, but influential, lay Conservatives had pushed the party to abandon its strict laissez-faire or limited government doctrine for a more reform-oriented, "middle of the road" approach.[240] In September 1942, these visionaries organized a well-publicized conference at Port Hope, Ontario, to construct a new party platform. One of the four policy committees was dedicated to labour relations. Advised by Norman Dowd of the CCL, the labour committee recommended the passage of a federal collective bargaining policy, the creation of a National Labour Relations Board, and the penalization of unfair labour practices.[241] Although the labour proposals allowed for non-union plant committees and included compulsory arbitration provisions, they were a stark contrast to existing labour policies. Fred Gardiner, the committee chair, later commented: "Unions ... have demonstrated the useful place they can occupy in our social structure ... No employer can any longer reasonably oppose collective bargaining."[242]

Back in Ottawa, it was beginning to dawn on Mackenzie King that some kind of policy action was needed. From January to September 1942, political support for the federal Liberals had fallen by sixteen points.[243] As the increased popularity of the CCF and the remarkable metamorphosis of the Conservative Party demonstrated, the political temperament of the country was shifting. What's more, Humphrey Mitchell was alienating the labour movement. Alex "Sandy" Skelton, a high-ranking civil servant, warned King that the labour minister was a serious liability who "did not follow through on things he promised to undertake."[244] The highly publicized resignation of Elliot Little, the NSS director, brought Mitchell's unpopularity into full play. Within the week, the prime minister received a joint letter from Percy Bengough and A.R. Mosher. Citing the delays in the proposed collective bargaining policy, the labour leaders wrote:

> Mr. Mitchell's attitude and activities have been unsatisfactory to the workers ... Labour relationships are worse off than they were when he was appointed, and it has become evident that he has lost the confidence of the organized workers of Canada ... [We] are demanding not only a satisfactory Labour policy, but the appointment of a Minister of Labour who will be strong enough to administer that policy without fear or favour.[245]

A few days later, the Liberals lost two of three scheduled federal by-elections. The prime minister attributed the large size of the CCF victory in Winnipeg North Centre to Little's resignation.[246]

What happened next was very telling. Under increased pressure, King took steps to placate the popular demands for a collective bargaining policy. But he did it in a way that was consistent with his principles. In early December 1942, the cabinet passed Order in Council PC 10802, which granted collective bargaining rights to workers in Crown corporations. Government agents were allowed to negotiate contracts with unions that represented a majority of the workers. The labour minister would resolve representation and jurisdiction disputes; conciliation boards would deal with all other conflicts.[247] The DOL later hailed PC 10802 as "a significant development," and both Bengough and Mosher applauded its passage.[248] Within a short time, collective agreements covered 18,000 government employees in four firms.[249] It seemed like a huge breakthrough for organized labour. As more astute labour leaders quickly realized, though, King had merely expanded the boundaries for collective bargaining, not abandoned his commitment to conciliatory methods. PC 10802 contained the same familiar elements of voluntary compliance as PC 2685. The language used was suggestive, not forceful. Labour law expert Bora Laskin, who had finally become a University of Toronto professor, noted: "[T]here [is] no compulsion upon [Crown corporations] to bargain collectively if they choose to ignore representative unions."[250]

A few days after the passage of PC 10802, King also thought seriously about replacing Humphrey Mitchell with Charles (Chubby) Power, the minister of national defence for air and a corporate lawyer by training. Given that Mitchell "had not really fought for labour as he should," the prime minister believed his dismissal would go a long way to appeasing the labour movement.[251] The Conservative Party's recent convention in

Winnipeg served as a catalyst. At this historic conference, the delegates adopted a near replica of the Port Hope platform, including the labour policy recommendations, and changed the party name to the Progressive Conservatives.[252] Although King likened the Conservative Party's embrace of reformism to the mixing of "oil and water," he worried that "Mitchell had got in quite wrong with Labour and would be a target at the next session."[253] Power, on the other hand, was not only a seasoned, bilingual parliamentarian, but also an outspoken supporter of civil liberties.[254] The idea proved fleeting. Uneasy about representing the interests of the labour movement, Power eventually talked King out of making the change. With the government's labour policies under increased scrutiny, however, the prime minister felt that he was only "postponing the evil day as far as Mitchell is concerned."[255]

By the end of 1942, most labour leaders agreed that the campaign for a compulsory collective bargaining policy had fallen flat. The only bright note was the increase in popular support. As the upscale weekly, *Saturday Night*, observed:

> On the part of government, we find piecemeal legislation, reluctantly granted bit by bit at times when the voice of labour becomes uncomfortably loud, in an effort to lull the working population into a sense of security. On the part of industry, we find an attitude of economic royalism ... that the employer is the only party capable of conducting an enterprise, and that the way he conducts it is of no concern to anyone but himself.[256]

Unlike earlier in the war, many middle-class commentators had begun to blame federal labour policies and the hostile behaviour of employers, not the militancy of workers, for the deterioration in industrial relations. Their views were complex, both varied and overlapping: some worried about war production; some sought workplace justice; some believed in the constancy of democratic principles. But they all agreed that a Wagner-like act would foster industrial order and stability. As Fred Gardiner of the newly named Progressive Conservative Party put it, a collective bargaining policy would create "a spirit of confidence and co-operation between employers' and employees' organizations leading to the establishment of sound labour relations."[257] These sentiments served as both the cause and effect of a larger shift in political values. On the one hand, voters drifted leftward to the CCF because the social democratic party supported a Canadian Wagner Act. On the other hand, the Conservative Party and regional Liberal Parties constructed collective bargaining planks to attract left-leaning voters. Either way, collective bargaining had become one of the leading topics of discussion in the country. In August, for example, the Canadian Institute on International Affairs, an influential, non-partisan policy forum, invited David Lewis of the CCF and Roger Brossard of the Université de Montréal to speak on the constitutional ramifications of a Canadian Wagner Act.[258]

Still, in December 1942, a dejected Patrick Conroy seemed ready to give up the chase. When asked by a regional organizer about the likelihood of a Wagner-like act in the near future, the CCL leader replied: "We do not feel it worthwhile to raise people's hopes when the record of the federal government is as it has been."[259] Why the pessimism? It was mainly due to Mackenzie King's stranglehold on the policymaking process. Earlier in the year, while preoccupied with other matters, he probably arranged for the shelving of the Richardson recommendations. Later, after refocusing on industrial relations, he had the DOL's draft proposal revised. Instead of compulsory collective bargaining, the country received PC 10802, an ideologically consistent policy that continued to ignore the realities of power in the workplace. A reformer at heart, the prime minister genuinely supported the goal of a more humane and democratic industrial order where workers enjoyed improved conditions and a greater voice in the workplace – what he referred to as the "task that lies ahead." But King continued to adhere to the supposedly even-handed principles of conciliation and persuasion. He remained convinced that if the government implemented policies that forced employers to recognize and bargain with unions, the ensuing backlash would harm workers' rights, incite industrial upheaval, and undermine national unity. Unwilling to introduce a policy that unambiguously favoured the labour movement, the wartime administration simply broadened the scope of what already existed. In short, the status quo prevailed. In the year ahead, an increasing number of people would call for more forceful government intervention in industrial relations. Instead of mounting social and political pressures, however, it would take the findings and recommendations of a reconstituted National War Labour Board to convince the prime minister that it was time to overhaul the existing labour policy framework. As one newspaper editor observed, the board would be much like "a child showing up its parent."[260]

Chapter Four

A Code of Labour Relations, Fall 1942–Spring 1944

On the windy, snowy evening of 4 December 1943, Mackenzie King rushed through the doors of the CBC Radio studio in Ottawa. He had only a few minutes to spare before giving his address to the nation. It had been a grueling day at Laurier House, sifting through pages of confusing, incomplete notes from different departments and agencies in order to finish the speech. His perfectionist tendencies added to the difficulties. At one point, the prime minister had felt so unprepared that he considered cancelling the broadcast. He was only able to piece together a final draft with the last minute help of two aides. There was no time to practice or even read through the speech beforehand; he hoped his voice wouldn't show "any sign of fatigue." After greeting the three CBC staff in the room, King positioned himself in front of the microphone and, at eight o'clock, was given the "On Air" signal. Making an effort to speak "slowly, clearly, and forcibly," he began explaining to the nation why the most critical challenge on the home front was the battle against inflation. He described how the economy had suffered after the Great War and warned that the government was going to do a much better job of enforcing the wage freeze. He promised, however, that it would include "the removal of gross injustices and inequities." Midway through the broadcast, the prime minister felt "that the speech itself was going well." He had only stumbled over a few words and was speaking with "a good deal of strength." He also knew that he had saved some of the best news for last. After talking for nearly half an hour about wage controls, King made the following announcement: "A code of labour relations is ... in the final stages of preparation." It will "define and prohibit unfair labour practices ... provide for compulsory collective bargaining ... [and] be enforced by a national wartime labour relations board."[1]

What had happened? For over thirty-five years, the prime minister had proselytized about conciliation mechanisms and government impartiality. Just a year earlier, he had orchestrated the passage of the benign PC 10802. How could he possibly reconcile a new "code of labour relations" with his political convictions? As most scholars agree, there is little doubt that expediency was at play. Throughout 1943, workers continued to join unions in large numbers, walk off their jobs at unprecedented rates, and shift their allegiances to the social democratic Co-operative Commonwealth Party (CCF). During these turbulent times, the Liberal government needed to take some kind of action, not only to promote industrial peace but also to bolster its support among workers. Yet the "code of labour relations" was much more than a knee-jerk reaction to social, economic, and political pressures. The prime minister had actually remained wedded to the status quo for the first half of 1943. It took three industrial relations experts on a reconstituted National War Labour Board (NWLB) to convince him that a compulsory collective bargaining policy was both desirable and necessary. Nor was King jettisoning his principles for the sake of self-interest. The "code of labour relations" was built on some of the same concepts as earlier policies, re-emphasizing the government's "neutral" role in industrial relations and the value of conciliation procedures. To be sure, the new labour policy, which became known as PC 1003 or the Wartime Labour Relations Regulations, was a significant development. By requiring contractual negotiations, the government curbed the arbitrary powers of employers and indirectly sanctioned the role of unions. But it was not a Wagner Act.

The Impetus

Robert "Bob" Haddow, the Grand Lodge representative of the International Machinists Union in Montreal, stood in front of a large group of shop committee members from Lodge 712 who had gathered at the Assistance Public Hall. Looking out over the audience with his one good eye, the Scottish-born toolmaker announced that the NWLB had denied the union's request for bonus pay in the aircraft industry. Despite a huge ten-day strike in the summer, the workers were not going to win any significant gains. Just as Haddow had anticipated, the hall erupted in shouts of anger and frustration. He quickly and skilfully changed topics and began talking about the prime minister's compulsory collective bargaining announcement two days earlier. The labour leader underscored how this was a huge development for the labour movement. He also questioned the integrity of the policymakers. Would they follow through on the undertaking? Haddow urged everyone in the hall to push hard for the implementation of the labour code. It will be one of "the biggest victories of the labour movement, if, and as long as the workers put enough pressure on the Government and on Mr. King to put these promises into effect." "You and I, the common workers of this country," he continued, "[must] compel our Government to apply these policies." Haddow's call to arms was not empty rhetoric. Although he was trying to divert attention from the NWLB's wage decision, he also understood that the labour movement wielded unprecedented influence. Certainly workers and their unions were not going to win every battle on the factory floor or before the NWLB. When effectively mobilized, however, they were a force to be reckoned with.[2]

In 1943, the labour movement had grown considerably. The overall union membership level rose by 15 per cent and the union density rate by another 2 per cent.[3] Local unions with more than one thousand members had increased from 79 to 108.[4] To be sure, some workers sought collective representation through independent affiliations. As the secretary-treasurer of the National Steel Car Employees' Association explained, they believed that these types of organizations upheld "individual rights and freedoms" and "true and honest cooperation with management."[5] Still, there was no denying that more and more wage-earners wanted to tap into the collective strength of the labour movement. No longer willing to let employers define the rules of the game, many co-opted existing employee associations to launch recognition drives. In late 1942, for example, steel mill workers at Stelco in Hamilton, Ontario, elected union members to eight of the eleven employee positions on a well-established works council. When the company refused to accede to council requests to recognize the United Steelworkers (USW), nine of the employee representatives resigned their positions. Management shut down the council, adopted the union's wage demand, and established a plant committee. But two years later a large majority of the workers chose the USW over the plant committee in a government-supervised vote.[6]

For many Canadians, the labour movement, especially the industrial unions, had become a more legitimate force. The general public expressed a much greater tolerance, if not appreciation, for collective action. Although by no means a consensus, much of the country felt that trade unions were capable of responsible behaviour, played an important representative role in Canadian society, and deserved legislative protection. In April 1943, for example, a Gallup poll revealed that 53 per cent of the country supported compulsory recognition.[7] It was also clear that the business community no longer enjoyed the confidence of the citizenship. Still blaming morally bankrupt employers for the Great Depression and appalled by the pre-tax profit levels, which had averaged 17 per cent since the beginning of the war, Canadians expressed considerable skepticism about business motives and activities.[8] "The simple unpleasant fact," J.M. Macdonnell, the president of National Trust, observed "is that they distrust us and regard us as selfish and incompetent."[9] When another Gallup poll asked whether Canadians preferred to have trade unions or large corporations controlling the government, nearly twice as many respondents chose organized labour.[10]

What was particularly impressive about 1943 was the raw economic and political power of the workers. Confronted with hardline employers and emboldened by full employment conditions, the wartime labour force was rocking the country with strikes.[11] Never before had so many Canadians participated in work stoppages – often in defiance of their unions and the wartime labour policies. Although recognition strikes made up only 11 per cent of the total, they were among the most turbulent and disruptive.[12] Over 600 workers at Dominion Glass in Wallaceburg, Ontario, engaged in an illegal strike for forty-five days to force the company to recognize and bargain with the United Auto Workers.[13] For two weeks, 500 loggers in the Queen Charlotte Islands of British Columbia curtailed the supply of spruce logs to both the airplane and Western pulp and paper industries, striking against the advice of their union leaders for recognition of the International Woodworkers.[14] More sympathetic to workers' rights, afraid that production levels were declining just when a final push was needed to win the war, conditioned by government actions like wage and price controls, and perhaps aware of the lower strike rate in the United States, the general public looked to legislators to produce a clear, comprehensive set of regulations that would restore the industrial order. As the *Financial Times* stated: "[T]he immediate settlement of the labour problem [is] probably the most important task for Canada at the moment."[15]

The CCF also continued to make remarkable advances at the expense of the two mainstream parties. On 4 August 1943, the social democratic party became the official opposition in Ontario's legislature when they won thirty-four seats compared to thirty-eight for the Progressive

Conservatives and only fifteen for the incumbent Liberals in the provincial election; more than half of the party's victorious candidates were union members.[16] A few days later, on 9 August, the CCF won two of four federal by-elections. By September, the CCF surpassed both the Liberals and the Progressive Conservatives in popular support throughout the country.[17] David Lewis and Frank Scott, the national secretary and chair of the party, respectively, rejoiced: "This war is becoming a people's war."[18] Of course, not all the CCF's support derived from wage-earners. In recent months, as Allied victories multiplied, many Canadians had begun to express concerns about "reconstruction" or the impending post-war period. The Wartime Information Board, the government's propaganda agency, reported that much of the country faced the reconstruction period with a feeling "akin to dread."[19] Haunted by memories of the economic turmoil that followed World War I, only just recovered from the Great Depression, and impressed with the implementation of wartime controls, many Canadians believed that the CCF's innovative program of socio-economic reforms offered the best hope for continued prosperity. According to one poll, 71 per cent of the English-speaking population wanted the government to make "many changes or reforms" after the war.[20] Nevertheless, as Paul Martin, the Liberal MP for Windsor, Ontario, recalled: "No one could deny that the major strength of the CCF was the crusading spirit of its workers."[21] Ralph Maybank, the Liberal MP from Winnipeg, concurred, writing in a letter to Mackenzie King that the leftward shift of the workers mainly reflected "a positive dislike, almost amounting to hatred, of federal labour policies."[22]

The Canadian Congress of Labour (CCL), which represented many of the industrial unions in the country, continued to lead the charge for a compulsory collective bargaining policy. After the false promises of previous years, the congress had regrouped and become much more openly critical of the Liberal administration. "[The] government has come to be distrusted in the minds of the mass of the workers," announced Pat Conroy, the secretary-treasurer, "who have come to regard [it] as merely an agency of opposition created by employers."[23] Moderate CCL leaders redoubled their efforts to convince the country that the more aggressive industrial unions could make positive contributions to society, often resorting to heavy-handed disciplinary actions in the name of responsible unionism. Confronted with a rash of illegal strikes in Ontario, for example, President Aaron Mosher threatened to resign unless affiliates disciplined their members.[24] When communist activists on the West Coast created an "unhealthy, chaotic state of affairs," the executive committee suspended charters and froze funds.[25] And, in March, the CCL briefly suspended the United Electrical Workers for challenging one of its jurisdictional decisions.[26] The congress also became much more politically active, strengthening its ties with the CCF. Although some CCL leaders and numerous local unions had long associations with the social democrats, the annual convention in September 1943 marked the CCL's first formal alliance with the CCF – much to the dismay of communist members.[27] Conroy, who normally disliked political affiliations, told delegates, he "was sick and tired of going cap in hand to Mackenzie King."[28]

Meanwhile, the Trades and Labour Congress (TLC), which represented most of the craft unions, had become much more vocal in its demands for a collective bargaining policy. In the spring, Percy Bengough, the acting president, bluntly told Mackenzie King that "the frustrations and interference of the employees' right to organize and bargain collectively through their chosen representatives is a state of affairs that should not be permitted in a democratic country at any time."[29] The election of Pat Sullivan, the communist president of the Canadian Seamen's Union and an internment camp veteran, to vice-president in August 1942 and secretary-treasurer in September 1943 symbolized how the congress was becoming more broad-minded.[30] Ten of the nineteen trade unionists who won seats in the recent Ontario election as CCF candidates belonged to TLC unions.[31] To be sure, a large divide still existed between the TLC and CCL. With high-ranking, old-school craft unionists like Tom Moore, the elected but bedridden president, voicing objections, the TLC stopped short of mounting a full-fledged crusade for collective rights.[32] Instead of affiliating with the CCF, the congress also established a non-partisan Political Action Committee to support favourable candidates from any party.[33] And with the CCL rapidly closing the membership gap between the two organizations, jurisdictional disputes limited once promising joint representations to the government. Despite local and regional collaborations, the TLC leadership refused most of the CCL's requests to work together.[34] Yet, impressed observers noted that the TLC and the CCL demanded the same kind of policy action. In the spring of 1943, the *Financial Times* headlined: "Collective Bargaining Seen Unifying Labour."[35]

Searching for ways to restore the industrial order and/or accommodate the restless electorate, provincial politicians latched onto the labour movement's demands for a collective bargaining policy. With active legislatures, slim leads over opposition parties, relatively light administrative loads, and no particular allegiance to Mackenzie King, the provincial governments proved more sensitive than the federal government to changes in the political climate. True, the provinces had lost much of their jurisdictional authority over industrial relations at the beginning of the war. But Ottawa's unwillingness or inability to address the current crisis seemed to oblige provincial action. As Adam Bell, the deputy minister of labour for British Columbia, observed in May 1943: "The Dominion Government is trailing ... behind. It is hardly up to the times."[36] Three types of labour policy activity took place in the provinces. First, collective bargaining bills were introduced and successfully opposed in the legislatures of Manitoba and Saskatchewan. Despite the defeats, both governments appointed commissions to conduct further investigations on the question. Saskatchewan would enact a far-reaching collective bargaining law the following year that clearly favoured workers.[37] Second, Alberta and British Columbia added compulsory provisions to their existing labour laws. Both governments began to fine employers up to $500 for refusing to negotiate contracts with employee representatives. They also made it illegal for employers to dominate or interfere with employee organizations.[38] Even the Consolidated Mining and Smelting Company in Trail, British Columbia, had to disband its much vaunted Workmen's Co-operative Committee.[39] From organized labour's standpoint, the amendments in British Columbia and Alberta were far from ideal. Instead of establishing an independent administrative agency like the National Labor Relations Board in the United States, the two provinces relied on labour ministers to implement the laws. Although British Columbia granted automatic certification to all unions with majority representation, workers had to belong to a union for more than three months prior to certification, and employers could challenge certifications after six months. The two provinces also continued to allow non-union organizations to represent workers.[40] Still, the revisions were a big step in the right direction. As Nigel Morgan of the International Woodworkers of America said triumphantly in British Columbia, the amendments represented a "new deal" for workers.[41]

Third, Ontario and Quebec enacted completely new collective bargaining laws. In early February, outspoken labour lawyer J.L. Cohen had resigned as the original author of Ontario's bill when business opposition bogged down the policymaking process. With an election pending, Premier Gordon Conant, who served briefly as Mitchell Hepburn's hand-picked successor, appointed a union-friendly Select Committee of the Legislature to conduct public hearings and draw up a new policy. The Collective Bargaining Act was subsequently passed on 14 April 1943.[42] Several months later, on 4 February 1944, Quebec's General Assembly passed the Labour Relations Act after the Prévost Commission investigated inter-union rivalries and recommended the passage of collective bargaining legislation.[43] Both of these new acts forced employers to negotiate contracts with employee representatives, prohibited employers from engaging in unfair labour practices, and outlawed employer-dominated or influenced employee organizations. Unlike Ontario, Quebec allowed for the certification of minority bargaining units – a concession to the Confédération des travailleurs catholiques du Canada (CTCC). There was also a significant difference in the administration of the two acts. Quebec adopted machinery that closely resembled the three-person National Labor Relations Board in the United States. Ontario created a Labour Court, which individual justices from the provincial Supreme Court presided over for two-week stints.[44] Although, in both cases, non-union employee associations were allowed to operate, the laws appeared to represent major breakthroughs for organized labour. E.J. Young, the director of Canadian National Railways, protested that "the real objective" of the Ontario act was "to deliver workers, bound and gagged, into the hands of the unions."[45]

Despite the loud objections of employers, one of the most striking aspects of this provincial policymaking was the ineffective opposition of the business community. As a Western member of the Canadian Manufacturers' Association lamented: "The B.C. Division made representations to the Legislature and to the Cabinet ... but we got nowhere."[46] This comment is not to suggest that corporate interests lacked influence in legislative circles. In Ontario, for example, lawyers for the auto companies managed to diminish J.L. Cohen's role in the drafting of the Collective Bargaining Act.[47] Yet, in four of the provinces – including the two largest industrial provinces – employers were not able to use their economic power and leverage to block collective bargaining provisions that directly threatened their managerial prerogatives. Why? There were two related reasons. First, fewer provincial politicians appreciated the anti-union rhetoric of belligerent employers. Given the swelling popularity of the unions and the CCF, not to mention the strike wave, they realized that some kind of policy innovation, not stagnancy or regression, was needed. Indeed, James Clark, the chair of Ontario's Select Committee, who represented the industrial riding of Windsor-Sandwich, abruptly terminated Stelco's presentation during the hearings for the new Collective Bargaining Act because the company demonstrated "a stubborn disregard for the social facts."[48]

Second, the business community had become more divided about the question of compulsory collective bargaining.[49] On the one hand, traditionalists argued that Canada should follow the laissez-faire example of Great Britain – where unions won contracts without statute enforcement – not the United States. Otherwise, the Ontario Branch of the Canadian Manufacturers' Association (CMA) asserted, the passage of a new labour policy "would have a disturbing effect on employer-employee relations and on war production efficiency."[50] On the other hand, a growing number of employers believed that collective bargaining encouraged industrial stability and order; they were more open or at least less closed to the idea of compulsion. In recent months, a few influential consulting firms had emerged to promote this ostensibly open-minded viewpoint. J.C. Adams of the Central Ontario Industrial Relations Institute explained to the Association of Canadian Advertisers that a collective agreement with binding rules and regulations "should be as much the aim of employers as it is of trade unions."[51] But there was an important caveat. These more "enlightened" employers were still anti-union. Indeed, they subscribed to a definition of collective bargaining that circumscribed organized labour's influence. They insisted that provincial labour policies allow for "freedom of association" – that employees be allowed to organize into non-union associations or plant committees. They also denounced the inclusion of union security provisions – provisions that safeguarded membership levels and eased dues collection. Anxious to assuage popular opinion and probably hesitant to promulgate unionism, the provinces included these corporate stipulations in their laws and amendments.

There was a stark contrast between these regional developments and the stasis in Ottawa. Throughout 1943, social and political pressures provided the impetus for new collective bargaining policies in the provinces. Politicians could no longer ignore the growing labour movement, the escalating strike rate, the overlapping demands of the main labour bodies, the rise of the CCF, and the groundswell of popular support. Despite wide variations in shape and scope, all the new policies involved some form of compulsion that forced employers to recognize and bargain with unions. As Peter Heenan, Ontario's labour minister, put it: "[Y]ou must have some teeth with which to bite them ... if they do not carry on according to the law."[52] But the impetus for labour policy reform fell short in Ottawa – at least initially. Some federal politicians recognized compulsory collective bargaining as a subject of national importance. In spring 1943, for example, Brooke Claxton, a Liberal MP from Montreal, announced in the House of Commons that "the time has come when it is desirable ... that [a labour] code should be passed."[53] Preoccupied with the larger war effort and/or indifferent to labour concerns, however, Mackenzie King and his colleagues were too ossified, obstinate, and unconcerned to react directly to the external pressures. Although aware of the shifting political climate and the increased militancy of workers, they were not about to pursue labour policy innovations on their own accord. Many critics blamed the prime minister for the torpor. In the words of an appalled and somewhat mystified Eugene Forsey, the CCL research director: "He has absolutely no conception of what he is up against, and what he is letting this country in for; or if he has he doesn't care."[54]

The Experts

On the morning of 3 February 1943, four men sat talking in Mackenzie King's east block office in the parliament buildings. Thick, red curtains and old, heavy furniture made the room feel dark and gloomy. A full-length portrait of Wilfrid Laurier looked down from one wall; a large stone fireplace loomed behind the prime minister's oak desk. But these dull surroundings belied the intensity of the conversation. In his usual forthright manner, Justice C.P. McTague of the Ontario Supreme Court had just stated his two conditions for becoming the new chair of the National War Labour Board (NWLB). First, he wanted to turn the board into an industrial court that developed its own jurisprudence. Second, he wanted to have J.L. Cohen and J.J. Bench sit on the board with him. The three other men in the room – Mackenzie King, Humphrey Mitchell, and C.D. Howe – were stunned. The politicians had absolutely no problem with changing the structure of the NWLB, which was badly in need of an overhaul. But Cohen and Bench? Although careful not to antagonize McTague, they immediately countered with objections. King questioned the political soundness of having all three members from Ontario; the board would be vulnerable to criticisms of regional bias. Given the Protestant affinity of much of the country, he also disliked that both McTague and Bench were Catholics. Mitchell and Howe voiced strong concerns about appointing Cohen. First of all, they did not like that the labour lawyer was Jewish; like many Canadians, they were profoundly anti-Semitic. Second, they could not stomach Cohen's close association with organized labour, especially the CCL; he was one of the country's most vociferous critics of federal labour policy. McTague refused to back down, insisting that Cohen and Bench were the best people for the job. He would not consider becoming the new NWLB chair without them. After further discussion, the three politicians eventually assented. "Politically this is not a good division," King acknowledged. But it was more important to appease McTague and tap "the special knowledge which these men have of industrial problems." Little did the prime minister realize that he had inadvertently triggered the policymaking process. "In" but not "of" the government, this intermediary body of experts would take it upon itself to push the federal government towards a compulsory collective bargaining policy in the next six months.[55]

Illegal strikes by 13,000 workers at three key steel mills in Sault Ste Marie, Ontario, and Sydney and Trenton, Nova Scotia, triggered the reconstitution of the NWLB. Confronted with severe regional wage differentials, the United Steelworkers had been calling for a high uniform base rate for all steel employees since late 1941. Besides improving the material well-being of lower paid workers and attracting new members, the union hoped to launch industry-wide bargaining. During the summer of 1942, however, the regional war labour boards in Ontario and Nova Scotia had rejected applications for wage increases and full cost-of-living bonuses – even though the government had allowed the steel companies to raise their prices. In September 1942, with strikes threatening to shut down two-thirds of the country's steel production, Mackenzie King appointed a royal commission, chaired by Justice F.H. Barlow, to hold public hearings on the merits of the dispute. A few months later, Justice Barlow and James T. Stewart, the employer representative, released a majority report that refused to classify steel as a national industry and upheld the decisions of the war labour boards. J. King Gordon, the employee representative, submitted a minority report that supported the union's demand for a high uniform wage rate. After waiting more than a year for a wage increase, the steel mill employees were, in the words of one CCL official, "blazing angry" with the majority report, and they walked off their jobs. The labour leader called the strikes "a rank-and-file affair if ever there was one."[56]

Worried that the steel strikes would play into the hands of the CCF, yet wanting a fair outcome, Mackenzie King spent most of January 1943 trying to find some way to appease the workers and maintain the wage controls. It was no easy task. Although he personally supported the recommendations of the minority report, his cabinet refused to concede or even negotiate the union's demands. There was a complete "lack of disposition to try and find a way of reaching a settlement," the prime minister despaired. "The attitude of most of the ministers is so reactionary to Liberal principles and policies."[57] With aircraft workers threatening another industry-wide wage strike, King finally managed to convince his cabinet and the USW leaders to agree to a seven-point "Memorandum of Understanding." The government proposed to recognize steel as a national industry and guarantee a relatively high minimum wage rate of fifty-five cents per hour for the industry. First, though, the union had to resubmit its case to a reconstituted NWLB so that the legal foundation for the minimum wage could be established. Unlike the old NWLB chaired by Humphrey Mitchell, the new NWLB would act independently of the Labour Department. This was a key point for the union leaders. Like most of the labour movement, they despised the labour minister. Despite serious misgivings, the steel mill workers returned to their jobs in late January. With some justification, King noted that "the strike would not have been settled but for my taking the matter in hand as I did."[58] It was at that point that he decided to ask C.P. McTague to become the chair of the new NWLB.

It never occurred to the prime minister that the reconstituted NWLB might become a policymaking force. With newspaper headlines blaring "Strike Imperils War Work," he was only concerned about resolving the immediate steel crisis.[59] But McTague had other plans. Originally from Guelph, Ontario, he was the son of Irish immigrants and had made his living early on as a teacher and accomplished baseball player. Admired for his "fine legal brain" and "ebullient Celtic humour," he had built up a successful corporate law firm in Windsor, Ontario, in the 1920s and eventually had received an appointment to the Supreme Court of Ontario in the midst of the Great Depression. Since the onset of war, the fifty-three-year-old jurist had served the federal government in a number of capacities, most notably chairing several important conciliation boards like Great Lakes shipping and Kirkland Lake gold mines, which dealt directly with the divisive issue of union recognition.[60] Although McTague was a committed member of the Conservative Party, King considered him "a real find" because the two men shared many similar views about industrial relations. Like King, he had little tolerance for the hardline stands of union officials who rejected compromise and conciliation; he blamed many of the wartime strikes on the "agitational and opportunistic ambitions of [labour] leaders." McTague also agreed with King that employers had to take a more enlightened approach to dealing with workers' rights. "It is my view," he told a Montreal audience, "that the industry's day of being paternalistic and deciding ... what type of union it will deal with has long gone by." Unbeknownst to King, however, the justice had serious questions about the effectiveness of the country's labour policies. His conciliation board experiences and the escalating strike rate had convinced him that both the Industrial Disputes Investigation Act and PC 2685 were too permissive.[61]

As part of their agreement, King gave McTague the authority to make some big changes to the NWLB. When originally established under PC 8253 in late 1941, the board's main responsibility had been to oversee several regional boards that administered the wage controls. With Humphrey Mitchell as chair, this cumbersome body of eight to ten labour and employer representatives had failed to create clear-cut procedural rules for the allowance or rejection of wage increase applications. Long delays and lax enforcement resulted. McTague immediately tightened control over the regional boards by establishing a formal appeals process. As promised, he also turned the NWLB into a three-person industrial court that developed its own jurisprudence, corralling the former board members into an advisory body. Guided by the traditions of law, his goal was to "abolish secrecy and to hold open and free discussions to obtain the basic facts [so that] the recommendations made by this board will be based on decency and justice."[62] McTague also followed through on his plan to ask J.J. Bench and J.L. Cohen to join him on the board. Discharged from the military a few years earlier for medical reasons, thirty-eight-year-old Bench, an Osgoode Hall Law School graduate, King's Counsellor, and the country's youngest senator, was to serve as the employer representative. One of the first corporate lawyers to focus on the employment relationship, he had helped to found the Niagara Industrial Relations Institute. Bench made the connection between collective bargaining and industrial stability, but he remained anti-union, insisting on "freedom of association" or the right to create non-union plant committees.[63] Forty-five-year-old Cohen, widely recognized as the pre-eminent labour lawyer of the wartime period, was to serve as the employee representative. During World War II, the intensely driven, impassioned labour lawyer had fought relentlessly for the rights of workers in the courts, on conciliation boards, and even in union headquarters. Although disliked by many for his caustic, self-important, and autocratic manner, he was also respected for his intelligence, expertise, and dedication.[64]

A contemporary described him as "a man of great ability and genuine devotion to the labour movement ... [who] did not think of himself as a mere advisor but rather as a force, a guru, a leader."[65] After serving with Cohen on several conciliation boards, McTague recognized that the labour lawyer's participation on the NWLB was critical to winning the support of the labour movement.[66]

Although the business community applauded the appointments of McTague and Bench, it was extremely critical of Cohen's nomination. Employers could not fathom why the prime minister had agreed to the selection of a "CIO lawyer."[67] As the editor of the *Globe and Mail* wrote in a scathing commentary, it was difficult for them to accept the labour lawyer's appointment "as a public service."[68] On the other side of the labour-capital equation, the unions expressed cautious optimism about the new NWLB. Although labour leaders disliked Bench's appointment, they considered McTague to be a distinct improvement over Humphrey Mitchell. Despite his rigid views on wage controls, the justice had publicly demonstrated his support for compulsory collective bargaining as the chair of the Great Lakes shipping and Kirkland Lake gold mining conciliation boards. Not surprisingly, organized labour also welcomed Cohen's appointment.[69] Throughout the war, the labour lawyer had proven time and again where his sympathies lay. As Cohen announced to a gathering of TLC unions in Montreal, he planned to follow a simple edict as a NWLB member: "Serve labour and thereby serve the nation; serve the nation and thereby serve labour."[70] In subsequent months, he would invite both Pat Conroy of the CCL and Percy Bengough of the TLC to his room at the Chateau Laurier "when basic matters had to be discussed."[71]

Bench's motives for joining the board are not known. It is clear, however, that McTague and Cohen intended to use the NWLB to push the federal government in a new direction. Not long after accepting the position, the justice openly admitted that he wanted a compulsory collective bargaining policy that "would introduce a leaven of responsibility into the whole field of labour relations which is lacking in certain places on either side."[72] It was well within the McTague's purview as NWLB chair to pursue labour policy innovations. As a quid pro quo to the labour movement, PC 8253, the original wage control order, allowed the NWLB to investigate and make policy recommendations to the minister of labour. PC 1141, which formally reconstituted the NWLB on 11 February 1943, contained the same allowance.[73] Up to this point, the board had rarely used this authority. Besides sponsoring the Richardson

Report in the spring of 1942 to examine collective bargaining in Crown corporations, the Mitchell NWLB had given little consideration to policymaking. But McTague was confident of his board's expertise in industrial relations – of its ability to offer a pragmatic, technical solution to current troubles. Instead of focusing solely on wage questions, he planned to use the NWLB to restore, if not reconstruct, the industrial order. This was the main reason why Cohen, who was hardly a supporter of the Liberal administration, agreed to join the board. As the labour lawyer later reminded McTague: "You and I were both agreed before I stepped on the Board that the government labour policy was bad, whether reflected in existing legislation, lack of legislation, or in the administrative policy. We both agreed that it would be our job ... to change this ... firstly by interpreting the laws themselves in a temperate manner, and secondly by recommending changes or additions to legislation."[74]

It is important to note that McTague and Cohen advocated compulsory collective bargaining for very different reasons. After emigrating from England at the age of nine and growing up under adverse conditions in Toronto's Jewish community, where his dad organized cap makers into a union and left-leaning organizations flourished, Cohen was deeply committed to increasing the economic and political power of working people.[75] Although originally involved in commercial law, "Cohen was a socialist," writes his biographer Laurel Sefton MacDowell, "appalled by the economic hardship in the Depression years and by the state's inadequate response."[76] Convinced that unions were one of the best vehicles for achieving social justice, he equated a Canadian Wagner Act with industrial citizenship. "The ultimate objective of collective bargaining," wrote Cohen, "is to secure for labour generally the right to participate, and by trade unions, the means of participating, in shaping the pattern and progress of society."[77] McTague, on the other hand, was more interested in industrial peace and stability than industrial democracy. A practicing Catholic, his writings and speeches echoed the call made by Pope Pius XI in his 1931 encyclical, *Quadragesimo anno*, for a middle way between free-market capitalism and socialism. It was the justice's view that compulsory collective bargaining could serve as a springboard to more cooperative relations between responsible labour and business organizations – to a more stable, humanized form of capitalism. Unlike Cohen, he linked collective bargaining to industrial harmony and the greater common good, not to working-class interests.[78] This was a major ideological divide that would eventually contribute to the board's demise. In spring 1943, however, the two men were prepared to overlook their differences to focus on the task at hand.

The new board members understood that they were to act as an independent body, free of governmental interference. For McTague and Cohen, at least, this was a critical point. They believed that any association with Humphrey Mitchell and the Labour Department would alienate the increasingly cynical labour movement. They also worried that the misguided, often expedient, actions of politicians would derail their efforts to resolve the industrial relations crisis. In late February, Cohen became very upset when he learned that the government might make unilateral changes to the board's membership. This incident stemmed from the overwhelmingly negative response of French Canadians to the anglophone makeup of the new NWLB. Liberal premier Adélard Godbout of Quebec wrote a public letter to King lamenting the lack of French-Canadian representation, and Gérard Picard of the Confédération des travailleurs catholiques du Canada, who had sat on the original NWLB, resigned in protest from the new board's advisory body.[79] Rumours spread that the government planned to remedy the situation by expanding the NWLB to five members. Although Cohen agreed that the NWLB should have a French-Canadian member, he sought reassurances that the matter be left to the board's discretion.[80] After considerable discussion, the NWLB and the King cabinet arrived at a solution that seemed to reaffirm the board's independence. In late April, under the pretense of declining health, J.J. Bench resigned his seat so that Léon Lalande, a corporate lawyer from Montreal, could join the board. In his late thirties, Lalande had worked as a young man in the mines and pulp mills near his hometown of Sault Ste Marie, Ontario. Since the beginning of the war, he had served as a solicitor for the Wartime Prices and Trade Board, travelling extensively to report on international tariffs.[81] Perhaps because of his earlier experiences as a wage-earner, he had more than a passing interest in industrial relations. In 1941, with the help of Margaret Mackintosh in the Labour Department, Lalande gave a talk to the Canadian Bar Association, later published in the *Canadian Bar Review*, on "The Status of Organized Labour." After comparing the legislative histories of England, the United States, and Canada, he concluded:

> The Federal Government could well consider the advisability of legislation, under its wartime emergency powers, to give practical effect to the exhortation contained in Order in Council P.C. 2685 concerning the

maintenance of the freedom of the institutions and practices of collective bargaining.[82]

Given that Lalande had worked in McTague's law firm in Windsor, Ontario, in the early 1930s and shared his former employer's views on labour policy, his appointment not only reaffirmed the board's independence, but also strengthened its resolve to pursue a compulsory collective bargaining policy.[83]

The NWLB's autonomy also came into question when it considered the original steel strike settlement. In late March, the McTague board released a unanimous decision that deviated significantly from the government's "Memorandum of Understanding." Since it was now possible for any local wage dispute to be appealed at the national level, the NWLB determined there was no need for steel to be designated as a national industry. To conform to the wage control policy, it also reduced the minimum wage rate to fifty cents per hour and instead added a nine cent cost-of-living bonus. Finally, the board ruled that the workers in Trenton could not be included in the award since they did not produce basic steel like workers in the other two mills.[84] Stunned by the decision, the leaders of the USW quickly demanded that the government live up to the terms of the original agreement. An outraged Charlie Millard prepared his membership for massive strike action.[85] Although Humphrey Mitchell indicated his willingness to negotiate, McTague warned the prime minister that the NWLB's independence must be respected. With the general public watching closely to see if the board was, in the words of one commentator, "no more than a tool of the government," the justice would not tolerate Mitchell reviewing and possibly revising decisions.[86] Since King had little confidence in his minister's abilities, he agreed to let the ruling stand. Soon after, Mitchell wrote Millard, in a letter released to the press, that the Labour Department "will not interfere with decisions of the NWLB nor will the Government interfere as long as the Board retains the confidence of the Government."[87] Although Mitchell would continue to encroach on the NWLB's jurisdiction, the board's credibility as an independent body was established in the public eye.

Most puzzling to labour leaders was why J.L. Cohen supported the steel decision. The probable answer was that the labour lawyer remained focused on the bigger picture. He was not happy about the changes. After carefully researching the language and back story of the earlier "Memorandum of Understanding," he had shared with McTague that

4.1 National War Labour Board, 1943. This photo of the newly reconstituted NWLB in March 1943 is remarkable for the self-assured, almost disdainful poses of the members. Clearly they believed they were riding to the rescue of a broken industrial relations system. From left to right: J.L. Cohen, Charles McTague, and J.J. Bench

Source: National Film Board of Canada, Still Photography Division, Library and Archives Canada, PA-112763.

"we perhaps have no right to alter it."[88] At the same time, however, Cohen felt strongly that the NWLB must establish its credibility as an independent agency. Otherwise, when it came to challenging the decrepit labour policy framework, the board's integrity would be questioned and undermined. Politicians, like Mackenzie King, would feel free to manipulate recommendations, while opponents would accuse the NWLB of playing politics. In order to make a difference, the board had to be recognized as a voice of authority – a tripartite of experts not accountable to the government or special interests. Although a tough

4.2 Léon Lalande, April 1943. Lalande joined the NWLB in April 1943 after J.J. Bench stepped down, ostensibly for health reasons. At thirty-nine years old, Lalande was not only the youngest, but also the only bilingual member of the board.

Source: *Montreal Gazette*, 31 May, 1943, Second Section, 13, Library and Archives Canada, Amicus No. 7979376.

predicament for Cohen, the USW's case wasn't compelling enough for him to take a stand against wage controls and jeopardize the influence of the NWLB. Besides, it was difficult to justify national representation for the union when the largest producer, Stelco, remained unorganized. And, even though the USW's base rate of fifty-five cents an hour was annulled, eligible workers still received increased wages with the cost-of-living bonus. As a result,"Cohen found himself defending the tribunal's independence," writes Laurel Sefton MacDowell, "but at the expense of the union."[89]

In early April, with the NWLB's independence firmly established, the members announced a public inquiry into the government's wage

4.3 Gerard D. Reilly, US National Labor Relations Board. Reilly would later influence how the NWLB's recommendations were shaped into policy.

Source: Harris and Ewing Collection, Library of Congress, Prints and Photographs Division, LC-H22-D2005.

and labour policies.[90] Neither Mackenzie King nor the Labour Department had anything to do with initiating the investigation. As Cohen later recalled, "[T]he decision of the Board to institute and conduct the Enquiry was reached without any consultation with any government authority, let alone permission or instructions."[91] Although the NWLB claimed that its main objective was to "hold open and free discussions to obtain the basic facts," it seems evident that the members planned to follow their own predetermined agenda when it came to compulsory collective bargaining. Confident that the submissions would reveal the deep malaise in wartime industrial relations, they called the inquiry to legitimize and promulgate, not to inform, their views. As McTague acknowledged in an interview, "I intend to convert something that's been in the field of pious hope into reality."[92] Unaware that the board was following a game plan, most observers expected it to become bogged down with information. With more Canadians than ever before participating in work stoppages and most labour and business leaders confounded by the existing labour policies, a high number of submissions were expected. Sifting through the mounds of paper to create a coherent set of recommendations was going to be, in the words of one newspaper editor, "a large and thorny undertaking."[93] What few people realized, however, is that the industrial relations experts on the NWLB regarded the inquiry as a means to an end.

We can only speculate about Mackenzie King's reaction to the announcement. The early part of 1943 was a relatively quiet period for him. Besides the usual exigencies of the war, there was not much else going on to divert his attention. Yet, he made no mention of the pending inquiry in his diary, correspondence, or memoranda. Nor did he share his views with reporters. His silence may have reflected poor health. Battling bad colds, sore eyes, and a deadening fatigue throughout April, he made few comments about any subject at that time.[94] So, given the void in the historical record, researchers are left to make educated guesses. One possibility is that political pressures had already reconciled King to the NWLB's goal of securing a collective bargaining policy. Concerned about losing working-class votes to the CCF and impressed that the more mainstream TLC had joined the call for a Wagner-like act, he might have finally realized that he had little choice but to move beyond his cherished conciliatory measures. And, given his social science background, he may have applauded the fact-finding of the NWLB as an important precursor to reform, hoping it would win over resistant cabinet colleagues.

Perhaps – but not likely. It is hard to imagine that King would suddenly turn his back on more than four decades of championing a consensual, ostensibly even-handed approach to intervention. The very recent passage of PC 10802 in December 1942, which granted collective bargaining rights to workers in Crown corporations, suggested nothing different about his take on labour policy. His deeply rooted principles – principles that involved clearing away misunderstandings and encouraging compromise rather than imposing solutions – still made it inconceivable that he would consider a Wagner Act for Canada. Indeed, rather than acquiescence, King's response to the NWLB inquiry was probably one of weary self-satisfaction. He had long been a champion of using the act of investigation to shift attitudes and resolve conflicts. As the prime minister had written many years earlier in *Industry and Humanity*:

> Investigation is the letting in of light. It does not attempt to award punishments or to affix blame; it aims simply at disclosing facts. Its efficacy lies

> in what it presupposes of the power of Truth to remedy evil itself ... [I]t assumes that collective opinion will approve the right, and condemn the wrong.[95]

Proud of his industrial relations legacy, hardly prone to modesty, and too tired to consider alternative scenarios, King almost certainly thought the NWLB was going to emulate his conciliatory model by (1) conducting an examination of the facts; (2) releasing findings to the general public; and (3) relying on public opinion to help restore industrial stability in the country. Although the inquiry was much wider in scope than a single labour dispute, the principle remained the same: by informing and educating, the NWLB investigation would move towards industrial peace. Blinded by a mix of conceit and exhaustion, in other words, it is more likely that King didn't comprehend the true motives of the board members, especially when the public announcement of the inquiry made no mention of policy reforms. What he probably anticipated was advice on how to tighten up the existing labour policies – how to reinforce, not to shift, his conceptual framework for industrial relations.[96]

Of course, this is all conjecture. What is much better established is that both the labour movement and the business community responded enthusiastically to news of the inquiry – though for different reasons. On the one hand, after years of frustrated appeals to the government, labour leaders looked forward to airing grievances about inadequate labour laws, unfair wage controls, anti-union practices, and plant committees. Probably receiving privileged information from Cohen, they anticipated movement towards a collective bargaining policy. Indeed, worried about displays of aggressive unionism, Charlie Millard and other USW leaders chose not to lead their angry members out on strike to protest the NWLB's controversial steel decision.[97] On the other hand, business leaders anticipated stricter laws for workers and unions. Convinced that the increase in illegal strikes was due to "irresponsible" labour leaders and "jurisdictional warfare," several pro-business papers applauded McTague for having "the courage and foresight ... to remedy the wrongs that he knows exists."[98] At a preliminary session in mid-April, which was mainly organizational in nature, over 150 labour and business representatives called for very different goals and priorities, but unanimously expressed their confidence in the NWLB and their praise for the upcoming inquiry.[99]

The NWLB conducted its actual inquiry from early May to mid-June. Over 100 labour organizations and business associations presented briefs on wage conditions and labour relations in widely publicized sessions.[100] For our purposes, three general observations may be made about the proceedings. First, the labour movement was almost completely unified in its opposition to current policies and its support for a Canadian Wagner Act. Despite ideological, geographical, and organizational differences, labour leaders virtually spoke with one voice, driving home how their unions were capable of responsible contractual relations and how a workplace rule of law would diminish industrial strife. The lone exception was the nationalistic CTCC, which lamented the ineffectiveness of PC 2685, but stopped short of endorsing a federal policy that encroached on provincial responsibilities.[101] Labour leaders also demanded that Ottawa improve on recent provincial legislation. Singling out Ontario's groundbreaking Collective Bargaining Act, which was enacted just a few weeks earlier, they called for stricter prohibitions against company unions. Convinced that the new Labour Court arrangement in Ontario would entangle their organizations in excessive legalism, they also expressed a preference for administrative machinery like the National Labor Relations Board in the United States. In the words of A.R. Mosher and Patrick Conroy: "Labour has always endeavoured to keep out of legal entanglements, and the whole procedure connected with this Labour Court is nothing more than a picnic for lawyers."[102] Labour leaders also questioned whether the judges in the Labour Court had enough background in industrial relations to make rulings that were informed and impartial. They anticipated heightened antagonism rather than industrial order. "With a genuine Collective Bargaining bill and an adequate administration board along the lines of the Wagner Act," C.S. Jackson of the United Electrical Workers offered, "the characteristics of the unions ... will change from that of militancy ... to that of statesmanship, self-discipline, [and] the acceptance of responsibility."[103]

Second, the business community revealed how divided it still was over the issue of compulsory collective bargaining.[104] Along with the Canadian Construction Association, the Toronto Board of Trade, and various companies like Stelco and Cominco, the Canadian Manufacturers' Association (CMA) maintained an uncompromising position. Once again pointing to the British example, CMA equated compulsory collective bargaining legislation to "put[ting] the cart before the horse – i.e. to giv[ing] the unions greatly increased power before they have developed the self-discipline and sense of responsibility which alone can ensure the proper use of power."[105] Other employers and business groups, however, expressed some willingness to accept compulsory collective bargaining. By no means advocates of unionism, they wanted the federal government to implement uniform standards of conduct that ensured continuous production across the country. As the Canadian Chamber of Commerce argued: "What is needed is a comprehensive labour code which would make plain the intention to avoid disputes and provide the machinery to deal effectively with them before they reach the strike stage."[106] Along similar lines, R.L. Beattie, the president of Inco, explained that an even-handed labour policy, which forced employers to bargain collectively but also outlawed closed shops, required the incorporation of trade unions, and imposed heavier penalties for illegal strikes, would go a long way towards restoring industrial stability.[107]

Third, the proceedings exposed the limited tolerance of the NWLB members, especially J.L. Cohen, for intransigent employers. Confronted with the rigid attitudes of the CMA, the labour lawyer asked "how trade unions are supposed to develop self-discipline and a sense of responsibility unless the employers recognize them and give them the opportunity to acquire one or more of these virtues?"[108] He also questioned how the Ontario Mining Association could condemn the leaders of CCL unions as "foreigners" when most mine owners lived outside of Canada.[109] Although more restrained, Justice McTague displayed a similar impatience. When Bert Lang, a management consultant, demanded "safeguards against international unions securing a dictatorial position over Canadian workers," McTague pointed out that many international unions had been in Canada for over fifty years.[110] The justice also challenged the contention of the legal counsel for the Toronto Board of Trade that company unions could engage in bona fide collective bargaining.[111] This comparable line of questioning by the board members did not escape the media's attention. When the inquiry drew to a close and the NWLB retired to prepare a report on the submissions and testimonies, most commentators anticipated unanimous labour policy recommendations.[112]

Two months later, on 17 August 1943, Cohen submitted a lengthy minority report to the Department of Labour. A couple of days after that, McTague and Lalande submitted a much briefer majority report.[113] Why two reports? The most serious differences involved wage policy. McTague and Lalande wanted to fold current cost-of-living bonuses, which ranged from sixty cents to $4.25 a week, into wage rates and then either discontinue the system or start it anew.[114] Rather than perpetuate existing inequalities, Cohen recommended leveling up all bonuses to the maximum and then continuing the system on a parity basis. Not one to mince words, he was "unable to comprehend, let alone agree with, the recommendations of my colleagues that the principle of cost-of-living bonus should be abandoned."[115] Another disagreement concerned family allowances. Both reports agreed that there should be a wage floor of fifty cents an hour, below which workers should be free to bargain collectively for wages (workers above the floor would still have frozen wages). It "is hardly defensible, politically and morally" to apply wage controls to earnings below fifty cents an hour, observed McTague and Lalande. Recognizing that a wage floor might contribute to inflation, however, the majority report proposed family allowances as an alternative way to supplement low wages.[116] Cohen firmly rejected the idea of family allowances, convinced not only that unions would cry foul but also that collective bargaining was more beneficial to low-income workers.[117]

Just as the newspapers had predicted, the two reports strongly concurred on the matter of labour policy. Both supported the passage of a compulsory collective bargaining law, underscoring the inadequacy of voluntary compliance. "The guests invited to the feast under PC 2685 scorned the invitation," wrote McTague and Lalande. "Now they must be gathered in from the streets and lanes, the highways and byways, and compelled to get along together."[118] The NWLB members also recommended the suspension of the Industrial Disputes Investigation Act. As Cohen put it, King's cherished conciliation mechanisms were "most ineffective, and even provocative and harmful, as a means of dealing with strikes in wartime."[119] There were important differences in the reports. Blaming the current unrest on irresponsible labour leaders, McTague and Lalande claimed that contractual relations would increase responsible unionism, diminish the appeal of militant tactics, and ensure industrial peace and stability. In contrast, Cohen blamed the strike wave on a "policy of exclusion" and linked collective bargaining to industrial citizenship or democracy.[120] In addition, McTague and Lalande recommended that an expert board administer the code, while Cohen called for a representative body with equal numbers of labour and management seats. The majority report also listed unfair labour practices for both employers and unions, and called on the courts, through the Defence of Canada Regulations, to impose penalties for infractions. The minority report limited unfair labour practices to employers and gave the administrative board the power to enforce the code. Finally, McTague and Lalande proposed compulsory arbitration for all bargaining disputes – including those that concerned contract determination – while Cohen limited compulsory arbitration to grievance disputes or contract interpretation.[121] Still, as one government official observed: "There would seem to be little difficulty in ironing out the differences of detail."[122] Certainly, no one could dispute that the NWLB members were in agreement when it came to the need for a collective bargaining policy.

At first, the reports gathered dust at the Labour Department. No one made an effort to carry out a comparative analysis. Rather than return to Ottawa to consider the recommendations, Humphrey Mitchell decided to continue a two-week vacation in New Brunswick. This neglect may have been due to bureaucratic pettiness. Mitchell and the Labour Department deeply resented the NWLB's interference in their affairs. Conciliation services, for example, had always been their purview; they did not want some outside agency telling them how to do their business.[123] Two weeks after the release of the reports, Mackenzie King took charge. Although busy hosting Winston Churchill and Franklin D. Roosevelt in Quebec City, he found the time to examine the NWLB reports during a short visit to Ottawa. Appalled by the negligence of his Labour Department and sensing the urgency of the situation, the prime minister made two immediate decisions. First, he would not release the reports to the public until the government could consider its policy options. Second, he would back the board's unanimous recommendations. He intended to use the proposals not only to devise new wartime policies, but also to establish "the basis of what might become permanent in times of peace."[124] In terms of labour relations, this decision meant that King was at long last prepared to set aside his deep aversion to compulsion and support a collective bargaining policy. Despite his past preference for voluntary compliance, he would use the government's emergency powers to force employers to sit down at the negotiating table. As Arthur MacNamara, the deputy minister of labour, shared privately with a newspaper reporter: "Willie left no doubt ... that we are going to have a new deal for labour."[125]

Why now? Why at this point in time did the prime minister finally commit to a compulsory collective bargaining policy? Clearly, he was politically motivated. The board's investigation had made plain how the Liberal government's disaffected approach to labour policy had alienated much of the labour movement and a good deal of the general public. Throughout King's career, he had always relied on the patronage of the mainstream labour movement. Given his background in industrial relations, he considered his close associations with more traditional labour leaders, like Tom Moore, to be a form of self-validation. As the recent Ontario election and the federal by-elections suggested, however, his government's extensive efforts to win the war had failed to translate into working-class votes. Even moderate unions were aligning themselves with the CCF.[126] In early September 1943, the prime minister was even given what one journalist described as "the icy brush-off" at the TLC's annual convention in Quebec City.[127] With a federal election looming, King admitted that "much work will have to be done" to regain the confidence of labour and return the Liberals to office.[128] Grant Dexter, the Ottawa reporter for the *Winnipeg Free Press*, wrote to his editor: "King feels that he has lost labour – his lifelong sweetheart, the ladder on which he mounted to fame. He's going to win her back – dash hang it."[129]

In a bizarre turn of events, J.L. Cohen's dismissal from the NWLB also increased the political saliency of a compulsory collective bargaining policy. Shortly before the reports were submitted to the Labour Department, the labour lawyer had begun to worry about bureaucratic delays in both publishing and implementing the recommendations. "[A]ction is timely!" he argued. "Canada dare not continue any longer a policy which cripples its effectiveness and endangers its future."[130] Cohen also wondered how he could, in good conscience, continue to do the work of the NWLB when he had just produced a twenty-three page document that criticized government policy. Already outmanoeuvred once with the drafting of Ontario's Collective Bargaining Act, he decided the best strategy was to share his concerns with the media. On 18 August, the day after the submission of his minority report, Cohen advised McTague in a public letter that he refused to hear any more cases on wage conditions until the government moved forward on the recommendations.[131] The NWLB chair was embarrassed and outraged. Convinced that the recent victories of the CCF had inspired the labour lawyer, McTague accused Cohen of playing politics, promised the board's continued operation in his absence, and suggested that he submit his resignation.[132] In a much-quoted statement that not only revealed how labour issues had become common parlance in the country but also implied unlawful behaviour, McTague told the press that Cohen "appears to be on a sit-down or slow-down strike."[133] Fully supported by the labour movement for "his courageous stand," Cohen refused to resign.[134] On 1 September, when Cohen spoke about the reports at the TLC's convention in Quebec City,

McTague took the matter to King, calling the labour lawyer "a political intriguer" and demanding his removal from the board. At first, King hesitated. He was sensitive to the political fallout, especially after Percy Bengough of the TLC and A.R. Mosher of the CCL made a joint representation in support of Cohen. On 9 September 1943, however, the cabinet decided to dismiss Cohen from the board. J.A. Bell of the Order of Railroad Telegraphers was soon appointed in his place. Organized labour called the ouster "a flagrant insult," while King blamed the incident on a CCF scheme to portray him as anti-labour and worried about making amends.[135]

Without discounting the importance of these political pressures, there were other mitigating factors that contributed to the prime minister's surprising embrace of compulsory collective bargaining. Since January, King, along with many politicians and civil servants, had given a lot more thought to what life in Canada would be like after the war. Not wanting to repeat the hard times experienced after World War I or during the Great Depression, they began to wrestle with the idea of establishing, in the words of Mitchell Sharp in the Finance Department, "a system of social security that would minimize the poverty and hardship that had been all too prevalent in the pre-war years."[136] Encouraged by the successes of the war effort, many believed that the time had arrived for a peacetime government to assume a more assertive role in managing the country. But not everyone agreed, and those who did often found themselves divided over how to make it happen. Throughout 1943, heated discussions about socio-economic reforms filled the offices, chambers, and halls of the parliament buildings. Although the prime minister had always self-identified as a reformer, he himself was conflicted. In January, King wrote in his diary: "I should be happy indeed if I could round out my career with legislation in the nature of social security."[137] During the spring, he also made several references to the importance of social security in talks and speeches.[138] At the same time, however, King worried about implementing sweeping changes too quickly, paying for these new programs, and dealing with the provinces over the division of powers. He responded cautiously in March when the Advisory Committee on Reconstruction released Leonard Marsh's landmark *Report on Social Security for Canada*, which promoted a wide range of socio-economic reforms.[139] And he expressed impatience with Liberal Party members who wanted to bring about immediate change.[140] Still, by the time the NWLB submitted its recommendations in mid-August, the prime minister did seem ready to commit his government to more activist policies.[141] He even began dreaming in his sleep about how "the important thing now is the whole social insurance scheme and social betterment generally."[142]

It was ultimately King's decision to move towards compulsory collective bargaining – to accept that the government had to intervene to a greater degree in the private ordering of the employment relationship. But there were two previously mentioned rising stars in the Liberal Party who helped to push him towards this realization. Shortly before the prime minister received copies of the NWLB reports, Paul Martin, the MP from the riding of Essex East, near Windsor, Ontario, had sent him a confidential memo that stressed the importance of acting on the board's recommendations.[143] Appointed parliamentary assistant to the minister of labour in May, Martin was a staunch reformer with a long history of supporting the collective rights of workers. In an interesting coincidence, he had once worked in Justice McTague's law firm in Windsor with Léon Lalande. He also believed that pro-business cabinet members like C.D. Howe were exerting an undue influence over Humphrey Mitchell.[144] Only recently elected to Parliament in 1940, Brooke Claxton, the MP from the riding of St Lawrence-St George in Montreal, who became King's parliamentary assistant in May, also urged the prime minister to follow up on the NWLB reports. Intent on shifting the Liberal Party leftwards, he linked compulsory collective bargaining to a broader program of socio-economic reforms. "What is needed," he told the prime minister, "is a labour policy which is part of a comprehensive plan of reform."[145] Clearly sympathetic to the plight of workers and well connected to prominent civil servants like Jack Pickersgill in the Prime Minister's Office or Arnold Heeney, the clerk of the Privy Council, these two future cabinet ministers believed that compulsory collective bargaining should be one of the cornerstones of a post-war Canada. They were willing to use their relatively recent access to the inner circles of power to achieve this goal. As Martin later recalled, "Brooke Claxton and I felt that what was required was a sympathetic understanding of labour's general needs."[146]

Most importantly, the NWLB deserves credit for breaking down the prime minister's rigid views on labour policy. Despite ideological differences, the reconstituted board managed, rather impressively, to use its jealously guarded independence, industrial relations expertise, and expansive powers to push a compulsory collective bargaining policy to the top of the Liberal administration's agenda. Perhaps King would have eventually moved beyond his cherished conciliation machinery without the urging of the NWLB. The social, economic, and political pressures made the likelihood of a compulsory collective bargaining policy seem almost inevitable. Yet, the basic historical fact remains that King ignored or rejected demands for labour policy innovations until McTague, Cohen, and Lalande produced their respective reports. Humphrey Mitchell had even announced in mid-July that no new labour policies would be forthcoming.[147] Although not anticipating the NWLB's recommendations, the prime minister greatly respected the knowledge and proficiency of its members. Back in February, when Liberal Party members questioned the appointment of two Catholics and a left-leaning Jew to the board, he had responded that "the time had come in dealing with some war questions when we [cannot] consider anything but ability and capacity."[148] Given his penchant for the social sciences, King appreciated how the two reports involved an incredible amount of fact-finding. He might also have been struck by their moral or ethical underpinnings – how they linked the uplift of Canadian society to compulsory collective bargaining. Finally, it is important to remember that the prime minister cared deeply and genuinely about working-class conditions and circumstances. When the NWLB reports forced King to confront the inherent shortcomings of the existing labour policy framework, he embraced compulsory collective bargaining, not just to win votes, though that was important, but also to improve the lives of Canadian workers. As he told his cabinet in early September: "I [have] not ... given my life to better [the] conditions of labour in order to end it as one who had gone back on all the principles for which he had fought ... I [propose] to fight openly for labour having its just dues." [149]

But what of King's beloved principles? Had the mounting pressures and the NWLB revelations finally forced him to abandon them? Not at all. Still concerned with national unity and employer backlash, he made sure the new collective bargaining policy reflected his particular approach to conflict resolution – that there was more of the same. A decade earlier, Senator Robert Wagner and his colleagues in the US Congress had explicitly drafted the National Labor Relations Act to encourage the spread of unions. In the act's preamble, they argued that trade unions helped not only to stabilize the industrial order and prevent economic downturns, but also to promote more equitable wealth distribution and achieve industrial democracy. As legal scholar Karl Klare writes, the Wagner Act "was perhaps the most radical piece of legislation ever enacted by the United States Congress."[150] Thanks to Mackenzie King's principles, however, the new Canadian policy would not be an abrupt departure. North of the US border, policymakers paid little attention to questions of industrial justice and shop floor power. Instead, they focused on the process or function of collective bargaining, folding in the decades-old mechanisms of investigation and conciliation. In short, continuity prevailed over change. And, ironically, by taking a more moderate approach that emphasized the common good over special interests, Canada's new collective bargaining policy would prove more advantageous than the Wagner Act to workers and their unions in the long run.

The Code

Bryce Stewart placed the phone back in the cradle, inhaled deeply on the British Consul cigarette in his holder, and looked out the window of his office in the thirty-one storey RKO building at the northwest corner of the Rockefeller Center. It was midway through the afternoon of 29 November 1943, and he was taking a couple of minutes to think about the call he had just received. After two hectic, demanding, and frustrating years in Ottawa as deputy minister of labour, Stewart was now back at his old job of research director at Industrial Relations Counselors, Inc. (IRC) in New York City. Eager to focus once again on in-depth analyses of the employment relationship, the sixty-year-old economist had already published a study of maintenance of membership clauses in fifty-nine union contracts.[151] Returning to his research interests, living in affluent Scarsdale, and having just recently become a US citizen, he had little desire to return to the strains and burdens of public service in Ottawa.[152] But it wasn't every day that the prime minister of Canada rang with a personal appeal. Apparently the policymaking process for the new labour code had bogged down. Numerous drafts had been rejected, Justice McTague and Humphrey Mitchell were at each other's throats, and the general public was becoming impatient. As the prime minister explained on the phone, he wanted his former deputy minister to come back to Ottawa and weave together a final draft that could be presented to the provinces, employers' associations, and labour movement for approval.[153]

The request made sense. Stewart was one of the few people with the right combination of skills and aptitude for the job. As a quasi-outsider who no longer worked in the Labour Department, he could claim some semblance of objectivity. He also had an intimate familiarity with existing labour policies and a track record of competency. And it didn't hurt that Stewart and King shared similar views about industrial relations. King was, after all, one of the muses behind the founding of the Rockefeller-funded IRC. Despite having left the federal government on a "disgruntled and disaffected" note, the former deputy minister agreed to make the trip north in a few days' time.[154] Gazing out the window at mid-town Manhattan, he probably felt a mix of emotions: flattered to be asked, excited about the challenge ahead, and relieved that it would be a short visit.

When Stewart arrived in Ottawa in early December, he discovered that the prime minister had not been exaggerating. Although the passage of a compulsory collective bargaining policy was no longer in question after the submission of the NWLB reports, it was taking an unusually long time to come to fruition. Keep in mind that the King cabinet enjoyed extraordinary wartime powers – it had the authority to circumvent the legislative entanglements of Parliament. In late 1941, for example, the government had drafted and enacted PC 8253, which imposed the initial wage freeze and created the original NWLB, in just a few months. But the collective bargaining policy was not on the same kind of fast track. Both the business community and the labour movement were at a loss to explain the whereabouts, not to mention the content, of the new labour policy. The *Financial Post* characterized the policymaking process as an inordinate amount of "backing and filling."[155] In late January 1944, an incredulous Patrick Conroy of the CCL complained: "We have no knowledge when [the] government will issue [the] labour code."[156] By the time the Liberal administration finally produced the Wartime Labour Relations Regulations or PC 1003 in February 1944, nearly half a year had passed since King's decision to act on the NWLB's recommendation. Why such a long gap? Although overlapping, three distinct factors were responsible for the delayed outcome: (1) the resistance of cabinet members; (2) the passage of another wage order; and (3) the inclusion of various interest groups in the policymaking process.

Cabinet members first discussed the question of the labour code on 14 September 1943, two weeks after the prime minister's decision to act on the joint recommendations of the NWLB. It was an extremely heated exchange, as hardliners like Alphonse Fournier, the minister of public works, voiced strong opposition. With Humphrey Mitchell saying little to defend the policy initiative, King had to fend off much of the criticism by himself, "dumbfounded at the reactionary attitude of some of [his] colleagues."[157] Rather than enforce the collective rights of workers, many of the ministers called for more stringent restrictions on union behaviour. C.D. Howe even tried to appeal to King's finely tuned political sensibilities, arguing that Ontario's new collective bargaining law "had done more than anything to defeat the Liberals in Ontario" just a few weeks earlier. Clearly unimpressed, the prime minister refused to back down, noting privately that Howe "knows nothing whatever about politics."[158] After a few more days of deliberation, King managed to convince reluctant colleagues that their political futures depended on the passage of a collective bargaining policy.[159] It was a temporary reprieve. During the drafting process, various cabinet members kept, in the words of newspaper reporter Grant Dexter, "tossing [in] monkey wrenches."[160] Although Angus MacDonald, the minister of national defence for naval services, initially expressed support, he became more narrow-minded as the fall progressed. He "does not favor appeasement of labour," observed Dexter. "He thinks that under firm treatment labour would steady down."[161] King parried every attack, confident that a collective bargaining policy not only made political sense, but was also the right thing to do for workers. Yet, his ministers persisted with their condemnations. As late as 17 February 1944, just a few hours before PC 1003 was tabled in the House of Commons, T.A. Crerar, the minister of mines and resources, urged the prime minister to reconsider how much "trouble" (by which he meant union activism) the government was inviting with the labour code. Fed up with the political dullness and recalcitrance of his cabinet, King experienced a rare lapse of composure, snapping back at Crerar that "the trouble would be brief compared with the period of exile the party would have in years to come if we did not do these things in these times ... I [do] not intend to be put into a false position further in relation to my attitude to labour."[162]

The government's conflicted approach to the NWLB's wage proposals also slowed the passage of PC 1003. Back in March 1943, Clifford Clark, the hard-working deputy minister of finance who formulated most of the government's socio-economic policies, had asked different departments to prepare reports on the effectiveness of the wartime wage and price controls.[163] Like many economists of that time, he feared that the return of peace would bring post-war inflation and high unemployment to Canada. Upon learning from various sources that the wage ceiling had holes, Clark convened the extremely influential Economic Advisory Committee (EAC) to discuss repairs. Created at the outbreak of war and regularly utilized by cabinet ministers, the EAC was an interdepartmental body of high-ranking civil servants that both evaluated and developed policy proposals, especially in regards to post-war planning.[164] Perhaps for the sake of efficiency or to avoid interest groups, the more surreptitious committee had assumed the labour policy responsibilities of the Interdepartmental Committee on Labour Co-ordination.[165] At two meetings in June and July, while McTague, Cohen, and Lalande drafted their respective reports, the EAC members debated how to make wage controls more palatable to workers. Although they clashed over what to do with people who made less than forty cents an hour and whether family allowances should enter into the equation, the members held similar concerns about the country's future, and everyone agreed it was critical to tighten wage controls; they were a very tight-knit, like-minded group who even belonged to the same fishing club, thirty miles outside of Ottawa.[166] The EAC members also worried about the pending wage policy recommendations of the NWLB. What would be the impact on inflation if McTague, Cohen, and Lalande, who had no background in economics, publically questioned the need for a wage freeze? Apprehension shifted to dismay when the NWLB members finally released their two reports in mid-August. A perturbed Clark wrote to J.L. Ilsley, the finance minister, that "they [are] very bad and … the situation [is] in a mess."[167]

A showdown soon took place between Clark and the NWLB chair. Justice McTague felt strongly that poorly paid workers should remain free of wage controls. Locking them into subpar wages would only perpetuate inequities in the wartime wage system. Clark, however, insisted that wage controls should be enforced for all workers.[168] He also argued, much like J.L. Cohen in his minority report, that family allowances should not be tied to wage policy, but become part of a much broader social security program. "I believe this situation is quite serious," Grant Dexter reported. "A real crisis has blown up over the wage ceiling."[169] Unlike many of his colleagues, the prime minister sided with McTague, observing: "Economists do not have human understanding of labour situations."[170] Although policymakers managed to piece together a draft order by the end of October, wage strikes erupted at sixty-six coal mines in Alberta and British Columbia a week later, and everything was put on hold. Still upset about the concessions made during the January steel crisis, C.D. Howe and J.L. Ilsley demanded that the military be called out to force miners back to work and preserve the wage ceiling. Tempers once again flared as ministers argued about what to do. King even threatened to resign his office if the hardliners didn't back down. Eventually, Howe and Ilsley relented, and the prime minister negotiated a compromise with the strikers that gave them a one-dollar-a-day increase.[171] Attention shifted back to policymaking, and King announced the pending wage freeze, along with the surprise announcement of the labour code, in his national radio broadcast on 4 December. A few days later, the cabinet enacted PC 9384, which imposed stricter wage controls for all workers but allowed the NWLB to correct for unfair wage levels.[172] An acceptable compromise had been reached.

Unlike the internally derived PC 9384, the making of PC 1003 involved a lot of outside participation. Up to this point in the war, the federal government had not really consulted with interest groups before creating labour policies. The only exception was when King conferred informally with Tom Moore of the TLC. But the stakes were higher this time. Policymakers were not only treading on managerial prerogatives, but also encroaching on provincial jurisdictions. At a number of levels, the status quo was being fundamentally challenged. Although the historical record offers little information about the prime minister's specific contributions to the order in council, not much would have happened without his knowledge or direction. Lacking confidence in Humphrey Mitchell, convinced that this was now the right thing to do for workers, and worried about political fallout, he would not have sat idly by while less informed public servants put together one of the most important Canadian labour policies of the twentieth century. Given the waning popularity of the Liberal Party, King wanted to show, in the words of a labour commentator, that it was "possible for a white kitten to walk out of the coal bin."[173] And, given his concerns about national unity, he wanted to minimize dissension and backlash; the collective bargaining policy needed to receive the widespread approval of all affected parties – at least as much as possible. As a result, policymakers took a very cautious, inclusive approach to drafting PC 1003, acutely aware of the significance of their actions. Rather than simply announce the labour policy as a done deal, they asked for input, made numerous revisions, and then requested feedback once again. It was a long process that often stalled as different details were debated and reconsidered.

Although the EAC closely monitored developments, three DOL officials took the lead on writing the numerous drafts for the labour policy: Arthur MacNamara, the deputy labour minister; Murdock (Kay) Maclean, the director of industrial relations; and Vincent MacDonald, the assistant deputy labour minister. They were an interesting mix. After serving for years as a public servant in Manitoba, the soft-spoken, cigar-smoking MacNamara had arrived in Ottawa at the beginning of the war and quickly earned a reputation as a capable, disinterested administrator.[174] Raised on a farm in Pictou, Nova Scotia, Maclean had spent over twenty-five years as Aaron Mosher's right-hand man in the Canadian Brotherhood of Railway Employees, All-Canadian Congress of Labour, and the CCL before joining the DOL in 1942, just a year after his youngest son was killed in the war.[175] MacDonald also became a DOL official in 1942, taking a leave of absence from his position as dean of the Law School at Dalhousie University in Halifax. Employed as the prime minister's secretary for a brief period in the 1920s, he had a penchant for bow ties and was known for his clear, coherent observations and opinions.[176] Despite their different backgrounds and personalities, these three officials shared enlightened but moderate views about the shape and direction of the new labour policy. Although sympathetic to calls for industrial democracy, they did not want to emulate the pro-labour Wagner Act, which extolled the citizenship rights of workers. Instead they let the guiding principle of "evenhandedness" inform their work as they completed over twenty versions of the labour code or, as MacDonald sheepishly described, "many drafts on many models."[177]

There were two important influences on their efforts to create an "impartial" collective bargaining policy. Clearly, the three DOL officials belonged to the Mackenzie King school of thought when it came to labour policy. Since the turn of the century, the prime minister had made a point of treating workers and employers equally so that they would be more inclined to negotiate and compromise. Of course, given the imbalance of power in the workplace, this "even-handed" approach had always favoured employers (hence the quotation marks). But King's approach endured, becoming the hallmark for the Labour Department. Even with his recent embrace of compulsory collective bargaining, he remained convinced that "class legislation" – policies that favoured wage-earners – did more harm than good. Antagonizing the business community and inciting a hostile counterattack would not only make things worse for workers, but also fracture the country – his worst nightmare.

Another little known influence on the policymakers was Gerard D. Reilly of the National Labor Relations Board (NLRB) in the United States, who assisted with some of the early drafts of PC 1003. As the chief law officer for the US Labor Department in the late 1930s, Reilly had witnessed first-hand how the pro-labour bias of the Wagner Act had produced loud, reactionary demands for congressional investigations and revisions. Indeed, in 1939, House conservatives attacked

Reilly and Francis Perkins, the labor secretary, for refusing to deport Harry Bridges, the left-leaning, Australian-born leader of the International Longshoremen's Association. Although initially a diehard New Deal liberal, Reilly gradually became disillusioned with what he considered to be the NLRB's antipathy to business and the power mongering of labour leaders. As he put it, "the pendulum had swung too far the other way."[178] Appointed to the NLRB in October 1941, he decided to make it his calling to correct the "one-sidedness" of the Wagner Act, initiating or supporting decisions that gave employers more leeway. In his exchanges with DOL officials like Vincent MacDonald, he no doubt shared that an "impartial" collective bargaining policy was the key to minimal opposition and long-term success. Later, after leaving the NLRB, Reilly would become one of the main architects of the 1947 Taft-Hartley Act, which, in the words of one scholar, "sought to diminish the influence and power of trade unions quite in contrast to the creators of the Wagner Act."[179]

In early October 1943, Grant Dexter of the *Winnipeg Free Press* wrote to his editor that the government would soon announce the completion of the labour code.[180] He was mistaken. Another delay ensued when the provinces raised objections. Given the constitutional ramifications of PC 1003, Ottawa had always intended to include the provinces in the policymaking process. But George Drew, the recently elected Progressive Conservative premier of Ontario, forced the matter when he demanded copies of the still unreleased NWLB reports and insisted he be informed about the status of the labour code. King quickly instructed Humphrey Mitchell to send out the reports and organize a conference of provincial labour officials for 8 November.[181] Both the collective bargaining policy and the wage controls would be on the agenda. During the three-day in camera or closed sessions, the provincial representatives, who sat in geographical order around the table from east to west, expressed serious concerns about the vagueness of the most recent labour policy draft.[182] W.D. King of Alberta complained: "It is a good bit like asking a man to buy a new type of car without seeing what the car will do, where it is to go and what is to be expected of it." There was also a lot of disagreement about the policy's scope. Officials from Quebec and British Columbia insisted their provincial legislation did a better job of addressing the special conditions of their particular regions. Participants from Ontario countered that coverage of all industries in the country, including non-war industries, "would eliminate a great many headaches." Humphrey Mitchell responded that the policy was only meant to cover war industries. The federal government was not going to encroach further on provincial jurisdictions because "[t]he provinces are just like nine children in a family. They do not all look alike ... and they do not have the same temperament." After three days of discussion and a dinner hosted by Mackenzie King at the Chateau Laurier, where he talked at length about the history of the DOL, most of the conference attendees agreed to support the draft. When MacNamara offered further reassurances about respecting the constitutional division of powers, Quebec and British Columbia softened their positions and a consensus was created. In a small concession to Ontario, one change was made allowing an individual province to request coverage of all of its non-war industries. All in all, Paul Martin recalled, it was "a rather pro forma affair."[183]

Winning the cooperation of the provinces was huge. But the endpoint was still not in sight. Just two weeks later, on 25 November, an angry exchange between Justice McTague and Humphrey Mitchell brought the policymaking process to a full stop. There was no love lost between the two men. As the chair of several pivotal conciliation boards and the head of the NWLB, the justice had developed a deep antipathy to the minister. Disturbed by the inefficiency, if not the incompetency, of the DOL, McTague may have even been gunning for Mitchell's job.[184] The labour minister, who was an electrician by training and a lifelong member of the labour movement, disliked how an Osgoode Hall Law School graduate presumed to know what was best for workers. As King noted, there was "a certain jealousy and lack of sympathy and co-operation" on both their parts.[185] Although the prime minister failed to disclose the details of the dispute, the NWLB chair may have questioned the inclusion of conciliation procedures in all the drafts. Both reports had criticized the conciliation process, pointing to "long delays and complicated methods."[186] But DOL officials, under the watchful eye of King, insisted that "the techniques and devices applied by [conciliation officers and boards] in composing or aborting labour disputes can well find a place in the newer and improved mechanisms of a Code designed to facilitate collective bargaining."[187] Whether out of bureaucratic self-interest or genuine belief in their effectiveness, they were not willing to consider their exclusion. The prime minister, who was already exhausted, found it difficult to reconcile the two sides. The confrontation put him in a real bind. On the one hand, he held McTague in high regard. If not worried about losing another by-election, the prime minister would probably have asked the justice to become his new labour minister.[188] On the other hand, King still believed that the government had a responsibility to try and get the disputing parties to resolve their differences. Perplexed, he phoned Bryce Stewart in New York City for help.[189]

During the first week of December, Stewart conferred with leading DOL officials, Humphrey Mitchell, Justice McTague, and Mackenzie King, and then wrote his own version of the labour code.[190] What really stands out about his draft is how closely it aligned with the principles of the prime minister. Despite some grumbling from Kay Maclean and others about the lack of "directness and clarity" in this most recent policymaking effort, the former deputy minister did provide for the continued use of conciliation services.[191] Unlike the 1907 Industrial Disputes Investigation Act, however, these mechanisms would now be used when collective bargaining failed to achieve the desired results.[192] Stewart also placed a lot more emphasis on the "even-handed" role of the government. Nowhere was this latter point better exemplified than in the area of unfair labour practices. In previous drafts of the labour code, policymakers had prohibited both employers and employees from engaging in coercive or intimidating activities. But they only defined the employer unfair labour practices in specific terms. Stewart's draft held employees and employers equally accountable for unfair labour practices, listing egregious practices for both sides. An appalled Bernard Wilson in the Industrial Relations Branch of the DOL wrote Maclean that Stewart's draft made "a fundamental error" because it "perpetuate[d] the existing bargaining inequality of the two parties." Wilson agreed that workers should have "duties," but not "equal" to employers.[193] Given the prevailing views of the prime minister, however, the conciliation officer's argument was not given serious consideration. In late December, after some legal tweaking by the Justice Department, Stewart's draft was sent out to labour organizations, business associations, and the provinces for comments.[194]

By late January 1944, Stewart's version of the labour code had elicited a variety of responses. Just two months had passed since the Ottawa conference, so the provinces called for relatively few changes. While Ontario still wanted coverage to include all industries, Edgar Rochette, a former Rhodes Scholar and Quebec's labour minister, asked for Mitchell's personal assurance that the order would apply only to war industries and would not change the federal government's jurisdiction over industrial relations in peacetime. To protect Quebec's Catholic labour organizations, he also wanted to make sure that two or more unions could bargain with an employer. Another area for clarification was non-union employee associations or plant committees. British Columbia suggested that a clearer distinction be made with bona fide trade unions, while Nova Scotia took a harder line, refusing to give its assent unless non-union employee organizations enjoyed the same rights and privileges as trade unions.[195]

Unlike earlier representations, the business community seemed resigned to the fact that compulsory collective bargaining was going to happen. But employer associations still offered varying degrees of feedback. While the Canadian Chamber of Commerce only called for similar employer, employee, and union penalties, the CMA submitted a six-page memorandum that mainly involved damage control.[196] Offering to send "a small Committee to Ottawa to discuss some of the more important points," the CMA stressed its opposition to multi-employer bargaining, called for greater limits on union activities, and tried to establish loopholes for company unions. It also wanted a more precise definition of a war industry, the exclusion of supervisory staff from union membership, an increase in the amount of time allowed for bargaining, and the continuation of the no-strike provisions that had been in effect under PC 7307. Finally, the CMA called for the administrative board to be like the Industrial Court in Ontario, rather than like the National Labor Relations Board in the United States, because its primary function would be judicial.[197]

In many ways, the labour movement's replies were predictable. Worried about encroachments on French-Canadian culture, the Confédération des travailleurs catholiques du Canada (CTCC) initially protested that "Ottawa should not legislate in labour matters, except with the approval of the Provinces." The confédération then moved on to call for the certification of both minority and majority unions in a designated bargaining unit and to oppose submitting its financial statements to the government. Given the pro-CIO biases of the early National Labor Relations Board in the United States, the TLC urged that craft workers be allowed to form their own unions and bargain on their own behalf, even if they comprised the minority of workers in a plant. The TLC also wanted to use the language of British Columbia's collective bargaining law to more precisely outlaw company unions. In a brief submission, the railway brotherhoods mainly expressed concern about the rights of craft unions and the need to report financial statements. In contrast to the other labour organizations, the CCL provided a much lengthier response that delved into almost every aspect of Stewart's draft. It called for greater protection from union discrimination and objected to some registration clauses. It strongly opposed a provision that held unions liable for the actions of their members, denouncing this effort to encourage responsible unionism as "nothing short of tyranny." Another contentious issue was whether certification depended on a majority of workers being union members or not. Despite all these questions and concerns, however, the labour movement proved surprisingly acquiescent.[198] Although each congress called for stronger language to outlaw company unions, for example, McTague observed: "I would have gone a little further in making the way very difficult for company unions."[199] The labour leaders also failed to contest an extensive ban on strikes. Perhaps they viewed the limits on economic action as a necessary quid pro quo for compulsory collective bargaining, or perhaps they welcomed the government's effort to keep more militant workers in line. Either way, the no-strike provisions remained unchallenged.[200]

In late January, a special committee of DOL officials began to reconcile all the different recommendations into a final draft. Conspicuously absent from the policymaking process was Justice McTague. After Stewart's draft, which clearly favoured the views of the DOL, the NWLB chair became more and more antagonistic towards the Liberal administration. Still feuding with Mitchell, he refused the labour minister's request to help fashion a new clause about company unions.[201] McTague also became very "annoyed" when he learned that the provinces were told he had approved the final draft – when he had yet to see it.[202] Shortly after the passage of PC 1003 in mid-February, the disgruntled justice finally resigned his position as NWLB chair to become the chair of the Progressive Conservative Party. Mackenzie King was outraged. "Taken into the confidence of the administration [and then] deserting the administration ... to come out and spend the remainder of his time trying to destroy the administration," he railed, "is about as contemptible as the action of any man could be."[203] Now only Léon Lalande remained from the tripartite board that had conducted the public inquiry and pushed for the compulsory collective bargaining policy. He would resign shortly after the end of the war in November 1945.[204] Although Justice Maynard Archibald of the Nova Scotia Supreme Court became the new chair in March 1944, the NWLB became a shadow of its former self. It would quickly earn the wrath of the labour movement for its narrow interpretations of the wage controls, an animosity that lasted until the agency disbanded in March 1947.[205]

During the closing stages of the policymaking process, King finally allowed Mitchell to table the NWLB reports in the House of

Commons.[206] As a DOL report explained later, the prime minister had withheld their release because they (1) lacked consensus; (2) were "of a contentious nature"; and (3) involved Cohen's dismissal.[207] Worried about public controversy, he had decided that the less people knew about the contents the better. But the reports had to have been one of the worst kept secrets of the war. As newspaper reporter Grant Dexter admitted several months earlier, "I think I know the contents pretty well."[208] With innumerable copies circulating within the federal government and then, at George Drew's insistence, sent out to the provinces, it was difficult to keep the findings and recommendations of the two reports under wraps. The various discussions with interest groups about the new labour code made it even more challenging. By the time King decided to table the reports in Parliament, most interested people already knew what they contained. In the words of a *Financial Post* editor, their public release "came more as an echo than as news."[209]

In the early afternoon of 17 February, the cabinet convened to discuss the latest draft of the labour code. A special subcommittee, which included Humphrey Mitchell, former labour minister Norman McLarty, and Justice Minister Louis St Laurent, had already gone through it carefully. But there was still pushback from colleagues. King "spoke out very clearly" that if "we were to be a liberal government at all we must recognize that it was part of our duty to see that we moved forward in helping to meet labour's demands." After some further discussion about coverage, the prime minister finally asked if anyone was strongly opposed to the passage of the collective bargaining policy. When no one spoke up, he decided on the spot to sign the order and be done with it, probably aware that the Progressive Conservative Party planned to make a labour policy announcement the next day. King was tremendously relieved to have the policymaking process completed, convinced that "we had at last done the right thing." He also believed that his principled stand with his colleagues was one of the main reasons for the order's successful conclusion. Later that evening, he congratulated himself with the words: "[H]ere is another battle won for what I have fought for so strongly through my life."[210]

Worried about Mitchell's bombastic oratory skills, King told his labour minister to table PC 1003 in the House of Commons, but "not to make any speech."[211] It would be left to more competent and articulate DOL officials to "explain its particulars to the press." Over the next few days, the country learned that there were several main components to the new order: [212]

- *Coverage*: PC 1003 automatically included all war industries and industries normally under federal jurisdiction, but a province could make arrangements to have the policy apply to its non-war industries. Only Alberta, Quebec, and Prince Edward Island refrained, so the new system of compulsory collective bargaining involved most of the country.
- *Administration*: The order created a Wartime Labour Relations Board (WLRB) to administer the regulations. The members included a chair, vice-chair, and no more than four pairs of representatives from the labour movement and business community. Although regional boards were created by the provinces to deal with most of the cases brought under PC 1003, the WLRB not only had the authority to hear appeals, but also to set precedents and make revisions.
- *Certification*: Unlike the Wagner Act, where certification eventually depended on representation votes, PC 1003 only required a written request by the majority of workers in a bargaining unit. The board could, however, conduct an investigation by checking dues payments or authorization cards to validate the claim of majority support. Another difference with the Wagner Act was that the order allowed craft unions to co-exist with industrial unions at a workplace. And, following a rather bizarre practice in British Columbia, the war labour boards certified individual representatives, not trade unions, to bargain on behalf of workers. If the majority of workers were union members, the union could appoint the representatives and, in effect, conduct the bargaining.
- *Non-Union Employee Associations*: The order allowed workers to organize into non-union employee associations, but they had to be free of all employer interference. Unlike unions, they also had to win the votes of the majority of the workers affected to earn certification.
- *Compulsory Bargaining*: Employers were obliged, after ten days' notice, to negotiate with the certified bargaining representatives of their workers.
- *Compulsory Conciliation*: Although PC 1003 discontinued the IDIA or Industrial Disputes Investigation Act of 1907, the labour minister could still appoint, in succession, a conciliation officer and conciliation board if the collective bargaining process bogged down.
- *Strikes*: The order contained an extensive strike ban. Not only were strikes still illegal during conciliation procedures, but they were

also not allowed during the process of certification (which meant no more recognition strikes) or during the life of a contract. And PC 7307 – the strike vote requirement – remained in effect.

- *Unfair Labour Practices*: The order made a long list of unfair labour practices for both employers and employees illegal.
- *Compulsory Grievance Arbitration*: Every contract was required to include a clause that outlined the resolution of grievances in a way that was final, binding, and without work stoppages.

By compelling employers to recognize and bargain with the representatives of their employees' choosing, PC 1003 marked the beginning of a new era in Canadian industrial relations. But it also bore the stamp of Mackenzie King's well-entrenched principles. Rather than impose a new legislative framework and risk alienation, for example, policymakers incorporated many of the suggestions and concerns of the provinces, labour organizations, and business associations. Informed by the Liberal imperatives of "evenhandedness" and national unity, policymakers had tried to reconcile the views and agendas of all the interested parties. As Humphrey Mitchell noted: "Compromise ... played a large part in the creation of the new Labour Relations Code."[213] Indeed, in response to the CCL's submission, the regulations excluded some of the more stringent provisions for responsible unionism. Although unions could still be sued for authorizing illegal strikes, they were not liable for the actions of their members. Eugene Forsey, the CCL's research director, calculated that PC 1003 satisfied thirty-four of the forty-eight criticisms the congress had listed in its reply to the Stewart draft. "This is not a bad score," he conceded, "especially as some of those not met are of slight importance."[214]

Yet, in contrast to the Wagner Act, it would be difficult for critics to construe the order as "class legislation." Although PC 1003 forced employers to sit down at the bargaining table, its main focus was not the self-determination of workers or the justice and fairness of outcomes. The order's preamble made no reference to industrial democracy or union growth. Instead, the first paragraph read: "[I]t is deemed to be in the public interest ... that employers and employees collaborate for the advancement of the enterprises in which they are engaged." Informed by Mackenzie King's principles, PC 1003 rose above the fray of class relations to promote the general welfare of the country. The emphasis was on process – on achieving peace and stability – not on basic rights.[215]

The mainstream media applauded the passage of PC 1003 as a positive development. As mentioned in the introduction, one reporter wrote: "Canadian labour has stepped out of its short pants for good."[216] But more perceptive observers reserved judgment. With the government determined to maintain its allegedly "neutral" position in industrial relations, the compulsory collective bargaining policy contained several measures that weakened union power. Perhaps obviously, the strike restrictions were debilitating. With workers unable to take economic action for a minimum of three months after the application for certification and then only with a strike vote, the unions lost much of their leverage at the bargaining table. The ban on strikes during the life of a contract also gave employers less incentive to respond to grievance complaints. Instead of acting quickly to resume or maintain production, they could let the problem languish in arbitration. At the same time though, PC 1003 made it much more difficult for employers to resist organizing drives. By allowing unions to appoint bargaining representatives without an election, the regulations insulated workers from numerous intimidation and delay tactics. Deprived of a forum, employers had fewer opportunities to discredit organized labour, not to mention the process of collective bargaining. The War Labour Relations Board still had to be convinced that the majority of workers wanted a union. But PC 1003's simplified certification procedure almost guaranteed that most well-orchestrated campaigns would result in recognition and agreements.[217] Did organized labour come out ahead in the end? Mackenzie King certainly thought so. It remained to be seen, however, whether workers and their unions agreed.

Chapter Five

A Fine Conclusion, Spring 1944–Summer 1948

On the evening of 14 July 1948, the seventy-three-year-old prime minister and his dear friend Joan Patteson walked through the freshly mown fields of Kingsmere, his estate in the Gatineau Hills. It was a bucolic scene. In "the soft light" of the setting sun, horses were grazing gently on hay and long shadows were forming on distant hills. As the couple gradually made their way towards the far gate, King described to Patteson how he had just averted a wage strike of over 120,000 railway workers. It had been a real crisis. Lacking an extensive highway network, the Canadian economy depended heavily on the smooth operation of its railroads. As one newspaper editor put it: "[I]f the strike had gone ahead ... an incalculable amount of hardship and suffering would have been inflicted upon the Canadian people."[1] Given the ongoing Soviet blockade of Berlin and the very real possibility of more warfare, the prime minister had also worried that a national railway strike might inspire "Russia to take some precipitate action." When two conciliation boards and the direct intervention of Humphrey Mitchell failed to produce a compromise, King stepped into the fray, meeting with both sides to clear away misunderstandings and appeal to reason. Respectfully, but firmly and candidly, he negotiated a deal for a wage increase. As N.R. Crump, vice-president of Canadian Pacific Railway, later admitted, he "had no alternative but to accept the ... settlement."[2] After hearing what had happened, Patteson, who had known King for thirty years, remarked how wonderful it was that "one of [his] last achievements as Prime Minister should be the avoidance of a railway strike." King couldn't have agreed more. Next month, he would relinquish the leadership of the Liberal Party after twenty-nine years at its helm. On 15 November, he would resign as prime minister of Canada after nearly twenty-two years in office, the longest serving head of government in the history of the British Commonwealth. Given his pioneer work as a government conciliator in the early 1900s, he was elated that the railway settlement "would link the close of my career with the opening and make the circle complete."[3]

The averted railway strike wasn't the only reason for King's euphoric mood on that summer evening. He was also delighted with the recent enactment of a peacetime labour law that finally replaced the Wartime Labour Relations Regulations. Initially, responses to PC 1003 had been either positive on the part of organized labour or muted on the part of the business community. As the number of certifications and contracts climbed, Canadian industrial relations became fairly stable, especially compared to the high level of unrest in the United States. With the return of peace in 1945, however, pressures mounted to amend the collective bargaining policy. Labour leaders, worried about post-war setbacks, had called for more effective safeguards against reactionary employers and destabilizing business cycles. Employers, angered by a wave of wage strikes in 1946, had demanded greater legal and financial responsibilities for unions. But the federal government refused to consider proposals that would impugn its self-ascribed "neutral" role in industrial relations. Of course, PC 1003 was only a temporary wartime measure. Even though the National Emergency Transitional Powers Act of December 1945 prolonged several wartime orders and regulations, including the Wartime Labour Relations Regulations, until 31 March 1947, the provinces would eventually regain their normal authority over most industrial relations. So the onus was on federal policymakers to enact a peacetime statute that replicated the basic structure of PC 1003 and encouraged a uniform pattern of labour legislation in the country. The Industrial Relations and Disputes Investigation Act (IRDIA), which went into effect in September 1948, was much narrower in coverage than PC 1003 and contained some modifications. But the new labour law ensured that Mackenzie King's unique approach to compulsory collective bargaining, which emphasized process and function over rights and responsibilities, prevailed in the post-war years. Along with a few other select statutes, the prime minister believed that IRDIA made "a fine conclusion to my record in Parliament on constructive measures that will run into the future, affecting the well-being of the people." Looking out over the tranquil Gatineau Hills, in other words, he felt not just a sense of triumph about the averted railway strike, but also a sense of completeness about his life's work in Canadian industrial relations. By remaining true to his principles, he had been able to guide and shape what had been accomplished; or, as he wrote in his diary: "[By] standing alone, I ... feel that my life has played a part in what has been achieved." Two years later, at the same serene location, he would die from a heart attack.[4]

Tempering

Sitting in her office in the hulking, V-shaped Confederation Building just west of Parliament Hill in late November 1945, Margaret Mackintosh began to write a memorandum to Kay Maclean, the industrial relations director. It concerned the labour movement's recent demand to add more compulsory features to PC 1003. Described by contemporaries as "mercurial in mind" and "unusually quick of apprehension," Mackintosh's expertise in labour policy was beyond question. Unlike the many fresh-faced staff walking the halls, Mackintosh had joined the Department of Labour (DOL) way back in 1916 as a clerk in the statistics branch. Making the most of her "colourless" post, she not only assumed responsibility for reorganizing and enlarging the DOL library, but also became renowned as "the Canadian authority on labour legislation and trade union law." After publishing widely in periodicals and helping to establish the Canadian Association of Administrators of Labour Legislation, she was appointed the first chief of the Legislative Branch in the DOL and, in 1943, was made a Member of the Order of the British Empire for her contributions to legislative research.[5] Given the gender expectations of that time, Mackintosh may have had to rely on less aggressive or less confrontational communication skills to avoid marginalization in the male-dominated DOL. But nothing in her background suggests that she was docile or deferential. Raised in Madoc, Ontario, fifty miles northeast of Kingston, Mackintosh was one of only a handful of women, including her sister, who attended Queen's University in the early 1910s.[6] A decade later, she played a key role in overcoming opposition to the building of a women's residence hall at her alma mater.[7] Throughout her career, she also attended and spoke at international conferences about women's issues. In other words, the legislative chief felt no inhibitions about sharing her opinion with a colleague. "I cannot say that I am very enthusiastic," she wrote to Maclean about the demands for changes to PC 1003. "While compulsion may be tried as a last resort," she continued, "it provokes opposition in the minds of the persons compelled to a certain line of action."[8] Although initially supportive of a collective bargaining policy, Mackintosh did not want the government getting further involved in industrial relations with the return of peacetime conditions.[9] As the labour movement soon discovered, she spoke for most of the movers and shakers in the federal government, especially the prime minister.

A year and a half earlier, most labour leaders had felt quite positive about the passage of PC 1003, which came into force on 20 March 1944. Percy Bengough, the president of the Trades and Labour Congress (TLC), informed affiliates that the new order met most of the demands of the congress and deserved its support.[10] Norman Dowd, the executive secretary of the CCL, wrote to union members that "in a great many respects, [PC 1003] is along the lines which we have asked for on numerous occasions."[11] Granted, this praise was sometimes qualified. The Confédération des travailleurs catholiques du Canada (CTCC) still wanted the government to limit the coverage of the new order so that the provinces could retain control over most industrial relations.[12] Many labour leaders also expressed frustration that wage controls, especially with the recent passage of PC 9384, prevented the true realization of "free" collective bargaining. As J.A. "Pat" Sullivan, the outspoken president of the Canadian Seamen's Union, former Petawawa internee, and secretary-treasurer of the TLC, derided, PC 1003 "is like taking a starving man to a banquet table," while PC 9384 "is putting a strait jacket on him and telling him to go ahead and eat." Still, even Sullivan welcomed the Wartime Labour Relations Regulations because they would make it much easier to organize workers. "Take Hamilton," he offered. "Every Trade Union that's gone into Hamilton plants has been smacked right between the eyes by company unions ... Now the men will get protection."[13] As Mackenzie King noted with considerable ebullience, "The labour code has brought a lot of kudos to the government." [14]

The labour leaders had good reason to celebrate PC 1003. With the exception of Prince Edward Island and Alberta, the provinces had agreed to assume responsibility for administering the order, increasing the possibility of winning recognition and contracts. There was a range of approaches. Although most provinces established their own regional labour relations boards, British Columbia invested its labour minister with the authority to oversee the implementation of compulsory collective bargaining. Moreover, Quebec and Saskatchewan only applied the regulations to war industries. They preferred to have non-war industries, which were broadly defined in Quebec, covered by their own legislation.[15] Regardless, between March 1944 and July 1946, the newly established labour relations boards granted 2,773 or 76 per cent of the 3,628 applications for certification.[16] Although some of these petitions involved independent employee associations or plant committees, the high approval rating mainly reflected how unions or, more accurately, their appointed bargaining representatives were able to win certifications without representation votes. The Ontario Labour Relations Board, for example, awarded 1,271 certifications, but ordered only 229 representation votes – and most of these were probably for plant committee setups.[17] The labour movement did shrink in size between 1944 and 1945. As the war came to an end, massive layoffs depleted union ranks. The United Steelworkers (USW), alone, lost twenty-thousand members when the federal government cancelled wartime contracts.[18] Once manufacturers began to convert to peacetime production, however, most unions recovered, and some even experienced tremendous growth. By 1946, nearly 28 per cent of the wage-earning labour force belonged to a union – a 5 per cent jump since 1943.[19]

The labour movement also found it easier to secure contracts with the new compulsory collective bargaining policy. Between March 1944 and July 1946, only 12 per cent of the certifications granted by the labour relations boards required the intervention of a conciliation officer or conciliation board because the parties could not negotiate a contract on their own. Conciliation procedures failed to result in collective agreements in just 29 per cent of these cases. In other words, the failure rate for contract negotiations was a low 3.5 per cent.[20] Over a two-year period, the United Electrical Workers (UE) increased its number of plant contracts by over 70 per cent.[21] As many scholars rightly emphasize, the strike restrictions in the new collective bargaining law did make it increasingly difficult for workers to wield their economic power either spontaneously or politically. With PC 1003's rigid emphasis on industrial peace, there was a trade-off, as legal scholars Judy Fudge and Eric Tucker write, of "legal right for industrial might."[22] Still, it is hard to deny that contracts also provided workers with protection from the insecurities and uncertainties of the marketplace. The number of unjust dismissals, layoffs, and disciplinary actions, though never eliminated, did decrease. And, with the eventual removal of wartime controls, wages, conditions, and benefits improved. Certainly, labour leaders considered collective agreements to be the ultimate measure of success. Although the wage freeze made it so "you couldn't bargain for very much at all," Ray Stevenson of the International Union of Mine, Mill, and Smelter Workers (Mine Mill) recalled, a contract did signal that "[t]he union was there to stay."[23]

By the end of the war, with fewer recognition and collective bargaining conflicts, not to mention the extensive strike ban, the strike rate fell to its lowest level in five years.[24] It appeared that PC 1003 was having its desired effect. Noting the much higher level of unrest in the United States, an American diplomat reported to Washington that there was "a marked contrast between the strike situations in the two countries."[25]

Yet, the regulations did elicit early criticisms from a few influential corners of the labour movement. Within a week of the order's passage, J.L. Cohen, the former member of the National War Labour Board who had been conspicuously shunned by policymakers during the passage of PC 1003, declared that "the document itself is a very inadequate one."[26] In a widely publicized press release, which caught the attention of the DOL and numerous unions, the labour lawyer listed several shortcomings of the new collective bargaining policy.[27] After consulting with Cohen, the Co-operative Commonwealth Federation (CCF) also went on the attack, keen to regain ground lost to the Liberal Party.[28] Arthur Williams, the former CCL organizer, announced in the Ontario legislature that "[t]he leopard has added a little spot here and a little spot there, but it's the same old leopard." George Grube, Ontario's CCF leader and a University of Toronto classics professor, wrote that "we are still in the same atmosphere of distrust and chicanery as we found ourselves in under previous orders-in-council."[29] As well, in early March, the communist-led United Electrical Workers sent a critical analysis of PC 1003 to the Department of Labour. Still eager to cooperate with the federal government in the war effort, most communist labour leaders had hailed the regulations as a Magna Carta for workers. Harvey Murphy, the gruff, Polish-born Mine Mill official and internment camp veteran, was apparently so jubilant that he went "off the deep end on this Labour Code."[30] The UE declared, however, that it would be "remiss in its obligation ... to its own members if it did not point out some of the evident weaknesses of this legislation."[31]

The critics had six main questions about PC 1003:[32] (1) Why was the collective bargaining policy a temporary wartime order and not a permanent law? Employers would expect to regain their absolute power after the war ended. (2) What about the "looseness" of certifying individual bargaining representatives, not unions? This stipulation not only confused workers and perhaps encouraged company unionism, but also undermined the legitimacy of the labour movement. Although the labour relations boards ignored the distinction in practice, it was a basic question of legitimacy and status. (3) Why were outdated, ineffective conciliation mechanisms still being used? The lag times and indefinite outcomes that accompanied them motivated employers to stall during collective bargaining proceedings. As Cohen explained to Eugene Forsey, the CCL's research director: "Any employer ... can put up a plausible front for thirty days ... after which the conciliation board machinery preempts the situation."[33] (4) How were workers supposed to wield bargaining power when there was an extensive ban on their "only, basic effective weapon?" Employers were not going to be in any hurry to bargain in good faith because legal strikes could only take place after several weeks of drawn-out negotiations and conciliation procedures. Not only did the workers' resolve weaken by the time they were allowed to go out legally, but the lack of leverage also hindered negotiations. (5) Didn't the order implicitly encourage company unionism by allowing for the certification of independent employee associations or plant committees? "There are cases," Grube observed, "where employees' organizations may exist which are not controlled or dominated by the employers, but they are very few."[34] (6) Why did representation votes require bargaining representatives to win the majority of workers affected, not the majority of the workers actually voting? When the UE won 71 of the 124 ballots cast in a vote at the Philco Corporation, for example, the Ontario Labour Relations Board refused certification because less than half of the eligible voters had voted for the union.[35] "If the principle embodied in the Board's rulings had been applied to the Dominion general election of 1940," the CCL's Research Department pointed out, "exactly six members would have been elected to the House of Commons."[36]

Several local district councils echoed these complaints.[37] But A.R. Mosher, the CCL president who, according to Forsey, always liked to be "in complete control," dismissed the questions about PC 1003 as "more froth than substance."[38] "It is my firm belief," he wrote to Charlie Millard of the USW, "that any defects in the code which become apparent in its administration can be readily adjusted."[39] As an industrial statesman who relished the opportunity to work on an equal footing with business and government, Mosher put his faith in the order's administrative machinery. His reasons were two-fold. First, unlike the National Labor Relations or Wagner Act in the United States, which allowed employers to appeal the decisions of the National Labor Relations Board to the federal circuit courts of appeals, PC 1003 limited the role of the courts in industrial relations to unfair labour practice judgments.[40] The certification rulings of the Canadian Wartime Labour

Relations Board (WLRB), which not only decided cases that normally fell under federal jurisdiction but also heard appeals about decisions of the provincial labour boards, were, for the most part, "final and conclusive."[41] The courts did not have much leeway to re-examine evidence or overturn verdicts. For Mosher, like most labour officials, this restriction on judicial review was crucial. Not only were employers deprived of an effective delay tactic, but organized labour escaped the upper middle-class biases and remote formalism of judge-made law. Second, the labour relations boards at both the national and provincial levels of operation were representative. This feature was another contrast to the United States, where three professionals sat on the National Labor Relations Board. On 16 March 1944, the labour movement and the business community had each nominated four delegates to the WLRB, including Mosher. The government appointed Justice G.B. O'Connor of Alberta's Supreme Court to represent the "public" as the chair. His role was to act as an umpire between the two groups, casting a vote when partisan ties prevented decisions.[42] Mosher clearly valued this setup. After many years of demanding adequate representation on government bodies, union leaders could finally look after labour's interests at the highest level of power.

The representative principle of the WLRB did have significant limits. In mid-March, Constance Garneau, a CBC commentator and president of the Montreal League for Women's Rights (who much later starred in the 1990 National Film Board movie *A Company of Strangers*), wired a telegram to Mackenzie King:

> WE ARE AMAZED AND INDIGNANT TO NOTE IN THE PRESS THAT THE GOVERNMENT HAS APPOINTED THE WAR LABOUR RELATIONS BOARD WITHOUT CONSIDERING REPRESENTATION OF WOMEN ... STOP THE WOMEN OF CANADA HAVE CONTRIBUTED TO THE WAR EFFORT IN ALL ITS PHASES STOP ... WE FEEL THAT THE GOVERNMENT HAS BEEN MOST UNFAIR IN IGNORING WOMEN IN SETTING UP THE WAR LABOUR RELATIONS BOARD[43]

The lack of female representation on the WLRB was a serious concern for many leading women in the country. Even before the passage of PC 1003, Margaret Wherry, president of the Federation of Business and Professional Women's Clubs, had written to Humphrey Mitchell about the appointment of at least one woman to the board.[44] Shortly afterwards, Ursilla Macdonnell, president of the Canadian Federation

5.1 Demobilized soldiers. The Reinstatement in Civil Employment Act (1942) guaranteed demobilized veterans their old jobs.

Source: Ronny Jaques, National Film Board of Canada, Still Photography Division, Library and Archives Canada, C-049434.

of University Women and dean of women at Manitoba University, who had given several talks about the plight of female war workers, made a similar appeal.[45] And US-born Laura Hardy, president of the National Council of Women of Canada since 1942, followed suit a few months later.[46] Well-educated and affluent, these spokeswomen shared little in common with the female labour force in the factories and mills. Hardy, for example, had just been made Commander of

5.2 Subcommittee on the Post-War Problems of Women. The hastily assembled subcommittee wanted to expand the scope of PC 1003 so that workers in traditionally female occupations could experience the benefits of union representation.

Source: *Winnipeg Tribune*, 26 April 1943, 10, Library and Archives Canada, Amicus No. 3821471.

the Order of the British Empire.[47] Given their mandate to improve the status of all women, however, they worried that women workers were going to miss out on the benefits of unionism without proper representation on the WLRB. Wherry, a big proponent of equal pay for equal work, had long urged her membership of business owners and professionals to "work in close co-operation with the woman in industry and ... strive to find a solution to the many problems confronting her."[48] Well aware that female wage-earners had enjoyed unprecedented advances and opportunities during the war, these middle- and upper-class reformers believed that union membership would help to entrench improvements and ultimately produce greater gender equality. "We must not let ourselves slip back into old provincialisms," entreated Hardy.[49]

As Jeffrey Keshen writes in his study of daily life in wartime Canada: "[T]oo much had changed for too many women to permit a return to the antebellum status quo."[50] Despite a wide gender disparity in wages

5.3 War Labour Relations Board, March 1944. With demobilized veterans guaranteed their old jobs, women's rights activists and their organizations (see figures 5.4, 5.5, 5.6, and 5.7) called for female representation on the War Labour Relations Board to help protect the wartime advances of wage-earning women.

Source: National Film Board of Canada, Still Photography Division, Library and Archives Canada, PA-112761.

5.4 Constance Garneau, Montreal League for Women's Rights

Source: *CBC Program Schedule*, 27 May 1945, 7, Old Time Radio Researchers Group.

5.5 Laura Hardy, National Council of Women of Canada

Source: *Winnipeg Tribune*, 28 March 1946, 12, Library and Archives Canada, Amicus No. 3821471.

5.6 Ursilla Macdonnell, Canadian Federation of University Women

Source: *Winnipeg Tribune*, 3 March 1944, 11, Library and Archives Canada, Amicus No. 3821471.

5.7 Margaret Wherry, Federation of Business and Professional Women's Clubs

Source: *Winnipeg Tribune*, 20 April 1943, 11, Library and Archives Canada, Amicus No. 3821471.

and the indifferent gender sensitivities of employers and unions, social commentators noted that women had derived a great deal of pride and self-assurance from working in wartime jobs. "Four years of war have challenged women and they have risen magnificently," observed a newspaper editor in early 1944. "Not the least of their achievements has been the growth in … confidence in their capabilities."[51] A lot of Canadians agreed that women had proven themselves just as capable as men in the wartime workplace. "[T]o cling to the … notion that a woman is somehow inferior to a man in her ability," a columnist wrote a few months earlier, "is to fly in the face of demonstrated proof."[52] Indeed, as a result of war work, women now questioned the reason customarily given for their exclusion from higher paying blue collar jobs – their lack of mental and physical stamina. Although more traditionally female occupations, like domestic and laundry work, were equally arduous and demanding, it had become readily apparent that women could operate machinery and assemble goods for extended periods of time just as well as men.

As several local surveys suggested, a large number of single and married women with industrial jobs planned to continue working after the war.[53] To be sure, wage-earning women were not a new phenomenon in Canada. As historian Ruth Frager documents, women from low-income families, especially those from cultures that supported female wage-earning like Eastern European Jews, had always worked out of economic necessity.[54] Before the war, though, most Canadians tended to view female wage-work as disreputable and implausible; a proper woman was supposed to lack the inclination and ability to forgo her domestic responsibilities and join the paid labour force. In early 1945, the participation of nearly a third of the female population over the age of fourteen in war production confused these popular notions of gender and class.[55] Although not ideal, it was now considered conceivable and more legitimate for women to work outside the home for wages. "So, Mr. Soldier and husbands in general, do not expect Jane and the other little women who have done a grand job in industry during this war to docilely go back home," warned Grace Hyndman, a prominent social worker and personnel director at the General Engineering Company. "If you are a boss in industry, don't think you can label jobs 'Women's Work' and as such, pay the traditionally poorer wages. Women have given good account of themselves on man-sized jobs during wartime."[56] Or, as Norah Stevens of the YWCA put it: "Women who have enjoyed economic independence will feel resentment at being pushed to the background in a 'man's world.'"[57]

The concerns of the women's organizations were well founded. Most indicators suggested the country was going to retreat from, rather than build on, wartime advances for working women. After all the uncertainties of the early 1940s, not to mention the Great Depression, many Canadians wanted to see a return to traditional gender relations where men assumed the role of breadwinner and women assumed the role of domestic housewife. This demand for "normalcy" had two dimensions. First, there was a widespread belief that married women needed to leave the paid labour force to save their families. Politicians throughout the country were blaming female workers for increased levels of juvenile delinquency and infant mortality during the war years.[58] So were regular Canadians. "We find there is a growing disease among mothers of today," one woman wrote to the *Ottawa Citizen* in early 1945, "the shirking of the family life at home."[59] Concern about the plight of children at home even extended to some women's organizations like the National Council of Women, which also called for married women to relinquish their jobs.[60] Second, given the strong possibility of an economic downturn after the war, most people agreed that women workers, especially married women workers, should give up their jobs to returning servicemen.[61] Female wage-earners often shared this view. "To say that because we were employed during an emergency we should be kept employed indefinitely," a women worker shared, "shows a very selfish attitude."[62] Most of the male-dominated unions also supported the return of women war workers to the home or at least to more traditional female jobs. At both De Havilland Aircraft and Massey-Harris, for example, the UAW invited employers to ignore the seniority rights of female workers so that men, including men of colour and men with non–Anglo-Celtic backgrounds, would be given preferential treatment in hiring and layoff decisions.[63] And, as historian Jennifer Stephen reveals, the federal government played an important role in reproducing these gender expectations. Under the purview of middle-class white women like Fraudena Eaton in the NSS, who failed to see how their own salaried positions challenged gender conventions, government officials had initially pushed women to take wartime jobs, while they reassured the country about the virtues of feminine domesticity. Now, with the war drawing to a close, they began to steer women workers back into the homes and low wage, traditionally female jobs. As one politician criticized, the general sentiment was as follows: "[W]e appreciate what you have done for us; but just run along; go home; we can get along without you very nicely."[64] By early 1945, companies involved in war production had already dismissed 30 per cent of their female workers.[65]

With the more well-paid economic opportunities for women workers quickly disappearing, it was probably no coincidence that the leaders of the national women's organizations called for female representation on the WLRB shortly after the Subcommittee on the Post-War Problems of Women released its final report. Created in January 1943 at the insistence of Margaret Wherry, Constance Garneau, and their respective organizations, the subcommittee was an offshoot of the all-male General Advisory Committee on Reconstruction, which the government had established much earlier in the spring of 1941. Allowed only eight months to conduct research, convene meetings, and publish recommendations, the ten female members of the subcommittee, who included Wherry, walked a fine line between calling for equal job opportunities for women and upholding the virtues of marriage and domesticity.[66] Their final report, while favourably reviewed in the mainstream media, failed to impress Mackenzie King and his cabinet.[67] What is significant, however, is that the subcommittee wanted to amend PC 1003 so that the collective rights of women workers in the traditionally female occupation of domestic service would also receive protection. To be clear, their ultimate goal was to make household help more readily available for middle-class women to allow them to pursue careers and voluntarism outside the home.[68] The subcommittee members largely viewed gender relations through a class lens. Still, they did seem to recognize the importance of expanding the scope of PC 1003 so that women workers could also gain material benefits and industrial citizenship. Despite the resegregation of the job market, women did not have to remain secondary workers in the post-war world. Citing the report, Dorise Nielson, the left-leaning politician from Saskatchewan, drove home this point a few months later in Parliament when she demanded an "equal pay for equal work" clause in PC 1003.[69] Indeed, the calls for female representation on the WLRB appeared to be part of a larger, concerted effort to use PC 1003 to improve conditions for women. A female WLRB member, for example, might push for the merging of male and female seniority lists so women workers could hold onto higher paying industrial jobs.

Perhaps not surprisingly, the petitions for female representation elicited evasive, patronizing replies. As Humphrey Mitchell wired back to Macdonnell:

> WE LIKE THE IDEA OF HAVING A WOMAN ON BOARD BUT OUR HANDS ARE PRETTY MUCH TIED BECAUSE OF FACT THAT WE HAVE TO ASK FOR NOMINATION.[70]

In other words, it was up to the employer associations and labour organizations to put forward a female representative, not the government. And, as Mitchell well knew, there was little chance of that happening. At that time, women comprised 9.5 per cent of total union membership, a conservative figure since most unions didn't report the sex of their membership. But the male leaders of the labour organizations were not prepared to nominate female unionists to positions on the WLRB. Percy Bengough had the decency to explain that the TLC had only one seat on the board; he couldn't possibly nominate a woman when most union members were men. Most other labour leaders simply ignored the question of female representation.[71] In desperation, Macdonnell called on Mitchell to create a dedicated seat for women on the WLRB, suggesting the appointment of the DOL's own Margaret Mackintosh.[72] Wherry made a similar, emphatically worded request to Mackenzie King.[73] Both demands proved futile. Beneath all the pleasantries, it was clear that the federal government viewed women workers as ancillary and temporal. Although female wage-earners might help to supplement the family income, their primary responsibilities remained in the home. It was the men as the main providers – the presumably bona fide workers – who were entitled to high wages and job security.

This gendered understanding of wage-work had unfortunate repercussions for the long term. Over the next thirty years, the labour force participation rate of women doubled to 40 per cent.[74] In what the Labour Department called "a revolutionary development," even the number of married women in the labour force increased by a significant amount in the post-war period.[75] Largely confined to traditionally female jobs with small firms in the highly competitive service sector, however, most women workers experienced low wages, poor conditions, and limited job security. Despite repeated efforts to organize collectively, like at Simpsons in the late 1940s and Eaton's in the early 1950s, they discovered that Canada's new collective bargaining regime made it difficult for them to win union certifications.[76] As labour and gender studies scholar Anne Forrest explains, one of the main problems was that PC 1003 gave the authority to determine bargaining units (the group of employees to be represented by a union) to labour relations boards. Focused more on the large factories, camps, mills, and mines, where men typically worked as full-time employees, the male-centric boards usually defined bargaining units by single workplaces, not entire companies. But this model was a poor fit for women-dominated industries like laundry, banking, or retail, where workplaces were smaller, part-time workers were prevalent, and job descriptions were fluid. Not only did a single retail store or bank branch with a handful of employees lack much bargaining power or economic clout, but the labour relations boards often had to deliberate for months to figure out which workers actually belonged in the bargaining unit, effectively undermining union support. Some unions also balked at spending the time and money to organize and win agreements for such small bargaining units. Although PC 1003 itself was gender neutral, it helped to buttress, if not expand, a two-tiered labour market that marginalized women workers.[77]

Meanwhile, despite Mosher's call for patience, the CCL affiliates were becoming increasingly critical of PC 1003. In August 1944, the United Auto Workers, with the assistance of J.L. Cohen, published a pamphlet that detailed the order's shortcomings.[78] A month later, Local 1005 of the United Steelworkers in Hamilton, Ontario, demanded that Ottawa initiate a number of changes to the regulations.[79] In mid-October, delegates at the CCL convention discussed policy improvements at length, eventually sending a list of resolutions to Humphrey Mitchell in December.[80] Given that union memberships had plummeted by nearly 40 per cent after World War I, labour leaders were extremely apprehensive about the near future.[81] They expected massive layoffs to decimate their ranks. In addition, no one knew how hundreds of thousands of demobilized veterans, who were guaranteed their old jobs under the Reinstatement in Civil Employment Act, would respond to calls for organization. And CCL leaders were convinced that more reactionary employers would try to rebuild the industrial order of the late 1930s when managerial prerogatives reigned supreme. They wanted to see improvements made to PC 1003 that would safeguard the future of their unions. They also wanted to push federal policymakers to convert an amended PC 1003 into a permanent peacetime law.

It is important to underscore this last point. Although Mackenzie King did not truly believe the end of war was near until September 1944, a myriad of government agencies had already given extensive consideration to the question of post-war reconstruction.[82] For example, Margaret Mackintosh's younger brother, Bill, a highly regarded economist in the Finance Department, had chaired a subcommittee of the influential Economic Advisory Committee in early 1943 to examine constitutional impediments to solving anticipated problems in the reconstruction period.[83] Post-war planning wasn't an overriding concern of government bureaucrats alone. Many people remembered the disarray and upheaval that had followed the end of the Great War.

When the Advisory Committee on Reconstruction released the *Report on Social Security for Canada* or Marsh Report in the spring of 1943, Gallop polls discovered that Canadians were discussing the need for post-war reforms to a much greater extent than their American neighbours.[84] There was much talk throughout the country about making a new social order after the war. Even the ever-cautious Mackenzie King enthused: "The task of Liberalism will not be finished when the war is won. That great moment will but mark a place of new beginning."[85] With the creation of the Department of Reconstruction in late 1944, which Bill Mackintosh joined for a short period, labour leaders wanted to make sure that an amended PC 1003 with all its legal protections for workers and unions became one of the cornerstones of the new post-war order and not a casualty of opposition or apathy. "It is no exaggeration to say," Pat Conroy told Humphrey Mitchell, "that many thousands of workers are literally afraid of what will happen in the post-war world."[86]

The recent passage of the Saskatchewan Trade Union Act helped ramp up criticisms of PC 1003. On 15 June 1944, the CCF had won the provincial election in Saskatchewan in an unexpected sweep. In the words of David Lewis, the party's national secretary, the victory was the "crowning achievement of three years of CCF progress."[87] Almost immediately, the new government with its large CCF majority passed the Trade Union Act. The provincial labour law deviated in many ways from PC 1003: trade union growth was encouraged in both the private and public sectors; trade unions were certified, not individual bargaining representatives; the majority of ballots cast determined the outcome of a representative vote; strikes during negotiations or the tenure of a contract were not outlawed; there were no stipulations for grievance arbitration clauses in contracts; unions could require the inclusion of membership maintenance and compulsory check-off clauses; the list of unfair labour practices for employers was extended; and, finally, the administrative board was given both remedial and punitive powers.[88] Although the CCF government proved reluctant to enforce some of the more far-reaching provisions of the Trade Union Act, most labour leaders agreed that PC 1003 should be brought into line with the provincial labour law.[89]

By early 1945, the CCL unions were assailing the wartime labour regulations. Unlike earlier, they no longer raised tactful questions about the content of PC 1003. Now they expressed anger and frustration about its application. Take the WLRB's handling of "run-off" elections, for example. In a key certification contest between the International Union of

Mine, Mill, and Smelter Workers and intervening employee associations at two gold mines in Kirkland Lake, Ontario, the union won a majority of the votes cast, but not the majority of the votes affected. Since the miners had demonstrated their desire for collective representation, the Ontario Labour Relations Board ordered a second election with only the union's name on the ballot. But the mine operators and employee associations appealed to the WLRB, and it ruled that the second vote was needless because the first election had already determined that the union lacked the support of a majority of the workers. With the miners now deprived of any representation whatsoever, J.L. Cohen declared that the ruling "completely stultifies the whole Order-in-Council."[90]

Besides certification issues, Allan McLean, the Liberal Party's chief strategist, heard "a considerable rumbling of discontent" in labour circles because employers were engaging in an "endless and futile pretense at negotiations."[91] Although the failure rate for contractual relations was quite low, some unions mistakenly believed that the regulations made it, in the words of the Shipyard Federation of British Columbia, "compulsory upon the employer to enter into a signed agreement."[92] This was not the case. Employers were only required to bargain in good faith with their employees' certified representatives. Still, the expectation generated considerable resentment when employers proved reluctant to sign an agreement. The WLRB also seemed to lack the authority and/or will to challenge employers who tried to undermine the bargaining process. A particularly high-profile dispute between the UAW and Ford Canada in Windsor, Ontario, made this clear. The UAW had tried to secure a new contract for months, but the company adamantly refused to concede ground. Instead, Ford used dubious tactics, like insisting on the attendance of every bargaining representative at every meeting and questioning the wording in different pieces of correspondence, to bog down negotiations. It was obvious that the company did not intend to make a reasonable effort to conclude a collective agreement. Yet, the WLRB did nothing.[93] As Paul Martin, parliamentary assistant to the labour minister and an MP for Windsor, remarked to Arthur MacNamara, deputy minister of labour, there was a "lack of authority in the Code to deal with this very kind of situation ... The Board is helpless."[94]

On a related note, the CCL unions also believed that the enforcement powers of the labour relations boards were "one of the most unsatisfactory features of the present Regulations."[95] To level an unfair labour practice charge against an employer, a union had to obtain a board's leave to prosecute the matter in police court. This process was not only time consuming, but ineffective. Labour leaders were convinced that most magistrates lacked the experience to rule on industrial relations issues; disliked how the onus of proof rested with the plaintiff; and regarded the fines of no more than $500 as inadequate. "By paying a small license fee," the CCL noted, "[the employer] secures the right to refuse to bargain with his employees' representatives." Instead, the UE argued: "The Boards must be given full powers of enforcement including cease and desist in cases of unfair labour practices by employers." The order also needed to be reworded so that "the onus is on the employer to disprove allegations of discrimination."[96]

Finally, in terms of contract content, the CCL unions had two objections. The first involved grievance arbitration. In a recent case that involved Automotive Trim and the UAW, the WLRB had determined that the mandatory grievance procedure was only applicable to issues covered by the collective agreement.[97] In other words, given the ban on midterm strikes, employees had no recourse for action if their grievances fell outside the provisions of the contract. Management rights prevailed in these circumstances. Recognizing that union negotiators could not possibly foresee every grievance, the CCL wanted to extend the scope of compulsory grievance arbitration to all disputes that arose during the term of a contract.[98] Second, the CCL believed, as Norman Dowd wrote to Harold Padget of the USW, that "union security measures such as maintenance of membership, union shop and check-off should be provided for."[99] For the sake of clarification, maintenance of membership means that workers must remain dues-paying union members for the life of a contract; union shop means that all new employees must become union members within an established time period; and check-off means that employers must deduct union membership dues automatically from pay cheques. Like union recognition, union security seemed to be a zero-sum issue that defied negotiation and conciliation. Employers didn't want to give up more control over their workplaces or do anything to sustain the existence of unions. Labour leaders believed that union security clauses were critical to surviving a post-war collapse.[100] Justice O'Connor, the WLRB chair, wrote to Humphrey Mitchell that the CCL unions appeared ready "to strike for considerable periods in the hope of obtaining a 'union shop' provision."[101] Two of the most protracted, bitter strikes of 1944, which involved streetcar workers in Montreal and shipyard workers in Halifax, centred on compulsory check-off provisions.[102] At a conference, Charles Millard, the forceful

USW leader, warned MacNamara that only government-mandated union security clauses would prevent further strife.[103]

In early 1945, the CCL invited its affiliates to send in suggestions for changes to PC 1003. The leadership was not just worried about policy issues that spring. Internecine differences, both political and jurisdictional, were consuming a lot of time and energy. "Ninety per cent of our trouble is between different branches of CIO International Unions who cannot agree among themselves on any basic issue," complained Pat Conroy. "Frankly, I am becoming pretty tired of being a buffer in between a number of irresponsible union groups all claiming to represent the workers."[104] The CCL's increasingly fraught relationship with the Congress of Industrial Organizations (CIO) in the United States was also a cause of concern. As Conroy and Dowd told an American diplomat, the CCL resented being treated as some kind of "colonial adjunct" with no representation at international conferences; having American organizers, often with communist backgrounds, foisted upon it; and receiving criticism for its support of the CCF.[105] Despite these important challenges, however, CCL leaders agreed that their primary goal should be to win amendments to PC 1003.[106] In mid-January, after receiving a good deal of input, they convened a special meeting to discuss the issues and decided to hire J.L. Cohen to draw up a legal document for submission to the federal government.[107]

It would be Cohen's last assignment for the CCL. His hefty invoice for services rendered would upset several affiliates and lead to the increased use of in-house lawyers.[108] But it was the labour lawyer's tragic demise that ultimately ended his long association with the congress. Since, as Cohen put it, his "unfortunate disagreement" with Justice McTague and resignation from the National War Labour Board, he had continued to maintain a hectic schedule. In 1944, he served as counsel to innumerable labour organizations and nearly became the CCF candidate for Essex West (Windsor), Ontario, for the next federal election. Only an embarrassing clash between local CCF and communist-led factions prevented his nomination. In 1945, Cohen not only worked on the PC 1003 submission for the CCL, but also investigated the coal-mining industry in Nova Scotia for the Carroll Commission, counselled the UAW in a landmark Ford dispute about union security clauses, and represented several unions during the LeBel Commission Inquiry about a secret police force in Ontario. Although still the top labour lawyer in the country, his highly professional, supremely confident persona masked profound insecurities. He needed to stay busy – to work sixteen-hour days and travel incessantly – to keep his personal demons at bay. No one, however, could endure such an unrelenting pace for so many years without paying a heavy price. By the time the CCL hired Cohen to work on the PC 1003 submission, he was addicted to sedatives and alcohol, and constantly on the verge of physical and psychological collapse. He would soon be arrested for sexually assaulting his mistress, sentenced to six months in prison, and disbarred for "conduct unbecoming a lawyer." In just five years, he would die a broken man at the age of fifty-three. But all this remained in the future.[109] On 23 March 1945, the CCL submitted Cohen's report to the federal government, still applauding the passage of PC 1003 but also noting that "experience has brought out a number of defects."[110] Local and regional CCL unions followed with a barrage of telegrams and letters that demanded action.[111]

Around the same time, the TLC also began to pressure the government for policy changes. Aside from some resolutions about union shop clauses and representation votes at the 1944 convention, the congress had remained relatively quiet on the subject of amendments to PC 1003.[112] Unlike the American Federation of Labor with the Wagner Act in the late 1930s, the TLC leadership seemed relatively satisfied that PC 1003 protected the craft privileges of its members. In late January 1945, however, the Workers' Educational Association in Toronto hosted a symposium on PC 1003, inviting local labour leaders from both TLC and CCL unions. After listening to Cohen's keynote address, the participants formed the Joint Committee for Revisions to PC 1003 and drafted a "Ten-Point Program of Action." Although Cohen dismissed the document as vague and polemic, it was sent out to all the union locals in Ontario, signaling the increased activism of local TLC leaders.[113] A couple of months later, the International Association of Machinists (IAM) organized another joint conference in Quebec to discuss PC 1003's shortcomings. "I was damned if I was going to sit by and let the CIO take over the whole thing," an IAM official wrote to Percy Bengough, "while our own people ... were sitting doing nothing."[114] After reading Cohen's report and meeting with Patrick Conroy, Bengough decided to broach the matter with the King cabinet.[115] On 23 April, the congress submitted its own memorandum to the government that largely reiterated the CCL's demands, except that there was an underlying note of voluntarism in its criticisms. Calling for a return to the less legalistic ways of the IDIA, the TLC submission singled out the cumbersome WLRB for going against the "intent of the Act."[116]

The Rand Formula

Early on the cold, overcast morning of Monday, 5 November 1945, Thomas (Tommy) MacLean, the assistant regional director for the UAW, drove his car up Drouillard Road in the west end of Windsor, Ontario, and parked in front of the main gates of the huge Ford Motor Company complex. Approaching middle age with a heavy-set build and receding hairline, he had long lamented how the union always "capitulated to the company."[117] Now, with the auto workers in the midst of a three-month strike, he took the keys out of the ignition, stepped out of the car, and walked away. Within a few minutes other union members followed suit, parking their cars tightly together to block any access to the Ford entrance. Soon after, the Drouillard Road transit bus, commandeered by Joe McBride, a twenty-five-year-old millwright, wedged in behind the cars.[118] A union sound truck began to direct commuters travelling along Sandwich Street (now Riverside Drive), a main thoroughfare that connected the suburbs and downtown, to join the congestion, threatening to overturn the vehicles of anyone (besides doctors) who resisted. As the strikers stood on the running boards of the cars and rocked them into place, hundreds of people, including thirty previously alerted newspaper reporters, gathered along the sidewalks to watch the blockade unfold. A union brass band appeared and began to play "Rule Britannia" and "Solidarity Forever." Another group of musicians with a bagpiper joined the festivities. At least seven other transit buses, two Greyhound buses, and several trucks loaded with goods fused into the traffic jam. The parked vehicles spread all the way down Drouillard Road and onto the perpendicular Sandwich Street, obstructing the entrance to Ford's power plant. Told their buses had reached the "end of the line," passengers disembarked and joined the swelling number of bystanders.[119] No police officers arrived to deal with the situation, possibly because of laxatives put in their coffee the evening before.[120] Lasting three days, the Ford Windsor park-in ended up covering twenty city blocks and proved to be one of the most dramatic events in Canada's labour history. And the cause? According to Ford Canada, it was "the uncompromising demand of the union for what it terms 'union security.'"[121]

In September 1944, the Liberal administration had amended PC 1003 to provide conciliation procedures during contract renewals and revoke the unnecessary PC 7307 or strike vote requirement.[122] But the government was not prepared to make any further changes. It largely ignored Cohen's comprehensive report. The DOL did send the report to the provinces and business community for comments. There was also some talk of a federal-provincial conference of labour ministers. But nothing of substance happened. When pushed for an explanation, Arthur MacNamara blamed the pending federal election of 11 June 1945 for the lack of "definite commitment."[123] More to the point, however, Mackenzie King believed that the existing regulations already allowed labour and capital to negotiate contracts as evenly matched competitors. He did not want his government put in a position where it had to influence outcomes or redress power imbalances. "[L]abour relations are primarily the concern of workers and employers," Humphrey Mitchell explained to CCL leaders on King's behalf. "[T]hey should not depend upon the government to solve their problems."[124] Nowhere was this quasi-voluntarism – this limited approach to intervention – better illustrated than with the issue of union security and Crown or government-owned companies. In late 1944, the USW had demanded the inclusion of a voluntary check-off clause in its contract with Research Enterprises Limited (REL), which manufactured optical equipment in a Toronto suburb. Although DOL officials were open to the idea, C.D. Howe, who now held the additional title of reconstruction minister, rejected any consideration of union security provisions. At a testy cabinet meeting in February 1945, Mackenzie King made it clear to Howe that the government would neither block nor mandate union security clauses in contracts.[125] As he later explained to Conroy, it didn't matter whether negotiations involved a private or Crown corporation, only management and labour could determine the content of agreements.[126] Howe put it somewhat less diplomatically when later confronted by REL employees on a golf course: "[W]hat happens to your Union is up to you. Get the hell off the course."[127]

The election results in June 1945 failed to shift the federal government. The Liberal Party won only the slimmest majority of 127 seats. Many soldiers overseas voted for the CCF, and Mackenzie King actually lost his seat in Prince Albert, Saskatchewan (he won another in a September by-election). Still, the prime minister wrote in his diary that he now had "peace of heart."[128] Despite six years of wartime austerity and hardships, the opposition parties had proven unequal to the task of toppling his government. The Progressive Conservatives managed to secure sixty-seven seats, and their leader, John Bracken, finally won a seat in Parliament, but they were disappointed, if not distressed, with the results.[129] Much to King's delight, Justice McTague failed to be elected as the Progressive Conservative candidate in Wellington County, Ontario. In truth, it wasn't much of a setback for the former NWLB chair. Quickly appointed chair of the Ontario Securities Commission, McTague would eventually sit on twenty-six company boards, chair Canada's Royal Commission on Transportation, and survive a hockey puck to the face at a Maple Leaf's game before his death in the mid-1960s.[130] Never good at forgiving disloyalty, however, the prime minister was almost gleeful that McTague's political career had come to an abrupt halt. What he found particularly gratifying about the election results was the relatively poor showing of the CCF. Although the social democrats more than tripled their number of seats in the House of Commons, they had expected a substantially larger gain. Joe Noseworthy, the only CCF MP from Ontario, actually lost his seat. Moreover, just a few days earlier, the CCF had suffered a devastating loss in the Ontario election when a Progressive Conservative landslide reduced its seats from thirty-four to eight. At least politically, the general public, including the labour movement, had demonstrated its support for the status quo.[131] "As the end of the war grew closer," David Lewis, the CCF's national secretary, later recalled, "one sensed a weariness mixed with the relief which Canadians felt. The spirit of adventure which induced them to try a new political party was giving way to an almost universal desire for tranquility."[132]

With the federal government lacking the political or ideological will to intervene further in industrial relations, a key contractual development of the post-war period, the "Rand formula," was for the most part an exercise in voluntarism. It followed the complete breakdown of negotiations at Ford Canada in Windsor, Ontario, in September 1945. With the WLRB determining union recognition questions and the National War Labour Board (NWLB) still governing wage increases, union security had become the pre-eminent bargaining issue of the day. Since March 1944, when PC 1003 was first implemented, over 90 per cent of the appointed conciliation boards had to some degree discussed the topic.[133] As J.L. Cohen explained:

> When workers are menaced on one side by a fear that their employer may not continue to recognize the union in the post-war era while at the same time they feel insecure about employment or pay or working conditions, union leaders and union policy become marked by a determination that unions must be so strongly established that there can be no doubt about this survival.[134]

Granted, not all labour leaders agreed that union security was beneficial. Art Schultz of UAW Local 222 in Oshawa, Ontario, worried rather perceptively that check-off provisions, where personnel offices not the shop stewards collected worker-authorized dues, would weaken the links between the local leadership and the rank and file.[135] But many unions were prepared to fight for a more definite permanency. Germany's surrender in early May sharpened this determination. A few months later, for example, the government was forced to appoint a controller at American Can in Vancouver when a USW strike over the union shop threatened to devastate British Columbia's food processing industry.[136]

In the United States, Ford had agreed to a union shop and compulsory check-off four years earlier. Despite a conciliation board's recommendation of voluntary check-off, however, Ford Canada refused to include union security provisions in its new contract with the UAW.[137] Aside from some minor changes to grievance procedures and seniority lists, the company wanted no new innovations.[138] On 12 September, ten days after the Japanese surrender and the return of peace, the union ordered 10,000 auto workers off the job. Mackenzie King blamed the company for "chiseling down the collective bargaining agreement." Wallace Campbell, the Ford Canada president, retorted: "If the government felt that the union shop and checkoff was good for the people of Canada then they should pass Legislation."[139] Through October and into November, the strike gained national attention as workers resorted to innovative picketing techniques, thousands of supporters turned up at a huge fundraising rally in Maple Leaf Gardens, the Ontario government sent in provincial police, the mayor tried to use public monies for strike benefits, and the renowned African-American singer Paul Robeson played a benefit concert. In November, the well-publicized blockade of 1,000 cars and buses around the Ford plant seemed to symbolize a renewed sense of labour solidarity, not only in Windsor, but throughout the nation. Often for the first time, CCL and TLC unions in different parts of the country worked together to raise funds for the strikers.[140] Eight thousand women and men from a different UAW local also went out on well-publicized sympathy strikes in the Windsor area.[141]

Missing the services of Norman McLarty, the former labour minister and Windsor MP who had just died at his daughter's wedding, Humphrey Mitchell and the other Windsor MP, Paul Martin, who had recently become the secretary of state, appealed directly to Henry Ford II and George Addes of the International UAW.[142] Secretly,

5.8 Aerial view of the Ford strike park-in. The Ford strike of 1945 involved a well-orchestrated "park-in," some failed police efforts to enter the plant, and a groundswell of sympathy strikes. As one of the first big strikes for union security provisions, it also demonstrated the limits of PC 1003 (see also figure 5.9).

Source: Walter Reuther Library, Archives of Labor and Urban Affairs, Wayne State University, Image 6646.

government officials also promised Pat Conroy that Mitchell would appoint an open-minded arbitrator to resolve the conflict if workers went back to their jobs. Despite serving as the head of the National Ford Strike Committee, the CCL leader welcomed the news. He worried that more sympathy strikes would undermine the legitimacy of the labour movement.[143] As A.R. Mosher put it, employers were not going to adhere to contracts if unions treated them like "mere scraps of paper."[144] Just recently returned from the World Trade Union Federation in Paris, Conroy travelled to Windsor and, according to newspaper accounts, "worked sanely and bravely for 10 days to find a way of peace."[145] Communist hardliners initially frustrated his efforts, but the membership finally agreed to binding arbitration in mid-December. Most observers agreed that the union had little other choice. Although impressive, the seizing of privately owned cars for the park-in and

5.9 Close-up view of the Ford strike park-in

Source: City of Toronto Archives, *Globe and Mail* Fonds, Fonds 1266, Item 99991.

5.10 Justice Ivan Rand. As the arbitrator selected by the Labour Department, Justice Ivan Rand formulated a long-term solution, which was essentially an exercise in voluntarism.

Source: *Ottawa Journal*, 20 February 1952, 28, Microfilm, Ottawa City Library, Main Branch.

5.11 *Stelco Strike: Steelworkers from Local 105 Used "The Whisper" to Stop Stelco Taking in Supplies and Strikebreakers by Water.* During the turbulent year of 1946, Stelco was perhaps the most widely publicized strike for higher wages and union security provisions. The United Steelworkers (USW) used two boats to prevent the delivery of supplies and strikebreakers by water.

Source: W.H. Partridge, Library and Archives Canada, PA-120526.

calls for a nationwide one-day "solidarity strike" had actually backfired, generating a lot of negative publicity and drying up financial contributions. As George Burt, the UAW director for Canada, later recounted: "There was a lot of pressure on us. People were starting to lose their homes. We didn't have enough money." [146]

With the workers back at their jobs, Humphrey Mitchell announced that Justice Ivan Rand of the Supreme Court of Canada would serve as arbitrator. The son of a master railroad mechanic who had joined the Supreme Court in 1943, sixty-one-year-old Rand was a former attorney general of New Brunswick and a leading lawyer for the Canadian

5.12 *Stelco Strike: The Picket Line That Kept the Stelco Plant Shut Tight*. A huge turnout at the picket line also proved effective at limiting access to the Stelco plant. Mackenzie King had to draw on all of his conciliatory skills to resolve the conflict, but the Stelco strike revealed, just like the Ford strike, how the federal government was not open to amending PC 1003.

Source: Photographs, Library and Archives Canada, PA-120521.

National Railway. Mackenzie King thought very highly of the Harvard-trained attorney, nearly asking him to join his cabinet.[147] So did Paul Martin, who believed that "Rand's views on the rights of labour were encompassed with a progressive social outlook."[148] The justice was actually more of a civil libertarian than a progressive reformer. Conservative in outlook and inclined to cultural stereotyping, he placed a high priority on defending individual rights and freedoms. He was also a problem-solver – someone known for creative, original thinking. On 29 January 1946, after a series of supervised talks and a six-day hearing, Justice Rand announced his award at Toronto's Royal York Hotel. As an advocate of individual rights, he had found it difficult to accept the concept of a union shop where a worker had to join a union as a condition of employment. Yet, largely thanks to Pat Conroy's eloquent testimony, he also didn't like the idea of non-union workers benefiting from collective agreements as free riders. Consequently, Rand ordered the inclusion of a compulsory check-off clause in the Ford contract – the employer would deduct union dues from every worker's pay cheque. To protect the individual rights of workers and the prerogatives of management, there would be no union shop. But all workers in a bargaining unit would "take the burden along with the benefit" of unionism. In addition, Rand stipulated that the union had to agree to conduct a secret ballot of the workers before it ordered a strike, and, most significantly, the union would lose its check-off privileges if it called an illegal strike or failed to repudiate the actions of wildcat strikers.[149]

David Croll, Toronto's only Liberal MP and the former labour minister of Ontario who had resigned from his office during the 1937 General Motors strike, called the award "a great milestone in the development of labour-management relations."[150] George Burt of the UAW applauded the "Rand formula" as a "work of literary craftsmanship."[151] Indeed, most mainstream labour leaders responded favourably to the Rand formula because it offered a semblance of union security and made more militant union members think twice before engaging in illegal activities.[152] Kay Maclean in the DOL agreed that "Rand's observation that responsibilities are co-relatives of rights" was critical.[153] By linking union security to industrial discipline, the justice recognized the labour movement as a legitimate partner in industrial relations, but only as long as it played by the rules. There is some indication that Arthur MacNamara may have instructed Rand to include a quid pro quo in the award when they met privately back in December.[154] But the decision was consistent with the justice's balanced approach to conflict resolution. It is also important to emphasize that Rand's decision applied only to the Ford dispute. Since the federal government refused to amend PC 1003, the inclusion of the formula in subsequent contracts depended on the bargaining power of the respective parties. Although the award would eventually become a mainstay in Canadian industrial relations, its early utilization was limited to larger employers. Over the next two years, only eleven of the ninety-five contracts signed across the country contained the compulsory check-off provision.[155] When more widely implemented, as law scholar William Kaplan and others discuss, the Rand formula trade-off of financial well-being for contract adherence did become one of the cornerstones for the post-war settlement between labour and capital. To continue to enjoy membership dues, labour leaders had to serve as "the guarantors of industrial peace."[156] Just like PC 1003, Rand's decision encouraged unions to emphasize responsible, not militant, action, heightening stability, productivity, and consumerism. Of course, as the tremendous wave of wage strikes in 1946 demonstrated, the rank and file sometimes had other ideas.

Post-war Tumult

In the late afternoon of 7 August 1946, Pat Conroy, the forty-nine-year-old secretary-treasurer of the Canadian Congress of Labour (CCL), took his seat at one end of the open rectangle of tables in the crowded meeting room. Directly across from him sat Maurice Lalonde, the Liberal MP who served as chair of the House of Commons Standing Committee on Industrial Relations. Along the extended side of the rectangle, on Lalonde's right, sat government members of the committee, including Humphrey Mitchell and C.D. Howe. Along the other side, on the chair's left, sat the opposition members. The press and spectators sat or stood behind Conroy.[157] When everyone had settled, the labour leader opened up his twenty-nine page document and began reading. The room had terrible acoustics, but he knew how to project his voice after years of speaking in cavernous union halls.[158] Born to Irish parents and raised in a Scottish coal-mining village, Conroy had emigrated to Canada at the age of twenty. While working in the coal mines of Alberta and Colorado in the 1920s, he joined the United Mine Workers and eventually became vice-president of District 18 in Western Canada. He lacked a formal education, but a friend described him as "a remarkable man, possessing one of the profoundest and most original minds I have ever met."[159] Conroy could also be unrepentantly blunt. As a newspaper reported the next day, he "read a brief, dripping with irony and sarcasm, in which he flayed the Government's labour policies."[160] The labour leader lamented the failure of both government and business to recognize labour's position in industry as an equal partner; blamed the government's rigid stand on wage controls for the current strike wave; and justified contracts with union security clauses. It was a forceful, compelling presentation that prompted a UAW official to effuse: "We have found in you: the devotion of Hardie, the thoroughness of Jaurès, the ruggedness of Debs." [161]

What Conroy's bold delivery barely concealed, however, was his deep concern about the future of the labour movement. With the return of peacetime conditions, it seemed very possible that employers were going to regain control of industrial relations. There were two main reasons why. First, post-war economic disruptions in manufacturing were depleting the ranks of the CCL unions. With the loss of war contracts, the number of Canadians employed in direct and indirect war-related work had plunged by almost 50 per cent, and the membership rate for CCL unions had dropped by 10 percent.[162] Meanwhile, the government was discharging thousands of women and men from the armed services on a daily basis. Since the Reinstatement in Civil Employment Act, as part of the Veterans Charter, guaranteed returning soldiers their old civilian jobs, employers now enjoyed access to a much larger non-unionized work force: a work force that often lacked the same kind of vested interest in unionism.[163] Second, a lot of employers seemed to be eagerly anticipating the expiration of PC 1003, which, after all, was a temporary wartime order. As the federal government shut down its Crown corporations and began what C.D. Howe called "orderly decontrol" or reducing its presence in private industry, one labour journalist wrote: "[T]he honeymoon is over ... Now these employers are showing their teeth."[164] Clearly remembering how they had been free to stymie organizing drives and reject demands for collective bargaining before the war, some business leaders began to call for the return of laissez-faire–like conditions where the only compulsion was to participate in, but not abide by, conciliation proceedings.[165]

Up to this point, the business community had remained fairly mute about PC 1003. Although US employers bitterly protested the passage of the National Labor Relations or Wagner Act in the 1930s, Canadian employers, like the labour movement, offered few criticisms of PC 1003 between 1944 and 1946. As the *Financial Post* observed: "[T]here is an apparent absence of serious objection on any important account."[166] In part, this noticeable silence was due to apathy. Despite the impressive spread of unionism, many companies still paid scant attention to industrial relations. One business reporter lamented:

> [There is] a smug indifference ... which renders [management] either completely blind to the constantly disrupting causes, or, if aware of them, lacking in the necessary amount of vital interest to up and do something about it.[167]

More concerned about securing supplies and winning market shares, employers continued to deal with their workers on an individual ad hoc basis. Harry Taylor, one of the business representatives on the WLRB and president of Canadian National Carbon, could not believe how unconcerned employers were about the regulations. "Some authority has ... been transferred from manufacturers to Government," he chastised members of the Canadian Manufacturers' Association (CMA), "and, in some cases at least, further transferred from Government to trade unions."[168] But his clarion call seemed to fall on deaf ears. A CMA poll of over 200 members found that only one-third "had any opinion respecting PC 1003."[169] There seemed to be a general sense of fait accompli or even fatalism that permeated the business community. In the minds of many, it was futile to resist the impetus of compulsory collective bargaining. What was done was done – time to adjust and move on. As another business journalist noted: "The few employers who have tried to fight before the board have found that they might as well spare the time and effort. The state and the law have entered the labour picture on the side of the unions."[170] Those employers who did pay attention to industrial relations actually believed the regulations were fair and reasonable or, at least, not as bad as they could be. After witnessing how the Wagner Act had encouraged trade unionism and handcuffed managerial practices, they appreciated PC 1003's claim of evenhandedness. Some actually felt that the order's stringent restrictions on strike action and other union behaviour would go a long way to ensuring stable industrial relations; they considered PC 1003 to be a positive development. As a CMA official later recalled: "The position that the Association took [was that] it would be better to carry on with the regulations."[171]

This stance did not mean that employers embraced the pluralistic spirit of PC 1003. Some vocal members of the business community, like

Harry Taylor, were convinced that the compulsory collective bargaining policy was a major setback for "free enterprise." Many companies hired corporate lawyers and industrial relations experts to help them control or temper union advances. By 1945, for example, 123 companies in British Columbia were linked to the anti-union Stuart Research Service.[172] There were numerous instances where employers blatantly resisted or ignored PC 1003. The Steel Company of Canada or Stelco in Hamilton, Ontario, refused to bargain in good faith with the United Steelworkers, while Dominion Textile in Quebec relied on various delay tactics to beat back the advances of the United Textile Workers.[173] CCL organizers reported from various corners of the country that companies were using the order's non-union employee association allowance to thwart bona fide unionism.[174] Union intimidation also remained rampant. When the United Rubber Workers began to organize 200 workers at Asbestonos Corporation in St Lambert, Quebec, the management posted notices that warned "heads which are more or less hot ... will be eliminated."[175] And Ben's Ltd., a large bakery and confectionery employer in Halifax, Nova Scotia, used spies to infiltrate union meetings.[176] As a business magazine reported, some managers still feared "the humanizing and democratizing efforts of modern industry lest it should lead to the eventual loss of the time-honoured privilege of ruling the industrial roost." They held to the "attitude which still reflects the master-servant idea of medieval industry."[177] In line with Pat Conroy's apprehension, some reactionary employers did hope for a return to the industrial order of the 1930s when managerial rights had prevailed in the workplace. As Neil Peterson, the president of Canadian Acme Screw and Gear, proclaimed: "We have the right to expect a return to equal rights for all ... It should be the prerogative of the employer to decide whether he wishes to recognize a union which may claim to represent all his employees."[178]

For the most part, however, the business community made few formal criticisms of PC 1003 from 1944 to early 1946. When the government decided to extend its wartime powers into the reconstruction period, there were no outcries or protests from employer groups about the continued operation of the order. Another CMA poll found that most members who held an opinion on labour policy "thought that the Regulations were generally satisfactory, and should not be changed ... Those that favoured PC 1003 pointed out collective bargaining was here to stay, and that these Regulations seemed to be fairly reasonable to both employer and employee."[179] In September 1945, a wave of sympathy strikes in the packinghouse industry did provoke some protest.

Although the government appointed a controller to resolve the conflict, the business press wanted to know why PC 1003 had failed to prevent such "irresponsible" actions.[180] But this open disapproval was exceptional. Generally satisfied that the collective bargaining policy limited militant union behaviour without seriously undermining managerial prerogatives, employers and their organizations offered little resistance to the introduction of formal, mutually determined rules and regulations in the workplace.

That is, until mid-1946, when a massive strike wave swept across Canada.[181] Earlier in the year, after a series of meetings with affiliates, the CCL leadership had decided to launch a nationwide campaign to increase wages and establish a forty-hour week, ideally on an industry-wide basis. Conroy, as the chair of the Wage Coordinating Committee, explained in a public announcement that "there will be at least 200,000 members of affiliated Congress unions involved in wage issues."[182] Although the congress carefully avoided endorsing economic action, its members were ready for a showdown, especially given that hundreds of thousands of mass production workers in the United States were already engaged in wage strikes. Indeed, thanks to rank-and-file activism and more maverick labour leaders, the CCL found it challenging to exert control over the campaign. In mid-May, the International Woodworkers of America (IWA) led the charge when it called out over 30,000 woodworkers in British Columbia.[183] A few days later, Mine Mill shut down Canada's only brass mill when it struck Anaconda American Brass in New Toronto. Over 12,000,000 pounds of brass and copper were lost.[184] On 16 June, 4,000 Chrysler workers in both Chatham and Windsor, Ontario, walked off their jobs. The following week over 10,000 rubber workers at ten different Ontario plants began a four-month strike. In mid-July, the United Electrical Workers called out 3,500 workers at Canadian Westinghouse in Hamilton, as well as 3,200 workers at four smaller companies.[185] And, from 14 July until 1 October, the United Steelworkers struck three big steel producers: Stelco in Hamilton, Ontario; Dosco in Sydney, Nova Scotia; and Algoma in Sault Ste Marie, Ontario.[186] "Here in Canada," a newspaper reported, "the reconversion programme ... is bogged down. If the situation continues, we shall find ourselves in chaos."[187] Or, in the words of a concerned C.D. Howe, stoppages "have shaken the system."[188]

The strikes were not confined to the CCL unions. Although most TLC affiliates remained peaceful, some found themselves caught up in the general fervour for higher wages. In late May and early June, compositors at several Southam newspapers in Ottawa, Hamilton, Edmonton, and Vancouver went out on sympathy strikes to support the wage demands of their fellow typesetters at the *Winnipeg Tribune*.[189] From late May until late June, the Canadian Seamen's Union and several Great Lakes shipping companies engaged in a violent battle over wages and the eight-hour day.[190] Throughout the summer in Quebec, the United Textile Workers led strikes of over 5,000 Dominion Textile employees for wage increases and, in one particularly fierce struggle, for recognition.[191] In the fall, 6,000 bush workers in Northern Ontario, members of the Lumber and Sawmill Workers Union, struck for increased wages and improved camp conditions.[192] Nearly every key industry in the country was under siege. Although the actual number of disputes remained low compared to 1942 or 1943, they were remarkable for their size and duration. There were more person days lost than ever before in Canadian history.[193]

According to Kay Maclean in the DOL, the strikes were as much against the government as they were against employers.[194] Although the Wartime Prices and Trade Board (WPTB) had recently lifted the price ceilings on steel, lumber, paper, textiles, and various food stuffs, the government had not made any real move to relax wage controls. Donald Gordon, the WPTB chair, who was deeply concerned about post-war inflation, warned that if wage increases "are large and widespread they will make price control impracticable."[195] In late January, the government did amend PC 9384 so the National War Labour Board (NWLB) could grant increases that were consistent with the maintenance of existing prices.[196] But the NWLB, which was now presided over by Justice Maynard Archibald, continued to interpret the wage controls very narrowly, rejecting most applications for increases. "The unions feel," Maclean told an American diplomat, "that the Government is deliberately discriminating against them and favoring the employers, and this has done more to arouse their ire than anything else." He also noted that the communist and non-communist unions were competing for the post-war allegiances of unorganized workers.[197]

Maclean was right on both counts. Given the rescinding of some price controls, a 10 per cent drop in real earnings since Germany's surrender, and a massive amount of strike activity in the United States, many Canadian unions were primed for action, demanding increases of at least fifteen cents an hour.[198] "We cannot believe that any such wage-increases can be inflationary," Conroy told Humphrey Mitchell in late May. "[The] union proposals merely call for maintained purchasing power, plus a moderate compensation for increased living costs due to price-increases already permitted."[199] At the same time, Mosher, Conroy, and Millard struggled to contain communist influences in the UE, Mine Mill, and IWA. Despite the recent spy allegations of Igor Gouzenko, the appointment of the Royal Commission into Espionage, and considerable discussion in CCL executive meetings about suspending communist affiliates, left-wing labour leaders like C.S. Jackson, the outspoken, contentious UE president, still enjoyed a lot of clout. Indeed, they were the main impetus behind the CCL's national wage drive.[200] At their insistence, the CCL's annual memorandum to the federal government in April contained harsh, critical language – so much so that Conroy actually apologized to King before reading it. But to no avail. A "red-faced" Mackenzie King gave "perhaps the most terrific tongue-lashing ever given representatives of labour by a prime minister." The prime minister was so incensed by the belligerent, insulting language of the submission that he refused to have his photo taken with the CCL delegates after the meeting.[201] With the alienation of the normally even-tempered King and the solidifying of Cold War sentiments, more mainstream union officials wanted to make sure they outshone the communists in the wage battles.

What made the conduct of communists especially troublesome to more moderate CCL leaders like Mosher, Conroy, and Millard was that they had hoped the industry-wide strikes of 1946 would help spawn liberal corporatist relations where the government, capital, and labour worked together on an equal footing. "If there is going to be a foundation laid for peace," Conroy told the House Standing Committee on Industrial Relations, "the best thing to do is for each partner in industry to recognize the other at the same level to overcome the present attitude of contempt by the employer for the union and the attitude of resentment by the union for the employer."[202] Rather than limit bargaining to the level of the plant, where "Labour is still being regarded and treated as a commodity," union officials wanted to negotiate with employers on a more interdependent and cooperative basis at the level of the industry, preferably in industrial councils. Not only would workers' issues be discussed on these councils, but so would questions of production and sales. It was a utopian vision that, in many ways, echoed the themes of organic unity or organizational pluralism that Mackenzie King had written about in *Industry and Humanity* decades earlier. As Charlie Millard explained: "[I]t seems to me that if the employers in the industry sit in with us on the council where the public is represented as well that the relationship would be so strong that there would be no more fear or suspicion on either side, that collective bargaining would achieve its successful end there and would not need to go beyond there."[203] But all the talk about industrial councils fell upon deaf ears. "It is difficult to see," argued H.G. Hilton, the Stelco president, "[how] such a committee is necessary or even likely to further these admittedly desirable ends to any extent." [204]

What the business community cared about was the here and now, not some noble ideal that smacked of socialism. And the here and now was the wave of wage strikes. With capital expenditures up by more than 30 per cent thanks to double depreciation allowances and rumours circulating that frustrated foreign buyers were cancelling contracts with Canadian firms, most employers were livid about the work stoppages.[205] "Instead of a year of progress," the *Globe and Mail* reported, "reconversion has been delayed and production retarded."[206] What made the strikes particularly unconscionable was, in the words of one CMA officer, "the continued attitude of the Government in refusing to or failing to invoke the law against trade unions."[207] Technically, under PC 9384, labour organizations were not allowed to challenge the wage decisions of the NWLB; wage strikes were illegal. As A.H. Brown of the Department of Labour admitted, however, "the Government has not considered it advisable to initiate prosecution against union leaders for illegal strikes."[208] Preferring to leave enforcement to local officials and worried about inciting a mass protest, Ottawa chose to overlook these transgressions. In the minds of most employers, this attitude was an egregious double standard. Although the government had forced companies to recognize and negotiate with unions, it was allowing labour to defy the law. After two years of relative complacency, J.S. Vanderploeg, president of Anaconda Brass, wrote to H.G. Hilton that it was time "to get up on our hind legs and make it plainly known that we are tired of being pushed around by radical minorities and weak-kneed law enforcement officers."[209]

In June 1946, the business community began to barrage the Labour Department with complaints about labour leaders and demands for policy changes. "Does the Canadian government tolerate a system," Wilson M. Southam, the newspaper baron, asked sardonically, "whereby Canadian labour ... is forced into the position of having to strike in violation of legislation for dealing with industrial disputes?"[210] Employers wanted two types of changes made to PC 1003. First, they called for the prohibition of union-sponsored strike votes during negotiations. Although the regulations already imposed extensive bans on economic action, labour leaders often tried to compensate for the loss of bargaining power with strike threats. When the IWA entered into negotiations with management consultants from the Stuart Research Service in late March, for example, 93 per cent of its membership had already indicated that it would support a strike if the parties failed to sign a contract.[211] As Wilfred Heffernan, a corporate lawyer from British Columbia, complained: "Such a tactic is holding a loaded gun over the employer's head."[212] Second, the business community insisted that the government incorporate or license unions. Convinced that ordinary rank-and-file workers were being led astray by unscrupulous, if not despotic, labour leaders, employers wanted to make the unions more accountable for their actions. If union officials initiated or supported illegal strikes, their organizations should not only be sued for damages but also have their bargaining rights revoked. "Collective bargaining will never fulfill the hopes held out for it," argued the Canadian Chamber of Commerce, "unless the increased rights accorded to organized labour are accompanied by the assumption of increased responsibilities."[213] By seeking more stringent limits on union behaviour, employers sought to "equalize" power between labour and capital – to surmount what were considered the more prejudicial aspects of PC 1003. As the CMA's British Columbia Division put it, they wanted "definite action designed to place industrial relations in Canada on a sound footing."[214]

With the strike wave nearly disabling the post-war economy, government officials were sympathetic to the corporate demands. Within the Labour Department, A.H. Brown, the fairly moderate solicitor and future chair of the governing body of the International Labour Organization, argued that there should be greater obligations and accountability for the unions.[215] Arthur MacNamara, the deputy minister of labour, also agreed that the order should go further in preventing strikes. "There are grounds for saying," he wrote to a Liberal MP from British Columbia, "that some organizations do not feel bound by the terms of the contract nor regulations if in a particular situation they consider it to their advantage to go on strike."[216] In late July 1946, shortly after the death of Tom Moore, the former TLC leader and Mackenzie King confidant who had personified old-school business unionism, Humphrey Mitchell became so frustrated with the new generation of "extremist" labour leaders calling illegal strikes that he took the unprecedented step of appealing directly to 10,000 workers at several tire plants to accept the award of a conciliator, completely bypassing the United Rubber

Workers. He also stated during the Great Lakes shipping strike that the National Employment Service would process the requests of strike-ridden companies for replacement workers.[217] His reaction was mild compared to some incensed colleagues. C.D. Howe and J.L. Ilsley, the minister of finance, wanted to send in armed troops to restore order in the big steel strike at Stelco, Dosco, and Algoma.[218]

Despite all the commiserating, however, the federal government failed to make significant changes to PC 1003. Thanks to hindsight, we now know that Conroy's deep-seated concerns about the future of the labour movement – while understandable – were largely unwarranted. A year earlier, the Liberal administration had shelved the CCL's amendments. Now, in the summer and fall of 1946, it either ignored or rebuffed the business community's recommendations. Although frustrated and angered by the strike wave, officials in Ottawa were not prepared to take one-sided action that placed labour at a serious disadvantage. They were convinced that this kind of knee-jerk reaction would only serve to undermine the collective bargaining process. In particular, demands for the incorporation of unions fell flat. "[M]aking unions legally accountable," Mitchell explained to Wilson Southam, "will only hold up matters in courts and not induce industrial peace and stability. [It] serves only to intensify antagonism."[219] Certainly government officials wanted to encourage responsible unionism. But they also believed that the unions had to participate freely in contractual relations. It would be a mistake to use the judiciary to force behaviour. "No effective means have been devised yet except in totalitarian states," Mitchell responded to another inquiry, "to keep a large body of men at work when they have made up their minds not to accept either the terms offered by the employers or the terms imposed upon them by some outside authority."[220]

Mackenzie King played a pivotal role in deflecting corporate demands and limiting government reactions. Nowhere was his steady hand more evident than when he helped to settle the national steel strike. In response to an increase in steel prices, a breakdown in negotiations, and the appointment of a hard-nosed government controller, the USW had called out workers at the three largest steel producers in the country in mid-July 1946, demanding higher wages, shorter hours, union security, and an industry-wide agreement. Most attention focused on Stelco in Hamilton, Ontario, where the company president, H.G. Hilton, claimed not to be opposed to collective bargaining but to "the policy of coercion and violation of the law which has prevailed since the C.I.O. started operations."[221] Anticipating a long strike, he had stockpiled food and supplies at least a month in advance so non-striking workers could live in the plant and avoid picket lines. Meanwhile, with the support of Hamilton's mayor and much of the city, the union laid siege to the plant, patrolling the harbour, preventing the delivery of coal shipments, and playing loud music to disrupt the sleep of workers inside.[222] Just about to embark on a lengthy trip to London and Paris, Mackenzie King was appalled when C.D. Howe, J.L. Ilsley, and even Humphrey Mitchell began talking about using the military to end the strike. Regretting the appointment of the government controller and "far from believing that the wrong is all on one side," he quickly agreed in the House of Commons when a member proposed that the Standing Committee on Industrial Relations hold a public inquiry. Rather than "attempt force," the prime minister reminded colleagues, "[It is] better [to] apply reason at every turn and bring recalcitrant people before a parliamentary committee."[223] He left for Europe feeling fairly confident that the House Committee investigation would help to revive negotiations between the workers and management, not to mention pre-empt more thoughtless reactions in the cabinet.

When King returned to Ottawa several weeks later, he learned that a month of presentations to the Standing Committee on Industrial Relations, including Pat Conroy's eloquent testimony, had done little to end the conflict. What's more, C.D. Howe along with George Drew, the imposing Ontario premier, still wanted to come down hard on the strikers, while Humphrey Mitchell, exhausted and suffering from nose bleeds, hoped only to escape to England for a holiday.[224] About to begin revisions on *Industry and Humanity* for re-publication, the prime minister took charge, confident that he could use his well-honed conciliation skills to, as he wrote in his 1918 book, "make self-evident wherein interests are common and not opposed."[225] On 5 September 1946, he met with a strike committee and learned that the union leadership wanted to end the walkout, but felt it necessary to match a sixteen cent an hour increase won by the communist-led IWA in British Columbia.[226] Throughout the month, King tried to convince the USW to settle for less, while he repeatedly muzzled C.D. Howe and his "rough arbitrary methods." When the stalemate persisted, he eventually made arrangements for the government to recommend compulsory arbitration. Although ostensibly "to put both parties on the spot," King was well aware that, unlike the union, neither Howe nor the companies wanted binding arbitration. He also knew that the union, thanks to his powers of persuasion and a dwindling strike fund, was finally willing to settle for less money.[227] In early October, the two sides reached an agreement, and the workers ended their long strike at the three mills. Although the wage increase fell well short of initial demands, the USW won an agreement at Stelco and some semblance of industry-wide union security. Steel executives, on the other hand, believed that they had not only managed to dampen wage demands, but also to hold firm on more extensive union security provisions like compulsory check-offs.[228] With both sides relatively satisfied, the prime minister must have been delighted with the result. To borrow again from *Industry and Humanity*, he had once again shown iron-fisted colleagues that "[t]here is a power superior even to Force, and that is Reason."[229]

There was only one exception to the federal government's labour policy inertia. In late August 1946, the King cabinet created PC 3689, which allowed Humphrey Mitchell "at the request of either party or if he deems fit" to order a strike vote before or during a strike.[230] Why would the prime minister support the new order? One reason was that the House Committee on Industrial Relations had just recommended a government-mandated strike vote in its recent report. In the midst of a national strike wave, King knew it would be politically foolish to ignore the suggestion. But PC 3689 also fell in line with his particular approach to labour policy. Instead of using force to settle strikes, the order tried to check the "irresponsible" behaviour of labour leaders who might be leading hapless members astray. It helped to defuse militancy and encourage collective bargaining without impugning the government's "impartial" role in industrial relations. Not surprisingly, the labour movement strenuously disagreed. Unions feared that Mitchell would bend to the tactical demands of employers.[231] As Emily Burnham, a Canadian Westinghouse worker, explained, a company could request a vote when it "considered the workingman's belt drawn into the last notch or at any propitious moment."[232] CCL leaders also worried that the ambiguous wording of the new labour policy made it possible for everyone from officer workers to strike breakers to cast votes. It was a legitimate concern and perhaps explains why Mitchell displayed some "gingerliness" in applying PC 3689 to the steel strike.[233] Regardless, the order was an empty vessel. Strike votes had long proven ineffective in deterring walkouts. During the war, 85 per cent of the workers casting ballots had supported strikes in compulsory votes. The government-mandated strike votes actually strengthened the bargaining positions of the unions.[234] Perhaps by design, PC 3689 was ineffectual. It amounted to little more than a token gesture on the part of the government.

Recognizing the limits of the new order, members of the CMA's Industrial Relations Committee debated whether to push for a cooling-off period after a government strike vote. They supported the "principle" of PC 3689, but believed "that in most cases strike votes do not represent the views of the majority of the employees."[235] In the end, the committee opted against a government representation, no doubt aware of its minimal influence on labour policy. Certainly, by the fall of 1946, the business community had learned that when it came to industrial relations it lacked the muscle to bully government officials. The King cabinet's tepid response to the massive strike wave was a severe disappointment. "Whether we realize it or not," the *Financial Times* admitted, "this is a most serious and morale-killing state of affairs."[236] Still, with the shape and direction of the post-war order at stake, many employers refused to succumb to fatalism. Uncertain of their managerial prerogatives and fearful of lengthy production interruptions, they began to refocus their attention on both labour policy and industrial relations. Resigned to the inevitability of unionism, most were willing to work within the new collective bargaining system – to call for policy reforms. But there were also more reactionary employers who agreed with William Southam that "[t]he labour situation in Canada ... needs a complete overhaul if justice is to be done."[237] Either way, the business community realized that it needed to do a better job of limiting union power and influencing collective bargaining outcomes. During the next two years, as the government worked towards replacing PC 1003 with a peacetime policy, employer groups would redouble their efforts to define the rules and regulations for post-war industrial relations.

The Middle of the Road

In the late afternoon of 6 April 1948, Humphrey Mitchell rose from his seat in the House of Commons and began to introduce Bill 195 as the peacetime replacement for PC 1003. The fifty-three-year-old labour minister cut a fine figure as he addressed the speaker of the House to his left and members of the opposing parties across the aisle. Tall and burly with the broad shoulders of a former competitive swimmer and a "determined looking British jaw," Mitchell projected the confident bearing of someone who had accomplished a great deal since becoming an apprentice electrician at the age of fourteen in England.[238] Perhaps his most impressive achievement was to retain his post as labour minister for several years. Although like-minded when it came to labour policy, King had nearly replaced Mitchell on more than one occasion because he made poor decisions, kowtowed to C.D. Howe, and infuriated the labour movement.[239] It was a tribute to Mitchell's work ethic and resolve that he managed to weather these storms. It also didn't hurt that he had a cheery, affable disposition. As a newspaper columnist wrote, his "geniality in the House often served to blunt what have been sharper thrusts at his department from opponents."[240] Still, even Mitchell's gregariousness couldn't compensate for mediocre oratory skills. An extensive reader and world traveller, Mitchell was, according to one friend, "brilliance personified" in private discussions. But "his formal utterances were dull and ofttimes involved." Or, as the prime minister put it: "Mitchell is always a little vague in the way he speaks."[241] Given this deficiency, it seems likely that the labour minister was well coached by King for his presentation on Bill 195. Looking out over his glasses at colleagues in the House of Commons, he offered an unusually eloquent explanation for the underlying principles of the proposed bill, capturing not only the uniqueness but also the constancy of Canadian labour policy since the turn of the century:

> I believe that when you swing too far to the left at one time you are bound to swing to the right the next time ... [T]o maintain stable labour relations it is far better to go down the middle of the road and to be as fair as humanly possible both to the employer and employee organizations ... My hon. friend the member for Winnipeg North Centre ... is smiling, but he knows what happened in the country to the south of us when the Wagner Act was put on the statute books. Some people thought that it swung too far to the left. They now have the Taft-Hartley law which, in the opinion of some people, is causing a great deal of industrial strife in the United States ... [I]f we in this dominion travel down the middle of the road, take the moderate course in the establishment and maintenance of labour relations, we shall be making a great contribution to the life of our time.[242]

It had been a long, arduous process to convert PC 1003 into Bill 195. Fearing a return "to the horse-and-buggy age" of the 1930s, CCL leaders had begun to push for a national labour code to take the place of the order as soon as the war ended in mid-1945.[243] They were acutely aware that the King cabinet would soon lose its extraordinary wartime authority; all remaining orders in council would expire; the House of

Commons would once again become the centre for legislative activity; and the provinces would regain jurisdiction over property and civil rights laws. If Ottawa failed to pass new legislation that incorporated the compulsory recognition and bargaining features of PC 1003, it would be left with the largely ineffective Industrial Disputes and Investigation Act (IDIA) of 1907 on its statute books. Unless the government took action to amend the constitution or to create some kind of special arrangement to increase its peacetime jurisdiction over industrial relations, labour and management would once again be subject to a plethora of uneven provincial labour laws. As Pat Conroy explained in a letter to affiliates in the late summer of 1945: "It is essential ... that to guide and stabilize Labour relationships in the years ahead and to stimulate a national consciousness among our people, *Labour must have a permanent Federal Labour Code enacted into law*" (emphasis in the original). To avoid legislative chaos, he urged all CCL unions to make the strongest possible representations for a national labour law to provincial governments. It was "political action of the most important kind."[244]

Despite all the entreaties, the federal government failed to discuss a peacetime labour code until a year later in 1946. Given the post-war imperatives of heightened productivity and low unemployment, DOL officials focused instead on implementing Ottawa's broader reconstruction program. But they did recognize that stable labour relations was one of the keys to economic prosperity and, in late 1945, convinced the provinces to agree to an extension of PC 1003 until 31 March 1947 as part of the larger National Emergency Transitional Powers Act.[245] The DOL also continued to extol the virtues of the compulsory collective bargaining policy. To be sure, when the number of working days lost to strikes began to climb from 1.1 per 1,000 in 1945 to 5 per 1,000 in 1946, some high-ranking people within the DOL, like Solicitor A.H. Brown, grumbled about the need for corrective measures.[246] Under the watchful eye of Mackenzie King, however, most of the staff considered it far wiser to stand by the wartime labour regulations and enhance the process or function of negotiation, not to modify the rights and responsibilities of unions and employers. Certainly DOL officials were well aware that the provinces would expect to resume their jurisdictions over industrial relations when PC 1003 expired. Short of an amendment to the BNA Act, they did worry that a national labour code in peacetime would only cover a handful of Canadian industries.[247]

It was the escalating strike rate that helped to refocus attention on a peacetime labour code. In September 1946, both the House Committee on

Industrial Relations and George Drew, the Ontario premier, demanded an inquiry to secure permanent legislation that would prevent further strife.[248] Almost immediately, the DOL organized a conference of federal and provincial labour officials for 15 October to discuss a hastily drawn-up proposal. It involved a mix of old and new ideas. Initially, officials had planned to create a whole different bill and toss out the IDIA. Out of deference to the prime minister, however, they decided to affix the substantive provisions of PC 1003 and PC 4020, which had established Industrial Dispute Inquiry Commissions during the war, to the IDIA.[249] "Naturally," as "the author of the I.D.I. Act," King was delighted to have his policy legacy remain intact.[250] The DOL also hoped to interest the provinces in an innovative administrative arrangement. Although well aware that the labour movement, some business groups, and the general public wanted a national labour code that covered all industries, the federal government realized that it lacked the leverage to win a constitutional amendment. Just a few weeks earlier, the Dominion-Provincial Conference on Reconstruction had revealed how several provinces were adamantly opposed to surrendering their policymaking powers to Ottawa.[251] As a compromise, the DOL proposed that it cover larger industries like steel, mining, and meatpacking, which operated on a national basis, in addition to its normal slate of interprovincial industries like shipping, railways, and communications. All other industries would remain under provincial jurisdiction. For the sake of uniformity, the Dominion would also encourage the provinces to include provisions from the new federal labour policy in their own labour laws. The new peacetime code would serve as a model statute for the provincial legislatures.[252]

Everyone knew that the compromise proposal would be a hard sell. As historians Robert Bothwell, Ian Drummond, and John English describe, the provincial premiers were like "sleeping dogs" who were "yawning and stretching" after several years of somnolence under the War Measures Act.[253] Eager to reassert their jurisdictional authority, few were in the mood to act conciliatory or make concessions. At an early meeting of the Dominion-Provincial Conference on Reconstruction, for example, George Drew of Ontario gave "a blustering and even at times truculent speech" about refusing to cede ground to Ottawa.[254] Much like with Mitchell Hepburn ten years earlier, recently re-elected Maurice Duplessis of Quebec joined Drew in the fight to defend provincial rights, openly questioning whether Canada was moving towards fascism. Even Liberal premiers like Angus Macdonald of Nova Scotia, a former cabinet minister, expressed deep reservations about Ottawa's centralist post-war planning.[255] These jurisdictional enmities flowed over into talks about labour policy. Duplessis did not want the federal government interfering with Quebec's Labour Relations Act, which, as Madeline Parent and Kent Rowley of the Textile Workers had discovered first-hand, was an effective weapon against unionism.[256] With an abundance of natural resource and manufacturing industries, the provinces of Ontario and British Columbia also wanted to retain control of their labour policies. As Drew insisted, "Ontario has the best, the fairest, and the most workable labor legislation in Canada."[257] Given these forceful sentiments, it seemed evident that acrimony, not productivity, was going to prevail at the labour policy conference.

On 15 October 1946, the labour ministers of all the provinces except Prince Edward Island met around a rectangle of tables with Mitchell, MacNamara, and other DOL officials in the Railway Committee Room of the House Commons. The stark, cold chamber, which lacked eye-level windows, set the tone for the frank, intensely focused discussions of the three-day in camera or closed session conference. The talks went as well as could be expected. On the first day, after Mitchell welcomed everyone with an emphatic statement about the importance of stable labour relations, MacNamara read the federal government's proposal for a national labour code, which included several possible amendments to PC 1003. Hoping to leave the conference with some kind of agreement, but also unwilling to cede authority, most of the provincial labour ministers immediately balked at the idea of Ottawa encroaching on their jurisdictions. They reminded the federal officials that industrial disputes usually involved circumstances specific to a province and required responses that reflected regional differences. Although Mitchell tried to explain that his only objective was "to have an Act of Parliament … that might be called a model," the participants spent the rest of the afternoon debating the sanctity of the constitution or British North America (BNA) Act. That evening, at a country club dinner, Mackenzie King spoke about the continued significance of the IDIA and seemed to ease the tension. It was clear, though, that the DOL's request for jurisdiction over larger interprovincial industries had fallen flat. "Given that," Lachlan Currie of Nova Scotia, a former coal miner, stated bluntly, "let's face the facts and endeavour to work as uniform a policy as possible across the country."[258]

For the next two days, federal officials focused on winning support for minor changes to PC 1003. The discussions remained cordial, though at one point Mitchell and C.C. Williams of Saskatchewan had to go off record to resolve an argument about union security provisions. Some of the DOL's suggestions, like lowering the percentage of votes for representation elections or increasing the application of government-supervised strike votes, reflected the more moderate demands of the labour movement and the business community. Other proposals, like freezing the terms and conditions of employment during negotiations for contract renewals or bestowing more legitimacy on plant committees, were government inspired. On the whole, the DOL recommendations were efforts to improve the operation of the collective bargaining machinery, not to modify rights and responsibilities. But the provincial representatives had different agendas and approaches. Although federal officials hoped that the provinces would adopt their modifications "and in this way provide a pattern which might bring about uniformity throughout Canada," they often found themselves caught between the Charybdis of more progressive provinces like Saskatchewan and the Scylla of more reactionary provinces like Quebec. According to one journalist, the DOL officials only succeeded in "holding a mouse by the tail."[259] Still, there was a positive outcome: everyone seemed to agree that the innovative, two-pronged approach of PC 1003, which combined the compulsory recognition and bargaining of unions with the compulsory conciliation of disputes and stoppages, offered the best framework for their provincial policies.[260]

Following the conference, an exhausted Mitchell left on a doctor-recommended holiday to the West Indies, leaving his staff to piece together a draft bill that reconciled the various viewpoints of the provinces.[261] In December, the DOL sent out a version to the labour movement and the business community for comments.[262] Some union leaders responded favourably. Given that conservative forces in the United States were busy revising the Wagner Act, one labour commentator wrote: "There is no evidence that the draftsmen have been carried away by the anti-labour hysteria of the new American Congress."[263] Percy Bengough's first reaction was that "in the main it is very good."[264] Although the TLC president would have preferred wider coverage, he also recognized that there were severe constitutional restrictions on the Dominion's authority. Upon closer study of the bill's eighty-eight clauses, the TLC did end up calling for some changes. To avoid excessive legalism, for example, it wanted a provision that limited the role of lawyers, especially corporate lawyers, in labour board hearings. When the government accommodated most of these demands, the TLC threw its full support behind the draft bill.[265] Both the railway brotherhoods and the CTCC, which appreciated the decentralized nature of the draft, soon followed suit.[266]

In contrast, the CCL denounced the DOL's initial effort to draft peacetime labour legislation. The congress had two main criticisms. First, CCL leaders decried the federal government's acquiescence to the jurisdictional demands of the provinces. They wanted a centralized labour code that not only kept the door open to multi-employer bargaining in nationally designated industries, but also allowed them to avoid less developed, if not repressive, labour laws in some provinces.[267] As far as they were concerned, the BNA Act was only an obstacle; it could be surmounted. There should not be "ten ways to solve one problem," Pat Conroy hammered home in a radio broadcast. "Constitutional difficulties are nominal in the sense that they are man-made, and can be removed when there is a will and a desire to do so."[268] Drawing on a recent J.L. Cohen article in *Saturday Night*, the congress pointed out how the British Privy Council had just decided in *A.G. Ontario v. Canada Temperance Federation* that the federal government did not need a national emergency to make laws for the peace and order of the country. Although, in reality, the decision was a constitutional anomaly, the congress felt it paved the way for the enactment of a national labour code.[269] Second, the CCL leaders protested how the draft bill "disregards entirely many important recommendations made by the Congress to the Department of Labour in the form of amendments to ... PC 1003, more than two years ago" or, in other words, the Cohen submission.[270] They called for the inclusion of more effective enforcement methods, penalties for lack of good faith bargaining, more inclusive grievance arbitration, far greater restrictions on non-union plant committees, and some semblance of union security, especially given the recent development of the Rand formula. But their efforts to extend the collective rights of workers and unions went nowhere. Unwilling to give labour what it considered to be an undue advantage over management, the federal government refused to take into account the CCL's demands. In March 1947, Conroy recognized that "the prospects are not too good that we shall get" a substantive national labour code and began encouraging provincial labour bodies to lobby their respective governments for favourable laws. The final outcome will probably be "a skeleton code," he explained. "We want to strengthen the provincial codes to the greatest extent possible."[271]

Employer groups fared little better. Since the draft bill equated plant committees and trade unions, the CMA actually considered it "a little more favourable to employers than PC 1003."[272] As the organization's legal counsel pointed out: "It has been quite difficult to show that the company dominates any employees' association."[273] This statement did not mean, however, that the business community supported the proposed legislation. Some employers whose companies operated in more than one province had actually hoped the federal government would assume more responsibility for labour policy in the post-war years. Not only did they find it confusing and costly to deal with several different labour laws, but they also wanted a more moderate federal code to supersede burdensome legislation like the Saskatchewan Trade Union Act.[274] As the Canadian Chamber of Commerce declared, many employers also deplored the "lack of balance between the rights and responsibilities of employees and employers respectively."[275] The chamber ended up working closely with the CMA to draw up new recommendations.[276] Indeed, the federal government's draft bill seemed to spark an unprecedented level of corporate lobbying. No doubt inspired by the successful efforts of the Republican Congress in the United States to revise the Wagner Act, a large number of companies made either direct representations to government officials or indirect appeals through their business associations for greater freedom of speech, stronger enforcement of individual rights, bans on mass picketing and secondary boycotts, tighter certification procedures, and, most of all, union liability.[277] "It should be made clear," the CMA emphasized, "that the principle of equality before the law really requires that trade unions should be made legally responsible through incorporation."[278] Given "the serious strikes of 1946," a hardware store magnate informed Humphrey Mitchell, "it is hard to see why unions should not be ... subject to suits for damages ... In a word, why unions should not be made as responsible as management is."[279] Although DOL officials considered suggestions that emphasized industrial peace to be "a pretty constructive approach," they once again ignored corporate demands to "equalize" rights and responsibilities. Given their long-time commitment to what they considered "middle of the road" policymaking, like the IDIA or PC 1003, they believed their draft bill offered the best prospect for industrial stability and economic prosperity.

Ongoing events south of the Canadian border confirmed how important it was to avoid extremes or take sides. Mackenzie King and the Liberal administration had long believed that the more pro-union slant of the Wagner Act would result in a reactionary backlash and industrial turmoil. For Canadian policymakers, the US labour law served as a shining example of what not to do. "God save us from the Wagner Act," proclaimed Mitchell.[280] What Mackenzie King especially disliked was how the US government often resorted to heavy-handed methods to try and restore the industrial order. In November 1946, for example, he couldn't believe it when the White House used a court injunction to try and coerce John L. Lewis and the United Mine Workers, heavily criticizing the Truman administration for making "a bad mess of things."[281] Canadian officials also felt that the Taft-Hartley Act of June 1947, which limited the right to strike, allowed the states to forbid union security arrangements, and forced union officers to sign anti-communist affidavits, needlessly raised the ire of the labour movement and threatened the industrial order. With some degree of smugness, they pointed out that this "corrective" legislation might have been avoided if policymakers had taken a more balanced and equitable approach to drafting the Wagner Act in 1935.[282] As W. Elliott Wilson, the deputy minister of labour for Manitoba, later told a conference of personnel administrators, Canada had no need to pass a Taft-Hartley–like act because "it has not gone to extremes. The pendulum has not swung so far in either direction."[283]

The prime minister was quite happy with the peacetime replacement for PC 1003. "What has happened in the United States," Mackenzie King observed, "has given our Bill more significance."[284] Due to delays in the policymaking process at both the federal and provincial levels of government, however, Humphrey Mitchell failed to submit the proposed legislation, which at that time was called Bill 338, to the House of Commons until 17 June 1947. Indeed, in the spring, he was forced to ask Parliament for another indefinite extension of PC 1003.[285] When the labour minister finally introduced Bill 338, he conveyed his hopes that the federal statute would act as a blueprint for the provinces. He stressed that Canada would not achieve lasting industrial peace and heightened productivity if there was widely varying labour legislation in the country. Mitchell also acknowledged that the government had paid scant attention to the more skewed representations of business and labour. "The essential purpose of the legislation," he asserted, "is to create the conditions favourable to the free exercise of the collective bargaining function ... [It] will fail in its fundamental objective if it introduces features of a punitive and coercive character which could only result in driving employers and employees further apart."[286] Bill 338 made it through a first and second reading in the House of Commons. But the measure bogged down in the hearings of the Standing

Committee on Industrial Relations – mainly due to the vociferous opposition of the CCL unions. Labour leaders, like Pat Conroy, voiced objections to several clauses in the bill. They criticized the section on unfair labour practices as too narrow and the section on the revocation of certification as too inviting to employers. But the bigger problem remained the limited coverage of the proposed labour law.[287] Equating the lack of uniformity in labour laws to the geopolitical mess of many years earlier in Southeastern Europe, Eugene Forsey, the CCL's research director, commented: "The present situation is one of Balkan chaos."[288] On 8 July, with the parliamentary session about to end, the committee recommended that the government introduce a similar bill early in the next session.[289] Hoping to be relieved of their duties, the current members of the WLRB seemed to express the most disappointment at the delay.[290]

The next year was one of troubled closure for Mackenzie King. Although he made arrangements with Louis St Laurent to become the new party leader at the next Liberal convention in August 1948, he found it challenging to relinquish control after so many years as the head of the government. Rationally, the prime minister understood that it was time to step down. If nothing else, his health needed to recover from the trials and tribulations of the war effort. A year earlier, he had fallen very ill while on holiday in Virginia Beach, Virginia.[291] He also found himself forgetting names and events. Emotionally, though, it was tough for the prime minister to let go, especially when the spectres of Franklin Roosevelt and Wilfrid Laurier visited him in spiritualist sittings and urged him "to continue in public life."[292] What helped ease the transition was when, in March 1948, the leaders of the main labour organizations offered an array of flattering, appreciative comments about his many contributions to industrial relations in their annual representations to the government. Legacy was important to King. Convinced that his grandfather, William Lyon Mackenzie, had never received proper credit for his reform efforts, the prime minister wanted future generations of Canadians to recognize and value his own "life's record of service." At each meeting, the labour leaders spoke highly of the prime minister, thanking him for everything he had done on behalf of their organizations and Canadian industrial relations as a whole. Despite the acrimonious conference of two years earlier, even the CCL leaders expressed "the kindest of feelings." King wrote that when he rose to respond to the accolades, "I found my own voice wavered just a bit." He "wished the world" could witness what wonderful "relations of gov't and Labour, good-will and co-operation there [were in Canada]." As he told the CCL delegates, he realized that the meetings were "rounding out ... the circle of [his] life's interests." "I had gone into politics," he said, "not because of politics, but because I was interested in labour questions." Clearly, it was a turning point for King. Later that evening, he reflected: "I went perhaps further in speaking about getting out of active politics than I have at any time up to the present."[293]

A month later, in April 1948, Humphrey Mitchell submitted Bill 195 to the House of Commons for its first reading with his "middle of the road" speech. "The provisions of the bill," he added, "are almost identical with those of Bill No. 338."[294] Once again, employer groups objected to the limited responsibilities bestowed on the unions, demanding the inclusion of corrective clauses. As Sharman Learie of the Niagara Industrial Relations Institute wrote to Mitchell: "[I]t was unwise to have granted [compulsory collective bargaining] without establishing requirements that the privilege be met with responsibility."[295] And the CCL continued to protest the decentralization of labour policy.[296] In early 1948, the congress had actually begun to present its own "National Labour Code" to the provincial governments to try and ratchet up support for industry-wide bargaining.[297] CCL representatives used a national strike of 14,000 meatpackers in the fall of 1947 to argue how difficult, if not absurd, it was to try and resolve a dispute that stretched across several provincial jurisdictions. To avoid utter confusion, Conroy had found himself wiring eight different premiers to arrange for the involvement of just one conciliator, not several.[298] If Bill 195 became law, G.S. Borgford, the CCL's regional director in Manitoba, worried, "we might have nine decisions on one struggle."[299] The provincial lobbying was a somewhat desperate action. The CCL owed a large overdraft and had begun to lay off organizers.[300] It needed to develop equitable wage standards across the country to reverse its fortunes. Several provinces, however, still disliked the idea of jurisdictional changes. George Drew, the imperious premier of Ontario, actually cut short his meeting with CCL delegates, accusing them of misrepresenting the "true feelings" of workers.[301]

The Industrial Relations Committee considered Bill 195 during the month of May, limiting outside representations to expedite the process. The responsibility for effective policymaking weighed heavily on the members. Just recently, the government in Prince Edward Island had passed an extremely draconian labour law. Although the provincial statute affected only a small number of workers, it demonstrated how, in the words of David Croll, the MP for Spadina in Toronto, the country was in "need of a national labour code to give guidance and to offset such ill-advise [*sic*] and retrograde legislation."[302] For the most part, the committee accepted Bill 195 in its entirety. On 17 June, when it reported back to the House, the one big change was the addition of a voluntary check-off clause. Dead set against the inclusion of a union security provision, however, Humphrey Mitchell carefully orchestrated its removal during the third reading in the House. Although employers had mounted a campaign to defeat the provision, the ubiquitous principles of Mackenzie King mainly explain the deletion.[303] Making overt references to the Taft-Hartley Act in the United States, Mitchell insisted that union security clauses interfered with the process of collective bargaining and deviated from the historical course of labour policy in Canada. "This bill is supposed to go down the middle of the road," he argued in the House. Swing "the pendulum" too far in the direction of labour and "you may get a government which swings much farther to the right, and which will take away from the labour organizations conditions which have existed for a good many years. That is why I say that the soundest approach to this problem is through negotiation."[304] Later that day, Bill 195 became the Industrial Relations and Disputes Investigation Act (IRDIA). The new statute came into effect on 1 September. Order in Council PC 1003, the path-breaking compulsory collective bargaining law, expired.[305]

The new federal labour code built upon the basic principles of PC 1003. It still compelled an employer to recognize and negotiate with a union that represented a majority of the workers. It continued to provide the conciliatory machinery for the settlement of industrial disputes. It kept in place strike restrictions or a "cooling-off period" until a conciliation officer tried to reconcile the two sides or a conciliation board submitted a report to the labour minister. Although the IRDIA created a Canada Labour Relations Board (CLRB) to replace the Wartime Labour Relations Board, the administrative machinery retained the representative precept of four labour members, four employer members, and a neutral chair. And the federal law still allowed the CLRB to certify unions on the basis of documentary evidence. The IRDIA also contained several new features that benefited the labour movement.[306] Unlike PC 1003, the new statute

- certified unions, not individuals, as bargaining agents;
- reduced the fourteen-day strike prohibition or "cooling-off" period that followed the report of a conciliation board to seven days;
- allowed the CLRB to invalidate any contract that involved an employer-dominated organization;

- gave the CLRB the power to investigate and remedy allegations of inferior bargaining practices;
- placed more restrictions on the freedom of speech of employers during the certification process;
- gave the courts the authority to force a company to pay compensation for lost wages if it was found guilty of dismissing a worker for union activities; and
- did not require union members to sign anti-communist affidavits.[307]

As Maurice Wright, the CCL legal counsel, wrote to Eugene Forsey: "The fact is that ... the new legislation does give some additional rights to labour."[308]

Employers offered halfhearted responses to the IRDIA. Although Ottawa ignored all sixteen of the CMA's recommendations for the IRDIA, E.R. Complin, the chair of the Industrial Relations Committee and former member of the WLRB, acknowledged that "it could have been worse."[309] Similarly, J.T. Stirrett, the CMA's general manager, counselled that, with just one exception, the IRDIA "should be given a fair trial before any changes are considered."[310] The exception was the lack of an anti-communist clause. Notwithstanding ideological questions about classless societies, employers had always found it difficult to deal with unyielding communist labour leaders. As the head of a small woodworking company put it, communists "regard relations between employees and management as a fight and not a co-operative venture ... [I]t is their intention ... to keep the pot boiling."[311] Fully agreeing with the CMA, the Canadian Chamber of Commerce called for an amendment to the IRDIA that disallowed coverage for any union that is "officered, dominated or controlled by Communists."[312] The recent staging of the Berlin blockade, the discovery of Soviet spies in Canada, and the public confession of Pat Sullivan, the TLC's secretary-treasurer, that he had "travelled with the Communist party," fuelled the corporate concerns about communist-led unions. Ignoring the law, Canada Steamship Lines actually voided an existing contract with the communist-led Canadian Seamen's Union and signed a new agreement with the more amenable Canadian Lake Seamen's Union.[313] Aside from this one problem and some empty rhetoric about union responsibilities, however, the business community generally accepted the IRDIA. In fact, the new labour code pushed employers to pay more attention to industrial relations. At conferences and in trade journals, the employment relationship became a major topic of discussion. Some employers hoped to learn new strategies for avoiding or weakening unions, but others realized that conditions had changed and they needed to embrace "a new management philosophy." For the sake of industrial stability and continuous production, they had to move forward and redefine their relationship with their employees. "It is management's *intent* that counts," lectured R.F. Hinton of Shell Oil Canada. "What are they out for? All they can get away with, or do they really care about the interests of their workers?"[314]

Despite the "additional rights" in the IRDIA, labour leaders proved much more vociferous in their objections. Even the normally benign TLC found it lacking. As Percy Bengough warned: "We can accept Bill 195 as worth a trial, subject to improvements by amendments."[315] What the TLC found particularly troubling about the new statute was that lawyers were still allowed to sit on conciliation boards. "In our opinion, lawyers are not so much interested in working out a solution to a labour dispute," Ford Brand of the Toronto District Labour Council wrote to Mackenzie King, "as they are in building up a case with all its legal aspects and interpretations."[316] The CCL leaders, mired in battles with communist affiliates, angrily denounced the new labour law because Ottawa had ignored their recommendations for amendments. Besides the absence of union security provisions, they condemned how the IRDIA made it much easier for legitimate employee associations to become certified; prohibited a union from holding a strike vote during conciliation proceedings; required paid-up membership dues, not signed authorization cards, as proof of majority representation; allowed the CLRB to mandate secret ballot elections for certification; still required a union to win over 50 per cent of workers eligible to vote, not a majority of workers who actually voted, in secret ballot elections; and gave the CLRB the authority to revoke certification when satisfied that a union had lost its majority. Most of all, the CCL denounced how "the Government simply handed back jurisdiction to the provinces, with the result that Labour legislation differs widely from one province to another."[317]

This last point resonated with many industrial relations experts. Stuart Jamieson, a sociology professor at the University of British Columbia and future author of the first English-language book to offer a general overview of Canadian industrial relations, wrote in 1951: "One of the greatest setbacks to trade unionism and collective bargaining in this country during the post-war period has been the failure to develop a national labour policy to replace that established by the Dominion

Government during the war."[318] By the early 1950s, most of the provinces, besides Saskatchewan and Quebec, did create labour laws that incorporated basic features of the IRDIA. But these policies varied widely, reflecting different political agendas and economic realities. Areas of divergence included enforcement, company unions, unfair labour practices, strike restrictions, mass picketing, and conciliation proceedings. With the addition of Newfoundland as a province in 1949, labour leaders now had to contend with ten provincial labour laws as well as the federal law, making industry-wide bargaining next to impossible. They also discovered that conservative provincial governments were not as concerned with balance and impartiality as Mackenzie King had been. Several legislatures imposed additional constraints on the rights of unions without prescribing similar limitations for employers. In British Columbia, for example, the labour board could order a vote of the workers on any settlement offer made by an employer during a strike and decertify any union that conducted an illegal strike. In Alberta, where a huge coal strike took place in early 1948, union organizers could not communicate with workers on company property without permission, and judges could rule contracts null and void if they involved illegal strikes.[319] As the British Columbia Federation of Labour protested in February 1952, the provincial government and the Labour Relations Board repeatedly ignored "the hard-won rights and established practices of the trade union movement."[320]

Compared to policy developments in the United States, however, the myriad of labour laws in the post-war period did reflect a uniquely Canadian approach to regulating industrial relations – an approach that built on the enduring, jealously guarded principles of Mackenzie King. Similar to PC 1003 and the IRDIA, most of the provincial policies embraced a two-stage system of certification and conciliation. As a whole, policymakers in the different provinces agreed that it was not enough to compel union recognition and collective bargaining. There also needed to be a compulsory procedure for resolving impasses and preventing conflicts. Despite a long history of mixed results, the provinces continued to believe that third party intervention or conciliation contributed to the ultimate goal of industrial stability.[321] As King had written long ago in *Industry and Humanity*: "[I]nvestigation prior to the lockout or strike marks the beginning of the introduction of Law and Order into Industry ... Private rights cease when they become public wrongs."[322] Like the federal government, the provincial policymakers also emphasized process and function, not rights. For the sake of peaceful labour relations and continuous production, their post-war laws contained rigid strike restrictions and high eligibility requirements for certification. But they also limited employer interference and supported union card certifications. Although some provincial labour policies targeted the labour movement, they generally produced more moderate and even-handed policies than the one-sided extremes of the Wagner Act or the Taft-Hartley Act in the United States.

Labour leaders enmeshed in organizational and financial difficulties failed to appreciate this difference. In the long run, however, their organizations benefited, especially when managerial opposition to unions intensified in the United States during the 1970s. This new surge of anti-unionism did sweep through Canada as well, but not to the same degree. Thanks to the wide-ranging, ripple effect of Mackenzie King's principles, Canada's less forceful approach to labour policy proved more favourable to organized labour. Certainly, the prime minister believed he had left his mark on Canadian industrial relations. In May 1949, a few weeks after relinquishing his seat in the House of Commons, he mused: "It has been a kind Providence that … has left me … with a record of which I need not be ashamed, and which has done credit to the name I bear, and above all has been of help to my fellow men. Of that I am sure when I think of the creation of the Department of Labour [and] all it has stood for, [and] what I have done for industrial … peace."[323]

Afterword

The passage of PC 1003 in 1944 created a new collective bargaining regime or legal framework for industrial relations in Canada. With fewer obstacles to union recognition and binding contracts, workers began to enjoy higher wages and benefits, improved working conditions and job security, and enhanced dignity and self-respect. A 1997 study discovered, for example, that about 80 per cent of unionized workers in Canada enjoyed extensive non-wage benefits, like pensions, compared to only 40 per cent of non-union workers.[1] As critics then and now argue, the new collective bargaining regime did contain notable limits. Although post-war labour laws encroached on managerial prerogatives, they did not significantly shift the balance of power in the workplace. In particular, the wide array of strike restrictions exemplified how policymakers approached the drafting process with preconceived notions and biases about private property and the sanctity of contracts that ultimately favoured employers. As a labour journalist recognized in 1947: "[T]here are some subtle attempts to hobble the well-organized and aggressively-led union."[2] In addition, while strikes still happened in the post-war period, the trade-off between militancy and legitimacy ensured that unions focused more on increasing material gains and maintaining production than winning greater decision-making authority for their members. Many scholars today refer to this arrangement as "Fordism."[3] And, as I experienced at Goodyear Tire in the early 1980s, it often contributed to union stagnancy and worker apathy. Canada's collective bargaining regime also excluded many workers from industrial citizenship or the right to join unions and win contracts. Reflecting and reproducing the predominant gender and racial constructs of the time, post-war labour laws targeted the higher paying mass production and natural resource industries, oblivious to the barriers to entry for women and people of colour. A segmented job market developed where many workers lacked the security and pay of union members. Still, by curtailing the arbitrary behaviour of employers, compulsory collective bargaining did greatly enlarge the ranks of the middle class. As Murray Cotterill, a wartime organizer and publicist for the Steelworkers, observed in the 1970s, collective bargaining "spread prosperity more effectively than any government plan. [It] pulled more Canadians out of the poverty bracket than all the speeches made by all the politicians."[4]

Thanks to the shape and form of Canada's collective bargaining regime, the labour movement has also proven more resilient over time than its counterpart in the United States. Of course, this is a relative statement. In recent years, Canadian unions have suffered serious setbacks with the evaporation of the manufacturing base, the proliferation of part-time workers, and the escalation of government back-to-work orders. Although the public sector maintained its unionization rate between 1997 and 2011, the private sector union density rate dropped from 21 per cent to 17 per cent. Despite this downward trajectory, however, the situation for organized labour in the United States has been far worse. South of the border, the private sector union density rate sank to less than 7 per cent in 2011, and only two states, New York and Alaska, possessed higher membership rates than Alberta, the least unionized province in Canada.[5] The sharpness and depth of the decline in the United States has prompted bloggers to debate whether a "slide of unions into nothingness" has taken place – whether the historic moment has passed for organized labour in the United States.[6]

What explains the cross-national divergence? Although analysts from the Fraser Institute, a conservative think tank, describe Canada's labour laws as "biased and prescriptive," it is actually their moderate tenor – PC 1003's legacy – that helps to explain the difference in union density rates.[7] Unlike the United States, for example, most Canadian jurisdictions allow for non-union employee representation plans. But it is also more difficult for Canadian employers to interfere in the certification process because membership card validations and expedited elections push the parties to the negotiating tables.[8] This "middle of the road" approach, which eschews rights talk for process and function, has limited attacks from reactionary forces in the judiciary, legislatures, and business community. A huge strike wave in the mid-1960s did result in the creation of expert commissions and additional powers for various administrative boards. Several provinces have made minor policy changes that encroach on the rights of workers and their unions, like the shift to mandatory certification elections from card check certifications. And, most recently, there have been well-publicized efforts to enact right-to-work and union disclosure laws. Compared to the Wagner Act in the United States, however, Canada's collective bargaining regime has not undergone significant changes – "the pendulum has not swung to the right" since the passage of PC 1003.[9]

There are other important developments besides the collective bargaining regime that influenced post-war industrial relations in Canada. Take the "Red Scare," for example. Although the communist purge in the United States was more relentless and extensive, both conservative and liberal forces in Canada worked diligently to check, if not eliminate, leftists in the labour movement.[10] It was a multifaceted effort. With Cold War tensions mounting, employers like Canadian Westinghouse and Canadair used red-baiting tactics to defeat organizing drives and terminate contracts.[11] Worried about self-image, fed up with hardline stands, and often pressured by US counterparts, more moderate labour leaders made it a priority to deal with leftists by consolidating their power over locals and removing "trouble-makers."[12] Pushed by Patrick Conroy and Norman Dowd, the executive of the Canadian Congress of Labour (CCL) used very questionable means to expel a number of communist affiliates, including Mine Mill and the United Electrical Workers, because, as the CCL's official newspaper explained, the communists were "anti-Christian, godless, materialistic, disloyal, and a menace to democracy."[13] Finally, even though political leaders like Lester Pearson, the external affairs minister, spoke out against "the black madness of witch hunts," government agencies also took steps to undermine left-leaning unionists. Besides RCMP spies infiltrating "suspicious" unions, the Labour Relations Board made the extraordinary decision in 1950 to decertify the Canadian Seamen's Union because it was dominated by communists. A few years later, in what would seem a throwback to the mid-1800s, the Combines Branch of the Justice Department decided to conduct investigations of more militant unions, like the United Fishermen, for "restraint of trade" or, in other words, picketing and slowdowns.[14] This "cleansing" proved costly to organized labour. As historian Irving Abella notes, the expunging of so many "energetic, zealous, and dedicated" activists sucked a good deal of vitality out of the mainstream labour movement and contributed to the more acquiescent and limited focus of many (though not all) union halls and offices in later years.[15] In short, PC 1003 was a significant influence on post-war industrial relations, but it was not the only significant influence.

Nor was PC 1003 inevitable. Many people sparred and quarrelled over the direction of Canadian labour policy in the 1930s and 1940s. Beneath all the legal language and protocols, the policymaking process involved real human beings with conflicting personalities and competing agendas. Everything from first-hand experiences, entrenched beliefs, and gut feelings to long-term strategies and expert judgments influenced the delay and then implementation of a compulsory collective bargaining policy. Whether the militancy of workers, the ambitions of labour leaders, the ascendancy of third parties, the burdens of wartime production, the belligerency of employers, the caution of Labour Department officials, or the intolerance of cabinet members, there were many contributing factors. For this reason, the passage of PC 1003 should not be reduced to a single set of causal forces. Rather than straightforward and predictable, the policymaking process was historically contingent and open-ended. Canadian industrial relations may have been listing in the direction of compulsory collective bargaining, especially with the passage of the Wagner Act in 1935. But nothing foreordained whether PC 1003 would happen or how it would happen. With all the interactions between the different participants and their organizations or agencies, it could have turned out much differently. What would have transpired if Justice McTague had refused to become chair of the National War Labour Board? Or if the steel workers had decided not to walk out at the three main steel mills in early 1943? Or if J.L. Cohen had not been such a vociferous voice for change? People living during the extraordinary years of the early 1940s certainly could not have predicted the passage of PC 1003. To repeat Patrick Conroy's weary words in late 1942: "We do not feel it worthwhile to raise people's hopes."[16]

Yet, even when we take all this messy causality into account, it is difficult to overlook the pivotal role that Mackenzie King played in the creation of Canada's collective bargaining regime. Part gatekeeper, part puppetmaster, and part soothsayer, he insisted that all labour policy innovations align with his well-entrenched principles or moral imperatives. There is no doubt that principles were a preoccupation with King. Consider this example. In October 1935, shortly before resuming office as prime minister and just a few months after the passage of the Wagner Act, he copied an aphorism of Ralph Waldo Emerson into his diary: "Nothing can bring you peace but the triumph of principles." Although the word "triumph" suggested impending struggles, the sentence seemed to reassure him that he would act with purpose and conviction in the years ahead. As long as he stayed true to his principles and didn't succumb to adversity or temptation, the country would be better off in the long run.[17] This diary entry was hardly an isolated incident. Informed by the religious and reformist currents of the late nineteenth and early twentieth century, the prime minister proselytized for the same set of principles all his personal and professional life. Indeed, they were the underpinnings for his particular brand of liberalism. Rather than force the pace or privilege one segment of society over another, he promoted moderation and interdependence. Unlike in the United States, where politicians emphasized individual rights, he focused on the unity and well-being of the general public. King did not develop his core principles in a vacuum; they were neither original nor his alone. Given his political longevity, righteousness, and single-mindedness, however, his convictions influenced not only the future, but also the collective identity of the country. Certainly, by insisting that PC 1003 adhere to the "middle of the road," the prime minister helped to create relatively viable, long-lasting conditions for unions in Canada.

Understanding the motives of politicians is no easy task. Most people today assume that expediency and self-interest drive politics. A 2002 poll of voters and non-voters in Canada discovered that well over half of the respondents did not believe "we can trust people in government to do what is right."[18] When it comes to sorting out the intentions of politicians, however, the most obvious explanation is not always the correct one. Political cynicism sometimes clouds our interpretations of why something actually happened. In the words of Stanley Baldwin, the British prime minister: "You will find in politics that you are much exposed to the attribution of false motive."[19] What makes it so difficult to untangle the Gordian knot of political intentions? First, the careers of politicians depend on electoral success. Ever mindful of self-image and popular appeal, they offer motives that are, in the words of psychologist David Winter, "subject to distortion, deception (including self-deception), and rationalization."[20] Second, as early twentieth-century sociologist Max Weber emphasized, politics is about "the art of compromise." Politicians do not operate in isolation, but in concert with each other. They negotiate and make concessions to resolve differences. Oftentimes, for strategic purposes or due to the realities of power, they find themselves supporting less-than-ideal policies. As a result, their actions can belie or disguise their motives. Finally, the true motives of politicians are particularly elusive when they are historical figures. It is hard enough to understand our own motives and behaviour, much less detect why someone did or did not take a certain action in the past. "[T]o enter into their inner life and character, whence all their actions originate," a German historian once observed, "presupposes so much knowledge of the human mind, so much self-denial and impartiality, requires such an expanded and detailed knowledge of the material … [that most studies] swarm with generalities and partial judgments."[21]

It is important to keep the enigmatic quality of political motives in mind when it comes to interpreting the career of Mackenzie King, especially in regards to labour policy. Ever since the mid-1950s, when Harry Ferns and Bernard Ostry offered the first critical assessment of the prime minister's life and accomplishments in their groundbreaking book, *The Age of Mackenzie King*, a long line of scholars and pundits have taken an almost Hobbesian view of his public service. Words like "self-interest," "opportunism," and "expediency" are usually employed to describe what he did or did not do. It is easy to understand why. The prime minister was a consummate politician, a pragmatist who proved willing to settle for compromise or to retreat from innovation when confronted with even the hint of opposition – an intentional strategy he referred to as "tacking and veering." King also engaged in a good deal of political manipulation to preserve, if not enhance, his power. Indeed, he had the remarkable ability to justify, even to himself, that his chicanery was morally sound. "With no trace of cynicism or deceit," notes historian Howard Gitelman, "he could transform the dross of self-interest into the finest gold of reasoned humanitarianism."[22] And let us not forget that his personality oscillated between self-absorption and obsequiousness. Few of his colleagues or staff enjoyed working with him because, as biographer Allan Levine writes, he was "a walking textbook example of an insecure passive-aggressive male."[23] Anxious about his legacy, obsessed with compliments and self-validation, and hypercritical about the perceived shortcomings of others, the prime minister's decision-making tended to revolve around his own personal and professional exigencies. Throw his spiritualist beliefs and superstitious peculiarities into the mix – what one twenty-first century reporter refers to as "his utter nuttiness" – and it is difficult not to have an overly cynical view of King's motives.[24]

Yet, a close reading of the primary sources from the late 1930s and 1940s reveals another side of the prime minister. A set of fairly fixed principles did guide, if not determine, his responses to social and political pressures – at least in regards to labour policy. Convinced that his principles provided the best framework for effective governance and the best results for the common good, he clung to them throughout the Great Depression and World War II, indirectly and directly asserting his authority over colleagues and subordinates. At all costs, he wanted to avoid insurrection, alienation, and fragmentation. Even when King finally agreed to support a compulsory collective bargaining policy, he made sure that what transpired was change within continuity. Recognizing the primacy of the prime minister's principles does not discount his presumptuousness or addiction to power. It takes a good deal of arrogance to impose your beliefs not only on a class of people but also on a whole country for such an extended period of time. There is also no denying that King worried constantly about the fate of the Liberal Party and his own political career. He enjoyed the status and clout that came with serving as prime minister, and proved extremely adept at self-preservation. By identifying and appreciating the saliency of his principles, however, we gain a more nuanced understanding of how he successfully led the country through two of the most turbulent decades of the twentieth century. Historian Louis Harlan writes: "The most important balance that a biographer can bring to [a] subject ... is the balance between sympathy and detachment." On the one hand, sympathy is needed to understand perspectives and motives. On the other hand, detachment is needed to deal with the "less savoury aspects" of a person's life. One of the goals of this book has been to add more "balance" to the historiography on Mackenzie King – to establish how his motives, just like those of everyone else, slid up and down on a continuum between idealism and self-interest.[25]

"Closing the circle" always appealed to the prime minister. As a spiritualist, he firmly believed that circles – the prominent metaphor in *Industry and Humanity* – were profound, transcendent symbols that represented unity, completion, devotion, and perpetuity. They also signified his unending commitment to principles. On the morning of 27 April 1949, when an ailing King, now in his mid-seventies, left Laurier House to attend his final meeting with the Liberal caucus, he looked forward to "closing the circle" of his life in public service. Arriving at the Railway Committee Room in the parliament buildings, his hand-picked successor, Louis St Laurent, took him by the arm and escorted him to a chair at the front as applause and table-thumping erupted around them. "I felt happier than I have felt for a long time," King later confided in his diary, "happy to be back again with 'the boys.'" St Laurent gave a short talk about the impending election and then called on his mentor to speak. After another "real, old time ovation," King took a few prepared notes out of his pocket and began thanking all the members for their support throughout his career. He told them that one of the reasons he had shown up that day was "to say a word of farewell to parliament itself" – that he would not be contesting the Glengarry seat he had held since 1945. After reminding the caucus how he had sat in nearly half of the parliamentary sessions since Confederation, he admitted that if given the opportunity to begin again, he would still choose "public life." Finally, following some discussion about the future of the Liberal Party, King once again conjured up an image of a circle, stating: "I would like to close where I began." He explained how William Gladstone's example of patient, visionary, and moral leadership had first inspired him to become involved in politics, referring to his hero as "the outstanding figure – the Liberal statesman in his day." Dwelling in particular on Gladstone's convictions and integrity, King offered a favourite quote as his parting words: "Be inspired with the belief that life is a great and noble calling. Not a mean and slovenly thing that we are to shuffle through as one can, but an elevated and lofty destiny." A somewhat sanctimonious, but sincere farewell from someone who had spent most of his life wielding power, playing politics, and trying to stay true to his principles – principles that ensured PC 1003 was no Wagner Act.[26]

Notes

Preface

1 Library and Archives Canada, *The Diaries of William Lyon Mackenzie King*, 16 August 1947, http://www.bac-lac.gc.ca/eng/discover/politics-government/prime-ministers/william-lyon-mackenzie-king/Pages/search.aspx.
2 Margaret Elizabeth Bedore, "The Reading of Mackenzie King" (PhD diss., Queen's University, 2008), 65, 194–6; Ruth Clayton Windscheffel, "Politics, Religion, and Text: W.E. Gladstone and Spiritualism," *Journal of Victorian Culture* (Spring 2006): 1–2.
3 *Diaries of William Lyon Mackenzie King*, 12 August 1900.
4 Ibid., 21 July 1939, 16 December 1939, 12 January 1944, and 14 April 1949; Allan Levine, *King: William Lyon Mackenzie King – A Life Guided by the Hand of Destiny* (Vancouver, BC: Douglas & McIntyre, 2011), 242.
5 *Diaries of William Lyon Mackenzie King*, 16 August 1947.
6 Bedore, "The Reading of Mackenzie King," 76, 115–16.
7 *Diaries of William Lyon Mackenzie King*, 12 August 1900.
8 Ibid., 16 August 1947.

Introduction

1 Joan Sangster, *Transforming Labour: Women and Work in Postwar Canada* (Toronto: University of Toronto Press, 2010), 5–6.
2 Bryan D. Palmer, *Capitalism Comes to the Back Country: The Goodyear Invasion of Napanee* (Toronto: Between the Lines, 1994), 78–89.
3 *Toronto Star*, 22 November 1986 and 12 May 1987.

4 Thomas A. Kochan, Harry C. Katz, and Robert B. McKersie, *The Transformation of American Industrial Relations* (Ithaca, NY: Cornell ILR Press, 1994), 45.
5 Nelson Lichtenstein, *State of the Union: A Century of American Labor* (Princeton, NJ: Princeton University Press, 2002), 99.
6 Richard P. Chaykowski and Anil Verma, "Adjustment and Restructuring in Canadian Industrial Relations: Challenges to the Traditional System," in *Industrial Relations in Canadian Industry*, ed. Richard P. Chaykowski and Anil Verma (Toronto: Holt, Rinehart and Winston, 1992), 21.
7 Christopher Huxley, David Kettler, and James Struthers, "Is Canada's Experience Especially Instructive?" in *Unions in Transition: Entering the Second Century*, ed. Seymour Martin Lipset (Los Angeles, CA: Institute for Contemporary Studies, 1986), 118; Joseph B. Rose and Gary N. Chaison, "Linking Union Density and Union Effectiveness: The North American Experience," *Industrial Relations* 35 (January 1996): 81.
8 See for example Seymour Martin Lipset, *Continental Divide: The Values and Institutions of the United States and Canada* (New York: Routledge, 1990).
9 John McIlroy and Richard Croucher, "The Turn to Transnational Labor History and the Study of Global Trade Unionism," *Labor History* 35, no. 5 (2013): 495.
10 Robert H. Babcock, *Gompers in Canada: A Study in American Continentalism before the First World War* (Toronto: University of Toronto Press, 1974), 36.
11 Taylor Hollander, "Making Reform Happen: The Passage of Canada's Collective-Bargaining Policy, 1943–1944," *Journal of Policy History* 13, no. 3 (2001): 299–300.
12 Michelle Brattain, "A Town as Small as That: Tallapoosa, Georgia and Operation Dixie, 1945–1950," *The Georgia Historical Quarterly* (Summer 1997): 395; Robert H. Zieger, *The CIO: 1935–1955* (Chapel Hill, NC: University of North Carolina Press, 1995), 234, 240.
13 August Meier and Elliott Rudwick, *Black Detroit and the Rise of the UAW* (Ann Arbor, MI: University of Michigan Press, 2007), 207.
14 Andrew Tillett-Saks, "Why the Labor Movement Must Join the Anti-Racist Struggle to Make Black Lives Matter," *Working In These Times* (*In These Times* blog), 6 April 2016, http://inthesetimes.com/working/entry/19038/unions-labor-black-lives-matter-anti-racist-racial-justice.
15 David Brody, "The Breakdown of Labor's Social Contract: Historical Reflections, Future Prospects," *Dissent* (Winter 1992): 35.
16 Kate Bronfenbrenner, "No Holds Barred: The Intensification of Employer Opposition to Organizing," *Economic Policy Institute Briefing Paper # 235* (20 May 2009): 2.

17 Kris Warner, "Protecting Fundamental Labor Rights: Lessons from Canada for the United States," Working Paper, Center for Economic and Policy Research (August 2012): 11, 25. http://cepr.net/documents/publications/canada-2012-08.pdf.

18 Reuel E. Schiller, "From Group Rights to Individual Liberties: Post-War Labor Law, Liberalism, and the Waning of Union Strength," *Berkeley Journal of Employment and Labor Law* 20, no. 1 (1999): 5–6.

19 Melvyn Dubofsky, *The State and Labor in Modern America* (Chapel Hill: University of North Carolina Press, 1994), 127; David Plotke, *Building a Democratic Political Order: Reshaping American Liberalism in the 1930s and 1940s* (New York: Cambridge University Press, 1996), 108–117; David Brody, "A Question of Rights," *New Labor Forum* (Fall–Winter, 1998): 131.

20 *New York Times*, 13 April 1937.

21 David Brody, "Labor Elections: Good for Workers," *Dissent* (Summer 1997): 72–4.

22 *New York Times*, 13 November 1937.

23 Dubofsky, *The State and Labor*, 146.

24 *New York Times*, 15 December 1939.

25 Dubofsky, *The State and Labor*, 201–7; Brody, "Labor Elections," 74–5.

26 Plato, *The Republic*, trans. Benjamin Jowett (New York: Modern Library, 1941), 510.

27 John M. Cammett, *Antonio Gramsci and the Origins of Italian Communism* (Palo Alto, CA: Stanford University Press, 1967), 84–5.

28 Christopher Tomlins, *The State and the Unions: Labor Relations, Law, and the Organized Labor Movement in America, 1880–1960* (New York: Cambridge University Press, 1985), 328.

29 Plotke, *Building a Democratic Political Order*, 111, 121.

30 David Brody, "Moving Past EFCA," *Labor* 7, no. 3 (2010): 27.

31 Richard W. Hurd, "Moving Beyond the Critical Synthesis: Does the Law Preclude a Future for US Unions?" *Labor History* 54, no. 2 (2013): 199; Jean-Christian Vinel, "Christopher Tomlins' *The State and the Unions* Today: What the Critical Synthesis Can Teach Us Now That the Unions Have Gone," *Labor History* 54, no. 2 (2013): 177–92.

32 Dubofsky, *State and Labor*, 220–1; National Council of State Legislatures, "Right to Work Resources," accessed 11 January, 2014, http://www.ncsl.org/research/labor-and-employment/right-to-work-laws-and-bills.aspx.

33 James A. Gross, *Broken Promises: The Subversion of U.S. Labor Relations Policy, 1947–1994* (Philadelphia, PA: Temple University Press, 1995), 285.

34 John Logan, "Permanent Replacements and the End of Labor's 'Only True Weapon,'" *International Labor and Working Class History* (Fall 2008): 175, 177.

35 David Macaray, "Union Strikes and Replacement Workers," *Counterpunch* (16 April 2008), accessed 25 November 2017, https://www.counterpunch.org/2008/04/16/union-strikes-and-replacement-workers/.
36 John Logan, "The Union Avoidance Industry in the United States," *British Journal of Industrial Relations* 44 (December 2006): 652, 655.
37 John Godard, "Labour Law and Union Recognition in Canada: A Historical-Institutionalist Perspective," *Queen's Law Journal* 38, no. 2 (2013): 392 fn. 2.
38 Joan Sangster, "'We No Longer Respect the Law': The Tilco Strike, Labour Injunctions, and the State," *Labour/Le Travail* 53 (Spring 2004): 47.
39 Eric M. Tucker, "Shall Wagnerism Have No Dominion?" Research Paper No. 30, *Osgoode Legal Studies Research Paper Series* 10, no. 8 (2014): 1–3, 12.
40 For in-depth examinations of PC 1003, see H.A. Logan, *State Intervention and Assistance in Collective Bargaining: The Canadian Experience, 1943–1954* (Toronto: University of Toronto Press, 1956); Daniel Coates, "Organized Labor and Politics in Canada: The Development of a National Labor Code" (PhD diss., Cornell University, 1973); Laurel Sefton MacDowell, "The Formation of the Canadian Industrial Relations System during World War Two," *Labour/Le Travail* 3 (1978): 175–96 ; Judy Fudge, "Voluntarism and Compulsion: The Canadian Federal Government's Intervention in Collective Bargaining from 1900 to 1946" (PhD diss., University of Oxford, 1988); Cy Gonick, Paul Phillips, and Jesse Vorst, eds. *Labour Gains, Labour Pains: 50 Years of PC 1003* (Winnipeg: Fernwood Publishing, 1995); Taylor Hollander, "'Down the Middle of the Road': The Canadian State and Collective Bargaining, 1935–1948" (PhD diss., Binghamton University, 1998); and Judy Fudge and Eric Tucker, *Labour Before the Law: The Regulation of Workers' Collective Action in Canada, 1900–1948* (Toronto: Oxford University Press, 2001), ch. 9–10.

Some studies that offer less detailed but informed considerations include H.D. Woods, *Labour Policy in Canada*, 2nd ed. (Toronto: Macmillan, 1973), ch. 3; Frederick David Millar, "Shapes of Power: The Ontario Labour Relations Board, 1944 to 1960" (PhD diss., York University, 1980), ch. 1–3; Peter Jon Warrian, "'Labour Is Not a Commodity': A Study of the Rights of Labour in the Canadian Postwar Economy" (PhD diss., University of Waterloo, 1986), ch. 1–2; Bob Russell, *Back to Work? Labour, State and Industrial Relations in Canada* (Toronto: Nelson Canada, 1990), ch. 6; Peter Stuart McInnis, *Harnessing Labour Confrontation: Shaping the Postwar Settlement in Canada, 1943–1950* (Toronto: University of Toronto Press, 2002), 36–42; Wendy Cuthbertson, *Labour Goes to War: The CIO and the Construction of a New Social Order, 1939–45* (Vancouver, BC: UBC Press, 2012), 45–9.

41 Bertrand Russell, "A Philosophy for You in These Times," *Reader's Digest* 39 (October 1941): 5–7. The magazine editors heavily edited Russell's original draft, so there is some question as to whether he actually wrote this sentence.
42 Hollander, "Down the Middle of the Road," 79–80, 287.
43 Library and Archives Canada (hereafter cited as LAC), MG2 I103, Canadian Labour Congress, vol. 155, "O'Brien, Daniel – Vancouver Correspondence – Part III," Patrick Conroy to Daniel O'Brien, 2 December 1942.
44 *Ottawa Citizen*, 8 May 1941.
45 H.F. Angus, "Review of *The Incredible Canadian: A Candid Portrait of Mackenzie King*, by Bruce Hutchinson," *Canadian Journal of Economics and Political Science* 20, no. 1 (February 1954): 121.
46 F.R. Scott, W.L.M.K.," Canada Poetry Online, accessed 24 May 2015, http://canpoetry.library.utoronto.ca/scott_fr/poem5.htm.
47 Ian McKay, "Review of *'An Impartial Umpire': Industrial Relations and the Canadian State, 1900–1911*, by Paul Craven," *Labour/Le Travail* 8/9 (Autumn 1981–Spring 1982): 364.
48 Lawrence Martin, "The Weirdo PM Who Showed the Way," *Globe and Mail*, 8 November 2011; Michael Hart, *A Trading Nation: Canadian Trade Policy from Colonialism to Globalization* (Vancouver, BC: UBC Press, 2002), 84.
49 Joy Esberey, *Knight of the Holy Spirit: A Study of William Lyon Mackenzie King* (Toronto: University of Toronto Press, 1980), 140.
50 LAC, *The Diaries of William Lyon Mackenzie King*, 15 August 1941, http://www.bac-lac.gc.ca/eng/discover/politics-government/prime-ministers/william-lyon-mackenzie-king/Pages/search.aspx.
51 James Farr, "The Historical Science(s) of Politics: The Principles, Association, and Fate of an American Discipline," in *Modern Political Science: Anglo-American Exchanges Since 1880*, ed. Robert Adcock, Mark Bevir, and Shannon C. Stimson (Princeton, NJ: Princeton University Press, 2007), 72–4.
52 Hugh P. MacDonald, "Principles: The Principles of Principles," *The Pluralist* 4, no. 3 (Fall 2009): 98.
53 Allan Levine, *King: William Lyon Mackenzie King – A Life Guided by the Hand of Destiny* (Vancouver, BC: Douglas & McIntyre, 2011), 15.
54 *Diaries of William Lyon Mackenzie King*, 7 July 1938.
55 Ibid., 3 February 1948.
56 *National Post*, 30 September 2011.
57 *Diaries of William Lyon Mackenzie King*, 27 July 1948.
58 Douglas How, "One Man's Mackenzie King," *The Beaver* 78, no. 5 (October/November 1998): 34.

59 House of Commons, *Debates (Hansard)*, 20th Parliament, 4th Session, vol. 3 (6 April 1948), 2710–11.
60 Fudge and Tucker, *Labour Before the Law*, 300.
61 Carmela Patrias, *Jobs and Justice: Fighting Discrimination in Wartime Canada, 1939–1945* (Toronto: University of Toronto Press, 2012), 82.

1. The Unity of Our Country, Fall 1935–Fall 1939

1 Clifford Odets, *Waiting for Lefty and Other Plays* (New York: Grove Press, 1994), 31.
2 *Ottawa Citizen*, 23 April 1936; Bonita Bray, "Against All Odds: The Progressive Arts Club's Production of *Waiting for Lefty*," in *Canadian Working-Class History: Selected Readings*, ed. Laurel Sefton MacDowell and Ian Radforth, 3rd ed. (Toronto: Canadian Scholars Press, 2006), 253–66
3 *Diaries of William Lyon Mackenzie King*, 22 April 1936.
4 Ibid., 9 December, 1895.
5 Ibid., 23 March 1895.
6 Ibid., 13 April 1937.
7 Ibid., 25 January 1919.
8 Ibid., 15 October 1901.
9 Fudge and Tucker, *Labour Before the Law*, 205–25.
10 LAC, Brooke Claxton Papers, MG32 B5, "Twenty Years of Liberal Leadership: Speech by W.L. Mackenzie King" (8 August 1939), 5.
11 Margaret Elizabeth Bedore, "The Reading of Mackenzie King" (PhD diss., Queen's University, 2008), 24, 34, 70–1.
12 *Diaries of William Lyon Mackenzie King*, 11 July 1894.
13 Ibid., 13 September 1904.
14 Ibid., 12 November 1896; Levine, *King*, 41–6.
15 Levine, *King*, 46–7, 50–1.
16 Kenneth Westhues, "Sociology for a New Century: Mackenzie King's First Career," in *Mackenzie King: Citizenship and Community: Essays Marking the 125th Anniversary of the Birth of William Lyon Mackenzie King*, ed. John English, Kenneth McLaughlin, and P. Whitney Lackenbauer (Montreal: Robin Brass Studio, 2002), 186–207.
17 Dorothy Ross, *The Origins of American Social Science* (New York: Cambridge University Press, 1991), 143–58.
18 *Diaries of William Lyon Mackenzie King*, 9 December 1895; Keith Cassidy, "Mackenzie King and American Progressivism," in *Mackenzie King: Widening the Debate*, ed. John English and J.O. Stubbs (Toronto: Macmillan, 1977), 118.

19 William Lyon Mackenzie King, *Industry and Humanity: A Study in the Principles of Industrial Reconstruction*, introduction by David Jay Bercuson (Toronto: University of Toronto Press, 1973), 328.
20 *Diaries of William Lyon Mackenzie King*, 20 October 1898; John Lewis Recchiuti, *Civic Engagement: Social Science and Progressive-Era Reform in New York City* (Philadelphia, PA: University of Pennsylvania Press, 2007), 26.
21 *Diaries of William Lyon Mackenzie King*, 25 January 1919; Bedore, "Reading of Mackenzie King," 26–8.
22 King, *Industry and Humanity*, 62.
23 *Diaries of William Lyon Mackenzie King*, 28 January 1904.
24 Reginald Hardy, *Mackenzie King of Canada: A Biography* (Toronto: Oxford University Press, 1949), 49.
25 King, *Industry and Humanity*, 10.
26 Levine, *King*, 54, 57, 68, 77, 79–85, 91–8, 104–6; Henry Ferns and Bernard Ostry, *The Age of Mackenzie King* (Toronto: James Lorimer & Co., 1976), ch. 2–7.
27 Jeremy Webber, "Compelling Compromise: Canada Chooses Conciliation Over Arbitration, 1900–1907," *Labour/Le Travail* 28 (Fall 1991): 19–29, 43–4.
28 King, *Industry and Humanity*, 21, 48, 140 (quotation), 144.
29 Fudge and Tucker, *Labour Before the Law*, 41.
30 King, *Industry and Humanity*, 11, 48, 63, 140, 144 (quotation).
31 Ibid., 137.
32 Richard Gillespie, *Manufacturing Knowledge: A History of the Hawthorne Experiments* (Cambridge: Cambridge University Press, 1991), 23–4.
33 *Diaries of William Lyon Mackenzie King*, 25 January 1919.
34 Ibid., 5 October 1901.
35 King, *Industry and Humanity*, 277–87; *Diaries of William Lyon Mackenzie King*, 15 April 1937; National Archives of the United States, RG59 vol. 6188, file 842.5045/159, Norman Amour to the Secretary of State, "Conversation with Prime Minister King," 17 April 1937.
36 Webber, "Compelling Compromise," 23–4, 27; C. Brian Williams, "Notes on the Evolution of Compulsory Conciliation in Canada," *Relations industrielles/Industrial Relations* 19 (1969): 314–17; Woods, *Labour Policy in Canada*, 21–2, 56–64; LAC, Public Records Committee, RG 35/7, vol. 21, file 18, "Wartime Activities of the Industrial Relations Branch," Report of the Department of Labour, March 1946.
37 Fudge and Tucker, *Labour Before the Law*, 53–61; US Government, Department of Commerce and Labor, *Bulletin of the Bureau of Labor* (Washington, DC: Government Printing Office, 1911): 65; King, *Industry*

and Humanity, 317; Bruno Ramirez, "U.S. Response to the Canadian Industrial Disputes Investigation Act," *Relations industrielles/Industrial Relations* 29, no. 3 (1974): 546.

38 King, *Industry and Humanity*, 142, 148, 320–1, 325–6, 328, 333.

39 LAC, Brooke Claxton Papers, MG32 B5, "Twenty Years of Liberal Leadership: Speech by W.L. Mackenzie King," 5.

40 W.L. Mackenzie King, "The Practice of Liberalism," in *The Dirty Thirties: Canadians in the Great Depression*, ed. Michiel Horn (Toronto: Copp Clark Publishing, 1972), 490.

41 *Diaries of William Lyon Mackenzie King*, 28 January 1937.

42 King, "The Practice of Liberalism," 496.

43 *Diaries of William Lyon Mackenzie King*, 11 May 1944; Hardy, *Mackenzie King of Canada*, 282–4.

44 Hardy, *Mackenzie King of Canada*, 283.

45 King, *Industry and Humanity*, 48, 334 (quotation).

46 Elizabeth R.B. Elliot-Meisel, "A Grand and Glorious Thing ... the Team of Mackenzie and Roosevelt," in *Franklin D. Roosevelt and the Formation of the Modern World*, ed. Thomas C. Howard and William D. Pederson (Armonk, NY: M.E. Sharpe, 2003), 140–1.

47 *Diaries of William Lyon Mackenzie King*, 8 September, 1933.

48 Ibid., 18 December 1936.

49 Ibid., 14 January 1938.

50 Ibid., 24 November 1933.

51 Ibid., 17 January 1934.

52 Ibid., 4 June 1935.

53 John Herd Thompson with Allen Seager, *Canada, 1922–1939: Decades of Discord* (McClelland & Stewart, 1986), Tables 1d and 1e.

54 C.E.S. Franks, *The Parliament of Canada* (Toronto: University of Toronto Press, 1987), 99–115; Richard Van Loon and Michael S. Whittington, *The Canadian Political System: Environment, Structure, and Process*, 3rd ed. rev. (Toronto: McGraw-Hill Ryerson, 1981), 619–22.

55 Paul Martin, *Far From Home*, vol. 1, *A Very Public Life* (Ottawa: Deneau Publishers, 1983), 167, 171, 217.

56 J.W. Pickersgill, *The Mackenzie King Record*, vol. 1, *1939–1944* (Toronto: University of Toronto Press, 1960), 9.

57 Thompson with Seager, *Canada, 1922–1939*, 277–8; John T. Saywell, *'Just Call Me Mitch': The Life of Mitchell F. Hepburn* (Toronto: University of Toronto Press, 1991), 307; Robert Bothwell and William Kilbourn, *C.D. Howe: A Biography* (Toronto: McClelland & Stewart, 1979), 65–6.

58 *Labour Gazette* 38 (January 1938): 24–7.

59 Ibid., 38 (May 1938): 521–3; *Winnipeg Free Press*, 5 August 1943.
60 Pickersgill, *The Mackenzie King Record*, 1:7.
61 *Diaries of William Lyon Mackenzie King*, 3 October 1937.
62 Christopher MacLennan, *Toward the Charter: Canadians and the Demand for a National Bill of Rights, 1929–1960* (Montreal: McGill-Queen's Press, 2003), 18.
63 D.E. Armstrong and Muriel Armstrong, "Third Party Intervention in the Alberta Coal Industry, 1900–1951," in *Patterns of Industrial Dispute Settlement in Five Canadian Industries*, ed. H.D. Woods (Montreal: McGill University, 1958), 68–9.
64 *Labour Gazette* 38 (February 1938): 148.
65 Peter Russell, ed., *Leading Constitutional Decisions: Cases on the British North America Act* (Toronto: McClelland & Stewart, 1976), 39–45.
66 Margaret Mackintosh, *Government Intervention in Labour Disputes in Canada*, Bulletin #11, Industrial Relations Series, Department of Labour (Ottawa: King's Printer, 1931), 13.
67 Van Loon and Whittington, *Canadian Political System*, 191–5, 243–57.
68 *Labour Gazette* 37 (November 1937): 1193.
69 Thompson with Seager, *Canada, 1922–1939*, 295–7; Robin Fisher, "The Decline of Reform: British Columbia Politics in the 1930s," *Journal of Canadian Studies* 25 (Autumn 1990): 83; Saywell, *Life of Mitchell F. Hepburn*, 338–43, 385–91, 396–406; Reginald Whitaker, *The Government Party: Organizing and Financing the Liberal Party of Canada, 1930–58* (Toronto: University of Toronto Press, 1977), 314–36.
70 Doug Owram, *The Government Generation: Canadian Intellectuals and the State, 1900–1945* (Toronto: University of Toronto Press, 1986), 170–1, 221–6, 238–42; J.L. Granatstein, *The Ottawa Men: The Civil Service Mandarins, 1935–1957* (Toronto: Oxford University Press, 1982), 2–4, 19–27, 58–61; James Struthers, *'No Fault of the Their Own': Unemployment and the Canadian Welfare State, 1914–1941* (Toronto: University of Toronto Press, 1983), 196–7.
71 LAC, Brooke Claxton Papers, MG32 B5, vol. 10, file: Constitution-Labour, Royal Commission on Dominion-Provincial Relations: Opinions on Constitutional Law, "Legal Difficulties Concerning Labour Legislation, B-a) Recognition of Unions" by L.M. Gouin; David Jay Bercuson, *True Patriot: The Life of Brooke Claxton, 1898–1960* (Toronto: University of Toronto Press, 1993), 82.
72 King, *Industry and Humanity*, 144.
73 *Diaries of William Lyon Mackenzie King*, 8 March 1939.
74 Note on the abbreviation CIO: The US organization, originally called the Committee for Industrial Organization, changed its name when it split

with the American Federation of Labor (AFL) in 1938 and became the Congress of Industrial Organizations.

75 *New York Times*, 9 April 1937; *Ottawa Citizen*, 14 April 1937; Irving Abella, *On Strike: Six Key Labour Struggles in Canada 1919–1949* (James Lorimer & Co., 1974), 95–109; Saywell, *Life of Mitchell F. Hepburn*, 309–29.
76 Saywell, *Life of Mitchell F. Hepburn*, 312.
77 *Financial Post*, 8 May 1937; Saywell, *Life of Mitchell F. Hepburn*, 327; Abella, *On Strike*, 116.
78 Saywell, *Life of Mitchell F. Hepburn*, 325; Laurel Sefton MacDowell, *Renegade Lawyer: The Life of J.L. Cohen* (Toronto: University of Toronto Press, 2001), 89.
79 David W.T. Matheson, "The Canadian Working-Class and Industrial Legality, 1939–1949" (Master's thesis, Queen's University, 1989), 40.
80 *Berkley Daily Gazette*, 4 June 1937.
81 *Ottawa Evening Citizen*, 21 January 1937.
82 Thompson with Seager, *Canada, 1922–1939*, Table XIIIa.
83 John Manley, "Canadian Communism, Revolutionary Unionism and the 'Third Period': The Workers Unity League, 1929–1935," Paper presented to the Canadian Historical Association, Calgary, AB, June 1994, 3, 10–20.
84 Irving Martin Abella, *Nationalism, Communism and Canadian Labour: The CIO, the Communist Party, and the Canadian Congress of Labour, 1935–1956* (Toronto: University of Toronto Press, 1973), 3–30.
85 Hollander, "Down the Middle of the Road," 81.
86 *Montreal Gazette*, 2 June 1937.
87 National Archives of the United States, RG59, State Department, vol. 6188, file 842.5045/169, Ely E. Palmer to the Secretary of State, "Memorandum of Conversation with Mr. Moore," 11 June 1937.
88 Abella, *Nationalism, Communism, and Canadian Labour*, 25.
89 Hollander, "Down the Middle of the Road," 79.
90 See, for example, the *Twenty-Seventh Annual Report on Labour Organizations in Canada* (Ottawa: King's Printer, 1938), 187–8.
91 Pamela Sugiman, "Privilege and Oppression: The Configuration of Race, Gender, and Class in Southern Ontario Auto Plants, 1939 to 1949," *Labour/Le Travail* 47 (Spring 2001): 88.
92 Ruth Frager and Carmela Patrias, *Discounted Labour: Women Workers in Canada, 1870–1939* (Toronto: University of Toronto Press, 2005), 133.
93 Ibid., 129.
94 Carmela Patrias and Larry Savage, *Union Power: Solidarity and Struggle in Niagara* (Edmonton: Athabasca University Press, 2012), 45–55.
95 *Financial Post*, 24 April 1937.

96 Laurel Sefton MacDowell, *"Remember Kirkland Lake": The History and Effects of the Kirkland Lake Gold Miners' Strike, 1941–42* (Toronto: University of Toronto Press, 1983), 61.
97 Statistics Canada, *Exploring the First Century of Canada's Consumer Price Index* (Ottawa: Minister of Industry, 2015), 8; Abdul Rashid, "Seven Decades of Wage Changes," *Perspectives on Labour and Income* 5, no. 2 (Summer 1993): Chart A.
98 Joan Sangster, *Earning Respect: The Lives of Working Women in Small-Town Ontario, 1920–1960* (Toronto: University of Toronto Press, 1995), 141.
99 Cuthbertson, *Labour Goes to War*, 14–15.
100 Doug Smith, *Cold Warrior: C.S. Jackson and the United Electrical Workers* (St John's, NL: Canadian Committee on Labour History, 1997), 57.
101 Sangster, *Earning Respect*, 98, 173–4.
102 Lara Campbell, *Respectable Citizens: Gender, Family, and Unemployment in Ontario's Great Depression* (Toronto: University of Toronto Press, 2009), 20, 34, 154–9; Warren Caragata, *Alberta Labour: A Heritage Untold* (James Lorimer & Co., 1979), 106.
103 Campbell, *Respectable Citizens*, 58; Leslie McCall, "The Complexity of Intersectionality," *Signs* 230, no. 3 (2005): 1173–4.
104 Craig Heron, "Boys Will Be Boys: Working-Class Masculinities in the Age of Mass Production," *International Labour and Working-Class History* (Spring 2006): 7, 26.
105 Sangster, *Earning Respect*, 165.
106 Patrias and Savage, *Union Power*, 48.
107 Frager and Patrias, *Discounted Labour*, 121–30; Laurie Mercier, "Gender, Labour, and Place: Reconstructing Women's Spaces in Industrial Communities of Western Canada and the United States, *Labour History* 53, no. 3 (2012): 389–91.
108 Abella, *Nationalism, Communism and Canadian Labour*, 20, 38.
109 Robert B. Bryce, *Maturing in Hard Times: Canada's Department of Finance through the Great Depression* (Kingston: McGill-Queen's University Press, 1986), 62; Thompson with Seager, *Canada, 1922–1939*, 350; Hollander, "Down the Middle of the Road," 79; Kenneth Norrie and Douglas Owram, *A History of the Canadian Economy* (Toronto: Harcourt Brace Jovanovich, 1991), 506.
110 Gloria Montero, *We Stood Together: First-Hand Accounts of Dramatic Events in Canada's Labour Past* (Toronto: James Lorimer & Co., 1979), 64.
111 Ibid., 72.
112 Norman Penner, *Canadian Communism: The Stalin Years and Beyond* (Toronto: Methuen, 1988), 107.

113 John Stanton, *Never Say Die! The Life and Times of a Pioneer Labour Lawyer* (Ottawa: Steel Rail Publishing, 1987), 41.
114 *Labour Gazette* 36 (October 1936): 895–6; Fudge and Tucker, *Labour Before the Law*, 195.
115 David Brody, *Workers in Industrial America: Essays on the 20th Century Struggle* (New York: Oxford University Press, 1980), 86; Christopher L. Tomlins, "AFL Unions in the 1930s: Their Performance in Historical Perspective," *Journal of American History* 65 (March 1979): 1029–30; John Manley, "Communists and Auto Workers: The Struggle for Industrial Unionism in the Canadian Automobile Industry, 1926–36," *Labour/Le Travail* 17 (Spring 1986): 115.
116 Robert Babcock, *Gompers in Canada*, 72–4.
117 Fudge and Tucker, *Labour Before the Law*, 211–25.
118 Stanton, *Never Say Die!*, 34.
119 Fudge and Tucker, *Labour Before the Law*, 211–25; *Labour Gazette* 39 (March 1939): 260 and 40 (March 1940): 219.
120 Abella, *Nationalism, Communism and Canadian Labour*, 34.
121 *Canadian Congress Journal* 17 (September 1938): 27–9.
122 Fudge and Tucker, *Labour Before the Law*, 196.
123 Abella, *Nationalism, Communism and Canadian Labour*, 35, 39–42; LAC, Labour Council of Metropolitan Toronto, MG28 I44, Microfilm Reel M2292, "Minutes of the Toronto District Labour Council," 16 February 1939.
124 Abella, *Nationalism, Communism and Canadian Labour*, 39–40.
125 "War Series: No. 1" (23 October 1939), in *R.C.M.P. Security Bulletins: The War Series, 1939–1941*, ed. Gregory S. Kealey and Reg Whitaker (St John's, NL: Committee on Canadian Labour History, 1989), 25.
126 Jeffrey Wilson, "Charles Millard and the Canadian Labour Movement" (Master's thesis, Wilfrid Laurier University, 1990), 70.
127 Abella, *Nationalism Communism and Canadian Labour*, 37.
128 Paul Craven, *'An Impartial Umpire': Industrial Relations and the Canadian State, 1900–1911* (Toronto: University of Toronto Press, 1980), 117–20; Hollander, "Down the Middle of the Road," 79; *Diaries of William Lyon Mackenzie King*, 28 September 1936; Desmond Morton with Terry Copp, *Working People* (Ottawa: Deneau Publishers, 1980), 142; *Canadian Congress Journal* 17 (January 1938): 7; 17 (February 1938): 10–17; and 18 (January 1939): 10.
129 Alexander Fraser Isbester, "A History of the National Catholic Unions in Canada, 1901–1965" (PhD diss., Cornell University, 1968), 138, 173–5, 246; Education Committees of the CSN and the CEQ, *The History of the Labour Movement in Quebec*, trans. Arnold Bennett (Montreal: Black

Rose Books, 1987), 91, 130–1; Jacques Rouillard, "Major Changes in the Confédération des travailleurs catholiques du Canada, 1940–1960," trans. Henri Malebranche, in *Quebec since 1945: Selected Readings*, ed. Michael D. Behiels (Toronto: Copp Clark Pitman Ltd., 1987), 112–13; Jacques Rouillard, "Le militantisme des travailleurs au Québec et en Ontario, niveau de syndicalisation et mouvement de grèves (1900–1980)," *Revue d'histoire de l'Amérique française* 37 (September 1983): 207; Alfred Charpentier, "La Grève du Textile dans le Québec en 1937," *Relations industrielles* 29 (January 1965): 86–127; and Alfred Charpentier, "La conscience syndicale lors des grèves du textile en 1937 et de l'amiante en 1949," *Labour/Le Travail* 3 (1978): 202–20.

130 Morton with Copp, *Working People*, 132; Hollander, "Down the Middle of the Road," 79.

131 LAC, J.L. Cohen Papers, MG30 A94, vol. 48, file 1, "ACCL Memorandum Submitted to the Government of Canada," 27 April 1934 and 20 January, 1935.

132 Abella, *Nationalism, Communism and the Canadian Labour*, 3, 44.

133 National Archives of the United States, RG59, The State Department, Volume 6188, File 842.5045/I69, Ely E. Palmer to the Secretary of State, "Memorandum of Conversation with Mr. Moore," 11 June 1937.

134 *Montreal Gazette*, 19 October 1936; *Ottawa Journal*, 30 October, 1936; LAC, Canadian Labour Congress, MG23 I130, vol. 206, file 7, "General Correspondence, Canadian Federation of Labour, 1945–47," Pat Conroy to Sir Walter Citrine, 8 January 1944; vol. 30, file 15, "Mine Mill General Part 1, 1944–47," Norman S. Dowd to Jack Stewart, 12 November 1946; and vol. 31, file 1, "Mine Mill, General, Part 2, 1944–47," Norman S. Dowd to William Kennedy, 4 March 1946.

135 Hollander, "Down the Middle of the Road," 79.

136 LAC, Department of Labour, RG 27, vol. 143, file 611.04:16, "Royal Commission of Inquiry into the Textile Industry," Norman McL. Rogers to G. Blair Gordon, 20 April 1938 and G. Blair Gordon to Norman McL. Rogers, 25 April, 1938.

137 Norrie and Owram, *History of the Canadian Economy*, 479–80, 485–6.

138 Toronto *Globe*, 3 January, 1935.

139 Duncan McDowall, *Steel at the Sault: Francis H. Clergue, Sir James Dunn, and the Algoma Steel Corporation, 1901–1956* (Toronto: University of Toronto Press, 1984), 176.

140 National Archives of the United States, RG 59, State Department, vol. 6188, file 842.5045/167, Report to the Secretary of State, "Labour Unrest in Canada," 27 May 1937; Alvin Finkel, *Business and Social Reform in the Thirties* (Toronto: James Lorimer & Co., 1979), 19.

141 Patrias and Savage, *Union Power*, 46.
142 LAC, Department of Labour, RG 27, vol. 143, file 611.04:16, G. Blair Gordon to the Deputy Minister of Labour, 27 August 1936.
143 Mark Cox, "The Limits of Reform: Industrial Regulation and Management Rights in Ontario, 1930–37," *Canadian Historical Review* 68 (December 1987): 552–75.
144 Ibid.; *Labour Gazette* 38 (September 1938): 1046.
145 Cox, "Limits of Reform," 565.
146 *Diaries of William Lyon Mackenzie King*, 15 April 1937.
147 Ibid., 3 October 1937.
148 Ibid., 27 October 1936.
149 Sanford Jacoby, "Masters to Managers: An Introduction," in *Masters to Managers: Historical and Comparative Perspectives on American Employers*, ed. Sanford Jacoby (New York: Columbia University Press, 1991), 12.
150 Thompson with Seager, *Canada, 1922–1939*, 140–1; Morton with Copp, *Working People*, 130–1.
151 Neil Fligstein, *The Transformation of Corporate Control* (Cambridge, MA: Harvard University Press, 1990), 27–8, 116–60.
152 *Industrial Canada* 40 (July 1939): 64–71.
153 *Canadian Business* 12 (June 1939): 24–6.
154 Margaret E. McCallum, "Corporate Welfarism in Canada, 1919–39," *Canadian Historical Review* 71 (March 1990): 48, 78–9; Joy Parr, *The Gender of Breadwinners: Women, Men, and Change in Two Industrial Towns, 1880–1950* (Toronto: University of Toronto Press, 1990), 39–49; Joan Sangster, "The Softball Solution: Female Workers, Male Mangers and the Operation of Paternalism at Westclox, 1923–60," *Labour/Le Travail* 32 (Fall 1993): 167–99; Robert Storey, "Unionization versus Corporate Welfare: The 'Dofasco Way,'" *Labour/Le Travail* 12 (Fall 1983): 7–42.
155 Cox, "Limits of Reform," 563.
156 McCallum, "Corporate Welfarism in Canada," 48.
157 Storey, "Unionization versus Corporate Welfare," 15–18.
158 McDowall, *Steel at the Sault*, 176; Jim Green, *Against the Tide: The Story of the Canadian Seamen's Union* (Toronto: Progress Books, 1986), 28; Kim Adair, Peter Pautler, and David Strang, "The URWA and the Struggle for Union Recognition, 1937–39," in Copp, *Industrial Unionism in Kitchener*, 2–6; Doug Smith, *Let Us Rise! A History of the Manitoba Labour Movement* (Vancouver, BC: New Star Books, 1985), 82–3.
159 Robert Storey, "The Struggle to Organize Stelco and Dofasco," *Relations industrielles/Industrial Relations* 42 (Spring 1987): 366–84.
160 Green, *Against the Tide*, 31–8.

161 *Canadian Forum* 19 (April 1939): 7–8.

162 Smith, *Cold Warrior*, 62.

163 MacDowell, *'Remember Kirkland Lake,'* 64.

164 Stephen C. Gray, "Woodworkers and Legitimacy: The IWA in Canada, 1937–1957" (PhD diss., Simon Fraser University, 1989), 34–5.

165 Patrias and Savage, *Union Power*, 53.

166 LAC, Canadian Labour Congress, MG28 I103, vol. 190, files 12 and 13: "Federal Deputy Minister of Labour Part 1, 1934–39," Norman S. Dowd to W.M. Dickson, 20 October 1938 and 21 February 1939.

167 Stanton, *Never Say Die!*, 30; Pamela Sugiman, *Labour's Dilemma: The Gender Politics of Auto Workers in Canada, 1937–1979* (Toronto: University of Toronto Press, 1994), 14.

168 *Ottawa Citizen*, 14 January 1937.

169 McInnis, *Harnessing Labour Confrontation*, 187.

170 Wayne Roberts and John Bullen, "A Heritage of Hope and Struggle: Workers, Unions, and Politics in Canada, 1930–1982," in *Modern Canada, 1930–1980s*, ed. Michael S. Cross and Gregory S. Kealey (Toronto: McClelland & Stewart, 1984), 106.

171 Don Wells, "Autoworkers on the Firing Line," in *On the Job: Confronting the Labour Process in Canada*, ed. Craig Heron and Robert Storey (Kingston and Montreal: McGill-Queen's University Press, 1986), 332.

172 Craig Heron and Robert Storey, "Work and Struggle in the Canadian Steel Industry, 1900–1950," in Heron and Storey, *On the Job*, 222.

173 MacDowell, *'Remember Kirkland Lake,'* 47; Green, *Against the Tide*, 34; Patrias and Savage, *Union Power*, 52; Saywell, *Life of Mitchell F. Hepburn*, 309.

174 Stanton, *Never Say Die!*, 43.

175 Ruth A. Frager, "Mixing with People on Spadina: The Tense Relations between Non-Jewish Workers and Jewish Workers," in *The History of Immigration and Racism in Canada: Essential Readings*, ed. Barrington Walker (Toronto: Canada Scholars' Press Inc., 2008), 151.

176 LAC, Ernest Lapointe Papers, MG27 III B10, vol. 35, file: "Unions – Amendments to the Criminal Code Concerning the Right of Association," Ross McMaster to Ernest Lapointe, 6 May 1939.

177 National Archives of the United States, RG59, State Department, vol. 6188, file 842.5045/176, "1930–39," Frederick Johnson to the Secretary of State, 9 November 1937.

178 Stephen Brooks, "Imagining Each Other," in *Canada and the United States: Differences That Count*, ed. David M. Thomas and David N. Biette, 4th ed. (Toronto: University of Toronto Press, 2014), 28–30.

179 Green, *Against the Tide*, 33–8; MacDowell, *'Remember Kirkland Lake,'* 63; Bryan Mahn and Ralph Schaffner, "The Packinghouse Workers in Kitchener: 1940–47," in Copp, *Industrial Unionism in Kitchener*, 30; Ian Radforth, *Bush Workers and Bosses: Logging in Northern Ontario, 1900–1980* (Toronto: University of Toronto Press, 1987), 130–1; Stanton, *Never Say Die!*, 3; Storey, "The Struggle to Organize Stelco and Dofasco," 371–2.
180 *Montreal Gazette*, 29 June 1938.
181 Montero, *We Stood Together*, 60.
182 *Canadian Business* 12 (June 1939): 15–16.
183 *Montreal Gazette*, 16 August 1937.
184 Stanton, *Never Say Die!*, 3; Andrew Parnaby, *Citizen Docker: Making a New Deal on the Vancouver Waterfront, 1919–1939* (Toronto: University of Toronto Press, 2008), 152–3.
185 Saywell, *Life of Mitchell F. Hepburn*, 306.
186 Abella, "Oshawa 1937," in Abella, *On Strike*, 107.
187 Morton with Copp, *Working People*, 27; A.W.R. Carrothers, E.E. Palmer, and W.B. Rayner, *Collective Bargaining Law in Canada* (Toronto: Butterworths, 1986), 16–30.
188 Craven, *An Impartial Umpire*, 197; Craig Heron, "Afterword: Male Wage-Earners and the State in Canada," in Earle, *Workers and the State*, 250; Bora Laskin, "Labour Law: 1923–1947," *The Canadian Bar Review* 26 (1948): 289.
189 *Canadian Forum* 16 (September 1936): 10–12; Fudge and Tucker, *Labour Before the Law*, 198, 211.
190 William D. Coleman, *Business and Politics: A Study of Collective Action* (Kingston: McGill-Queen's University Press, 1988), 6, 18, 22; Gray, "Woodworkers and Legitimacy," 23; Christopher Green, *Canadian Industrial Organization and Policy* (Toronto: McGraw-Hill Ryerson, 1980), 98.
191 Finkel, *Business and Social Reform*, 20.
192 Tom Traves, "Security without Regulation," in *The Consolidation of Capitalism, 1896-1929*, ed. Michael S. Cross and Gregory S. Kealey (Toronto: McClelland & Stewart, 1983), 32–9; Coleman, *Business and Politics*, 22; Craven, *An Impartial Umpire*, 100, 106–7, 123–31, 175–189.
193 Millar, "Shapes of Power," 8–11; Saywell, *Life of Mitchell F. Hepburn*, 359.
194 *Labour Gazette* 38 (June 1938): 618–19 and 39 (July 1939): 678–9; Fudge and Tucker, *Labour Before the Law*, 197; LAC, Canadian Manufacturers Association, MG28 I230, In Process 83/138, file: "Industrial Relations Committee Minutes," 22 September, 1938.
195 Coleman, *Business and Politics*, 197.
196 Ibid., 214; Finkel, *Business and Social Reform*, 20.

197 Michael A. Atkinson and William D. Coleman, *The State, Business and Industrial Change in Canada* (Toronto: University of Toronto Press, 1989), 35–9; Michael Howlett and M. Ramesh, *The Political Economy of Canada: An Introduction* (Toronto: McClelland & Stewart, 1992), 189; Carolyn J. Tuohy, *Policy and Politics in Canada: Institutionalized Ambivalence* (Philadelphia, PA: Temple University Press, 1992), 217.

198 *Labour Gazette* 39 (July 1939): 678–9.

199 MacDowell, *Renegade Lawyer*, 22; Philip Girard, *Bora Laskin: Bringing Law to Life* (Toronto: University of Toronto Press, 2005), 54, 103–17.

200 Bora Laskin, "The Legal Status of Trade Unions," in *Problems in Canadian Unity: Lectures Given at the Canadian Institute on Economics and Politics, August 6 to 19, 1938*, ed. Violet Anderson (Toronto: Thomas Nelson and Sons, 1938), 90–102.

201 *Montreal Gazette*, 11 September 1937; John Herd Thompson and Stephen J. Randall, *Canada and the United States: Ambivalent Allies*, 4th ed. (Athens, GA: University of Georgia Press, 2008), 131.

202 Queen's University, Industrial Relations Centre, *Industrial Relations at Queen's: The First Fifty Years* (Kingston, ON: Queen's University, 1987), 3, accessed 22 July 2011, http://irc.queensu.ca/sites/default/files/queens-irc-50-years-history.pdf.

203 Ian Radforth and Joan Sangster, "A Link between Labour and Learning: The Workers' Educational Association in Ontario, 1917–1951," *Labour/Le Travail* 89 (Autumn/Spring 1981/1982): 65.

204 R.C.B. Risk, *A History of Canadian Legal Thought: Collected Essays* (Toronto: University of Toronto Press, 2006), 38.

205 MacDowell, *Renegade Lawyer*, 24; Stanton, *Never Say Die!*, viii.

206 LAC, Royal Commission on the Textile Industry, RG33/20, *Report* (1938), 12, 191.

207 LAC, Department of Labour, RG27, vol. 143, file: 611.04:16, Norman Rogers to G. Blair Gordon, 20 April, 1938; *Financial Post*, 9 April 1938 and 17 September 1938.

208 Storey, "Unionization versus Corporate Welfare," 18.

209 *Canadian Congress Journal* 18 (September 1939): 26.

210 Michiel Horn, *The League for Social Reconstruction: Intellectual Origins of the Democratic Left in Canada, 1930–1942* (Toronto: University of Toronto Press, 1980), 62.

211 Robert A .Wright, "The Canadian Protestant Tradition," in *The Canadian Protestant Experience, 1760–1990*, ed. George A. Rawlyk (Montreal: McGill-Queen's University Press, 1990), 181.

212 Eugene Forsey, *A Life on the Fringe: The Memoirs of Eugene Forsey* (Toronto: University of Oxford Press, 1990), 133–4.
213 Thompson with Seager, *Canada, 1922–1939*, 285.
214 Abella, *Nationalism, Communism and Canadian Labour*, 29.
215 Green, *Against the Tide*, 30.
216 William Kaplan, *State and Salvation: The Jehovah's Witnesses and Their Fight for Civil Rights* (Toronto: University of Toronto Press, 1989), 19–25.
217 Ross Lambertson, *Repression and Resistance: Canadian Human Rights Activists, 1930–1960* (Toronto: University of Toronto Press, 2005), 51–66.
218 R. Douglas Francis, *Frank H. Underhill: Intellectual Provocateur* (Toronto: University of Toronto Press, 1986), 99.
219 Thompson with Seager, *Canada, 1922–1939*, 275; Horn, *League for Social Reconstruction*, 126; Walter D. Young, *The Anatomy of a Party: The National CCF, 1932–61* (Toronto: University of Toronto Press, 1969), 76–9.
220 Young, *Anatomy of a Party*, 81–2.
221 David Lewis, *The Good Fight: Political Memoirs, 1909–1958* (Toronto: Macmillan of Canada, 1981), 142, 147.
222 Ibid., 155; Young, *Anatomy of a Party*, 147–8; M. Earle and H. Gamberg, "The United Mine Workers and the Coming of the CCF to Cape Breton," in Earle, *Workers and the State*, 85–108.
223 Fudge and Tucker, *Labour Before the Law*, 225.
224 Ibid.
225 LAC, Ernest Lapointe Papers, MG27 III B10, vol. 35, file: "Unions – Amendments to the Criminal Code Concerning the Right of Association," Ernest Lapointe to Ross McMaster, 13 May 1939.
226 J.L. Cohen, *Collective Bargaining in Canada: An Examination of the Legislative Record and Policy of the Government of the Dominion of Canada* (Toronto: Steel Workers Organizing Committee, 1941), 16–24; *Canadian Forum* 19 (June 1939): 75.
227 LAC, Brooke Claxton Papers, MG32 B5, "Twenty Years of Liberal Leadership: Speech by W.L. Mackenzie King," 13.
228 *Diaries of William Lyon Mackenzie King*, 18 January 1939.

2. The Breastplate of Righteousness, Fall 1939–Fall 1941

1 Ibid., 9–10 June 1940.
2 Struthers, *No Fault of Their Own*, 142.
3 *Diaries of William Lyon Mackenzie King*, 9–10 June 1940. King did suggest that Rogers take a train, not a plane
4 Ibid.

5 Ibid., 19 September 1939 and 22 May 1940.
6 Martin, *Far From Home*, 150, 159, 215–16, 244–5.
7 *PM Magazine*, November 1941.
8 LAC, W.L. Mackenzie King Papers, MG26 J4, Microfilm C4273 C122980, "Memoranda and Notes," Memorandum to the Prime Minister from the Trades and Labour Council, 5 October 1939.
9 *Labour Gazette* 39 (September 1939): 883–4, 894–5 and 40 (February 1940): 115–17; Hollander, "Down the Middle of the Road," 160.
10 *Diaries of William Lyon Mackenzie King*, 5 October 1939.
11 The Canadian branch of the CIO, formed in October 1939, was called the Canadian Committee for Industrial Organization until it merged with the All-Canadian Congress of Labour (ACCL) to form the Canadian Congress of Labour (CCL) in 1940. Prior to 1939, Canadian "CIO unions" were loosely associated with the CIO in the United States but not a distinct entity.
12 Abella, *Nationalism, Communism, and Canadian Labour*, 41–3.
13 Hollander, "Down the Middle of the Road," 160.
14 Abella, *Nationalism, Communism and Canadian Labour*, 43
15 *Toronto Star*, 27 October 1939; *Hamilton Spectator*, 6 November 1939; "War Series: No. 4" (13 November 1939), in Kealey and Whitaker, *War Series, 1939–1941*, 47–8.
16 Abella, *Nationalism, Communism and Canadian Labour*, 43.
17 MacDowell, "The Formation of the Canadian Industrial Relations System," 179.
18 *Labour Gazette* 39 (November 1939): 1086–7; LAC, Public Records Committee, RG35/7, vol. 21, file 18: "Wartime Activities of the Industrial Relations Branch," Report of the Department of Labour, March 1946.
19 *Canadian Congress Journal* 19 (April 1940): 9; LAC, J.L. Cohen Papers, MG30 A94, vol. 26, file 2872A: "REX v. Clarence S. Jackson, Fall 1941," Transcript of Evidence Given Before the Defence of Canada Regulations Advisory Committee, 11 September 1941.
20 LAC, Labour Council of Metropolitan Toronto, MG28 I44, Microfilm Reel M2292, "Toronto District Council Minutes," 21 March 1940.
21 MacDowell, *'Remember Kirkland Lake,'* 65–72.
22 Green, *Against the Tide*, 54–72.
23 Stanton, *Never Say Die!*, 44–54.
24 *Labour Gazette* 40 (June 1940): 538–43.
25 C.P. Stacey, *Arms, Men and Governments: The War Policies of Canada, 1939–1945* (Ottawa: Supply and Services, 1970), 485–6, 503–4.
26 LAC, J.L. Cohen Papers, MG30 A94, vol. 50, file 1: "General Correspondence," Clarence Gilles to J.L. Cohen, 30 May 1940; LAC,

Labour Council of Metropolitan Toronto, MG28 I44, Microfilm Reel M2292, "Toronto District Council Minutes," 21 March and 27 March 1940.

27 Hardy, *Mackenzie King of Canada*, 335.

28 LAC, W.L. Mackenzie King Papers, MG26 J4, Microfilm Reel H1507 C207806, "Memoranda and Notes," W.J. Turnbull to Mackenzie King, 5 June 1940.

29 Hollander, "Down the Middle of the Road," 161.

30 LAC, Canadian Labour Congress, MG28 I103, vol. 190, file 5: "Federal Department of Labour Correspondence Part 2, 1939–1944," Memorandum with Respect to Meeting Held on June the 13th, 1940"; *Diaries of William Lyon Mackenzie King*, 13 June 1940.

31 *Diaries of William Lyon Mackenzie King*, 13 June, 1940.

32 Ibid., 17 June and 24 June 1940.

33 LAC, Department of Labour, RG 27, vol. 631, file 60: "NLSC Appointments and Resignations," Norman S. Dowd to Norman A. McLarty, 11 March 1941; vol. 631, file 61: "Minister of Labour," Norman McLarty to A.J. Hills, 21 March 1941; vol. 631, file 67: "Department of Labour," Gerald Brown to Norman A. McLarty, 26 June 1940.

34 LAC, Department of Labour, RG 27, vol. 632, file 85: "Minutes of the NLSC Meetings," 26 August 1940; LAC, Canadian Labour Congress, MG28 I103, vol. 330, file 16: "CCL Executive Council Minutes, 1940–41," 5 November 1940.

35 Cohen, *Collective Bargaining in Canada*, 39.

36 LAC, Privy Council, RG2, vol. 2, file: D-16, A.D.P. Heeney to Mackenzie King, 20 June 1940; *Diaries of William Lyon Mackenzie King*, 19 June 1940.

37 "War Series: No. 36" (26 August 1940), in Kealey and Whitaker, *War Series, 1939–1941*, 286–7.

38 LAC, Joseph Mackenzie Papers, MG31 B45, vol. 6, file 15: "Joseph Mackenzie to Ed Robins," 26 July 1940.

39 LAC, Ernest Lapointe Papers, MG27 III B10, vol. 35, "Unions-Amendments to the Criminal Code Concerning the Right of Association," Norman McLarty to Ernest Lapointe, 21 September 1941.

40 Cohen, *Collective Bargaining in Canada*, 35

41 *Canadian Congress Journal* 19 (August 1940); LAC, Arthur J. Hills Papers, MG31 E12, vol. 5, "National Labour Supply Council," Text of Talk Broadcast over CBC by Tom Moore, 1 November 1940.

42 *Labour Gazette* 41 (March 1941).

43 Norrie and Owram, *History of the Canadian Economy*, 525.

44 LAC, Department of Labour, RG 27, vol. 632, file 82: "Committee of the Cabinet on Labour Supply," Memorandum from the Labour Co-ordination Committee to Norman McLarty, 18 October 1940.

45 Abella, *Nationalism, Communism and Canadian Labour*, 44–5; Morton with Copp, *Working People*, 169.
46 Hollander, "Down the Middle of the Road,"160.
47 LAC, Canadian Labour Congress, MG28 I103, vol. 312, file 2–24: "Canadian Committee for Industrial Organization, 1939–1940," Charles Millard and Silby Barrett to Mackenzie King, 16 August 1940; Woods, *Labour Policy in Canada*, 76; LAC, Labour Council of Metropolitan Toronto, MG28 I44, Microfilm Reel M2292, Norman McLarty to J.W. Buckley, 22 October 1940.
48 LAC, Canadian Labour Congress, MG28 I103, vol. 114, file 14: "CCL Executive Council Minutes," 5 November 1940.
49 LAC, Canadian Labour Congress, MG28 I103, vol. 190, file 5: "Federal Department of Labour Correspondence Part 2, 1939–1944," Memorandum with Respect to Meeting Held on June the 13th, 1940.
50 J.W. Pickersgill, *The Mackenzie King Record*, 1:7.
51 Fudge and Tucker, *Labour Before the Law*, 237.
52 John Stanton, "Government Internment Policy, 1939–1945," *Labour/Le Travail* 31 (Spring 1993): 211–19.
53 Kaplan, *State and Salvation*, 33–4, 37, 43–4; Abella, *Nationalism, Communism and Canadian Labour*, 46–7.
54 LAC, Canadian Labour Congress, MG28 I103, vol. 22, file 11: "UAW Local 195, Windsor, 1940–43, Part 2," UAW Bulletin 12 November 1941 – Norman Dowd to George Burt, 25 November 1940; George Burt to Norman Dowd, 28 November 1940 and 18 February 1941; and Norman Dowd to Ernest Lapointe, 18 June 1941; MG28 I103, vol. 192, file 5: "Federal Labour Court," A.R. Mosher and Norman Dowd to Norman McLarty, 14 January 1941; LAC, J.L. Cohen Papers, MG30 A94, vol. 25, file 2858: "UAW, Local 195 v. Chrysler Corp., Windsor, 1940–41," IDIA Commission Report, 10 September 1941 and J.L. Cohen to George Burt, 19 September 1941.
55 LAC, Canadian Labour Congress, MG28 I103, vol. 22, file 11: "UAW Local 195, Windsor, 1940–43, Part 2," UAW Bulletin 12 November, 1941 – Norman Dowd to George Burt, 15 November 1940; George Burt to Norman Dowd, 18 November 1940 and 18 February 1941; and Norman Dowd to Ernest Lapointe, 18 June 1941; MG28 I103, vol. 192, file 5: "Federal Labour Court," A.R. Mosher and Norman Dowd to Norman McLarty, 14 January 1941.
56 Stanton, "Government Internment Policy," 234.
57 Ibid., 211–19; Kaplan, *State and Salvation*, 34; Gregory S. Kealey and Reg Whitaker, "Introduction," in *R.C.M.P. Security Bulletins: The War Series, 1939–1941*, ed. Gregory S. Kealey and Reg Whitaker (St John's, NL: Committee on Canadian Labour History, 1989),14.

58 Stanton, "Government Internment Policy," 234; MacDowell, *Renegade Lawyer*, 154, 162–3, 170–1; LAC, J.L. Cohen Papers, MG30 A94, vol. 31, file 2917 A8: "National Council for Democratic Rights," Released Internees Represented by J.L. Cohen, 2 September 1942; Rick Salutin, *Kent Rowley, the Organizer: A Canadian Union Life* (Toronto: James Lorimer & Co., 1980), 26, 29; Ian Radforth, *Bush Workers and Bosses*, 142.
59 LAC, Ernest Lapointe Papers, MG27 III B10, vol. 16, "Communisme: Les measures entrepris par le Gouvernment pour combattre la subversive #40," Ernest Lapointe to L. Aileen Larkin, 27 October 1941.
60 LAC, J.L. Cohen Papers, MG30 A94, vol. 20, file 2807: "Defence of Canada Regulations," J.L. Cohen, Address to the Civil Liberties Association of Toronto, 1 November 1940.
61 LAC, J.L. Cohen Papers, MG30 A94, vol. 19, file 2801-3: "CSU: Sullivan Internment" and vol. 20, file 2801-3: "Pat Sullivan, Habeas Corpus; MacDowell, *Renegade Lawyer*, 164, 171–5.
62 LAC, J.L. Cohen Papers, MG30 A94, vol. 26, file 2872A: "REX v. Clarence Jackson" and "UE and the Internment of C.S. Jackson, Fall–Winter 1941"; MacDowell, *Renegade Lawyer*, 176–9, 181–2.
63 LAC, J.L. Cohen Papers, MG30 A94, vol. 19, file 2801-2: "CSU: Sullivan Internment," Tom Moore, to J.L. Cohen, 6 August 1940.
64 LAC, Canadian Labour Congress, MG30 I103, vol. 114, file 15: "CCL Executive Council Meeting Draft Minutes," 13 May 1941; MacDowell, *Renegade Lawyer*, 167.
65 LAC, J.L. Cohen Papers, MG30 A94, vol. 26, file 2872A: "UE and the Internment of C.S. Jackson, Fall–Winter 1941," J.L. Cohen to Norman Dowd, 18 September 1941.
66 LAC, Ottawa and District Labour Council, MG28 I236, vol. 10, file 41: "TLC Conventions, 1940–44," Report on the 1941 Convention; LAC, Canadian Labour Congress, MG28 I103, vol. 32, file 16: "UMWA District 18, Calgary, Part 3, 1940–43," Resolutions 17–22 November, 1941.
67 LAC, Canadian Labour Congress, MG28 I103, vol. 185, file 1: "Toronto Labour Council Part 1, 1940–41," G.R. Hodgson to Norman Dowd, 29 October 1941.
68 *Toronto Daily Star*, 1 November, 1941 and 20 January, 1942; *Saturday Night*, 13 September 1941; *Toronto Telegram*, 7 November, 1940; LAC, Richard B. Hanson Papers, MG27 III B22, Microfilm Reel C3121 43785, George Drew to R.B. Hanson, 12 September 1940.
69 Kealey and Whitaker, "Introduction," 14.
70 Reginald Whitaker, "Official Repression of Communism during World War II," *Labour/Le Travail* 17 (Spring 1986): 137–8, 160; Kaplan, *State and Salvation*, 38–43.

71 *Diaries of William Lyon Mackenzie King*, 24 November 1939; Kaplan, *State and Salvation*, 15–29.

72 J.L. Granatstein, *Canada's War: The Politics of the Mackenzie King Government, 1939–1945* (1975; repr., Toronto: University of Toronto Press, 1990), 28–35.

73 LAC, J.L. Cohen Papers, MG30 A94, vol. 31, file 2917-A8: "National Council for Democratic Rights," List of Released Interns, October 1942.

74 LAC, Department of Labour, RG27, vol. 632, file 82: "Committee of the Cabinet on Labour Supply," Memo to Norman McLarty, 18 October 1940; *Labour Gazette* 40 (November 1940): 1101–2.

75 Industrial Relations Counselors, Inc., "History of IRC," accessed 18 July 2007, http://ircounselors.org/history/index.html; Queen's University, *Industrial Relations at Queen's*, 2–4, 8, 12.

76 Rockefeller Archive Center, RG2F, vol. 16, file 130: "Industrial Relations Counselors Inc.," Bryce Stewart to C.J. Hicks, November 1943.

77 Struthers, *No Fault of the Their Own*, 181–2.

78 *Financial Post*, 28 September 1940.

79 *Labour Gazette* 50 (September 1950): 1333–9.

80 Ibid., 47 (July 1947): 950–95.

81 Michael Bliss, *Northern Enterprise: Five Centuries of Canadian Business* (Toronto: McClelland & Stewart, 1987), 452–3.

82 Bothwell and Kilbourn, *C.D. Howe*, 140–1; LAC, Department of Labour, RG27, vol. 897, file 9-9-74 Part 1: "Labour Co-ordination Committee," H.B. Chase to the Labour Co-ordination Committee, 10 October 1940 and "Labour Co-ordination Committee Minutes," 26 October, 1940.

83 Thompson with Seager, *Canada, 1922–1939*, 76.

84 Bryce M. Stewart, "War-Time Labour Problems and Policies in Canada," *Canadian Journal of Economics and Political Science* 7 (August 1941): 434–6.

85 Ibid.

86 Struthers, *No Fault of the Their Own*, 197–207.

87 *Diaries of William Lyon Mackenzie King*, 16 January and 13 December, 1940.

88 LAC, Department of Labour, RG27, vol. 887, file 8-9-74 Part 1: "Labour Co-ordination Committee Minutes," 23 November 1940 and 30 November 1940.

89 Stewart, "War-Time Labour Problems and Policies," 430.

90 LAC, Canadian Labour Congress, MG28 I103, vol. 331, file 2: "CCL Executive Committee Minutes, 1940–41," 31 March 1941; H.A. Logan, "Government Control of Labour Relations," *Behind the Headlines* 2 (October 1941): 8–9, 12–13.

91 LAC, Canadian Labour Congress, MG28 I103, vol. 43, file 12: "USWA Dosco-Peck Montreal 1941," C.P. McTague to Norman McLarty, 7 April 1941; *Labour Gazette* 41 (April 1941): 372–85.

92 National Archives of the United States, State Department, RG59, vol. 5040, file 842.5045/18: "1940–1945," Pierrepont Moffat to the Secretary of State, 29 April 1941.
93 Fudge and Tucker, *Labour Before the Law*, 237; Laurel Sefton MacDowell, "The 1943 Steel Strike against Wartime Wage Controls," *Labour/Le Travail* 10 (Autumn 1982): 67.
94 LAC, Canadian Labour Congress, MG28 I103, vol. 330, file 16: "CCL Executive Council Minutes, 1940–41," Report of the Executive Council, n.d.
95 LAC, Canadian Labour Congress, MG28 I103, vol. 183, file 6: "Hamilton General Service Workers' Organizing Campaign Part 2, 1942," Memorandum by Arthur Williams for CCL Executive Committee, 20 March 1942.
96 Cuthbertson, *Labour Goes to War*, 57.
97 LAC, J.L. Cohen Papers, MG30 A94, vols. 25 and 26; LAC, Canadian Labour Congress, MG28 I103, vols. 38, 43, 114, 118, 190, and 197.
98 LAC, Arthur Meighen Papers, MG26 I, Microfilm Reel C3593 144000, Eugene Forsey to Arthur Meighen, 14 January 1942.
99 *Labour Gazette* 41 (October 1941): 1243, 1249.
100 MacDowell, *Renegade Lawyer*, 100.
101 *Saturday Night*, 4 October 1941.
102 LAC, W.L. Mackenzie King Papers, MG26 J4, Microfilm Reel H1536 C24946, "Memoranda and Notes," Criticisms of the Government's Labour Policies – Cohen's Book on Collective Bargaining, 16 September 1941.
103 Cohen, *Collective Bargaining in Canada*, 43, 74.
104 LAC, Public Records Committee, RG35/7, vol. 21, file 18: "Wartime Activities of the Industrial Relations Branch," Report by the Department of Labour, March 1946.
105 Granatstein, *Canada's War*, 179–80.
106 *Canadian Congress Journal* 20 (November 1941): 6–7.
107 LAC, Privy Council, RG2, vol. 2, file D-16: "Department of Labour, 1940–41," Proposed Amendment to PC 7440 and Establishment of National and Regional War Labour Boards, 9 October 1941.
108 LAC, Canadian Labour Congress, MG28 I103, vol. 238, file 4: "General Correspondence, TLC Part 3, 1930–1944," Report on the Conference of TLC Leaders Regarding PC 8253, 13 November 1941.
109 LAC, Canadian Labour Congress, MG28 I103, vol. 114, file 13: "CCL Executive Committee Meeting, Draft Minutes," 22 October 1941.
110 Hollander, "Down the Middle of the Road," 161.

111 *Financial Post*, 26 April 1941.
112 Stewart, "War-Time Labour Problems and Policies," 445.
113 LAC, Canadian Labour Congress, MG28 I103, vol. 238, file 4: "General Correspondence. Trades and Labour Congress, Part 2, 1930–44," TLC Annual Memorandum to the Government, 14 March 1941; *Labour Gazette* 41 (July 1941): 801.
114 *Hansard*, 19th Parliament, 2nd Session, vol. 4 (6 June 1941), 3628.
115 Pickersgill, *The Mackenzie King Record*, 1:145–6.
116 *Diaries of William Lyon Mackenzie King*, 23 May, 30 May, and 29 July 1941.
117 *Industrial Canada* 42 (October 1941): 63; LAC, C.D. Howe Papers, MG27 III B20, vol. 140, "Articles, Speeches, and Books, Part 2," R.A. Stapells to C.D. Howe, 24 April, 1941, C.D. Howe to R.A. Stappells, 29 April 1941, and Norman McLarty to C.D. Howe, 3 May 1941.
118 LAC, C.D. Howe Papers, MG27 III B20, vol. 143, "Articles and Biography, Ministers," C.D. Howe to Mackenzie King, 26 July 1941; *Diaries of William Lyon Mackenzie King*, 26 July 1941; LAC, Ernest Lapointe Papers, MG27 III B10, vol. 11, "Arvida – Grève á la Compagnie Arvida," C. Vaillancourt to Ernest Lapointe, 31 July 1941.
119 *Diaries of William Lyon Mackenzie King*, 27 July 1941.
120 LAC, Privy Council, RG2, vol. 2, file D-16: "Department of Labour, 1940–41," Royal Commission on Arvida Strike, October, 1941.
121 *Diaries of William Lyon Mackenzie King*, 6 June 1941.
122 LAC, Department of Labour, RG27, vol. 897, file 8-9-74 Part 1: "Labour Co-ordination Committee Minutes," 29 April 1941.
123 Cohen, *Collective Bargaining in Canada*,16–24.
124 LAC, Department of Labour, RG27, vol. 632, file 70: "Labour Conditions on War Contracts," Bryce Stewart to Norman McLarty, 22 February 1941.
125 LAC, J.L. Cohen Papers, MG30 A94, vol. 24, file 2848: "SWOC and National Steel Car, 1941," Eric Dalrymple to Norman McLarty, 30 January 1941; Everett Lymburner to Erie Dalrymple, 8 February 1941; G.D. Conant to Ernest Lapointe, 3 February 1941; Ruling of Magistrate H.A. Burbidge, 3 April 1941.
126 LAC, Public Records Committee, RG35/7, vol. 21, file 18: "History of Wartime Activities – Industrial Relations Branch," March 1946.
127 LAC, J.L. Cohen Papers, MG30 A94, vol. 25, file 2871: "Canadian Hosiery Workers Union Local 18 v. Schofield Woollen Co. Ltd. Re. Royal Commission to Investigate the Strike of April 7, 1941."
128 LAC, Canadian Labour Congress, vol. 238, file 4: "General Correspondence, TLC, Part 2, 1930–44," Memorandum Presented to the Prime Minister, 14 March 1941.

129 *Financial Post*, 19 and 26 April 1941.
130 LAC, J.L. Cohen Papers, MG30 A94, vol. 25, file 2870: "PWOC v. Dumart's Ltd.," Spring and Summer 1941.
131 LAC, Mackenzie King Papers, MG26 J13, Microfilm Reel H1497 C193441, A. Brunzlow to Mackenzie King, 5 August 1941.
132 LAC, Public Records Committee, RG35/7, vol. 21, file 18: "History of Wartime Activities – Industrial Relations Branch," March 1946.
133 LAC, Department of Labour, RG27, vol. 632, file 85, Part 1: "NLSC Minutes," 24 March 1941 and A.J. Hills to Norman McLarty, 20 May 1941.
134 LAC, Department of Labour, RG27, vol. 635, file 131, Part 1: "Dismissals for Union Activities," Memorandum on the Chronology of the Proposed Order, 8 April 1941 and Amended Draft of Proposed Measures for Dealing with Alleged Discrimination for Union Activity, 8 April 1941.
135 LAC, Canadian Labour Congress, MG 28 I103, vol. 114, file 9: "CCL Executive Committee Meetings, Draft Minutes," 25 March 1941 and vol. 191: "National Labour Supply Council, Part 1, 1941–42," Report of the Committee on Measures for Dealing with Alleged Discrimination for Union Activity, 1 April 1941.
136 LAC, Canadian Labour Congress, MG 28 I103, vol. 314, file 24: "Federal Government: Correspondence Concerning Wartime Relations with Organized Labour, 1939–41," Patrick Conroy to A.R. Mosher, 19 April 1941.
137 LAC, Canadian Manufacturers Association, MG28 I230, In Process 83/138: "CMA-Industrial Relations Committee Minutes," 17 April 1941; RG 27, Department of Labour, vol. 635, file 131: "Dismissals for Union Activities," J.M. Piggott to A.J. Hills, 6 May 1941 and J.H. Stovel to Humphrey Mitchell, 10 May 1941.
138 LAC, Department of Labour, RG 27, vol. 632, file 85, Part 1: "NLSC Minutes," A.J. Hills to Norman McLarty, 20 May 1941.
139 *Labour Gazette* 41 (May 1941): 527–30; *Ottawa Journal*, 10 March 1938.
140 *Diaries of William Lyon Mackenzie King*, 28 April 1941.
141 LAC, Richard B. Hanson Papers, MG27 III B22, Microfilm Reel C3099 29052, Bryce Stewart to Richard B. Hanson, 2 May 1941.
142 LAC, J.L. Cohen Papers, MG30 A94, vol. 24, file 2854: "SWOC and LACSCO," J.L. Cohen to Norman McLarty, 24 June 1941.
143 LAC, W.L. Mackenzie King Papers, MG26 J1, Microfilm Reel C262187 C4865, "Primary Correspondence," CMA Delegation, 5 May 1941; LAC, Department of Labour, RG27, Microfilm Reel T-10,109, vol. 121, file 601.2: "CMA Correspondence," Harold Crabtree to Mackenzie King, 5 May 1941.

144 *Diaries of William Lyon Mackenzie King*, 5 May 1941.
145 *Financial Post*, 10 May 1941.
146 LAC, Canadian Labour Congress, MG28 I103, vol. 114, file 15: Draft Minutes of the CCL Executive Council Meetings, 13 May 1941.
147 LAC, Department of Labour, RG27, Microfilm Reel T10, 179, vol. 254, file 721.02: "Illegal Strikes," Memorandum by Norman McLarty to W. Stuart Edwards, 9 June 1941.
148 LAC, J.L. Cohen Papers, MG30 A94, vol. 25, file 2871: "Canadian Hosiery Workers Union, Local 18 v. Schofield Woollen Co. Ltd. RE. Royal Commission to Investigate the Strike of April 7, 1941."
149 LAC, J.L. Cohen Papers, MG30 A94, vol. 26, file 2873: "REX v. Various Members of the UE," Trial Transcripts for 24 June, 4 July, and 15 July 1941.
150 *Diaries of William Lyon Mackenzie King*, 31 May 1941; LAC, Department of Labour, RG27, vol. 897, file 8-9-74, Part 1: "Labour Co-ordination Committee Minutes," 3 June 1941.
151 *Labour Gazette* 41 (July 1941): 801.
152 Fudge and Tucker, *Labour Before the Law*, 246–8; LAC, Department of Labour, RG27, vol. 897, file 8-9-74, Part 1: "Labour Co-ordination Committee Minutes," 3 June 1941.
153 LAC, Public Records Committee, vol. 21, file 18: "Wartime Activities of the Industrial Relations Branch," Report of the Department of Labour, March 1946.
154 LAC, Public Records Committee, vol. 21, file 18: "Wartime Activities of the Industrial Relations Branch," Appointments of Commissions under Section 5 of Order in Council PC 4020 of 6 June 1941. As Amended, March 1946.
155 LAC, Canadian Labour Congress, MG30 I103, vol. 330, file 16: "CCL Executive Council Minutes, 1940–41," n.d.
156 *Diaries of William Lyon Mackenzie King*, 31 May 1941.
157 LAC, Canadian Labour Congress, MG30 I103, vol. 314, file 24: "Federal Government: Correspondence Concerning Wartime Relations with Organized Labour, 1939–1941," A.R. Mosher to Patrick Conroy, 20 June 1941.
158 LAC, Canadian Labour Congress, MG30 I103, vol. 314, file 24: "Federal Government: Correspondence Concerning Wartime Relations with Organized Labour, 1939–1941," Norman Dowd to Patrick Conroy, 11 June 1941.
159 LAC, J.L. Cohen Papers, MG30 A94, vol. 24, file 2856: "CCL Re. Orders-in-Council 2685 and 7440, and General Correspondence," J.L. Cohen to M.M. Maclean, 9 June 1941; *Labour Gazette* 41 (July 1941): 801.

160 LAC, Canadian Labour Congress, MG30 I103, vol. 44, file 15: "USWA – Charles H. Millard, Part 4, 1940–42," Norman S. Dowd to Gerald Brown, 30 July 1941.
161 LAC, Labour Council of Metropolitan Toronto, MG28 I44, Microfilm M2292, Toronto District Labour Council, "Resolution Submitted by Archie Johnson," 19 June 1941; *Canadian Congress Journal* 20 (June 1941): 7.
162 Stuart Brandes, *American Welfare Capitalism, 1880–1940* (Chicago: University of Chicago Press, 1976), 125.
163 Daphne G. Taras, "Voice in the North American Workplace: From Employee Representation to Employee Involvement," in *Industrial Relations to Human Resources and Beyond: The Evolving Process of Employee Relations Management*, ed. Bruce E. Kaufman, Richard A. Beaumont, and Roy B. Helfgott (New York: M.E. Sharpe, 2003), 301–2; King, *Industry and Humanity*, 277–87; Paul Craven, *An Impartial Umpire*, 241–70; Howard M. Gitelman, *Legacy of the Ludlow Massacre: A Chapter in American Industrial Relations* (Philadelphia, PA: University of Pennsylvania Press, 1988), passim.
164 Rockefeller Archive Center, RG2F, vol. 16, file 127: "Industrial Relations Counselors Inc., 1926–1958," Raymond Fosdick to John D. Rockefeller Jr., March 1934 and file 130: "Industrial Relations Counselors Inc.," Bryce Stewart Memorandum to C.J. Hicks, November 1943.
165 *Labour Gazette* 41 (July 1941), 800.
166 LAC, Canadian Manufacturers Association, MG28 I230, In Process, 83/138, file "Industrial Relations Committee Minutes," 10 September 1941.
167 King, *Industry and Humanity*, 137–9, 279–87.
168 Bruce Kaufman, "Accomplishments and Shortcomings of Nonunion Employee Representation in the Pre-Wagner Act Years: A Reassessment," in *Nonunion Employee Representation: History, Contemporary Practice, and Policy*, ed. Bruce Kaufman and Daphne Gottlieb Taras (New York: M.E. Sharpe, 2000), 27–8, 32–5.
169 Stewart, "War-Time Labour Problems and Policies," 444.
170 Daphne Gottlieb Taras, "Portrait of Nonunion Employee Representation in Canada: History, Law, and Contemporary Plans," in Kaufman and Taras, *Nonunion Employee Representation*, 123.
171 *Diaries of William Lyon Mackenzie King*, 7 February 1919.
172 Kaufman, "Accomplishments and Shortcomings," 27.
173 LAC, J.L. Cohen Papers, MG30 A94, vol. 26, file 2878: "SLWOC v. L. McBrine Co.," SLWOC Submission to the L. McBrine, Sunshine Waterloo, and Dominion Trucking Conciliation Board, 22 May 1941.

174 Taras, "Portrait of Nonunion Employee Representation in Canada," 123–5.
175 *PM Magazine*, November 1941.
176 LAC, Department of Labour, RG27, vol. 638, file 202: "IDIC – Canada Packers," Bryce M. Stewart to Humphrey Mitchell, 7 July 1941.
177 Cuthbertson, *Labour Goes to War*, 44.
178 LAC, Canadian Manufacturers Association, MG28 I230, In Process 83/138, file: "Industrial Relations Committee Minutes," 10 September 1941.
179 *Canadian Forum* 21 (August 1941); *Labour Gazette* 40 (June 1940): 538–43.
180 *Diaries of William Lyon Mackenzie King*, 14 March, 1941.
181 LAC, J.L. Cohen Papers, MG30 A94, vol. 24, file 2854: "SWOC and NASCO," J.L. Cohen to Norman McLarty, 24 June, 1941 and H.B. Chase to J.L. Cohen, 15 July 1941.
182 LAC, J.L. Cohen Papers, MG30 A94, vol. 24, file 2854: "SWOC and NASCO," Charlie Millard to Norman McLarty, 24 July 1941.
183 *Diaries of William Lyon Mackenzie King*, 28 July and 31 July, 1941; LAC, Canadian Labour Congress, vol. 118, file 12: "Millard, Charles H." Charles Millard to Mackenzie King, 22 September 1941.
184 LAC, J.L. Cohen Papers, MG30 A94, vol. 24, file 2854: "SWOC and LACSCO," C.H. Millard to SWOC's Montreal Office, 1 August 1941.
185 *Hansard*, 19th Parliament, 2nd Session, vol. 4 (14 November 1941), 4404.
186 LAC, Public Records Committee, RG35/7, vol. 21, file 8: "History of Wartime Activities – Industrial Relations Branch," Industrial Disputes Inquiry Commissions Established under Order in Council PC 4020 of 6 June 1941, section 1, n.d.
187 LAC, Department of Labour, RG27, Access 83/84-206, box 1: George Hodge Memorandum to C.A.L. Murchison, 5 July 1946.
188 LAC, Department of Labour, RG27, vol. 638, file 202: "IDIC – Canada Packers," Bryce Stewart to Humphrey Mitchell, 7 July, 1941.
189 *Financial Post*, 28 November 1940 and 24 October 1941; MacDowell, *'Remember Kirkland Lake,'* 93–4.
190 NAC, Department of Labour, RG 27, vol. 637, file 188: "IDIC Case Reports," 24 July 1941 and 7 August 1941; *Labour Gazette* 41 (September 1941): 1085.
191 MacDowell, *'Remember Kirkland Lake,'* 75–96; LAC, Department of Labour, RG27, vol. 637, file 118: "IDIC Case Reports," 12 August 1941.
192 LAC, Arthur Meighen Papers, Microfilm Reel, C3593-144000, Eugene Forsey to Arthur Meighen, 14 January 1942.
193 MacDowell, *'Remember Kirkland Lake,'* 92.

194 *Canadian Congress Journal* 20 (September 1941).
195 Cohen, *Collective Bargaining in Canada*, 55, 59.
196 LAC, Privy Council, RG2, vol. 2, file 16: "Department of Labour, 1940–41," Norman McLarty to Mackenzie King, 16 September 1941.
197 *Labour Gazette* 41 (October 1941): 1209.
198 LAC, Bernard Wilson Papers, MG31 E16, vol. 2, file: "Wartime Labour Relations History," Manuscript by Bernard Wilson, n.d.
199 LAC, Public Records Committee, RG35/7, vol. 21, file 18: "Wartime Activities – Industrial Relations Branch," Strike Votes under Order in Council, PC 7307, n.d.
200 *Financial Post*, 27 September 1941.
201 LAC, Canadian Labour Congress, MG28 I103, vol. 314, file 24: "Federal Government: Correspondence Concerning Wartime Relations with Organized Labour, 1939–41," Norman Dowd to Mackenzie King, 19 September 1941.
202 Cohen, *Collective Bargaining in Canada*, 64.
203 *Labour Gazette* 41 (October 1941): 1244–9; *Toronto Telegram*, 22 September 1941; LAC, Ottawa and District Labour Council, MG28 I236, vol. 10, file 41: "TLC Conventions, 1940–44," Report of the 1941 TLC Convention, September 1941.
204 LAC, Canadian Labour Congress, MG28 I103, vol. 313, file 14: "Pat Conroy – Correspondence, 1941," Patrick Conroy to Norman Dowd, 8 August 1941.

3. The Task That Lies Ahead, Fall 1941–Fall 1942

1 King, *Industry and Humanity*, 257.
2 *Diaries of William Lyon Mackenzie King*, 15 December 1941.
3 Walter Galenson and Arnold Zellner, "International Comparison of Unemployment Rates," in *The Measurement and Behavior of Unemployment*, ed. National Bureau Committee for Economic Research (Princeton, NJ: Princeton University Press, 1957), 456.
4 Hollander, "Down the Middle of the Road," 232–3.
5 National Archives of the United States, RG 174, Department of Labor, vol. 160, file: "Frances Perkins – General Subject Files – State Department 1942," Cordell Hull to Frances Perkins, 12 February 1942.
6 LAC, Canadian Labour Congress, MG28 I103, vol. 192, file 3: "Federal Department of Labour, Part 2, 1940–43," Pat Conroy to Humphrey Mitchell, 12 May 1942.
7 *Diaries of William Lyon Mackenzie King*, 9 September 1942 and 9 December 1942.

8 LAC, Canadian Labour Congress, MG28 I103, vol. 114, file 16, "CCL Executive Council Draft Minutes, 22 October 1941 and vol. 192, file 4: "Federal Labour Department, Part 3, 1930–43," CCL Representation to the Government, 22 October 1941.

9 LAC, Canadian Labour Congress, MG28 I103, vol. 114, file 13: "CCL Executive Committee Meeting, Draft Minutes," 20–22 October 1941.

10 Joseph Stalin, "Broadcast to the People of the Soviet Union, July 3, 1941," Appendix 1 in *Assured Victory: How Stalin the Great Won the War But Lost the Peace,* by Albert L. Weeks (Santa Barbara, CA: Praeger, 2011), 229–34.

11 LAC, Canadian Labour Congress, MG28 I103, vol. 317, file 2: "Clarence S. Jackson, President, UE District 5 – 1942," C.S. Jackson to C.D. Howe, 20 May 1942.

12 LAC, Canadian Labour Congress, MG28 I103, vol. 313, file 25: "Pat Conroy Speeches," Speech on Bargaining Rights in Wartime to the Workers' Educational Association, 22 March 1942.

13 Hollander, "Down the Middle of the Road," 232.

14 MacDowell, *'Remember Kirkland Lake,'* 118–39.

15 *Northern News,* 8 October 1941; LAC, J.L. Cohen Papers, MG30 A94, vol. 26, file 2879: "Mine, Mill and Smelter Workers, Local 240 v. Assorted Gold Mines," Report of the Kirkland Lake Conciliation Board, 15 October, 1941.

16 LAC, Canadian Labour Congress, MG28 I103, vol. 114, file 13: "CCL Executive Committee Meeting, Draft Minutes," 20–22 October, 1941.

17 Abella, *Nationalism, Communism, and Canadian Labour,* 88.

18 MacDowell, *'Remember Kirkland Lake,'* 44, 173–82, 190–2.

19 *PM Magazine,* November 1941.

20 LAC, J.L. Cohen Papers, MG30 A94, vol. 28, file 2900: "Mine, Mill and Smelter Workers v. Kirkland Lake Mine Operators," Mackenzie King to William Simpson, 6 December 1941.

21 LAC, M Canadian Labour Congress, G28 I103, vol. 317, file 8: "Mackenzie King Correspondence," Patrick Conroy to Mackenzie King, 13 January 1942.

22 *Diaries of William Lyon Mackenzie King,* 2 December 1941.

23 LAC, J.L. Cohen Papers, MG30 A94, vol. 28, file 2900: "Mine, Mill and Smelter Workers v. Kirkland Lake Mine Operators," Reid Robinson to Philip Murray, 13 February 1942.

24 MacDowell, *'Remember Kirkland Lake,'* 173–7.

25 Ibid., 221.

26 *Canadian Congress Journal* 21 (February 1942): 19–24.

27 LAC, Canadian Labour Congress, MG28 I103, vol. 313, file 8: "CIO–Allan Haywood Correspondence, 1941–42," Patrick Conroy to Allan

Haywood, 2 April 1942; vol. 192, file 12: "Federal Minister's Consultative Committee, 1942," Humphrey Mitchell to A.R. Mosher, 8 April 1942.

28 Chaired by Humphrey Mitchell, the NWLB executive included R.H. Neilson, a Labour Department official, as secretary; George Hodge of Canadian Pacific Railroad; and J.A. McClelland of the International Association of Machinists. LAC, Records of Boards, Offices and Commissions, RG 36/4, "The National War Labour Board."

29 *Diaries of William Lyon Mackenzie King*, 27 February 1942; *Labour Gazette* 42 (March 1942): 291–5.

30 *Canadian Forum* 22 (April 1942): 21.

31 LAC, Canadian Labour Congress, MG28 I103, vol. 312, file 12: "George Burt Correspondence, 1942–46," Pat Conroy to Philip Murray, 5 March, 1942.

32 LAC, Canadian Labour Congress, MG28 I103, vol. 313, file 25: "Pat Conroy Speeches," Speech on Bargaining Rights in Wartime to the Workers' Educational Association, 22 March 1942.

33 MacDowell, *'Remember Kirkland Lake,'* 224.

34 LAC, Canadian Labour Congress, MG28 I103, Memorandum Submitted by Murray Cotterill to the CCL Executive Committee, 18 March 1942; Cuthbertson, *Labour Goes to War*, 58.

35 LAC, Canadian Labour Congress, MG28 I103, vol. 183, file 6: "Hamilton General Service Workers' Organizing Campaign, Part 2, 1942," Charlie Millard to Patrick Conroy, 16 March 1942.

36 LAC, Canadian Labour Congress, MG28 I103, Murray Cotterill to Patrick Conroy, 1 April 1942; vol. 76, file 2: "Textile Workers' Organizing Committee, Part 2, 1941–43," Arthur Williams to Patrick Conroy, 5 March 1942; and vol. 24, file 6: "UAW – Local 222, Oshawa, Part 1, 1940–43," Patrick Conroy to A.G. Schultz, 8 May 1942.

37 LAC, Canadian Labour Congress, MG28 I103, vol. 183, file 6: "Hamilton General Service Workers' Organizing Campaign, Part 2, 1942," Arthur Williams to Patrick Conroy, 11 May 1942.

38 LAC, Canadian Labour Congress, MG28 I103, vol. 313, file 25: "Pat Conroy Speeches," Speech on Bargaining Rights in Wartime to the Workers' Educational Association, 22 March 1942; and vol. 330, file 17: "CCL Executive Council Minutes, 1942–43," 21 November 1942.

39 Hollander, "Down the Middle of the Road," 233.

40 LAC, Canadian Labour Congress, MG28 I103, vol. 119, file 1: "Mosher, Aaron Roland, 1941–55," Labour Day Message, 1 September 1941.

41 Abella, *Nationalism, Communism, and Canadian Labour*, 67–70, 80.

42 LAC, Canadian Labour Congress, MG28 I103, vol. 45, file 11: "USWA, Alan Wright, 1941–44," Alan Wright to Norman Dowd, 29 January 1942.

43 Abella, *Nationalism, Communism, and Canadian Labour*, 176.

44 LAC, Canadian Labour Congress, MG28 I103, vol. 319, file 16: "TLC of Canada: Cooperation between the TLC and CCL, 1941–48," Tom Moore to A.R. Mosher, 19 December 1941; vol. 330, file 10: "TLC Executive Council Minutes, 1939–42," 10–13 February 1942; vol. 330, file 17: "CCL Executive Council Minutes," 26 February 1942.
45 LAC, Canadian Labour Congress, MG28 I103, vol. 192, file 12: "Federal Labour Department, Minister's Consultative Committee, 1942," Patrick Conroy to Tom Moore, 21 March 1942; vol. 319, file 34: "UE – 1942," Patrick Conroy to C.S. Jackson, 20 June 1942.
46 LAC, Canadian Labour Congress, MG28 I103, vol. 313, file 8: "CIO – Allan Haywood, Correspondence, 1941–42," Patrick Conroy to Allan Haywood, 2 April 1942.
47 *Toronto Telegram*, 8 May, 1942; *Globe and Mail*, 9 May, 1942.
48 LAC, Canadian Labour Congress, MG28 I103, vol. 177, file 1: "British Columbia Labour Council, Part I, 1942," Patrick Conroy to Harold Pritchett, 24 October 1942.
49 LAC, Canadian Labour Congress, MG28 I103, vol. 178, file 11: "British Columbia Vancouver Island Joint Labour Conference," James Robertson to Patrick Conroy, 6 March 1942; LAC, C.S. Jackson Papers, MG31 B54, vol. 2, file 26: "Wartime Labour Legislation, 1942–45, 1948–65," Proceedings of a Provincial Trade Union Conference Called by the Workers Educational Association and Endorsed by the TLC and CCL, 29 November 1942; *Toronto Daily Star*, 25 and 27 July 1942.
50 LAC, Canadian Labour Congress, MG28 I103, vol. 185, file 5: "Toronto Labour Council, Part 3, 1942–43," Murray Cotterill to Patrick Conroy, 14 July 1942.
51 Lewis, *The Good Fight*, 190, 204–5.
52 *Toronto Daily Star*, 26 May, 1942.
53 LAC, Canadian Labour Congress, MG28 I103, vol. 313, file 36: "CCF – General," Patrick Conroy to Charles Millard, 30 January 1942.
54 Abella, *Nationalism, Communism, and Canadian Labour*, 73–5; MacDowell, *'Remember Kirkland Lake,'* 233.
55 *Toronto Daily Star*, 25 and 26 March 1942; *Canadian Congress Journal* 21 (April 1942): 14–15.
56 *Financial Post*, 11 April 1942 and 2 May 1942.
57 LAC, Canadian Labour Congress, MG28 I103, vol. 211, file 6: "General Correspondence on Collective Bargaining, Part 1, 1928–42," Patrick Conroy to C.S. Jackson, 6 July 1942.
58 LAC, Canadian Labour Congress, MG28 I103, vol. 314, file 25: "Federal Government Correspondence," C.S. Jackson to E.M. Little, 18 June 1942; vol. 317, file 2: "Clarence S. Jackson," Patrick Conroy to C.S. Jackson,

20 June 1942; vol. 30, file 14: "IUMMSW – General, 1940–43," Patrick Conroy to Thomas McGuire, 17 August 1942.

59 LAC, Canadian Labour Congress, MG28 I103, vol. 44, file 13: "USWA – Charles H. Millard, Part 2, 1940–42," Patrick Conroy to Charles Millard, 20 July 1942.

60 *Diaries of William Lyon Mackenzie King*, 16 November 1942.

61 Hollander, "Down the Middle of the Road," 232.

62 *Canadian Business* 14 (November 1941): 32–4.

63 Ibid.

64 LAC, Brooke Claxton Papers, MG32 B5, vol. 170, "Labour II," U.S. Coordinator of Information, Restricted Bulletin No. 4, "Canadian Labour and the War," 9 January 1942.

65 *Financial Post*, 4 October 1941.

66 *Canadian Business* 14 (November 1941): 36–7, 98–9.

67 *Northern Miner*, 12 February 1942.

68 National War Labour Board, *Proceedings of the National War Labour Board Public Enquiry*, vols. 2–12 (Ottawa: King's Printer, 1943), 8:672–4 (hereafter referred to as *NWLB Proceedings*); LAC, J.L. Cohen Papers, MG30 A94, vol. 32, file 2940: "UAW Local 195, Windsor v. Garwood Industries, Canadian Bridge Company, Canadian Steel Corp. and Champion Spark Plug," 9 July 1942.

69 *Labour Gazette* 42 (November 1942): 1258–67.

70 *Labour Gazette* 43 (January 1943): 71–7.

71 *NWLB Proceedings*, 9:834.

72 LAC, J.L. Cohen Papers, MG30 A94, vol. 33, file 2962: "UE v. Taylor Electric Manufacturing Co. Ltd. – London, 1942–43," Employee Brief to the Conciliation Board, 16 November 1942.

73 Sanford M. Jacoby, "Reckoning with Company Unions: The Case of Thompson Products, 1934–1964," *Industrial and Labor Relations Review* 43 (October 1989): 39.

74 LAC, Canadian Labour Congress, MG28 I103, vol. 29, file 3: "International Fur and Leather Workers' Union – 1940–43," Patrick Conroy to M.M. Maclean, 24 December 1942.

75 Patrias, *Jobs and Justice*, 24.

76 *Windsor Daily Star*, 6 November 1941.

77 LAC, J.L. Cohen Papers, MG30 A94, vol. 28, file 2898: "UAW v. Ford"; *Windsor Daily Star*, 6 November 1941, 12 January 1942, and 16 January 1942; *Labour Gazette* 41 (November 1941): 1339; Montero, *We Stood Together*, 92–7; David Moulton, "Ford Windsor 1945," in Abella, *On Strike*, 131–2.

78 LAC, J.L. Cohen Papers, MG30 A94, vol. 29, file 2908: "UAW Local 195 v. Chrysler Corporation of Canada, Spring 1942"; Canadian Labour Congress, MG28 I103, vol. 22, file 10: "UAW Local Part 1, 1940–43"; Paul Martin, *Far From Home*, 292–3.
79 LAC, Canadian Labour Congress, MG28 I103, vol. 39, file 10: "United Rubber Workers – General, Part 1, 1940–44"; Bryan D. Palmer, *Capitalism Comes to the Backcountry*, 77–8.
80 Montero, *We Stood Together*, 97.
81 LAC, Canadian Labour Congress, MG28 I103, vol. 155, file: "O'Brien, Daniel – Vancouver Correspondence, Part 2, 1942," Daniel O'Brien to Patrick Conroy, 14 March 1942.
82 LAC, Canadian Labour Congress, MG28 I103, vol. 190, file 4: "Federal Department of Labour Correspondence, Part 2, 1939–1944," A.W. Crawford to Patrick Conroy, 26 January 1942.
83 LAC, Canadian Labour Congress, MG28 I103, vol. 22, file 8: "UAW Local 112, Toronto, Part 1, 1942–46," and file 9: "UAW, Local 112, Toronto, Part 2, 1942–43; LAC, Department of Labour, RG 27, vol. 863, file 8-4-5-1: "Industrial Disputes Investigation Committee," A. MacNamara to Norman McLarty, 16 January 1942; *Labour Gazette* 43 (July 1943): 924.
84 LAC, Canadian Labour Congress, MG28 I103, vol. 313, file 25: "Pat Conroy Speeches," Speech on Bargaining Rights in Wartime to the Workers' Educational Association, 22 March 1942; *Ottawa Citizen*, 17 December, 1941.
85 *Canadian Forum* 22 (October 1942): 210.
86 *Industrial Canada* 44 (January 1944): 95.
87 LAC, Canadian Labour Congress, MG28 I103, vol. 44, file 12: "USWA – Charles Millard, Part 1 – 1940–42," Charles Millard to M.M. Maclean, 27 November 1942.
88 Russell, *Back to Work?*, 175.
89 Jeffrey Keshen, *Saints, Sinners, and Soldiers: Canada's Second World War* (Vancouver, BC: UBC Press, 2004), 54.
90 *Montreal Gazette*, 12 May 1942.
91 MacDowell, *'Remember Kirkland Lake,'* 178–9; *Globe and Mail*, 5 January 1942.
92 *Toronto Daily Star*, 25 March 1942; *Canadian Congress Journal* 21 (April 1942): 20.
93 *Canadian Forum* 22 (July 1942): 110.
94 LAC, J.L. Cohen Papers, MG30 A94, vol. 39, file 3112-A: "CCL Reports on PC 1003," J.L. Cohen to Percy Bengough, 22 December 1943.
95 Michael Earle, "'Down with Hitler and Silby Barrett': The Cape Breton Miners' Slowdown Strike of 1941," in Earle, *Workers and the State*, 114.

96 LAC, J.L. Cohen Papers, MG30 A94, vol. 18, file 2790: "CSU v. Various Great Lakes Shipping Companies," Report of the Conciliation Board, 14 January 1941.

97 LAC, J.L. Cohen Papers, MG30 A94, vol. 26, file 2879: "Mine Mill, Local 240 v. Various Kirkland Lake Gold Mine Operators," 15 October 1941; MacDowell, *'Remember Kirkland Lake,'* 108–10.

98 Stephen C. Gray, "Woodworkers and Legitimacy," 96–7.

99 LAC, Canada Manufacturers Association, MG28 I230, vol. 15: "CMA Executive Council Minutes," 28 September 1942.

100 *Canadian Forum* 21 (November 1941): 232.

101 LAC, Canadian Labour Congress, MG28 I103, vol. 313, file 25: "Pat Conroy Speeches," Speech on Bargaining Rights in Wartime to the Workers' Educational Association, 22 March, 1942.

102 Hollander, "Down the Middle of the Road," 233.

103 Canada, Advisory Committee on Reconstruction, Subcommittee on Post-War Problems of Women, *Post-War Problems of Women: Final Report of the Subcommittee,* 30 November 1943 (Ottawa: King's Printer, 1944), 7.

104 Peter S. Li, "Cultural Diversity in Canada: The Social Construction of Racial Differences," Department of Justice Strategic Issues Series, rp02-83 (Ottawa: Research and Statistics Division, 2000), 2.

105 Patrias, *Jobs and Justice,* 20–7, 32–5, 154.

106 Pamela Sugiman, "Privilege and Oppression," 88, 91.

107 *Labour Gazette* 44 (April 1944): 462.

108 Ivana Caccia, *Managing the Canadian Mosaic in Wartime: Shaping Citizenship Policy, 1939–1945* (Montreal: McGill-Queen's University Press, 2010), 126.

109 Alison Prentice et al., *Canadian Women: A History* (Toronto: Harcourt Brace Jovanovich, 1988), 234; Ruth Roach Pierson, *'They're Still Women After All': The Second World War and Canadian Womanhood* (Toronto: McClelland & Stewart, 1986), 9.

110 Pierson, *They're Still Women,* 25–6; Canada, Advisory Committee on Reconstruction, *Post-War Problems of Women: Final Report of the Subcommittee,* 8.

111 Ibid., 7; *Labour Gazette* 45 (July 1945): 1042.

112 *Toronto Daily Star,* 25 March 1942; *Labour Gazette* 44 (April 1944): 456.

113 Canada, Advisory Committee on Reconstruction, *Post-War Problems of Women: Final Report of the Subcommittee,* 17, 19.

114 *Labour Gazette* 44 (April 1944): 457–8.

115 Pierson, *They're Still Women,* 26, 77.

116 Helen Smith and Pamela Wakewich, "Trans/Forming the Citizen Body in Wartime: National and Local Public Discourse on Women's

Bodies and 'Body Work' for Women during the Second World War," in *Contesting Bodies and Nation in Canadian History*, ed. Patrizia Gentile and Jane Nicholas (Toronto: University of Toronto Press, 2013), 311–12.

117 *Labour Gazette* 44 (April 1944): 457.

118 Sugiman, *Labour's Dilemma*, 70.

119 Canada, Advisory Committee on Reconstruction VI, *Post-War Problems of Women*, 8.

120 Pierson, *They're Still Women*, 78.

121 Jeffrey A. Keshen, "Revisiting Canada's Civilian Women during World War II," *Histoire sociale/ Social History* 30, no. 60 (1997): 256.

122 *The Canada Year Book, 1943–44* (Ottawa: King's Printer, 1944), 789; *Labour Gazette* 47 (February 1947): 136.

123 Keshen, *Saints, Sinners, and Soldiers*, 55.

124 Barry Broadfoot, *Six War Years, 1939–1945: Memories of Canadians at Home and Abroad* (Toronto: Doubleday Canada, 1974), 277.

125 Sugiman, "Privilege and Oppression," 93.

126 LAC, Public Records Committee, RG 35/7, vol. 20, file 10: "Historical Activities Re. Employment of Women in the War," Table I – Average Annual, Weekly, and Hourly Earnings of Female Wage-earners, 1939–45, n.d.; Bonnie J. Fox and John Fox, "Women in the Labour Market, 1931–81: Exclusion and Competition," *Canadian Review of Sociology and Anthropology* 23, no. 1 (1986): 7–8.

127 Broadfoot, *Six War Years*, 358.

128 Pamela Wakewich and Helen Smith, "The Politics of 'Selective' Memory: Re-visioning Canadian Women's Wartime Work in the Public Record," *Oral History* (Autumn 2006): 60.

129 J.L. Granatstein, *Canada's War*, 260.

130 Canada, Department of Trade and Commerce, Bureau of Statistics, *The Employment Situation at the Beginning of February, 1943 – Together with Payrolls for the Last Week in January* (Ottawa: King's Printer, 1943), 23–4.

131 Broadfoot, *Six War Years*, 168.

132 Patrias, *Jobs and Justice*, 74–8; Sugiman, "Privilege and Oppression," 93.

133 Keshen, *Saints, Sinners, and Soldiers*, 160.

134 Ellen Scheinberg, "The Tale of Tessie the Textile Worker: Female Textile Workers in Cornwall during World War II," *Labour/Le Travail* 33 (Spring 1994): 162–3.

135 *Ottawa Citizen*, 17 December 1941.

136 Caragata, *Alberta Labour*, 146.

137 Sugiman, "Privilege and Oppression," 87.

138 Ruth Frager, *Sweatshop Strife: Class, Ethnicity, and Gender in the Jewish Labour Movement in Toronto, 1900–1939* (Toronto: University of Toronto Press, 1992), 150, 153.
139 *Toronto Telegram*, 20 April 1942; *Financial Post*, 9 May 1942; *Canadian Forum* 22 (July 1942): 112.
140 *Canadian Business* 14 (November 1941).
141 Michael Kimmel, *Manhood in America: A Cultural History* (New York: The Free Press, 1996), 1–10, 210–13; Steven Maynard, "Rough Work and Rugged Men: The Social Construction of Masculinity in Working-Class History," *Labour/Le Travail* 23 (Spring 1989): 159–69.
142 *Labour Gazette* 40 (June 1940): 530–2; LAC, Labour Council of Metropolitan Toronto, MG28 I44, Microfilm Reel M2292: "Toronto District Labour Council – Minutes," 17 January 1941; *Financial Post*, 13 December 1941.
143 LAC, Canadian Labour Congress, MG28 I103, vol. 192, file 3: "Federal Department of Labour, Part 2, 1930–43," Patrick Conroy to Humphrey Mitchell, 23 January, 1942; LAC, J.W. Bruce Papers, MG31 B8, vol. 7: "What Labour Thinks," Transcript of Workers Educational Association Radio Broadcast, 24 April 1940; *Canadian Business* 16 (May 1943): 24; Cuthbertson, *Labour Goes to War*, 136.
144 Helen Smith and Pamela Wakewich, "Regulating Body Boundaries and Health during Wartime: Nationalist Discourse, Media Representations and the Experiences of Canadian Women War Workers," *Gender and History* 24, no. 1 (April 2012): 61.
145 *Labour Gazette* 44 (April 1944): 464.
146 Jean Bruce, *Back the Attack! Canadian Women during the Second World War – At Home and Abroad* (Toronto: Macmillan, 1985), 58.
147 Helen Smith and Pamela Wakewich, "'Beauty and the Helldivers': Regulating Women's Work and Identities in a Warplant Newspaper." *Labour/Le Travail* 44 (Fall 1999): 87–90.
148 Sugiman, *Labour's Dilemma*, 43–5; *Financial Post*, 5 December 1942; Cuthbertson, *Labour Goes to War*, 125–8.
149 Bruce, *Back the Attack!*, 69–71.
150 Alicja Muszynski, "The Organization of Women and Ethnic Minorities in a Resource Industry: A Case Study of the Unionization of Shoreworkers in the B.C. Fishing Industry 1937–1949," *Journal of Canadian Studies* 19 (Spring 1984): 102.
151 Cuthbertson, *Labour Goes to War*, 92; Sugiman, *Labour's Dilemma*, 29, 35, 37, 59–60; Julie Guard, "Fair Play or Fair Pay? Gender Relations, Class Consciousness, and Union Solidarity in the Canadian UE," *Labour/Le Travail* 37 (Spring 1996): 155–7.

152 Ruth Frager, "No Proper Deal: Women Workers and the Canadian Labour Movement, 1870–1940," in *Union Sisters: Women in the Labour Movement*, ed. Linda Briskin and Lynda Yanz (Toronto: Women's Educational Press, 1983), 55.
153 Bruce, *Back the Attack!*, 72.
154 Joan Sangster, *Earning Respect*, 139–65.
155 Sugiman, *Labour's Dilemma*, 60.
156 Jennifer A. Stephen, *Pick One Intelligent Girl: Employability, Domesticity, and the Gendering of Canada's Welfare State, 1939–1947* (Toronto: University of Toronto Press, 2007), 45.
157 Department of Labour, *Labour Organizations in Canada* (Ottawa: King's Printer, 1942), 12; Department of Labour, *Labour Organizations in Canada* (Ottawa: King's Printer, 1943), 18; Department of Labour, *Labour Organizations in Canada* (Ottawa: King's Printer, 1944), 18.
158 Patrias and Savage, *Union Power*, 62.
159 *Labour Gazette* 44 (April 1944): 456–64; Pierson, *They're Still Women*, 48–54, 149–50, 165.
160 *Labour Gazette* 44 (April 1944): 462.
161 Broadfoot, *Six War Years*, 193; Bruce, *Back the Attack!*, 58, 65, 115; Ellen Scheinberg, "The Tale of Tessie the Textile Worker," 174–5.
162 Alfred Edwards, "The Mill: A Worker's Memoir of the 1930s and 1940s," *Labour/Le Travail* 36 (Fall 1995): 294.
163 Patrias, *Jobs and Justice*, 145–8.
164 Ibid., 148–9; Sugiman, "Privilege and Oppression," 102.
165 Sugiman, "Privilege and Oppression,"103.
166 Cuthbertson, *Labour Goes to War*, 87.
167 Patrias and Savage, *Union Power*, 61.
168 LAC, Canadian Labour Congress, MG28 I103, vol. 38, file 7: "PWOC Dumart's, Kitchener, 1941–42," Dumart's Employees to Mackenzie King, 28 May 1942.
169 Laurel Sefton MacDowell, "Company Unionism in Canada, 1915–1948," in Kaufman and Taras, *Nonunion Employee Representation*, 113.
170 Marcus Klee, "Hands-off Labour Forum: The Making and Unmaking of National Working-Class Radio Broadcasting in Canada, 1935–1944," *Labour/Le Travail* 35 (Spring 1995): 107–32; Vancouver *Sun*, 6 November 1942.
171 Roberts and Bullen, "A Heritage of Hope and Struggle," 116.
172 *Hansard*, 19th Parliament, 3rd Session, vol. 2 (26 March 1942), 1679; *Toronto Daily Star*, 8 April 1942; *Toronto Telegram*, 20 June 1942.
173 J.L. Granatstein, *The Politics of Survival: The Conservative Party of Canada, 1939–1945* (Toronto: University of Toronto Press, 1970), 110 fn. 106.

174 John English, "Canada's Road to 1945," *Journal of Canadian Studies* 16 (Fall–Winter 1981): 103.
175 LAC, Brooke Claxton Papers, MG32 B5, vol. 31: "Correspondence with George V. Ferguson," Brooke Claxton to George Ferguson, 3 February 1942.
176 LAC, J. King Gordon Papers, MG30 C241, vol. 14: "General Correspondence, 1940–43," R.K. Finlayson to J. King Gordon, 30 March 1942.
177 *Canadian Forum* 22 (October 1942): 198.
178 *Diaries of William Lyon Mackenzie King*, 27 February 1942.
179 J.W. Pickersgill, *The Mackenzie King Record*, 1:278.
180 Ibid., 333–407; Granatstein, *Canada's War*, 201–43, 294–327.
181 *Diaries of William Lyon Mackenzie King*, 15 December 1941.
182 *Globe and Mail*, 15 December 1941.
183 *Ottawa Citizen*, 20 December 1941.
184 LAC, Canadian Labour Congress, MG28 I103, vol. 192, file 3: "Federal Labour Department, Part 3, 1930–43," A.R. Mosher to Norman A. McLarty, 13 August, 1941; LAC, Robert Haddow Papers, MG30 A118, vol. 1: "Reports – Montreal and District, 1942," Report by Robert Haddow on Collective Bargaining in Crown Corporations to the International Association of Machinists, January 1942; *Canadian Business* 15 (January 1942): 26–9.
185 Fudge, "Voluntarism and Compulsion," 203–4.
186 LAC, National War Labour Board, RG36/5, vol. 25, file 909-1-16: "Collective Bargaining Rights in Government Departments or Agencies," Humphrey Mitchell to R.H. Neilson, 12 January 1942.
187 Fudge, "Voluntarism and Compulsion," 204.
188 *Canadian Forum* 22 (August 1942): 138.
189 LAC, Canadian Labour Congress, MG28 I103, vol. 313, file 15: "Pat Conroy Correspondence – 1942," Pat Conroy to W.N. Davidson, 4 March 1942.
190 *Diaries of William Lyon Mackenzie King*, 19 January 1943; Bothwell and Kilbourn, *C.D. Howe*, 158, 166.
191 *Ottawa Citizen*, 10 March 1942.
192 LAC, Co-operative Commonwealth Federation, MG28 IVI, vol. 196: "USWA: Charles Millard to David Lewis, 21 December 1941.
193 LAC, Canadian Labour Congress, MG28 I103, vol. 192, file 3: "Federal Department of Labour, Part 2, 1930–43," Patrick Conroy to Murray Cotterill, 22 July 1942.
194 LAC, Canadian Association of Administrators of Labour Legislation, MG28 I127, vol. 1: "Proceedings," May 1942.

195 LAC, Public Records Committee, RG 35/7, vol. 21, file 18: "Wartime Activities of the Industrial Relations Branch," Report of the Department of Labour – Industrial Relations Branch, March 1946.

196 *Winnipeg Free Press*, 5 August 1943; LAC, Canadian Labour Congress, MG28 I103, vol. 114, file 10: "CCL Executive Committee Meeting Draft Minutes," 12 May 1941; vol. 114, file 16: "CCL Executive Council Meeting Draft Minutes," 22 October 1941.

197 *Toronto Telegram*, 1 September 1942; LAC, Eugene Forsey Papers, MG30 A25, vol. 5: "Personal Correspondence, 1921–51," V.C. MacDonald to Eugene Forsey, 18 March 1948.

198 Hollander, "Down the Middle of the Road," 233.

199 LAC, Gordon Graydon Papers, MG27 III C15, vol. 12, file L-100: "Bert Lang – Collective Bargaining – Labour," George Drew to R.A. Bell, 30 March 1943.

200 *NWLB Proceedings*, 3:207.

201 LAC, Canadian Labour Congress, MG28 I103, vol. 6, file 5: "Railway Carmen of America, Part 2, 1942–57," J.A. D'Aoust to Joseph Corbett, 9 September 1942.

202 LAC, C.S. Jackson Papers, MG31 B54, vol. 2, file 20: "Organizing Activities, Correspondence, Reports 1942–45," Resolutions Passed at Meeting of UE District 5, 23 August 1942.

203 LAC, Canadian Labour Congress, MG28 I103, vol. 211, file 6: "General Correspondence – Collective Bargaining, Part 1, 1928–42," Draft Recommendations of the National Selective Service Advisory Board – Subcommittee on Industrial Relations, 3 September 1942.

204 MacDowell, *'Remember Kirkland Lake,'* 227; *Labour Gazette* 42 (October 1942): 1147–52.

205 LAC, Canadian Labour Congress, MG28 I103, vol. 317, file 2: "Clarence S. Jackson," C.S. Jackson to Bryce M. Stewart, 26 September, 1942.

206 *Globe and Mail*, 28–29 August 1942; *Canadian Congress Journal* 21 (September 1942): 14–23; LAC, Ottawa and District Labour Council, MG28 I236, vol. 10, file 41: "TLC Conventions," Report of Art D. Ling, 18 September 1942.

207 LAC, Canadian Labour Congress, MG28 I103, vol. 192, file 3: "Federal Department of Labour, Part 2, 1930–43," Humphrey Mitchell to A.R. Mosher, 29 August 1942.

208 LAC, Canadian Labour Congress, MG28 I103, vol. 319, file 16: "TLC-CCL Correspondence," Patrick Conroy to J.A. D'Aoust, 7 July 1942.

209 LAC, Canadian Labour Congress, MG28 I103, vol. 211, file 6: "General Correspondence, Collective Bargaining, Part 1, 1928–1942," Draft

Submitted by the Department of Labour, October 1942; vol. 177, file 1: "British Columbia – Vancouver Labour Council, Part 1, 1942," Patrick Conroy to Harold Pritchett, 24 October 1942

210 LAC, Canadian Labour Congress, MG28 I103, vol. 7, file 23: "Teamsters, 1942–45," Percy Bengough to Birt Showler, 28 October 1942.

211 LAC, Canadian Labour Congress, MG28 I103, vol. 211, file 6: "General Correspondence, Collective Bargaining, Part 1, 1928–42," Comments by A.R. Mosher and Percy Bengough on the Draft Memorandum on Collective Bargaining, October 1942; vol. 211, file 6: "General Correspondence, Collective Bargaining, Part 1, 1928–42," Patrick Conroy to C.S. Jackson, 19 October 1942.

212 LAC, Canadian Labour Congress, MG28 I103, vol. 331, file 3: "CCL Executive Committee Minutes," 20 November 1942.

213 *Diaries of William Lyon Mackenzie King*, 1 October 1942 and 17 November 1942.

214 LAC, Canadian Labour Congress, MG28 I103, vol. 28, file 11: "UE International Office, Part 2, 1940–43," Patrick Conroy to George Harris, 4 November 1942 and vol. 317, file 2: "Clarence S. Jackson," George Harris to M.M. Maclean, 18 October 1942.

215 LAC, Canadian Labour Congress, MG28 I103, vol. 317, file 2: "Clarence S. Jackson, President, District 5 UE – 1942," Clarence Jackson to Humphrey Mitchell, 12 November 1942.

216 LAC, Canadian Labour Congress, MG28 I103, vol. 28, file 11: "UE International Office, Part 2, 1940–43," Patrick Conroy to George Harris, 19 November 1942.

217 LAC, Canadian Labour Congress, MG28 I103, vol. 44, file 12: "USWA – Charles Millard, Part 1, 1940–42," Charles Millard to M.M. Maclean, 27 November 1942.

218 *Globe and Mail*, 18 September 1942; *Diaries of William Lyon Mackenzie King*, 2 September 1942 and 17–18 November 1942; Frederick W. Gibson and Barbara Robertson, eds., *Ottawa at War: The Grant Dexter Memoranda, 1939–1945*, volume 11 of the Manitoba Record Society Publications (Winnipeg, MB: Manitoba Record Society, 1994), 368–9.

219 *Financial Post*, 28 November 1942.

220 Gibson and Robertson, *Ottawa at War*, 369.

221 *Diaries of William Lyon Mackenzie King*, 17–18 November 1942.

222 *Canadian Business* 16 (February 1943): 22.

223 *Ottawa Citizen*, 28 August 1942.

224 *Diaries of William Lyon Mackenzie King*, 23 September 1942.

225 Ibid., 19 September 1942.

226 Ibid., 9 October 1942.
227 LAC, Brooke Claxton Papers, MG32 B5, vol. 20, file: "Nominal Correspondence – 'P' – 1932–42," Brook Claxton to C.H. Peters, 11 September 1942.
228 *Diaries of William Lyon Mackenzie King*, 2 October 1942; LAC, W.L. Mackenzie King Papers, MG26 J4, "Memoranda and Notes," Microfilm Reel C156879 H-1471, AFL Convention – Toronto, Friday Morning Session, 9 October 1942.
229 *Toronto Daily Star*, 2 September 1942; *Globe and Mail*, 2 September 1942.
230 LAC, Gordon Graydon Papers, MG27 III C15, vol. 12, file L-100: "Bert Lang – Collective Bargaining – Labour," George Drew to R.A. Bell, 30 March 1943.
231 MacDowell, *'Remember Kirkland Lake,'* 228.
232 MacDowell, *Renegade Lawyer*, 110–17.
233 *Financial Post*, 10 October 1942.
234 LAC, Canadian Labour Congress, MG28 I103, vol. 178, file 11: "British Columbia Vancouver Island Joint Labour Conference," James Robertson to Patrick Conroy, 6 March 1942.
235 Gray, "Woodworkers and Legitimacy," 81.
236 Ibid., 33–4.
237 Ibid., 64; *Canadian Congress Journal* 18 (December 1939): 28–9 and 19 (December 1940): 22.
238 LAC, Canadian Labour Congress, MG28 I103, vol. 45, file 11: "USWA, Alan Wright, 1941–44," Alan Wright to Norman S. Dowd, 29 January 1942.
239 LAC, Canadian Labour Congress, MG28 I103, vol. 177, file 5: "British Columbia Vancouver Island Labour Council, Part 2, 1943," Memorandum Submitted by the Vancouver Labour Council to the Government of John Hart, 19 December 1942; *Canadian Congress Journal* 22 (February 1943): 24–30; Gray, "Woodworkers and Legitimacy," 114.
240 Granatstein, *The Politics of Survival*, 126–30.
241 Ibid., 133; *Globe and Mail*, 6 September 1942; *Toronto Telegram*, 8 September 1942; LAC, John Bracken Papers, MG27 III C16, vol. 43, file O-160-P: "Organization – Port Hope Conference," *Report of the Round Table on Canadian Policy*, 7 September 1942; LAC, Progressive Conservative Party, MG28 IV2, vol. 282, file: "Port Hope Conference," A Round Table on Canadian Policy – Committee on Labour Relations, September 1942.
242 *Toronto Daily Star*, 9 September, 1942; *Financial Post*, 3 October 1942.
243 Saywell, *Life of Mitchell F. Hepburn*, 489.
244 *Diaries of William Lyon Mackenzie King*, 17 November 1942.

245 LAC, Canadian Labour Congress, MG28 I103, vol. 314, file 25: "Federal Government Correspondence Concerning Wartime Relations with Organized Labour, 1942–45," Percy Bengough and A.R. Mosher to Mackenzie King, 27 November 1942.
246 *Diaries of William Lyon Mackenzie King*, 30 November 1942.
247 Fudge, "Voluntarism and Compulsion," 205.
248 *NWLB Proceedings*, 2:67, 122.
249 LAC, Public Records Committee, RG35/7, vol. 21, file 18: "Wartime Activities of the Industrial Relations Branch," *Report* of the Industrial Relations Branch, March 1946.
250 Fudge, "Voluntarism and Compulsion," 205.
251 *Diaries of William Lyon Mackenzie King*, 9 December 1942.
252 LAC, John Bracken Papers, MG27 III C16, vol. 40, file O-151: "Organization Policy," Policy Resolutions Adopted by the National Conservative Party at the National Convention at Winnipeg, 9–11 December 1942; Granatstein, *The Politics of Survival*, 137–50.
253 *Diaries of William Lyon Mackenzie King*, 9 December 1942.
254 Charles G. Power, *A Party Politician: The Memoirs of Chubby Power*, ed. Norman Ward (Toronto: Macmillan, 1966), 351.
255 *Diaries of William Lyon Mackenzie King*, 11 December 1942.
256 *Saturday Night*, 21 February 1942.
257 *Financial Post*, 3 October 1942.
258 *Globe and Mail*, 22 August, 1942.
259 LAC, Canadian Labour Congress, MG28 I103, vol. 155, "O'Brien, Daniel – Vancouver Correspondence – Part 3," Patrick Conroy to Daniel O'Brien, 2 December 1942.
260 *Toronto News*, 17 April 1943.

4. A Code of Labour Relations, Fall 1942–Spring 1944

1 *Diaries of William Lyon Mackenzie King*, 4 December 1943; *Montreal Gazette*, 6 December 1943.
2 *Montreal Gazette*, 6 December, 1943.
3 Hollander, "Down the Middle of the Road," 287.
4 *Labour Organizations in Canada* (Ottawa: King's Printer, 1943), 43.
5 *NWLB Proceedings*, 9:852–4.
6 Ibid., 8:682–91; *Labour Gazette* 44 (February 1944): 240–1; Robert H. Storey, "The Struggle to Organize Stelco and Dofasco," 377–8.
7 Millar, "Shapes of Power," 141, 164 fn. 123.

8 David A. Wolfe, "The Rise and Demise of the Keynesian Era in Canada: Economic Policy, 1930–1982," in *Modern Canada, 1930–1980s: Readings in Canadian Social History*, ed. Michael S. Cross and Gregory S. Kealey (Toronto: McClelland & Stewart, 1984), 66.
9 Bliss, *Northern Enterprise*, 455.
10 *Regina Leader-Post*, 10 December 1943.
11 Hollander, "Down the Middle of the Road," 288.
12 *Labour Gazette* 44 (March 1944): 320, 322.
13 LAC, Canadian Labour Congress, MG28 I103, vol. 24, file 12: "UAW, George Burt, Windsor 1940–43," To All Canadian Labour Unions from George Burt, 10 February 1943.
14 Gray, "Woodworkers and Legitimacy," 128–34.
15 *Financial Times*, 30 April, 1943.
16 Lewis, *The Good Fight*, 205.
17 Granatstein, *The Politics of Survival*, 162.
18 English, "Canada's Road to 1945," 104.
19 Granatstein, *Canada's War*, 251.
20 English, "Canada's Road to 1945," 104.
21 Paul Martin, *Far From Home*, 325.
22 Saywell, *Life of Mitchell F. Hepburn*, 509.
23 *NWLB Proceedings*, 9:893.
24 LAC, Canadian Labour Congress, MG28 I103, vol. 312, file 39: "CIO Correspondence," A.R. Mosher to Patrick Conroy, 6 February 1943.
25 "War Series: No. 7" (1 February 1943)," in *R.C.M.P. Security Bulletins: The War Series – Part II, 1942–45*, ed. Gregory S. Kealey and Reg Whitaker (St John's, NL: Canadian Committee on Labour History, 1993), 49; Stanton, *Never Say Die!*, 188–94.
26 Abella, *Nationalism, Communism, and Canadian Labour*, 176–7.
27 LAC, Canadian Labour Congress, MG28 I103, vol. 317, file 18: "C.H. Millard, 1943–44," Patrick Conroy to Charles Millard, 6 August, 1943.
28 Abella, *Nationalism, Communism, and Canadian Labour*, 75.
29 *Canadian Congress Journal* 22 (March 1943): 7–11.
30 Green, *Against the Tide*, 90–1; William Kaplan, *Everything That Floats: Pat Sullivan, Hal Banks, and the Seamen's Unions of Canada* (Toronto: University of Toronto Press, 1987), 35–6.
31 Gerald D. Caplan, *The Dilemma of Canadian Socialism* (Toronto: McClelland & Stewart, 1973), 105.
32 *Diaries of William Lyon Mackenzie King*, 1 September 1943.
33 Lewis, *The Good Fight*, 295.

34 Hollander, "Down the Middle of the Road," 287; LAC, Ottawa and District Labour Council, MG28 I236, vol. 2, file 4: "Minutes, February 1943–January 1945," 1 May 1943; LAC, Canadian Labour Congress, MG28 I103, vol. 4, file 5: "Brotherhood of Maintenance and Way Employees, 1943–45," J.J. O'Grady to Percy Bengough, 11 September 1943; vol. 23, file 4: "UAW Local 200 Ford, Windsor, 1942–43," Joint Resolution for the Passage of Genuine Labour Bill, 28 February 1943; vol. 238, file 3: "General Correspondence – TLC Part 1, 1930–44," Fred G. Steeve to Patrick Conroy, 16 June 1943; vol. 317, file 18: "C.H. Millard, National Director, USWA, Correspondence 1943–44," 21 January 1944; vol. 319, file 16: "Cooperation between the TLC and CCL, 1941–48," Percy Bengough to Patrick Conroy, 22 January 1943 and 15 June 1943; vol. 330, file 11: "TLC Executive Council Minutes, 1943–45," 14 January 1943 and 17–19 December 1943; *Canadian Congress Journal* 22 (February 1943): 24–30.

35 *Financial Post*, 13 March 1943.

36 LAC, Canadian Association of Administrators of Labour Legislation, MG28 I127, vol. 1: "Proceedings," 3–5 May 1943.

37 *Labour Gazette* 43 (May 1943): 557, 691–701 and 43 (June 1943): 848–58; Warrian, "Labour Is Not a Commodity," 90.

38 *Labour Gazette* 43 (May 1943): 691–701; Queen's University, Industrial Relations Section, *The Right to Organize: Recent Canadian Legislation*, Bulletin No. 8 (Kingston, ON: Queen's University, 1943).

39 "War Series: No. 12" (1 May 1943), in Kealey and Whitaker, *War Series – Part II, 1942–45*, 110.

40 Gray, "Woodworkers and Legitimacy," 115; Fudge, "Voluntarism and Compulsion," 238–9.

41 Gray, "Woodworkers and Legitimacy," 116.

42 Millar, "Shapes of Power," 78–81.

43 *Labour Gazette* 43 (December 1943): 1693–7; Education Committees of the CSN and the CEQ, *History of the Labour Movement in Québec*, 138–9; Isbester, "National Catholic Unions in Canada, 215, 228, 232–3.

44 *Labour Gazette* 44 (February 1944): 126–7; 44 (August 1944): 1046–7; and 44 (November 1944): 1443–5; Queen's University, *The Right to Organize*; Fudge and Tucker, *Labour Before the Law*, 271–2.

45 LAC, Canadian Labour Congress, MG28 I103, vol. 199, file 19: "Provincial Government of Ontario," A.R. Mosher to J.E. Michaud, 28 April 1943.

46 *Industrial Canada* 44 (July 1943): 230.

47 Millar, "Shapes of Power," 91–2.

48 LAC, Canadian Labour Congress, MG28 I103, vol. 211, file 8: "General Correspondence on the Ontario CB Act, Part 1, 1943," Bora Laskin to Patrick Conroy, 20 March 1943.

49 Millar, "Shapes of Power," 85–90.
50 LAC, Brooke Claxton Papers, MG32 B5, vol. 170, file: "CMA – Ontario," Submission of the Ontario Division of the CMA to the Select Committee Appointed by the Legislature of the Province of Ontario, 9 March 1943.
51 *Financial Post*, 6 November 1943.
52 LAC, Canadian Association of Administrators of Labour Legislation, MG28 I127, vol. 1, file: "Proceedings," May 1943.
53 *Hansard*, 19th Parliament, 4th Session, vol. 2 (6 April 1943), 1902.
54 LAC, Arthur Meighen Papers, MG26 I, Microfilm C3593-144301, Eugene Forsey to Arthur Meighen, 18 January 1943.
55 Hardy, *Mackenzie King of Canada*, 335–6; *Financial Post*, 10 April 1943; *Diaries of William Lyon Mackenzie King*, 3 February 1943.
56 LAC, Arthur Meighen Papers, MG26 I, Microfilm C3593-144301, Eugene Forsey to Arthur Meighen, 18 January 1943; MacDowell, "The 1943 Steel Strike," 65–73; *Canadian Forum* 22 (October 1942): 205–10; *Diaries of William Lyon Mackenzie King*, 26–30 August and 2–3 September 1943. See also:

- LAC, Mackenzie King Papers, MG26 J1, "Primary Correspondence," Microfilm C281721-C6810, Mackenzie King to Charles Millard, 26 August 1942; C81727-C6810, Mackenzie King to Charles Millard, 27 August 1942.
- LAC, Department of Munitions and Supplies, RG 28, vol. 138, file 3-E1-1: "Economic Advisory Committee," M.A. Hoey to Walter Patterson, 22 April 1943.
- LAC, Canadian Labour Congress, MG28 I103, vol. 43, file 1: "USWA, Local 2251, Sault Ste Marie, Part 1, 1940–44," Charles Millard to A.R. Mosher, 24 July 1942 and Charles Millard to Patrick Conroy, 6–7 August 1942; vol. 44, file 3: "USWA – Charles H. Millard, Part 2, 1940–42," Charles Millard to Algoma, Local 2251 Steward's Council, 13 August 1942; Charles Millard to Mackenzie King, 19 August 1942 and 27 August 1942; Charles Millard to Philip Murray, 26 August 1942.

57 *Diaries of William Lyon Mackenzie King*, 14 January 1943.
58 Ibid., 25 January 1943; MacDowell, "The 1943 Steel Strike," 73–80; *Canadian Forum* 23 (March 1943): 342; *Financial Post*, 16 January and 23 January 1943.
59 *Calgary Herald*, 13 January 1943.
60 *Montreal Gazette*, 31 May 1943; Martin, *Far From Home*, 100; *Ottawa Citizen*, 3 February 1943.

61 *Diaries of William Lyon Mackenzie King,* 2 February 1943; *Montreal Gazette,* 6 April 1943; *Financial Post,* 10 April 1943.
62 *Globe and Mail,* 12 April 1943; LAC, Public Records Committee, RG35/7, vol. 23, file 26: "NWLB History," Draft by R.H. Neilson, n.d.
63 *Ottawa Journal,* 9 December 1947; LAC, Department of Labour, RG 27, vol. 3520, file 3-26-10-1: "Strikes and Lockouts, Correspondence," Submission by the Niagara IR Institute to Humphrey Mitchell, April 1943.
64 MacDowell, *Renegade Lawyer,* 299.
65 Forsey, *A Life on the Fringe,* 92.
66 LAC, J.L. Cohen Papers, MG30 A94, vol. 34, file 3052-1: "Cohen Correspondence – NWLB," *Report on Problems of the Wartime Wages Control Policy,* 24 April 1943.
67 *Montreal Gazette,* 18 February 1943; *Financial Post,* 20 February 1943.
68 *Globe and Mail,* 15 February 1943.
69 LAC, Canadian Labour Congress, MG28 I103, vol. 153, file: "Marquette, Paul Emile – Montreal Correspondence, Part 6, 1943–45," Patrick Conroy to Paul Emile Marquette, 18 February 1943.
70 LAC, J.L. Cohen Papers, MG30 A94, vol. 34, file 3052-3, "NWLB Speeches," Address by J.L. Cohen to the Montreal RLC and Quebec Provincial Federation of Labour, 20 February 1943.
71 LAC, J.L. Cohen Papers, MG30 A94, vol. 34, file 3052-1: "NWLB Correspondence," J.L. Cohen to C.S. Jackson, 10 March 1943 and vol. 39, File 3112-A: "CCL Correspondence, Reports, Notes on PC 1003," J.L. Cohen to Patrick Conroy, 7 April 1945.
72 *Montreal Gazette,* 6 April 1943; *Financial Post,* 10 April 1943.
73 LAC, Privy Council, RG 2, vol. 2, file D-16: "Department of Labour, 1940–41," Proposed Amendment to PC 7440 and Establishment of a National and Regional War Labour Boards, 9 October 1941.
74 LAC, J.L. Cohen Papers, MG30 A94, vol. 34, file 3052-1: "NWLB Correspondence," J.L. Cohen to C.P. McTague, 19 August 1943.
75 *Montreal Gazette,* 31 May 1943.
76 MacDowell, *Renegade Lawyer,* 13–30, 80.
77 Cohen, *Collective Bargaining in Canada,* 63.
78 *Financial Times,* 9 April 1943; LAC, Canadian Labour Congress, MG28 I103, vol. 120, file 14: "Bishop's Committee for Social Questions Round Table Conference," *Report on Collective Bargaining Session,* 4–7 February 1944.
79 *Montreal Gazette,* 30 April 1943; Montréal *Matin,* 19 February 1943; Québec *Chronicle,* 20 February 1943; *Windsor Daily Star,* 27 February 1943.
80 LAC, J.L. Cohen Papers, MG30 A94, vol. 34, file 3052-1: "NWLB – Correspondence," J.L. Cohen to C.P. McTague, 11 March 1943; *Diaries of William Lyon Mackenzie King,* 23 February 1943.

81 *Montreal Gazette*, 31 May 1943.
82 Léon Lalande, "The Status of Organized Labour: An Outline of the Development of the Law in Great Britain, the United States, and Canada," *The Canadian Bar Review* 19 (November 1941): 679.
83 Martin, *Far From Home*, 101.
84 LAC, J.L. Cohen Papers, MG30 A94, vol. 34, file 3052-4: "NWLB Reasons for Judgments (1943)," Algoma Steel, Dosco, and Trenton Steel Works Ltd. v. the USWA, 31 March 1943.
85 MacDowell, "The 1943 Steel Strike," 84.
86 LAC, J.L. Cohen Papers, MG30 A94, vol. 34, file 3052-1: "Cohen Correspondence," C.P. McTague to Mackenzie King, 22 April 1943.
87 *Globe and Mail*, 8 April 1943.
88 MacDowell, *Renegade Lawyer*, 128–30.
89 Ibid., 130.
90 LAC, J.L. Cohen Papers, MG34 A90, vol. 34, file 3052-2: "NWLB Statements," Press Release by the NWLB, 8 April 1943.
91 LAC, J.L. Cohen Papers, MG34 A90, vol. 34, file 3052-3: "NWLB Speeches," Address to the Annual Convention of the Trades and Labour Congress of Canada, 1 September 1943.
92 *Globe and Mail*, 12 April 1943; *Montreal Standard*, 17 April 1943.
93 *Globe and Mail*, 10 April 1943.
94 *Diaries of William Lyon Mackenzie King*, 6 April 1943, 8 April 1943, and 22 April 1943.
95 King, *Industry and Humanity*, 142.
96 *Ottawa Citizen*, 8 April 1943.
97 MacDowell, "The 1943 Steel Strike," 84–5.
98 *Financial Times*, 17 April 1943; *Globe and Mail*, 10 April 1943.
99 *Globe and Mail*, 16 April 1943; *Montreal Daily Star*, 15 April and 16 April 1943.
100 LAC, Privy Council, RG 2, vol. 46, file D-16-2: "Department of Labour – Labour Relations Problems, 1942–43," Analysis of Submissions Re. Labour Relations and Wage Conditions in Canada, National War Labour Board Inquiry, 4 May to 18 June 1943.
101 *NWLB Proceedings*, 2:148–9.
102 LAC, Canadian Labour Congress, MG28 I103, vol. 199, file 20: "Provincial Government, Ontario Minister of Labour, 1938–44," A.R. Mosher and Patrick Conroy to Peter Heenan, 20 July 1943.
103 *NWLB Proceedings*, 9:825.
104 Fudge and Tucker, *Labour Before the Law*, 267–8.
105 *NWLB Proceedings*, 3:168.
106 Ibid., 3:186.

107 Ibid., 6:593–6; *Financial Post*, 5 June 1943.
108 *NWLB Proceedings*, 3:169.
109 Ibid., 5:392.
110 Ibid., 9:762.
111 Ibid., 9:859.
112 *Globe and Mail*, 5 June and 21 June 1943; *Financial Post*, 5 June 1943; *Financial Times*, 20 August 1943.
113 "Report of National War Labour Board Arising Out of Its Public Inquiry into Labour Relations and Wage Conditions Together with a Minority Report," *Labour Gazette – Supplement* 44 (February 1944): 3.
114 Ibid., 9.
115 Ibid., 30.
116 Ibid., 8.
117 Ibid., 27.
118 Ibid., 5.
119 Ibid., 17.
120 Ibid., 4, 16.
121 Ibid., 19–20.
122 LAC, Brooke Claxton Papers, MG32 B5, vol. 169, file: "Labour," National War Labour Board Reports: Attitude of the Government to the Recommendations, n.a., 3 September 1943.
123 *Diaries of William Lyon Mackenzie King*, 28 August 1943 and 1 September 1943; Gibson and Robertson, *Ottawa at War*, 423, 427.
124 *Diaries of William Lyon Mackenzie King*, 28 August 1943.
125 Gibson and Robertson, *Ottawa at War*, 427.
126 Granatstein, *Canada's War*, 265–72.
127 Gibson and Robertson, *Ottawa at War*, 425.
128 *Diaries of William Lyon Mackenzie King*, 31 August 1943.
129 Gibson and Robertson, *Ottawa at War*, 427.
130 "Report of National War Labour Board," 36.
131 LAC, J.L. Cohen Papers, MG30 A94, vol. 34, file 3052-1: "NWLB Correspondence," J.L. Cohen to C.P. McTague, 18 August 1943.
132 LAC, J.L. Cohen Papers, MG30 A94, vol. 34, file 3052-1: "NWLB Correspondence," C.P. McTague to J.L. Cohen, 19 August 1943.
133 *Montreal Daily Star*, 18 August 1943.
134 *Toronto Telegram*, 19 August 1943.
135 *Diaries of William Lyon Mackenzie King*, 3, 7–10 September 1943; *Montreal Daily Star*, 10 September 1943; *Globe and Mail*, 21 September 1943; MacDowell, *Renegade Lawyer*, 138–44.

136 Mitchell Sharp, *Which Reminds Me: A Memoir* (Toronto: University of Toronto Press, 1993), 20–1.
137 *Diaries of William Lyon Mackenzie King*, 10 January 1943.
138 Ibid., 12 January 1943, 26 January 1943, and 5 March 1943; Doug Owram, *The Government Generation*, 288–90.
139 Granatstein, *Canada's War*, 257–62.
140 *Diaries of William Lyon Mackenzie King*, 24 March 1943.
141 Bercuson, *True Patriot*, 116.
142 *Diaries of William Lyon Mackenzie King*, 17 October 1943.
143 Ibid., 28 August 1943.
144 Martin, *Far From Home*, 294, 317.
145 Bercuson, *True Patriot*, 117.
146 Martin, *Far From Home*, 296.
147 LAC, Canadian Labour Congress, MG28 I103, vol. 314, file 25: "Federal Government Correspondence Concerning Wartime Relations with Organized Labour, 1942–45," C.S. Jackson to Mackenzie King, 13 July 1943.
148 *Diaries of William Lyon Mackenzie King*, 17 February 1943.
149 Ibid., 1 September 1943.
150 Karl Klare, "Judicial Deradicalization of the Wagner Act and the Origins of Modern Legal Consciousness, 1937–1941," *Minnesota Law Review* 62 (1978): 265.
151 Princeton University, Industrial Relations Section, Selected References, No. 14, "Union Security" (1 March 1947), 2.
152 *PM Magazine*, November 1941; *New York Times*, 14 November 1956.
153 *Diaries of William Lyon Mackenzie King*, 29 November 1943.
154 Gibson and Robertson, *Ottawa at War*, 368.
155 *Financial Post*, 1 January 1944.
156 LAC, Canadian Labour Congress, MG28 I103, vol. 29, file 2: "UE, Toronto – Part 2, 1944–45," Patrick Conroy to C.S. Jackson, 22 January 1944.
157 *Diaries of William Lyon Mackenzie King*, 14 September 1943.
158 Ibid.
159 Ibid., 16 September 1943.
160 Gibson and Robertson, *Ottawa at War*, 444.
161 Ibid., 430.
162 *Diaries of William Lyon Mackenzie King*, 17 February 1944.
163 Robert A. Wardhaugh, *Behind the Scenes: The Life and Work of William Clifford Clark* (Toronto: University of Toronto Press, 2010), 247.
164 Granatstein, *The Ottawa Men*, 159–60.
165 Fudge, "Voluntarism and Compulsion," 200.

166 LAC, Department of Munitions and Supplies, RG 28, vol. 138, file 3-E1-1: "Economic Advisory Committee," William C. Clark to G.K. Shiels, 27 March 1943; Carl Goldenberg to R.A.C. Henry, 25 June 1943; and Carl Goldenberg to R.A.C. Henry, 9 July 1943; Wardhaugh, *Behind the Scenes*, 168.
167 Queen's University Archives, W.C. Clark Papers, RG 2207, vol. 6, file L-2-2: "Labour Problems," William C. Clark to J.L. Ilsley, 21 August 1943; Gibson and Robertson, *Ottawa at War*, 423–4, 426–7.
168 LAC, Department of Finance, RG 19, vol. 3579, file FM-01: "Memoranda to the Minister," W.A. Mackintosh to J.L. Ilsley, 6 October 1943.
169 Gibson and Robertson, *Ottawa at War*, 424; Wardhaugh, *Behind the Scenes*, 254.
170 *Diaries of William Lyon Mackenzie King*, 5 October 1943 and 7 October 1943.
171 Ibid., 2–4, 6–7, 9–10 November 1943; LAC, Department of Labour, RG 27, vol. 618, file 2: "War Appropriations for Debate Material," M.M. Maclean to Humphrey Mitchell, 1 February 1944.
172 *Diaries of William Lyon Mackenzie King*, 6 December 1943.
173 *Canadian Congress Journal* (November 1943): 5–6.
174 *Financial Post*, 28 September 1940.
175 LAC, Arthur Roebuck Papers, MG32 C68, vol. 5, file 2: "Labour – Wartime Labour Relations Regulations, 1943–45," Biography of M.M. Maclean.
176 Allan Blakeney, *An Honourable Calling: Political Memoirs* (Toronto: University of Toronto Press, 2008), 18.
177 *Labour Gazette*, 44 (March 1944): 368; LAC, Department of Labour, RG 27, "General Correspondence PC 1003," Access 83-84/206, box #1 F7-2-1-1 Part 1, Vincent MacDonald to Gerard Reilly, 28 December 1943.
178 Rick Wartzman, *The End of Loyalty: The Rise and Fall of Good Jobs in America* (New York: Public Affairs, 2017), 61–5.
179 LAC, Department of Labour, RG 27, "General Correspondence PC 1003," Access 83-84/206, box #1 F7-2-1-1 Part 1, Vincent MacDonald to Gerard Reilly, 28 December 1943; James A. Gross, *The Reshaping of the National Labor Relations Board: National Labor Policy in Transition 1937–1947* (Albany, NY: State University of New York Press, 1981), 240; Melvyn Dubofsky, *The State and Labor*, 149–61; 202–7.
180 Gibson and Robertson, *Ottawa at War*, 444.
181 LAC, Department of Labour, RG 27, vol. 866, file F-8-7-8-16: "Dominion-Provincial Conference: Labour Relations," George Drew to Mackenzie King, 16 October 1943 and Humphrey Mitchell to Canadian Premiers, 25 October 1943.

182 The following discussion and all excerpts are taken from LAC, Department of Labour, RG 27, vol. 621, file 3: "Dominion-Provincial Labour Conference," Minutes, 8–10 November 1943.

183 Martin, *Far From Home*, 298.

184 Gibson and Robertson, *Ottawa at War*, 423, 427.

185 *Diaries of William Lyon Mackenzie King*, 25 November 1943.

186 "Report of the National War Labour Board," 6.

187 LAC, Department of Finance, RG 19, vol. 4664, "Report to the Minister of Labour on Recommendations of the National War Labour Board," by V.C. MacDonald, M.M. Maclean, and A.H. Brown, 4 September 1943.

188 *Diaries of William Lyon Mackenzie King*, 30 August and 15 September 1943.

189 Ibid., 29 November 1943.

190 LAC, Privy Council, RG 2, vol. 46, file D-16-2: "Department of Labour, 1943–44," J.W. Pickersgill to A.D.P. Heeney, 6 December 1943.

191 LAC, Department of Labour, RG27, vol. 621, file 4: "Loose Correspondence, Memoranda, and Documentation," Memorandum, M.M. Maclean to Arthur MacNamara and Humphrey Mitchell, 13 December 1943.

192 LAC, Department of Labour, RG 27, Access 83-84/206, box #3, F7-2-2-1 Part 1, "General Correspondence RE PC 1003, 1942–44," Arthur MacNamara to F.P. Varcoe, 8 December 1943.

193 LAC, Department of Labour, RG27, vol. 621, file 4: "Loose Correspondence, Memoranda, and Documentation," Memorandum, Bernard Wilson to M.M. Maclean, 15–16 December 1943.

194 LAC, Privy Council, RG 2, vol. 46, file D-16-2: "Department of Labour, 1943–44, W.R. Jackett to F.P. Varcoe, 13 December 1943.

195 LAC, Paul Martin Papers, MG32 B12, vol. 1, file: "Labour Code, 1941–44," Edgar Rochette to Humphrey Mitchell, 5 January 1944; LAC, Department of Labour, RG 27, vol. 621, file 4: "Loose Correspondence, Memoranda, and Documentation," Recommendations by Labour Department Committee as to Desirable Amendments Arising Out of Provincial Submissions, January 1944 and Arthur MacNamara to Humphrey Mitchell, 24 January 1944.

196 LAC, Paul Martin Papers, MG32 B12, vol. 1, file: "Labour Code, 1941–44," Reply of the Canadian Chamber of Commerce and Comments by the Labour Committee, January 1944.

197 LAC, Canadian Manufacturers Association, MG28 I230, vol. 117: "Industrial Relations Committee, 1944–50," Interim Report, January 1944; vol. 15, file: "CMA Executive Council Minutes," 28 January 1944; RG 27, Department of Labour, vol. 621, file 4: "Loose Correspondence,

Memoranda, and Documentation," CMA Memorandum of Amendments Proposed to the Draft Wartime Labour Relations Regulations, 31 January 1944.

198 LAC, Department of Labour, RG 27, vol. 621, file 4: "Loose Correspondence, Memoranda, and Documentation," Replies of the Catholic Confederation of Labour, Trades and Labour Congress, and Canadian Congress of Labour, January 1944.

199 LAC, Department of Labour, RG 27, vol. 621, file 4: "Loose Correspondence, Memoranda, and Documentation," C.P. McTague to Humphrey Mitchell, 7 February 1944.

200 LAC, Paul Martin Papers, MG32 B12, vol. 1, file: "Labour Code, 1941–44," Replies of the Four Labour Congresses to the Draft of the Labour Code and Comments by the Labour Relations Committee, January 1944.

201 LAC, Department of Labour, RG 27, vol. 621, file 4: Humphrey Mitchell to C.P. McTague, 28 January 1944 and C.P. McTague to Humphrey Mitchell, 7 February 1944.

202 LAC, Mackenzie King Papers, MG26 J1, H1536 C250265, "Memoranda and Notes," J.W. Pickersgill to Mackenzie King, 5 January 1944.

203 *Diaries of William Lyon Mackenzie King*, 23 April 1944.

204 *Labour Gazette* 45 (November 1945): 1606.

205 National Archives of the United States, State Department, RG59, vol. 6013, file 842.5045/4-546: "1945–1949," Paul Norgren to the Secretary of State, 5 April 1946.

206 *Labour Gazette* 44 (February 1944): 124.

207 LAC, Public Records Committee, RG35/7, vol. 21, file 18: "Wartime Activities of the Industrial Relations Branch," March 1946.

208 Gibson and Robertson, *Ottawa at War*, 426.

209 *Financial Post*, 5 February 1944.

210 *Diaries of William Lyon Mackenzie King*, 17 February 1944; Fudge and Tucker, *Labour Before the Law*, 273.

211 *Diaries of William Lyon Mackenzie King*, 17 February 1944.

212 Canada, Department of Labour, "Wartime Labour Relations Order," *Labour Gazette* 44, no. 2 (1944): 135–43, accessed July 2012, https://archive.org/stream/labourgazette1944cana#page/134/mode/2up; Woods, *Labour Policy in Canada*, 86–93; Fudge and Tucker, *Labour Before the Law*, 273–5.

213 LAC, Paul Martin Papers, MG32 B12, vol. 1, file: "Labour Code, 1941–44," Humphrey Mitchell, "Explanatory Notes on the Wartime Labour Relations Regulations, P.C. 1003, February 17, 1944," n.d.

214 LAC, Canadian Labour Congress, MG28 I103, vol. 314, file 4: "CCF-General," Eugene Forsey to M.J. Coldwell, 18 February 1944.
215 Canada, Department of Labour, "Wartime Labour Relations Order," 136–7.
216 LAC, Paul Martin Papers, MG32 B12, vol. 1, file: "Labour Code, 1941–44," Clipping from *Montreal Standard*, n.d.
217 Paul Weiler, *Reconcilable Differences: New Directions in Canadian Labour Law* (Toronto: Carswell, 1980), 37–41.

5. A Fine Conclusion, Spring 1944–Summer 1948

1 *Saskatoon Star-Phoenix*, 15 July 1948.
2 *Montreal Gazette*, 15 July 1948.
3 *Diaries of William Lyon Mackenzie King*, 13–14 July 1948; *Ottawa Citizen*, 3 July 1948.
4 *Diaries of William Lyon Mackenzie King*, 26 May and 14 July 1948.
5 *Labour Gazette* 49 (May 1949): 246.
6 Garnet Pigden and Ardith McKinnon, *'Way Back When': Reflections of Madoc Village and Madoc County* (Madoc, ON: Privately Printed, 1975), 337.
7 Charlotte Whitton, "'All That It Stands For': Some Notes on How Ban Righ Hall at Queen's Came to Be and the Role of the Alumnae Therein," Unpublished manuscript, September 1958, 23–4.
8 LAC, Department of Labour, RG27, Access vol. 83-84/206, box #3, file 7-2-2-1, Part 2: "General Correspondence," Margaret Mackintosh to M.M. Maclean, 29 November 1945 and M.M. Maclean to Margaret Mackintosh, 44 December 1945.
9 LAC, Canadian Association of Administrators of Labour Legislation, MG28 I127, vol. 1: "Proceedings," May 1942.
10 LAC, Canadian Labour Congress, MG28 I103, vol. 238, file 3: "General Correspondence, Part 1, 1930–44," Percy Bengough to TLC Unions, 14 March 1944.
11 LAC, Canadian Labour Congress, MG28 I103, vol. 171, file 11: "Circulars, 1944," Norman Dowd to CCL Unions, 25 February 1944.
12 *Labour Gazette* (March 1944): 369–72.
13 LAC, Paul Martin Papers, MG32 B12, vol. 1: "Labour Code, 1941–44," *Montreal Standard*, n.d.
14 *Diaries of William Lyon Mackenzie King*, 25 February 1944.
15 Logan, *State Intervention and Assistance*, 30.

16 LAC, Department of Labour, RG 27, vol. 896, file 8-9-23, Part 1: "Standing Committee on Industrial Relations," *Report*, 16 July 1946.
17 Millar, "Shapes of Power," 336.
18 Ibid., 289; Sugiman, *Labour's Dilemma*, 52–3.
19 Hollander, "Down the Middle of the Road," 346.
20 LAC, Department of Labour, RG 27, vol. 896, file 8-9-23, Part 1: "Standing Committee on Industrial Relations," *Report*, 16 July 1946.
21 Doug Smith, *Cold Warrior*, 127, 138.
22 Fudge and Tucker, *Labour Before the Law*, 302.
23 Montero, *We Stood Together*, 86.
24 Hollander, "Down the Middle of the Road," 347.
25 National Archives of the United States, State Department, RG 59, vol. 6013, file 842.5045/I-946: "1945–1949," Lewis Clark to the Secretary of State, 9 January 1946.
26 LAC, J.L. Cohen Papers, MG30 A94, vol. 36, file 3065: "Study of PC 1003," J.L. Cohen to David Lewis, 24 February 1944.
27 LAC, J.L. Cohen Papers, MG30 A94, vol. 36, file 3063: "Press Releases Regarding PC 1003 and PC 9384," 25 February 1944.
28 LAC, Canadian Labour Congress, MG28 I103, vol. 199, file 21: "Provincial Government of Ontario, Leader of the Opposition, 1943–48," A.R. Mosher to E.B. Joliffe, 10 March 1944.
29 *Canadian Forum* 24 (April 1944): 8.
30 LAC, Canadian Labour Congress, MG28 I103, vol. 156, file: "O'Brien, Daniel. Vancouver Correspondence, Part 3, 1944," Daniel O'Brien to Patrick Conroy, 19 May 1944.
31 LAC, Department of Labour, RG 27, vol. 621, file 4: "Loose Correspondence, Memoranda, and Documentation," Submission by the UE, 3 March 1944.
32 LAC, Department of Labour, RG 27, vol. 621, file 4: "Loose Correspondence, Memoranda, and Documentation," UE-Evaluation of Wartime Labour Relations Regulations, 1 March 1944 and Memorandum Relative to the Newspaper Statement by Mr J.L. Cohen, 8 March 1944; J.L. Cohen Papers, MG30 A94, vol. 34, file 3052-10: "National War Labour Board, Miscellaneous," Memorandum on PC 1003 by the Regional Office and the District Council Committee of the United Auto Workers, 18 August 1944.
33 LAC, Co-operative Commonwealth Federation, MG28 IV1, vol. 191, file: "Unions-General, 1944–46," J.L. Cohen to Eugene Forsey, 1 March 1944.
34 *Canadian Forum* 24 (April 1944): 7.

35 LAC, MG28 IV1, vol. 195, file 3: "Submissions Regarding PC 1003 and PC 9384, Part 1, 1943–45," UE Brief, January 1945.

36 LAC, Co-operative Commonwealth Federation, MG28 IV1, vol. 197, file 14: "Memorandum to the Government, Part 2, 1945," Memorandum on Amendments to PC 1003, Prepared by the CCL Department of Research, 12 January 1945.

37 LAC, Canadian Labour Congress, MG28 I103, vol. 184, file 3: "Oshawa and District Labour Council, 1944," M.J. Fenwick to A.R. Mosher, 14 March 1944.

38 Forsey, *A Life on the Fringe*, 86; LAC, Canadian Labour Congress, MG28 I103, vol. 199, file 21: "Provincial Government of Ontario, Leader of the Opposition, 1943–48," A.R. Mosher to E.B. Joliffe, 17 March 1944.

39 LAC, Canadian Labour Congress, MG28 I103, vol. 40, file 22: "USWA General, Part 3, 1943–44," A.R. Mosher to C.H. Millard, 17 March 1944.

40 Douglas J. Feeney-Gallagher, "Battle on the Benches: The Wagner Act and the Federal Circuit Courts of Appeals, 1935–1942," *Seattle University Law Review* 23, no. 3 (2000): 507.

41 Millar, "Shapes of Power," 181; Laskin, "Labour Law: 1923–1947," 303.

42 NAC, Canadian Labour Congress, MG28 I103, vol. 192, file 7: "Federal Labour Department, 1944," Humphrey Mitchell to A.R. Mosher and Percy Bengough, 10 July 1944.

43 LAC, Department of Labour, RG 27, vol. 849, file 8-3-11-1, Part 2: "Administration, Wartime Labour Relations Board," Constance Garneau to Mackenzie King, 17 March 1944; *Montreal Gazette*, 13 September 1944 and 4 May 1962; Canadian Broadcasting Corporation, CBC *Program Schedule*, 27 May 1945, accessed 18 January 2016, http://www.otrr.org/FILES/Magz_pdf/CBC%20Program%20Schedule/CBC%20Program%20Schedule%20450527.PDF.

44 LAC, Department of Labour, RG 27, vol. 3540, file 3-26-51-1: "Suggestions and Recommendations Regarding PC 1003," Margaret M. Wherry to Humphrey Mitchell, 18 and 24 February 1944.

45 LAC, Department of Labour, RG 27, vol. 849, file 8-3-11-1, Part 2: "Administration, Wartime Labour Relations Board," Ursula M. Macdonnell to Humphrey Mitchell, 25 February 1944; *Lethbridge Herald*, 26 April 1944.

46 LAC, Department of Labour, RG 27, vol. 3489, file 1-10N-58, Part 1: "National Council of Women, Correspondence," Laura P. Hardy to Humphrey Mitchell, 3 July 1944; N.E.S. Griffiths, *Centennial History of the National Council of Women of Canada, 1893–1993* (Ottawa: Carleton University Press, 1997), 221.

47 *Montreal Gazette*, 24 April 1944.
48 Ibid., 29 September 1941.
49 Ibid., 17 June 1943.
50 Keshen, *Saints, Sinners, and Soldiers*, 146.
51 *Sherbrooke Telegram*, 6 January 1944.
52 Keshen, *Saints, Sinners, and Soldiers*, 161; *Toronto Daily Star*, 31 December 1942.
53 *Toronto Telegram*, 7 July 1944; *Toronto Daily Star*, 26 January 1945.
54 Frager, *Sweatshop Strife*, 113, 151.
55 Keshen, *Saints, Sinners, and Soldiers*, 150.
56 Canadian Broadcasting Corporation, "The Soldier's Return: A Digest of the Series Broadcast on the CBC Trans-Canada Network during the Winter of 1944–45" (Toronto: CBC Publications, 1945), 44.
57 *Globe and Mail*, 13 January 1944
58 Keshen, *Saints, Sinners, and Soldiers*, 204–5, 212; Julie Guard, "Womanly Innocence and Manly Self-Respect: Gendered Challenges in Labour's Postwar Compromise," in *Labour Gains, Labour Pains: 50 Years of PC 1003*, ed. Cy Gonick, Paul Phillips, and Jesse Vorst (Winnipeg: Fernwood Publishing, 1995), 126.
59 *Ottawa Citizen*, 3 February 1945.
60 Alvin Finkel, *Social Policy and Practice in Canada: A History* (Waterloo, ON: Wilfrid Laurier Press, 2006), 200–1.
61 *Calgary Herald*, 17 October 1945.
62 *Toronto Daily Star*, 18 August 1945.
63 Cuthbertson, *Labour Goes to War*, 142; Sugiman, "Privilege and Oppression," 94–7; Patrias, *Jobs and Justice*, 184, 192; Sangster, *Transforming Labour*, 35.
64 Stephen, *Pick One Intelligent Girl*, 4–6, 30–1, 135–6; Gail Cuthbert Brandt, "Pigeon-Holed and Forgotten: The Work of the Subcommittee on the Post-War Problems of Women, 1943," *Histoire sociale/ Social History* 15, no. 29 (May 1982): 259.
65 Pierson, *They're Still Women*, 77–9, 93.
66 Brandt, "Pigeon-Holed and Forgotten," 241–2, 253–4; Stephen, *Pick One Intelligent Girl*, 106.
67 Brandt, "Pigeon-Holed and Forgotten," 255–7.
68 Ibid., 250.
69 Ibid., 255.
70 LAC, Department of Labour, RG 27, vol. 849, file 8-3-11-1, Part 2: "Administration, Wartime Labour Relations Board," Constance Garneau to Mackenzie King, 17 March 1944, Ursula M. Macdonnell to Humphrey

Mitchell, 25 February 1944, and Humphrey Mitchell to Ursula M. Macdonnell, 25 February 1944.

71 LAC, Department of Labour, RG 27, vol. 3540, file 3-26-51-1: "Suggestions and Recommendations Regarding PC 1003," A. MacNamara to Margaret M. Wherry, 1 March 1944; LAC, Department of Munitions and Supply, RG 28, vol. 859, file: "Labour Surveys," January 1944; *Labour Organizations in Canada* (Ottawa: King's Printer, 1945), 22

72 LAC, Department of Labour, RG 27, vol. 849, file 8-3-11-1, Part 2: "Administration, Wartime Labour Relations Board," Ursula M. Macdonnell to Humphrey Mitchell, 26 February 1944.

73 LAC, Department of Labour, RG 27, vol. 3540, file 3-26-51-1: "Suggestions and Recommendations Regarding PC 1003," Margaret M. Wherry to Mackenzie King, 8 March 1944.

74 Sangster, *Transforming Labour*, 18.

75 *Montreal Gazette*, 27 May 1961.

76 Donica Belisle "Negotiating Paternalism: Women and Canada's Largest Department Stores, 1890–1940," *Journal of Women's History* 19, no. 1 (Spring 2007): 73–4.

77 Anne Forrest, "Hidden in the Past: How Labour Relations Policy and Law Perpetuate Women's Economic Inequality," *Canadian Woman Studies* 23, nos. 3–4 (2004): 67–9. See also Judy Fudge, "Rungs on the Labour Law Ladder: Using Gender to Challenge Hierarchy," *Saskatchewan Law Review* 60, no. 2 (1996): 254–9.

78 LAC, J.L. Cohen Papers, MG30 A94, vol. 36, file 3065: "Study of PC 1003," J.L. Cohen to George Burt, 8 August 1944 and vol. 34, file 3052-10: "National War Labour Board, Miscellaneous," Memorandum on PC 1003 by the Regional Office and the District Council Committee of the United Auto Workers, 18 August 1944.

79 LAC, Canadian Labour Congress, MG28 I103, vol. 44, file 12: "USWA-Hamilton, General, 1941–44," Patrick Conroy to Bert McClure, 27 September 1944.

80 LAC, Canadian Labour Congress, MG28 I103, vol. 192, file 7: "Federal Labour Department, 1944," Resolutions Sent to Humphrey Mitchell, 6 December 1944.

81 Bryan D. Palmer, *Working Class Experience: Rethinking the History of Canadian Labour, 1800–1991* (Toronto: McClelland & Stewart, 1992), 219–20.

82 Gibson and Robertson, *Ottawa at War*, 480.

83 Granatstein, *The Ottawa Men*, 164–5.

84 Peter Neary and J.L. Granatstein, eds., *The Veteran's Charter and Post-World War II Canada* (Montreal: McGill-Queen's University Press, 1998), 236.

85 J.L. Granatstein, *Canada's War*, 270–1.
86 *Labour Gazette* 45 (May 1945): 642.
87 Lewis, *The Good Fight*, 206.
88 LAC, Canadian Labour Congress, MG28 I103, vol. 198, file 14: "Saskatchewan: Plans for Progress," Published Pamphlet, 1945; LAC, Department of Labour, RG 27, vol. 3489, file 1-10N-44: "National Liberal Federation – Correspondence," M.M. Maclean to Allan G. McLean, 11 August 1945; Fudge and Tucker, *Labour Before the Law*, 272.
89 LAC, Canadian Labour Congress, MG28 I103, vol. 156, file: "O'Brien, Daniel, Vancouver Correspondence, Part 4, 1945–46," Daniel O'Brien to Patrick Conroy, 5 September 1945 and vol. 198, file 14: "Provincial Government of Saskatchewan, Part 3, 1945–53," A.R. Mosher to Kenneth Bryden, 25 September 1945.
90 LAC, J.L. Cohen Papers, MG30 A94, vol. 37, file 3080: "Mine Mill v. Wright-Hargreaves and Sylvanite Gold Mines," J.L. Cohen to R.H. Carlin, 3 March 1945; LAC, Department of Labour, RG 27, vol. 618, file 8: "War Appropriations Debate Material," Press Release, 8 March 1945.
91 LAC, Department of Labour, RG 27, vol. 3540, file 3-26-51-1: "Suggestions and Recommendations Regarding PC 1003," Allan G. McLean to Paul Martin, 29 December 1944.
92 LAC, Canadian Labour Congress, MG28 I103, vol. 195, file 3: "Submissions Regarding PC 1003 and PC 9384, Part 1, 1943–45," Shipyard Federation of British Columbia to the CCL Executive Council, 7 January 1945.
93 LAC, Canadian Labour Congress, MG28 I103, vol. 195, file 3: "Submissions Regarding PC 1003 and PC 9384, Part 1, 1943–45," Shipyard Federation of British Columbia to the CCL Executive Council, 7 January 1945; vol. 195, file 5: "Submissions Regarding PC 1003 and PC 9384, Part 1, 1943–45," H.J. Padget to Norman S. Dowd, 11 January 1945; and vol. 191, file 8: "Director of Industrial Relations and Registrar – M.M. Maclean, Part 1, 1942–44," George Burt to A.R. Mosher, 30 November 1944; LAC, Department of Labour, RG 27, Access 83-84/206, box 1, file 7-2-1-1, Part 1: Short Chronological History of Conciliation in Industrial Relations between the Ford Motor Company of Canada Ltd. and Local 200, UAW-CIO, Windsor, Ontario, by G.B. O'Connor, n.d.
94 LAC, Department of Labour, RG 27, vol. 3540, file 3-26-51-1: "Suggestions and Recommendations Regarding PC 1003," Paul Martin to A. MacNamara, 5 January 1945.
95 LAC, Canadian Labour Congress, MG28 I103, vol. 197, file 14: "Memorandum to the Government, Part 2, 1945," Memorandum on

Amendments to PC 1003, Prepared by the CCL Department of Research, 12 January 1945.

96 LAC, Canadian Labour Congress, MG28 I103, vol. 195, file 3: "Submissions Regarding PC 1003 and PC 9384, Part 1, 1943–45," UE Brief, January 1945.

97 Fudge and Tucker, *Labour Before the Law*, 278.

98 LAC, J.L. Cohen Papers, MG30 A94, vol. 38, file 3112(1): "CCL Correspondence, Reports, Notes on PC 1003," Report of the Special Committee of the Executive Council of the CCL on PC 1003 and PC 9384," 15 January 1945.

99 LAC, Canadian Labour Congress, MG28 I103, vol. 40, file 20: "USW-General, Part 1, 1943–44," Norman S. Dowd to Harold Padget, 19 December 1944.

100 Jeremy Webber, "The Malaise of Compulsory Conciliation: Strike Prevention in Canada during World War II," in *The Character of Class Struggle: Essays in Canadian Working-Class History, 1850–1985*, ed. Bryan D. Palmer (Toronto: McClelland & Stewart, 1986), 155.

101 LAC, Department of Labour, RG 27, Access 83-84/206, box 1, F-7-2-1-1, Part 1, "General Correspondence PC 1003," G.B. O'Connor to Humphrey Mitchell, 23 August 1944.

102 *Labour Gazette* 44 (August 1944): 971–3, 976–81 and 45 (July 1945): 986–7; LAC, Public Records Committee, RG35/7, vol. 21, file 18: "Wartime Activities of the Industrial Relations Branch," *Report*, March 1946; Jay White, "Pulling Teeth: Striking for the Check-Off in the Halifax Shipyards, 1944," in Earle, *Workers and the State*, 144–70.

103 LAC, Canadian Labour Congress, MG28 I103, vol. 41, file 1: "USWA – General, Part 1, 1944–45," Charles Millard to Pat Conroy, 17 April 1945.

104 LAC, Canadian Labour Congress, MG28 I103, vol. 129, file 60: "Haywood, Allan S., 1945–50," Pat Conroy to Allan S. Haywood, 26 May 1945.

105 National Archives of the United States, State Department, RG 59, vol. 6013, file 842.5043/6-2745: "1945–49," Paul Norgren to the Secretary of State, 27 June 1945.

106 LAC, Canadian Labour Congress, MG28 I103, vol. 330, file 18: "CCL Executive Council Minutes," 15 January 1945 and vol. 195, file 3: "Submissions Regarding PC 9384 and PC 1003, Part 1, 1943–45.

107 LAC, J.L. Cohen Papers, MG30 A94, vol. 38, file 3112(1): "CCL Correspondence, Reports, Notes on PC 1003," Report of the Special Committee of the Executive Council of the CCL on PC 1003 and PC 9384, 15 January 1945.

108 LAC, Canadian Labour Congress, MG28 I103, vol. 211, file 4: "General Correspondence, JL Cohen-PC 1003 Account, 1945," T.F. Stevenson to Norman S. Dowd, 14 May 1945.
109 MacDowell, *Renegade Lawyer*, 193–211, 223–66, 289–90.
110 LAC, J.L. Cohen Papers, MG30 A94, vol. 38, file 3112: "CCL Reports on PC 1003," Proposed Amendments to Wartime Labour Relations Regulations, 23 March 1945.
111 LAC, Canadian Labour Congress, MG28 I103, vol. 171, file 11: "Circular Letters, 1945," 30 April 1945 and vol. 330, file 18: "CCL Executive Council Minutes," 23 March 1945; LAC, RG 27, Department of Labour, vol. 3540, file 3-26-51-1: "Suggestions and Recommendations Regarding PC 1003," A. MacNamara to Humphrey Mitchell, 18 April 1945.
112 *Labour Gazette* 44 (November 1944): 1426–33.
113 LAC, J.L. Cohen Papers, MG30 A94, vol. 39, file 3112A: "CCL Reports on PC 1003," Press Release by the Workers' Educational Association, 21 January 1945; Workers' Education Association Joint Committee for Revisions to PC 1003, "The Wartime Labour Regulations: A Ten-Point Programme of Action," February 1945; Circular by the Workers' Education Association, 22 February 1945.
114 LAC, Canadian Labour Congress, MG28 I103, vol. 3, file 19: "IAM, 1942–45," Alex Reith to Percy Bengough, 16 March 1945 and "IAM, 1942–45," IAM Circular, April 1945.
115 LAC, J.L. Cohen Papers, MG30 A94, vol. 211, file 2: "General Correspondence JL Cohen Account, Part 1, 1944–45," J.L. Cohen to Patrick Conroy, 7 April 1945.
116 *Labour Gazette* 45 (May 1945): 636–9.
117 Walter P. Reuther Library, Wayne State University, "(6647) Ford, UAW, 1945 Strike Agreement, Windsor, Ontario," accessed 12 July 2015, http://reuther.wayne.edu/node/3408; *St Petersburg Evening Independent*, 2 May 1944.
118 Herb Colling, "Excerpts from *99-Days, the Ford Strike in Windsor, 1945*," *The Walkerville Time Magazine*, accessed 12 July 2015, http://www.walkervilletimes.com/27/ford-strike.html.
119 *Ottawa Citizen*, 5 November 1945; *Toronto Daily Star*, 5 November 1945; Moulton, "Ford Windsor 1945," 142.
120 Montero, *We Stood Together*, 105–6.
121 Winnipeg *Tribune*, 22 November 1945.
122 *Labour Gazette* 5 (May 1945): 640–3.
123 LAC, Canadian Labour Congress, MG28 I103, vol. 39, file 3112-A, "CCL Report on PC 1003," Arthur MacNamara to J.L. Cohen, 20 March 1945;

LAC, J.L. Cohen Papers, MG30 A94, vol. 39, file 3112: "CCL Report on PC 1003," Department of Labour Press Release, 29 May 1945; LAC, Department of Labour, RG 27, Access 83-84/206, file 7-2-2-1, Part 2: "General Correspondence Regarding PC 1003, 1944–47," A.H. Brown to M.M. Maclean, 30 May 1945.

124 LAC, MG28 I103, Canadian Labour Congress, vol. 171, file 16: Circular Letter No. 74," Norman S. Dowd to CCL Affiliates, 25 April 1945.

125 LAC, RG 2, Privy Council, vol. 46, file D-16-2: "Department of Labour, 1945," Cabinet Committee Minutes, 2 February 1945.

126 LAC, Canadian Labour Congress, MG28 I103, vol. 196, file 1: "W.L. Mackenzie King 1945–48," Mackenzie King to Patrick Conroy, 20 February 1945.

127 Bothwell, and Kilbourn, *C.D. Howe*, 206.

128 *Diaries of William Lyon Mackenzie King*, 12 June 1945.

129 Granatstein, *The Politics of Survival*, 192–7.

130 Windsor *Star*, 5 November1966; Susan Goldenberg, *Snatched! The Peculiar Kidnapping of Beer Tycoon John Labatt* (Toronto: Dundurn Press, 2004), 217.

131 John English, "Canada's Road to 1945," 106–7.

132 Lewis, *The Good Fight*, 267, 291.

133 *Labour Gazette* 46 (February 1946): 146.

134 LAC, J.L. Cohen Papers, MG30 A94, vol. 36, file 3605: "Study of PC 1003," by J.L. Cohen, August 1944.

135 Moulton, "Ford Windsor 1945," 150.

136 LAC, Public Records Committee, RG 35/7, vol. 21, file 18: "Wartime Activities of the Industrial Relations Branch," *Report*, March 1946.

137 LAC, Department of Labour, RG 27, Access 83-84/206, box 1, file 7-2-1-1, Part 1: "Short Chronological History of Conciliation in Industrial Relations between the Ford Motor Company of Canada Ltd. and Local 200, UAW-CIO, Windsor, Ontario," by G.B. O'Connor.

138 William Kaplan, "How Justice Rand Devised His Famous Formula," in *Work on Trial: Canadian Labour Law Struggles*, ed. Judy Fudge and Eric Tucker (Toronto: Irwin Law, 2010), 78.

139 *Diaries of William Lyon Mackenzie King*, 13 September 1945; Millar, "Shapes of Power," 257.

140 LAC, Canadian Labour Congress, MG28 I103, vol. 145, "Harm, Henry: Nova Scotia Correspondence Part 3, 1945–48," Henry Harm to Pat Conroy, 5 November 1945.

141 Kaplan, "How Justice Rand Devised His Famous Formula," 81.

142 LAC, Department of Labour, RG 27, Access 83-84/206, box 1, file 7-2-1-1, Part 1: "Short Chronological History of Conciliation in Industrial

Relations between the Ford Motor Company of Canada Ltd. and Local 200, UAW-CIO, Windsor, Ontario," by G.B. O'Connor.

143 Montero, *We Stood Together*, 108–9; Moulton, "Ford Windsor 1945," 146.

144 William Kaplan, *Canadian Maverick: The Life and Times of Ivan C. Rand* (Toronto: University of Toronto Press, 2009), 189.

145 *Toronto Daily Star*, 19 September and 22 November 1945; *Edmonton Journal*, 10 November 1945.

146 Montero, *We Stood Together*, 110.

147 *Diaries of William Lyon Mackenzie King*, 6 January 1944.

148 Martin, *Far From Home*, 395.

149 Kaplan, *Canadian Maverick*, 199, 205, 424–5, 430.

150 Moulton, "Ford Windsor 1945," 149.

151 Kaplan, *Canadian Maverick*, 216.

152 LAC, Co-operative Commonwealth Federation, MG28 IV, vol. 196, file: "USWA," Charles Millard to David Lewis, 16 February 1946.

153 Kaplan, *Canadian Maverick*, 210.

154 Ibid., 194.

155 LAC, Department of Labour, RG 27, vol. 3563, file 11-4-3-3-1 Part 2, "Working Conditions," Harry Hereford to M.M. Maclean, 10 January 1948.

156 Kaplan, "How Justice Rand," 104.

157 Robert Marleau and Camille Montpetit, eds., "Committees," in *House of Commons Procedure and Practices*, accessed 12 August 2012, http://www.parl.gc.ca/MarleauMontpetit/DocumentViewer.aspx?DocId=1001&Sec=Ch20&Seq=9&Language=E.

158 *Labour Gazette* (September 1946): 1331–59; Canada, House of Commons, Industrial Relations Committee, *Minutes of Proceedings and Evidence* (Ottawa: King's Printer 1946), 184.

159 Forsey, *A Life on the Fringe*, 81.

160 *Montreal Gazette*, 8 August 1946.

161 LAC, Canadian Labour Congress, MG28 I103, vol. 123, file 8: "House of Commons Industrial Relations Committee," Brief, 7 August 1946.

162 Hollander, "Down the Middle of the Road," 346; McInnis, *Harnessing Labour Confrontation*, 87–8.

163 McInnis, *Harnessing Labour Confrontation*, 90.

164 Ibid., 99.

165 LAC, Canadian Labour Congress, MG28 I103, vol. 123, file 8: "House of Commons Industrial Relations Committee," Brief, 7 August 1946.

166 *Financial Post*, 26 February 1944.

167 *Canadian Business* 17 (July 1944), 54; Bliss, *Northern Enterprise*, 456.

168 *Labour Gazette* 44 (July 1944): 927–32.

169 LAC, Canadian Manufacturers Association, MG28 I230, vol. 147, file: "Wartime Labour Relations Regulations," Memorandum in Reply to Circular 1614, August 1946.

170 *Canadian Business* 17 (October 1944): 36.

171 LAC, Canadian Manufacturers Association, MG28 I230, vol. 147, file: "Wartime Labour Relations Regulations," A.C. Thompson to W.R. Yendall, 26 September 1946 and In Process 83/138, "CMA – Industrial Relations Committee Minutes," 10 August 1945.

172 Gray, "Woodworkers and Legitimacy," 163.

173 LAC, J.L. Cohen Papers, MG30 A94, vol. 36, file 3065: "Study of PC 1003," T.W. McClure to Humphrey Mitchell, 11 September 1944; LAC, Canadian Labour Congress, MG28 I103, vol. 8, file 1: "United Textile Workers, 1943–45," Pamphlet on Organizing at Dominion Textiles, April 1944; Montero, *We Stood Together*, 119.

174 LAC, Canadian Labour Congress, MG28 I103, vol. 156, file: "O'Brien, Daniel, Vancouver Correspondence, Part 3, 1944," Daniel O'Brien to Patrick Conroy, 19 May 1944; vol. 139, file: "Borgford, G.S., Winnipeg, Manitoba Correspondence, Part 1, 1943–44," Patrick Conroy to G.S. Borgford, 29 August 1944.

175 "War Series: No. 25" (1 October 1945), in Kealey and Whitaker, *War Series – Part II, 1942–45*, 436–7; Storey, "Unionization versus Corporate Welfare," 34.

176 LAC, Canadian Labour Congress, MG28 I103, vol. 145, file: "Harm, Henry, Halifax, Nova Scotia Correspondence, Part 2, 1945–48," Henry Harm to Patrick Conroy, 27 February 1946.

177 *Canadian Business* 17 (July 1944): 54.

178 LAC, Canadian Manufacturers Association, MG28 I230, vol. 117, file: "Industrial Relations and Disputes Investigation Act #1, 1946–47," N. Peterson to E.R. Complin, 24 January 1947.

179 LAC, Canadian Manufacturers Association, MG28 I230, vol. 147, file: "Wartime Labour Relations Regulations," Memorandum in Reply to Circular 1614, August 1946.

180 *Montreal Daily Star*, 14 September 1945; LAC, Public Records Committee, RG35/7, vol. 21, file 18: "Wartime Activities of the Industrial Relations Branch," *Report*, March 1946.

181 Hollander, "Down the Middle of the Road," 347–8; Morton with Copp, *Working People*, 190–3; *Labour Gazette* 47 (March 1947): 421–51.

182 LAC, Canadian Labour Congress, MG28 I103, vol. 228, file 6: "General Correspondence, Labour Information Center, Part 2, 1945–47," Radio Broadcast by A.R. Mosher, 6 April 1946; *Montreal Gazette*, 21 March 1946.

183 Gray, "Woodworkers and Legitimacy," 210–55.
184 LAC, Department of Labour, RG 27, vol. 896, file 8-9-23: "Standing Committee on Industrial Relations," Donald Gordon to A. MacNamara, 16 July 1946.
185 LAC, Department of Labour, RG 27, vol. 896, file 8-9-23, Part 2: "Standing Committee on Industrial Relations," Submissions by the UAW, URW, and UE, 1 August, 1946.
186 William Kilbourn, *The Elements Combined: A History of the Steel Company of Canada* (Toronto: Clarke, Irwin, and Co., 1960), 182–99; McDowall, *Steel at the Sault*, 224–9.
187 *Ottawa Evening Journal*, 29 August 1946.
188 *Globe and Mail*, 24 September 1946.
189 LAC, Department of Labour, RG 27, vol. 3520, file 3-26-10-1, Part 1: "Strikes and Lockouts Correspondence, 1946," Wilson M. Southam to Humphrey Mitchell, 18 June 1946.
190 Green, *Against the Tide*, 139–50; Kaplan, *Everything That Floats*, 42–8.
191 Montero, *We Stood Together*, 114–32; Salutin, *Kent Rowley*, 37–52.
192 Ian Radforth, *Bush Workers and Bosses*, 145–6.
193 McInnis, *Harnessing Labour Confrontation*, 101–2; Hollander, "Down the Middle of the Road," 348.
194 National Archives of the United States, State Department, RG 59, vol. 6013, file 842.5045/4-546: "1945–1949," Paul Norgren to the Secretary of State, 5 April 1946.
195 LAC, Canadian Labour Congress, MG28 I103, vol. 123, file 8: "House of Commons Industrial Relations Committee," Brief, 7 August 1946, 1340.
196 Gray, "Woodworkers and Legitimacy," 203.
197 National Archives of the United States, State Department, RG 59, vol. 6013, file 842.5045/4-546: "1945–1949," Paul Norgren to the Secretary of State, 5 April, 1946.
198 *Labour Gazette* 47 (July 1947): 951; Gray, "Woodworkers and Legitimacy," 229.
199 *Labour Gazette* 46 (June 1946): 725.
200 Smith, *Cold Warrior*, 161–2.
201 *Windsor Daily Star*, 6 April 1946; *Diaries of William Lyon Mackenzie King*, 5 April and 5 September 1946.
202 LAC, Canadian Labour Congress, MG28 I103, vol. 123, file 8: "House of Commons Industrial Relations Committee, CCL Wage Co-ordinating Committee," Brief, 1 August 1946, 1343; McInnis, *Harnessing Labour Confrontation*, 140–1.
203 Warrian, "Labour Is Not a Commodity," 208.

204 *Labour Gazette* 46 (September 1946): 1354.

205 Norrie and Owram, *History of the Canadian Economy*, 536, 560; LAC, Canadian Manufacturers Association, MG28 I230, vol. 147, file: "Wartime Labour Relations Regulations," J.T. Stirrett to Hugh Macdonnell et al., 23 August 1946.

206 *Globe and Mail*, 18 September 1946.

207 LAC, Canadian Manufacturers Association, MG28 I230, vol. 147, file: "Wartime Labour Relations Regulations," Hugh Dalton to J.T. Stirrett, 27 August 1946.

208 LAC, Department of Labour, RG 27, Access 83-84/206, box #1, file 7-2-1-1, Part 1: "General Correspondence, PC 1003, 1943–47," A.H. Brown to A. MacNamara, 25 June 1946.

209 LAC, Canadian Manufacturers Association, MG28 I230, vol. 117, file: "Industrial Relations: Strikes 1946," J.S. Vanderploeg to H.S. Hilton, 18 October 1946.

210 LAC, Department of Labour, RG 27, vol. 3520, file 3-26-10-1, Part 2: "Strikes and Lockouts Correspondence," Wilson M. Southam to Humphrey Mitchell, 18 June 1946.

211 Gray, "Woodworkers and Legitimacy," 199–201. Kaplan, *Everything That Floats*, 42; Kilbourn, *The Elements Combined*, 188; Dan England, Robert England, and Del Stewart, "The 1946 Rubber Workers' Strike," in Copp, *Industrial Unionism in Kitchener*, 81.

212 LAC, Department of Labour, RG 27, vol. 3520, file 3-26-10-1, Part 2: "Strikes and Lockouts Correspondence," Wilfrid Heffernan to James Gardiner, 21 June 1946.

213 LAC, Canadian Chamber of Commerce, MG28 III 62, vol. 17, file: "*The Record*, 1940–52," August 1946.

214 LAC, Canadian Manufacturers Association, MG28 I230, vol. 147, file: "Wartime Labour Relations Regulations," Hugh Dalton to J.T. Stirrett, 27 August 1946.

215 LAC, Department of Labour, RG 27, vol. 3520, file 3-26-10-1, Part 2: "Strikes and Lockouts Correspondence," A.H. Brown to A. MacNamara, 23 July 1946.

216 LAC, Department of Labour, RG 27, Access 83-84/206, box #1, file 7-2-1-1: "General Correspondence PC 1003, 1943–47," A. MacNamara to Col. C.C.I. Merritt, 15 August 1946.

217 LAC, Department of Labour, RG 27, vol. 3520, file 3-26-10-1, Part 2: "Strikes and Lockouts Correspondence," Humphrey Mitchell to James Wiltze, 30 July 1946; England et al., "The 1946 Rubber Workers' Strike," 87; Kaplan, *Everything that Floats*, 44.

218 *Diaries of William Lyon Mackenzie King*, 15 July 1946.
219 LAC, Department of Labour, RG 27, vol. 3520, file 3-26-10-1, Part 2: "Strikes and Lockouts Part 2," Humphrey Mitchell to Wilson M. Southam, 20 June 1946.
220 LAC, Department of Labour, RG 27, vol. 3520, file 3-26-10-1, Part 2: "Strikes and Lockouts Part 2," Humphrey Mitchell to unknown respondent, 23 July 1946.
221 *Windsor Daily Star*, 23 July 1946.
222 Morton with Copp, *Working People*, 191–3.
223 *Diaries of William Lyon Mackenzie King*, 14–17 July 1946.
224 Ibid., 26 August 1946.
225 King, *Industry and Humanity*, 140.
226 *Diaries of William Lyon Mackenzie King*, 5 September 1946.
227 Ibid., 26 September 1946.
228 Kilbourn, *The Elements Combined*, 193–200.
229 King, *Industry and Humanity*, 144.
230 *Labour Gazette* 46 (September 1946): 1187.
231 *Labour Gazette* 46 (October 1946): 1386; LAC, Department of Labour, RG 27, vol. 3521, file 3-26-10-1, Part 3: "Strikes and Lockouts Correspondence," A.R. Mosher to Humphrey Mitchell, 21 August 1946.
232 LAC, Department of Labour, RG 27, vol. 3521, file 3-26-10-1, Part 3: "Strikes and Lockouts Correspondence," Emily Burnham to Humphrey Mitchell, 12 September 1946.
233 *Ottawa Citizen*, 5 September and 7 September 1946.
234 F.R. Anton, *Government Supervised Strike Votes* (Toronto: C.C.H. Canadian Ltd., 1961), 11.
235 LAC, Canadian Manufacturers Association, MG28 I230, In Process 83/138, file: "CMA – Industrial Relations Committee Minutes," 26 August 1946.
236 *Financial Times*, 9 August 1946.
237 LAC, Department of Labour, RG 27, vol. 3541, file 3-26-58-2, Part 2: "Suggestions and Representations Regarding the Industrial Relations and Disputes Investigation Act," Wilson Southam to Humphrey Mitchell, 20 January 1947.
238 *Windsor Daily Star*, 1 August 1950.
239 *Diaries of William Lyon Mackenzie King*, 26 September 1944.
240 *Ottawa Citizen*, 1 August 1950.
241 *Diaries of William Lyon Mackenzie King*, 11 October 1946.
242 *Hansard*, 20th Parliament, 4th Session, vol. 3 (6 April 1948), 2710–11.

243 LAC, Canadian Labour Congress, MG28 I103, vol. 228, file 6: "General Correspondence, Labour Information Centre, Part 2, 1945–47," Radio Broadcast by A.R. Mosher, 6 April 1946.

244 LAC, M Canadian Labour Congress, G28 I103, vol. 171, file 22: "Circular Letter No. 81," 29 August 1945.

245 LAC, Department of Labour, RG 27, vol. 866, file 8-7-8-8: "Dominion Provincial Conferences: Statement on War Labour Regulations," 30 November 1945 and Eric Stangroom to A. MacNamara, 3 December 1945.

246 *Labour Gazette* 47 (March 1947): 421; LAC, Department of Labour, RG 27, Access 83-4/206, box #1, file 7-2-1-1, Part 1: "General Correspondence PC 1003, 1943–47," A.H. Brown to A. MacNamara, 25 June 1946.

247 LAC, Department of Labour, RG 27, vol. 3528, file 3-26-17, Part 1: "Suggestions and Representations Re. Labour Legislation," Eric Stangroom to A. MacNamara, 28 September 1946.

248 *Labour Gazette* 46 (September 1946): 1331–56; LAC, Department of Labour, RG 27, vol. 866, file 8-7-8-8: "Dominion-Provincial Conference, Labour Relations Proposals," George Drew to Mackenzie King, 7 September 1946.

249 LAC, Department of Labour, RG 27, vol. 867, file 8-7-8-19-2: "Dominion-Provincial Conference, 1946," Memorandum for Consideration of Members of the Cabinet and for Discussion, 11 October 1946.

250 *Diaries of William Lyon Mackenzie King*, 11 October 1946.

251 Alvin Finkel, "Paradise Postponed: A Re-examination of the Green Book Proposals of 1945," *Journal of the Canadian Historical Association* 4 (1993): 120–42.

252 LAC, Department of Labour, RG 27, vol. 867, file 8-7-8-19-2: "Dominion-Provincial Conference, 1946," Memorandum for Consideration of Members of the Cabinet and for Discussion, n.d.

253 Robert Bothwell, Ian Drummond, and John English, *Canada since 1945: Power, Politics, and Provincialism*, rev. ed. (Toronto: University of Toronto Press, 1989; Reprint 2001), 74.

254 Bothwell and Kilbourn, *C.D. Howe*, 206.

255 Bothwell, Drummond, and English, *Canada since 1945*, 79.

256 Montero, *We Stood Together*, 133–5.

257 Winnipeg *Tribune*, 13 October 1944.

258 LAC, Department of Labour, RG 27, vol. 867, file 8-7-8-19-1, Part 1: "Dominion-Provincial Conference, 1946," Minutes, 15–17 October 1946; *Diaries of William Lyon Mackenzie King*, 15 October 1946.

259 Winnipeg *Tribune*, 18 October 1946.

260 LAC, Department of Labour, RG 27, vol. 867, file 8-7-8-19-2: "Dominion-Provincial Conference, 1946," Substantive Amendments to the Provisions of PC 1003 Proposed for Incorporation in Dominion Legislation, 15 October 1946 and vol. 867, file 8-7-8-19-1, Part 1: "Dominion-Provincial Conference, 1946," Minutes, 15–17 October 1946; *Diaries of William Lyon Mackenzie King*, 15 October 1946.
261 *Diaries of William Lyon Mackenzie King*, 31 October 1946.
262 LAC, Department of Labour, RG 27, vol. 3541, file 3-26-58-3: "Suggestions and Recommendations Regarding the Industrial Relations and Disputes Investigation Act," Humphrey Mitchell to the Provincial Labour Ministers, 27 December, 1946.
263 *Canadian Forum* 27 (February 1947).
264 LAC, Department of Labour, RG 27, vol. 3541, file 3-26-58-3: "Suggestions and Recommendations Regarding the Industrial Relations and Disputes Investigation Act," Percy Bengough to A. MacNamara, 7 January 1947.
265 LAC, Canadian Labour Congress, MG28 I103, vol. 330, file 12: "Trades and Labour Congress Executive Council Minutes, 1946–49," 26–29 March 1947.
266 LAC, Louis St Laurent Papers, MG26 L, vol. 24, file 135: "Labour 1944–48," Memorandum of the CTCC, 13 March 1947; LAC, Canadian Labour Congress, MG28 I103, vol. 172, file 31: "Circular Letters, 1947," 3 July 1947.
267 LAC, Department of Labour, RG 27, vol. 3542, file 3-26-58-4, Part 1: "Suggestions and Recommendations Regarding the Industrial Relations and Disputes Act," CCL Brief on the Draft Bill, n.d.
268 LAC, Canadian Labour Congress, MG28 I103, vol. 128, file 18: "Conroy, Pat – National Labour Code," Transcript of Radio Broadcast, n.d.
269 J.L. Cohen, "Dominion has the Power to Legislate for Labour," *Saturday Night*, 14 December 1946, 22; William Lahey, "Canada Temperance Act," in *Alcohol and Temperance in Modern History: An International Encyclopedia*, ed. Jack S. Blocker, David M. Fahey, and Ian R. Tyrrell (Santa Barbara, CA: ABC-CLIO, 2003), 1:130–1; LAC, Canadian Labour Congress, MG28 I103, vol. 123, file 13: "House of Commons Industrial Relations Committee. CCL Submissions on Bill 338," Memorandum, 30 June 1947.
270 LAC, Canadian Labour Congress, MG28 I103, vol. 172, file 31: "Circular Letters, 1947," 14 March 1947.
271 LAC, Canadian Labour Congress, MG28 I103, vol. 149: "MacDonald, Donald Sydney NS Correspondence, Part 2 , 1947," Pat Conroy to Angus MacLeod, 1 March 1947.
272 LAC, Canadian Manufacturers Association, MG28 I230, vol. 117, file: "Industrial Relations and Disputes Investigation Act," A.C. Thompson to Canadian Gypsum Co. Ltd., 14 February 1947.

273 LAC, Canadian Manufacturers Association, MG28 I230, vol. 117, file: "Industrial Relations and Disputes Investigation Act," A.C. Thompson to William R. Yendall, 7 July 1947.

274 LAC, Department of Labour, RG 27, vol. 3542, F3-26-58-6: "Suggestions and representations Re. IRDIA," A.H. Brown to Humphrey Mitchell, 17 April 1947.

275 LAC, Canadian Chamber of Commerce, MG28 III62, vol. 10, file: "Labour Relations Committee Meetings," Minutes, 8 January 1947.

276 LAC, Canadian Chamber of Commerce, G28 III62, vol. 10, file: "Labour Relations Committee Meetings," 26 February 1947.

277 LAC, Canadian Manufacturers Association, MG28 I230, vol. 117, file: "Industrial Relations and Disputes Investigation Act," Recommendations of the Ontario Mining Association, 30 December 1946; C.W. Findlow to H.W. Macdonnell, 9 January 1947; William R. Yendall to H.W. Macdonnell, 10 January 1947; N. Peterson to E.R. Complin, 24 January, 1947; J.S. Vanderploeg to A.C. Thompson, 3 February 1947; J.T. Stirrett to R.C. Berkinshaw, 12 February 1947; and W.D. Black to J.T. Stirrett, 19 February 1947; LAC, Department of Labour, RG 27, vol. 3541, file 3-26-58-2, Part 2: "Suggestions and Representations Regarding the Industrial Relations and Disputes Investigation Act," Wilson M. Southam to Humphrey Mitchell, 20 January 1947; and vol. 3542, file 3-26-58-6, Part 1: "Suggestions and Recommendations IRDIA," F.D. Shepherd to Humphrey Mitchell, 7 March 1947.

278 *Labour Gazette* 47 (August 1947): 1106.

279 LAC, Department of Labour, RG 27, vol. 3541, file 3-26-58-2, Part 2: "Suggestions and Representations Regarding the Industrial Relations and Disputes Investigation Act," Harry Ashdown to Humphrey Mitchell, 16 May 1947.

280 LAC, Department of Labour, RG 27, vol. 867, file 8-7-8-19-1, Part 1: "Dominion-Provincial Conference, 1946," Minutes, 15–17 October 1946.

281 *Diaries of William Lyon Mackenzie King*, 19–20 November 1946.

282 *Hansard*, 20th Parliament, 4th Session, vol. 3 (6 April 1948), 2710–11; LAC, Department of Labour, RG 27, vol. 3541, file 3-26-58-2, Part 1: "Suggestions and Representations Regarding the Industrial Relations and Disputes Investigation Act," Humphrey Mitchell to Paul Martin, 25 June 1947.

283 *Winnipeg Citizen*, 2 November 1948.

284 *Diaries of William Lyon Mackenzie King*, 24 June 1947.

285 *Hansard*, 20th Parliament, 3rd Session, vol. 3 (22 April 1947), 2290–2301.

286 *Hansard*, 20th Parliament, 3rd Session, vol. 5 (17 June 1947), 4231.

287 LAC, Canadian Labour Congress, MG28 I103, vol. 330, file 2: "TLC Executive Council Minutes, 1946–1949," 3 October 1947; vol. 182, file 8: "Ontario Federation of Labour, Part 1, 1945–47," W.F. Cleve to Various Unions, 10 November 1947; and vol. 123, file 13: "House of Commons IR Committee. CCL Submissions on Bill 338," Memorandum Submitted by the CCL, 30 June 1947.
288 LAC, Eugene Forsey Papers, MG30 A25, vol. 4, file: "Arthur Meighen, 1946–50," Eugene Forsey to Arthur Meighen, 17 June 1947.
289 *Labour Gazette* 47 (February 1947): 132–4 and 47 (August 1947): 1093.
290 LAC, Department of Labour, RG 27, vol. 849, file 8-3-11-1: "Wartime Labour Relations Board Correspondence," A.H. Brown to A. MacNamara, 10 July 1947.
291 *Diaries of William Lyon Mackenzie King*, 2 April 1947.
292 Levine, *King*, 386–7.
293 *Diaries of William Lyon Mackenzie King*, 4–5 March 1948.
294 *Hansard*, 20th Parliament, 4th Session, vol. 3 (6 April 1948), 2709.
295 LAC, Department of Labour, RG 27, vol. 3542, file 3-26-58-4, Part 2: "Suggestions and Recommendations Regarding the Industrial Relations and Disputes Investigation Act," Sharman Learie to Humphrey Mitchell, 6 April 1948 and Memorandum Submitted by the Canadian Chamber of Commerce, 3 March 1948.
296 LAC, Canadian Labour Congress, MG28 I103, vol. 115, file 16: "Baron, Sam. 1945–1951," Report by the CCL Executive Council, n.d.
297 LAC, Canadian Labour Congress, MG28 I103, vol. 178, file 15: "Alberta Provincial Committee of CCL Unions, Part 1, 1946–49," Report, 8 May 1948; vol. 182, file 12: Ontario Federation of Labour, Part 2, 1948–49.
298 LAC, Canadian Labour Congress, MG28 I103, vol. 139, file: "Borgford, G.S. Winnipeg Manitoba Correspondence, Part 2, 1945–48," Pat Conroy to G.S. Borgford, 19 September 1947.
299 Winnipeg *Tribune*, 28 January 1948.
300 LAC, Canadian Labour Congress, MG28 I103, vol. 130, file 29: "MacDonald, Donald Correspondence 1946–1952," Pat Conroy to Donald MacDonald, 10 March 1948.
301 LAC, Canadian Labour Congress, MG28 I103, W.F. Cleve Kidd to Ontario Federation of Labour Affiliates, 23 March 1948.
302 *Hansard*, 20th Parliament, 4th Session, vol. 3 (6 April 1948), 2760.
303 *Labour Gazette* 48 (July 1948): 695; LAC, Department of Labour, RG 27, vol. 3542, file 3-26-58-6, Part 2: "Suggestions and Representations IRDIA," H. Grenville Smith to Humphrey Mitchell, 4 June 1948.
304 *Hansard*, 20th Parliament, 4th Session, vol. 6 (17 June 1948), 5371.

305 *Labour Gazette* 48 (November 1948): 1255–6.
306 *Labour Gazette* 48 (October 1948): 1082 and 48 (November 1948): 1257–61.
307 LAC, Canadian Manufacturers Association, MG28 I230, In Process 83/138, file: "CMA-Industrial Relations Committee Minutes," 8 November 1948.
308 LAC, Canadian Labour Congress, MG28 I130, vol. 132, file 23: "Wright, Maurice W., 1946–1954," Maurice Wright to Eugene Forsey, 20 September 1948.
309 *Labour Gazette* 48 (August 1948): 839.
310 *Labour Gazette* 49 (September 1949): 1098.
311 LAC, Canadian Manufacturers Association, MG28 I230, vol. 118, file 5: "IRDIA 1948," N.L. Smith to H.W. MacDonnell, 25 October 1948.
312 LAC, Canadian Chamber of Commerce, MG28 III62, vol. 17, file: "Policy Declarations 1926–48," October 1948.
313 Kaplan, *Everything That Floats*, 61–2; *Ottawa Citizen*, 14 March 1947.
314 *Labour Gazette* 49 (September 1949): 1099.
315 *Labour Gazette* 48 (December 1948): 1367.
316 LAC, Department of Labour, RG 27, vol. 3542, file F3-26-58-6, Part 2, "Suggestions and Representations IRDIA," Ford Brand to Mackenzie King, 11 June 1948.
317 LAC, Canadian Labour Congress, MG28 I130, vol. 115, file 16: "Baron, Sam 1945–1951," CCL Executive Council Memorandum, March 1950; John Logan, "How 'Anti-Union' Laws Saved Canadian Labour: Certification and Striker Replacements in Post-War Industrial Relations," *Relations industrielles/Industrial Relations* 57, no. 1 (2002): 132.
318 Stuart Jamieson, "Industrial Relations and Government Policy," *Canadian Journal of Economics and Political Science* 17 (February 1951): 32–3; Bruce E. Kaufman, *The Global Evolution of Industrial Relations: Events, Ideas, and the IIRA* (Geneva: International Labour Organization, 2004), 280; Craig Riddell, Gideon Rosenbluth and Mark Thompson, "Tribute to Stuart Marshall Jamieson, 1914–2002," *Relations industrielles/Industrial Relations* 59, no. 2 (2004): 231.
319 Judy Fudge and Eric Tucker, "Pluralism or Fragmentation? The Twentieth Century Employment Law Regime in Canada," *Labour/Le Travail* 46 (Fall 2000): 278–80; Alvin Finkel, "The Cold War, Alberta Labour, and the Social Credit Regime," *Labour/Le Travail* 21 (Spring 1988): 135.
320 *Labour Gazette* 52 (March 1952): 280.
321 Woods, *Labour Policy in Canada*, 338, 345–7.
322 King, *Industry and Humanity*, 329.
323 *Diaries of William Lyon Mackenzie King*, 28 May 1949.

Afterword

1 Ernest B. Akyeampong, "A Statistical Portrait of the Trade Union Movement," Statistics Canada, Catalogue no. 75-001-XPE, *Perspectives on Labour and Income* (Winter 1997): 50–1.
2 *Canadian Forum* 27 (February 1947).
3 Don Wells, "The Impact of the Postwar Compromise on Canadian Unionism: The Formation of an Auto Worker Local in the 1950s," *Labour/Le Travail* 36 (Fall 1995): 147–52.
4 *Montreal Gazette*, 31 July 1972.
5 Kris Warner, "Protecting Fundamental Labor Rights," 7–8.
6 Evan Soltas, "Is the U.S. Better Off without Unions?" *Bloomberg View* (19 February 2014), accessed 5 August 2015, https://www.bloomberg.com/view/articles/2014-02-19/is-the-u-s-better-off-without-unions-; Brad DeLong, "Debate: Is There a Substitute for Unions in Achieving Equitable Growth? And Can Unions Be Saved?" Washington Center for Equitable Growth, 28 February 2014, accessed 5 August 2015, http://equitablegrowth.org/equitablog/debate-is-there-a-substitute-for-unions-in-achieving-equitable-growth-and-can-unions-be-saved/.
7 Hugh MacIntyre and Charles Lammam, *Labour Relations Laws in Canada and the United States: An Empirical Comparison (2014 Edition)* (Vancouver, BC: Fraser Institute, 2014), 29.
8 Warner, "Protecting Fundamental Labor Rights," 5, 10–11, 21, 24; Taras, "Portrait of Nonunion Employee Representation in Canada," 139; Logan, "How 'Anti-Union' Laws Saved Canadian Labour," 135–6, 151.
9 Judy Fudge, "After Industrial Citizenship: Market Citizenship or Citizenship at Work?" *Relations industrielles/Industrial Relations* 60, no. 4 (2005): 643.
10 Michael Goldfield and Bryan D. Palmer, "Canada's Workers Movement: Uneven Developments," *Labour/Le Travail* 59 (Spring 2007): 159.
11 Smith, *Cold Warrior*, 191; CBC, "The Red Scare," accessed 24 July 2016, http://www.cbc.ca/history/EPISCONTENTSE1EP15CH1PA2LE.html.
12 Montero, *We Stood Together*, 134, 156.
13 Sangster, *Transforming Labour*, 80; Morton with Copp, *Working People*, 208–12; Smith, *Cold Warrior*, 177, 194–203.
14 CBC, "The Red Scare"; Smith, *Cold Warrior*, 177; Sangster, *Transforming Labour*, 96; Montero, *We Stood Together*, 162.
15 Abella, *Nationalism, Communism, and Canadian Labour*, 220–2.
16 LAC, Canadian Labour Congress, MG28 I103, vol. 155: "O'Brien, Daniel – Vancouver Correspondence – Part 3," Patrick Conroy to Daniel O'Brien, 2 December 1942.

17 *Diaries of William Lyon Mackenzie King*, 22 October 1935; Bedore, "Reading of Mackenzie King," 165; David M. Robinson, *Emerson and the Conduct of Life: Pragmatism and Ethical Purpose in the Later Work* (New York: Cambridge University Press, 1993), 13.
18 Elections Canada, "Survey of Voters and Non-Voters, 2002," accessed 9 August 2015, http://search1.odesi.ca/#/details?uri=%2Fodesi%2Fsovnv-E-2002.xml.
19 Antony Jay, *Lend Me Your Ears: Oxford Dictionary of Political Quotations* (New York: Oxford University Press, 2010), 23.
20 David G. Winter, "Measuring the Motives of Political Actors at a Distance," in *The Psychological Assessment of Political Leaders: With Profiles of Saddam Hussein and Bill Clinton*, ed. Jerrold M. Post (Ann Arbor, MI: University of Michigan Press, 2003), 153.
21 Hermann Wimmer, "Catechism on Methods of Teaching," *American Journal of Education* 4 (1858), 514.
22 Gitelman, *Legacy of the Ludlow Massacre*, xiv.
23 Levine, *King*, 7–11.
24 *National Post*, 30 December 2011.
25 Raymond W. Smock, ed., *Booker T. Washington in Perspective: Essays of Louis R. Harlan* (Jackson, MS: University Press of Mississippi, 1988), 193.
26 *Diaries of William Lyon Mackenzie King*, 27 April 1949.

References

Archival Sources

Library and Archives Canada
- Arthur J. Hills Papers
- Arthur Meighen Papers
- Arthur Roebuck Papers
- Bernard Wilson Papers
- Brooke Claxton Papers
- Canadian Association of Administrators of Labour Legislation
- Canadian Chamber of Commerce
- Canadian Labour Congress
- Canadian Manufacturers' Association
- C.D. Howe Papers
- Co-operative Commonwealth Federation
- C.S. Jackson Papers
- Department of Finance
- Department of Labour
- Department of Munitions and Supply
- Ernest Lapointe Papers
- Eugene Forsey Papers
- Gordon Graydon Papers
- Ian Mackenzie Papers
- J. King Gordon Papers
- J.L. Cohen Papers
- John Bracken Papers
- John W. Bruce Papers
- Joseph Mackenzie Papers

Labour Council of Metropolitan Toronto
Louis St Laurent Papers
National War Labour Board
Ottawa and District Labour Council
Paul Martin Papers
Privy Council
Progressive Conservative Party
Public Records Committee
Richard B. Hanson Papers
Robert Haddow Papers
W.L. Mackenzie King Papers
National Archives of the United States
Labor Department
State Department
Queen's University Archives
T.A. Crerar Papers
W.C. Clark Papers
Rockefeller Archive Center
Office of the Messrs Rockefeller

Federal Government Documents

Advisory Committee on Reconstruction. *Report*, 1943.
Department of Labour. *Government Intervention in Labour Disputes*. Industrial Relations Series. Bulletin #11. By Margaret Mackintosh. 1938.
Department of Labour. *Labour Gazette*, 1935–1948.
Department of Labour. *Labour Gazette Supplement*, 1943.
Department of Labour. *Labour Organizations in Canada*, 1934–1948.
Department of Trade and Commerce. Bureau of Statistics. *The Employment Situation*, 1943.
Elections Canada. *Survey of Voters and Non-Voters*, 2002.
House of Commons. *Debates (Hansard)*, 1935–1948.
House of Commons. Standing Committee on Industrial Relations. *Report*, 1946.
National War Labour Board. *Proceedings*, 1943.
– *Reports*, 1944.
Orders in Council: PC 2483, PC 3495, PC 2363, PC 2686, PC 2685, PC 5922, PC 7440, PC 892, PC 4020, PC 4844, PC 5830, PC 7307, PC 8253, PC 1426, PC 10802, PC 1141, PC 9384, PC 1003, PC 6893, PC 3689.

Public Records Committee. *Wartime Activities of the Industrial Relations Branch,* 1946.
Royal Commission of Inquiry into the Textile Industry. *Report,* 1938.
Royal Commission of Inquiry on the Arvida Strike. *Report,* 1941.
Royal Commission of Inquiry on the Schofield Woollen Strike. *Report,* 1941.
Statistics Canada. *The Canada Year Book,* 1943–44, 1944.
Statistics Canada. *Exploring the First Century of Canada's Consumer Price Index,* 2015.
Subcommittee on the Post-War Problems of Women to the Advisory Committee on Reconstruction, *Report,* 1943.

Newspapers and Journals

Many clippings from the following newspapers may also be found in the J.L. Cohen Papers, vols. 53–5 at the Library and Archives Canada.
Berkley Daily Gazette
Calgary Herald
Canadian Congress Journal
Canadian Business
Canadian Forum
Canadian Tribune
CCF News Comment
Edmonton Journal
Financial Post
Financial Times
Globe and Mail
Hamilton Spectator
Industrial Canada
Lethbridge Herald
Montreal Daily Star
Montreal Gazette
Montreal Matin
Montreal Standard
National Post
New Commonwealth
New York Times
Northern Miner
Northern News
Ottawa Citizen

Ottawa Evening Citizen
Ottawa Evening Journal
Ottawa Journal
PM Magazine
Quebec Chronicle
Regina Leader-Post
Saskatoon Star-Phoenix
Saturday Night
Sherbrooke Telegram
St Petersburg Evening Independent
Toronto Daily Star
Toronto News
Toronto Telegram
Windsor Daily Star
Winnipeg Citizen
Winnipeg Free Press

Books

Abella, Irving Martin. *Nationalism, Communism, and Canadian Labour: The CIO, the Communist Party, and the Canadian Congress of Labour, 1935–1956*. Toronto: University of Toronto Press, 1973.

–, ed. *On Strike: Six Key Labour Struggles in Canada 1919–1949*. Toronto: James Lorimer & Co., 1974.

Anton, F.R. *Government Supervised Strike Votes*. Toronto: C.C.H. Canadian Ltd., 1961.

Atkinson, Michael A., and William Coleman. *The State, Business, and Industrial Change in Canada*. Toronto: University of Toronto Press, 1989.

Avakumovic, Ivan. *The Communist Party in Canada: A History*. Toronto: McClelland & Stewart, 1975.

Babcock, Robert H. *Gompers in Canada: A Study in American Continentalism before the First World War*. Toronto: University of Toronto Press, 1974.

Bercuson, David Jay. *True Patriot: The Life of Brooke Claxton: 1898–1960*. Toronto: University of Toronto Press, 1993.

–, ed. *Canadian Labour History: Selected Readings*. Toronto: Copp Clark Pitman, 1987.

Blakeney, Allan. *An Honourable Calling: Political Memoirs*. Toronto: University of Toronto Press, 2008.

Bliss, Michael. *Northern Enterprise: Five Centuries of Canadian Business*. Toronto: McClelland & Stewart, 1987.

Bothwell, Robert, Ian Drummond, and John English. *Canada since 1945: Power, Politics, and Provincialism*. 2nd ed. Toronto: University of Toronto Press, 1989. Reprint 2001.

Bothwell, Robert, and William Kilbourn. *C.D. Howe: A Biography*. Toronto: McClelland & Stewart, 1979.

Brandes, Stuart. *American Welfare Capitalism, 1880–1940*. Chicago: University of Chicago Press, 1976.

Broadfoot, Barry. *Six War Years, 1939–1945: Memories of Canadians at Home and Abroad*. Toronto: Doubleday Canada, 1974.

Brody, David. *Workers in Industrial America: Essays on the 20th Century Struggle*. New York: Oxford University Press, 1980.

Bruce, Jean. *Back the Attack! Canadian Women during the Second World War – At Home and Abroad*. Toronto: Macmillan, 1985.

Bryce, Robert B. *Maturing in Hard Times: Canada's Department of Finance through the Great Depression*. Kingston: McGill-Queen's University Press, 1986.

Caccia, Ivana. *Managing the Canadian Mosaic in Wartime: Shaping Citizenship Policy, 1939–1945*. Montreal: McGill-Queen's University Press, 2010.

Cammett, John M. *Antonio Gramsci and the Origins of Italian Communism*. Palo Alto, CA: Stanford University Press, 1967.

Campbell, Lara. *Respectable Citizens: Gender, Family, and Unemployment in Ontario's Great Depression*. Toronto: University of Toronto Press, 2009.

Caplan, Gerald D. *The Dilemma of Canadian Socialism*. Toronto: McClelland & Stewart, 1973.

Caragata, Warren. *Alberta Labour: A Heritage Untold*. Toronto: James Lorimer & Co., 1979.

Carrothers, A.W.R., E.E. Palmer, and W.B. Rayner. *Collective Bargaining Law in Canada*. Toronto: Butterworths, 1986.

Cawson, Alan. *Corporatism and Political Theory*. New York: Basil Blackwell, 1986.

Cohen, J.L. *Collective Bargaining in Canada: An Examination of the Legislative Record and Policy of the Government of the Dominion of Canada*. Toronto: Steel Workers Organizing Committee, 1941.

Cohen, Lizabeth. *Making a New Deal: Industrial Workers in Chicago, 1919–1939*. New York: Cambridge University Press, 1990.

Coleman, William D. *Business and Politics: A Study of Collective Action*. Kingston: McGill-Queen's University Press, 1988.

Copp, Terry, ed. *Industrial Unionism in Kitchener, 1937–47*. Elora, ON: Cumnock Press, 1976.

Craig, Alton W.J. *The System of Industrial Relations in Canada*. Toronto: Prentice-Hall, 1983.

Craven, Paul. *"An Impartial Umpire": Industrial Relations and the Canadian State, 1900–1911*. Toronto: University of Toronto Press, 1980.

Creighton, Donald. *The Forked Road: Canada, 1939–1957*. Toronto: McClelland & Stewart, 1976.

Cuthbertson, Wendy. *Labour Goes to War: The CIO and the Construction of a New Social Order, 1939–45*. Vancouver, BC: UBC Press, 2012.

Dubofsky, Melvyn. *The State and Labor in Modern America*. Chapel Hill, NC: University of North Carolina Press, 1994.

Dulles, Foster Rhea, and Melvyn Dubofsky. *Labor in America: A History*. 4th ed. Arlington Heights, IL: Harlan Davidson, 1984.

Dumas, Evelyn. *The Bitter Thirties in Québec*. Translated by Arnold Bennett. Montreal: Black Rose Books, 1975.

Earle, Michael, ed. *Workers and the State in Twentieth Century Nova Scotia*. Fredericton, NB: Acadiensis Press, 1989.

Education Committees of the CSN and the CEQ. *The History of the Labour Movement in Québec*. Translated by Arnold Bennett. Montreal: Black Rose Books, 1987.

Esberey, Joy. *Knight of the Holy Spirit: A Study of William Lyon Mackenzie King*. Toronto: University of Toronto Press, 1980.

Ferns, Henry, and Bernard Ostry. *The Age of Mackenzie King*. Toronto: James Lorimer & Co., 1976.

Finkel, Alvin. *Business and Social Reform in the Thirties*. Toronto: James Lorimer & Co., 1979.

– *Social Policy and Practice in Canada: A History*. Waterloo, ON: Wilfrid Laurier Press, 2006.

Fligstein, Neil. *The Transformation of Corporate Capital*. Cambridge, MA: Harvard University Press, 1990.

Forsey, Eugene. *A Life on the Fringe: The Memoirs of Eugene Forsey*. Toronto: University of Oxford Press, 1990.

Fox, Alan. *History and Heritage: The Social Origins of the British Industrial Relations System*. London: George Allen and Unwin, 1985.

Frager, Ruth. *Sweatshop Strife: Class, Ethnicity, and Gender in the Jewish Labour Movement of Toronto, 1900–1939*. Toronto: University of Toronto Press, 1992.

Frager, Ruth, and Carmela Patrias. *Discounted Labour: Women Workers in Canada, 1870–1939*. Toronto: University of Toronto Press, 2005.

Francis, R. Douglas. *Frank H. Underhill: Intellectual Provocateur*. Toronto: University of Toronto Press, 1986.

Franks, C.E.S. *The Parliament of Canada*. Toronto: University of Toronto Press, 1987.

Fudge, Judy, and Eric Tucker, *Labour before the Law: The Regulation of Workers' Collective Action in Canada, 1900–1948*. Toronto: Oxford University Press, 2001.

Gibson, Frederick W., and Barbara Robertson, eds. *Ottawa at War: The Grant Dexter Memoranda, 1939–1945*. Vol. 11 of the Manitoba Record Society Publications. Winnipeg, MB: Manitoba Record Society, 1994.

Gillespie, Richard. *Manufacturing Knowledge: A History of the Hawthorne Experiments*. Cambridge: Cambridge University Press, 1991.
Girard, Philip. *Bora Laskin: Bringing Law to Life*. Toronto: University of Toronto Press, 2005.
Gitelman, Howard M. *Legacy of the Ludlow Massacre: A Chapter in American Industrial Relations*. Philadelphia: University of Pennsylvania Press, 1988.
Goldenberg, Susan. *Snatched! The Peculiar Kidnapping of Beer Tycoon John Labatt*. Toronto: Dundurn Press, 2004.
Gonick, Cy, Paul Phillips, and Jesse Vorst, eds. *Labour Gains, Labour Pains: 50 Years of PC 1003*. Winnipeg, MB: Fernwood Publishing, 1995.
Gordon, Colin. *New Deals: Business, Labor, and Politics in America, 1920–1935*. Cambridge: Cambridge University Press, 1994.
Granatstein, J.L. *Canada's War: The Politics of the Mackenzie King Government, 1939–1945*. 1975. Reprint, Toronto: University of Toronto Press, 1990.
– *The Ottawa Men: The Civil Service Mandarins, 1935–1957*. Toronto: Oxford University Press, 1982.
– *The Politics of Survival: The Conservative Party of Canada, 1939–1945*. Toronto: University of Toronto Press, 1970.
Grant, Wynn, ed. *The Political Economy of Corporatism*. London: St Martin's Press, 1983.
Green, Christopher. *Canadian Industrial Organization and Policy*. Toronto: McGraw-Hill Ryerson, 1980.
Green, Jim. *Against the Tide: The Story of the Canadian Seamen's Union*. Toronto: Progress Books, 1986.
Greene, B.M. *Who's Who in Canada, 1943–44*. Toronto: International Press, 1944.
Griffiths, N.E.S. *Centennial History of the National Council of Women of Canada, 1893–1993*. Ottawa, ON: Carleton University Press, 1997.
Gross, James A. *Broken Promises: The Subversion of U.S. Labor Relations Policy, 1947–1994*. Philadelphia, PA: Temple University Press, 1995.
– *The Reshaping of the National Labor Relations Board: National Labor Policy in Transition 1937–1947*. Albany, NY: State University of New York Press, 1981.
Hardy, Reginald. *Mackenzie King of Canada: A Biography*. Toronto: Oxford University Press, 1949.
Hart, Michael. *A Trading Nation: Canadian Trade Policy from Colonialism to Globalization*. Vancouver, BC: UBC Press, 2002.
Heron, Craig, and Robert Storey, eds. *On the Job: Confronting the Labour Process in Canada*. Kingston and Montreal: McGill-Queen's University Press, 1986.
Horn, Michiel, ed. *The Dirty Thirties: Canadians in the Great Depression*. Toronto: Copp Clark Publishing, 1972.

– *The League for Social Reconstruction: Intellectual Origins of the Democratic Left in Canada, 1930–1942*. Toronto: University of Toronto Press, 1980.

Howlett, Michael, and M. Ramesh. *The Political Economy of Canada: An Introduction*. Toronto: McClelland & Stewart, 1992.

Hunter, Peter. *Which Side Are You On Boys? Canadian Life on the Left*. Toronto: Lugus Productions, 1988.

Jacoby, Sanford. *Employing Bureaucracy: Managers, Unions, and the Transformation of Work in American Industry, 1900–1945*. New York: Columbia University Press, 1985.

Jay, Antony. *Lend Me Your Ears: Oxford Dictionary of Political Quotations*. New York: Oxford University Press, 2010.

Jenson, Jane, and Rianne Mahon, eds. *The Challenge of Restructuring: North American Labour Movements Respond*. Philadelphia, PA: Temple University Press, 1993.

Jessop, Bob. *State Theory: Putting Capitalist States in Their Place*. University Park, PA: Pennsylvania University Press, 1990.

Kaplan, William. *Canadian Maverick: The Life and Times of Ivan C. Rand*. Toronto: University of Toronto Press, 2009.

– *Everything That Floats: Pat Sullivan, Hal Banks, and the Seamen's Union of Canada*. Toronto: University of Toronto Press, 1987.

– *State and Salvation: The Jehovah's Witnesses and Their Fight for Civil Rights*. Toronto: University of Toronto Press, 1989.

Kaufman, Bruce E. *The Global Evolution of Industrial Relations: Events, Ideas, and the IIRA*. Geneva: International Labour Organization, 2004.

–, Richard A. Beaumont, and Roy B. Helfgott, eds. *Industrial Relations to Human Resources and Beyond: The Evolving Process of Employee Relations Management*. New York: M.E. Sharpe, 2003.

–, and Daphne Gottlieb Taras, eds. *Nonunion Employee Representation: History, Contemporary Practice, and Policy*. New York: M. E. Sharpe, 2000.

Kealey, Gregory S., and Reg Whitaker, eds. *R.C.M.P. Security Bulletins: The War Series, 1939–1941*. St John's, NL: Committee on Canadian Labour History, 1989.

– *R.C.M.P. Security Bulletins: The War Series, Part II, 1942–45*. St John's, NL: Committee on Canadian Labour History, 1993.

Kennedy, J. de N. *History of the Department of Munitions and Supply: Canada in the Second World War*. Vol. 2. Ottawa: King's Printer, 1950.

Keshen, Jeffrey. *Saints, Sinners, and Soldiers: Canada's Second World War*. Vancouver, BC: UBC Press, 2004.

Kilbourn, William. *The Elements Combined: A History of the Steel Company of Canada*. Toronto: Clarke, Irwin, and Co., 1960.

Kimmel, Michael. *Manhood in America: A Cultural History*. New York: The Free Press, 1996.

King, William Lyon Mackenzie. *Industry and Humanity: A Study in the Principles of Industrial Reconstruction*. Introduction by David Jay Bercuson. Toronto: University of Toronto Press, 1973.

Kochan, Thomas A., Harry C. Katz, and Robert B. McKersie, *The Transformation of American Industrial Relations*. Ithaca, NY: Cornell ILR Press, 1994.

Lambertson, Ross. *Repression and Resistance: Canadian Human Rights Activists, 1930–1960*. Toronto: University of Toronto Press, 2005.

Levine, Allan. *King: William Lyon Mackenzie King – A Life Guided by the Hand of Destiny*. Vancouver, BC: Douglas & McIntyre, 2011.

Lewis, David. *The Good Fight: Political Memoirs, 1909–1958*. Toronto: Macmillan of Canada, 1981.

Lichtenstein, Nelson. *Labour's War at Home: The CIO in World War II*. New York: Cambridge University Press, 1982.

– *State of the Union: A Century of American Labor*. Princeton, NJ: Princeton University Press, 2002.

Lipset, Seymour Martin. *Continental Divide: The Values and Institutions of the United States and Canada*. New York: Routledge, 1990.

Lipton, Charles. *The Trade Union Movement of Canada, 1827–1959*. Montreal: Canadian Social Publications, 1966.

Logan, H.A. *State Intervention and Assistance in Collective Bargaining: The Canadian Experience, 1943–1954*. Toronto: University of Toronto Press, 1956.

MacDowell, Laurel Sefton. *"Remember Kirkland Lake": The Gold Miners' Strike of 1941–42*. Toronto: University of Toronto Press, 1983.

– *Renegade Lawyer: The Life of J.L. Cohen*. Toronto: University of Toronto Press, 2001.

Mackintosh, Margaret. *Government Intervention in Labour Disputes in Canada*. Bulletin #11. Industrial Relations Series. Department of Labour. Ottawa: King's Printer, 1931.

MacIntyre, Hugh, and Charles Lammam. *Labour Relations Laws in Canada and the United States: An Empirical Comparison (2014 Edition)*. Vancouver, BC: Fraser Institute, 2014.

MacLennan, Christopher. *Toward the Charter: Canadians and the Demand for a National Bill of Rights, 1929–1960*. Montreal: McGill-Queen's Press, 2003.

Maier, Charles S. *In Search of Stability: Exploration in Historical Political Economy*. New York: Cambridge University Press, 1987.

– *Recasting Bourgeois Europe: Stabilization in France, Germany, and Italy in the Decade after World War I*. 2nd ed. Princeton, NJ: Princeton University Press, 1988.

Martin, Paul. *Far from Home*. Volume 1 of *A Very Public Life*. Ottawa: Deneau Publishers, 1983.

McDowall, Duncan. *Steel at the Sault: Francis H. Clergue, Sir James Dunn, and the Algoma Steel Corporation, 1901–1956*. Toronto: University of Toronto Press, 1984.

McInnis, Peter Stuart. *Harnessing Labour Confrontation: Shaping the Postwar Settlement in Canada, 1943–1950*. Toronto: University of Toronto Press, 2002.

Meier, August, and Elliott Rudwick. *Black Detroit and the Rise of the UAW*. Ann Arbor, MI: University of Michigan Press, 2007.

Milkman, Ruth. *Gender at Work: The Dynamics of Job Segregation by Sex during World War II*. Urbana, IL: University of Illinois Press, 1987.

Montero, Gloria. *We Stood Together: First-Hand Accounts of Dramatic Events in Canada's Labour Past*. Toronto: James Lorimer & Co., 1979.

Morton, Desmond, with Terry Copp. *Working People*. rev. ed. Ottawa: Deneau Publishers, 1984.

Naylor, James. *The New Democracy: Challenging the Social Order in Industrial Ontario, 1914–25*. Toronto: University of Toronto Press, 1991.

Neary, Peter, and J.L. Granatstein, eds., *The Veterans Charter and Post–World War II Canada*. Montreal: McGill-Queen's University Press, 1998.

Nelles, H.V. *The Politics of Development: Forest, Mines, and Hydro-Electric Power in Ontario, 1849–1941*. Toronto: Macmillan of Canada, 1974.

Norrie, Kenneth, and Douglas Owram. *A History of the Canadian Economy*. Toronto: Harcourt Brace Jovanovich, 1991.

Odets, Clifford. *Waiting for Lefty and Other Plays*. New York: Grove Press, 1994.

Owram, Doug. *The Government Generation: Canadian Intellectuals and the State, 1900–1945*. Toronto: University of Toronto Press, 1986.

Palmer, Bryan D. *Capitalism Comes to the Backcountry: The Goodyear Invasion of Napanee*. Toronto: Between the Lines, 1994.

– *Working-Class Experience: Rethinking the History of Canadian Labour, 1900–1991*. Toronto: McClelland & Stewart, 1992.

Parnaby, Andrew. *Citizen Docker: Making a New Deal on the Vancouver Waterfront, 1919–1939*. Toronto: University of Toronto Press, 2008.

Parr, Joy. *The Gender of Breadwinners: Women, Men, and Change in Two Industrial Towns, 1880–1950*. Toronto: University of Toronto Press, 1990.

Patrias, Carmela. *Jobs and Justice: Fighting Discrimination in Wartime Canada, 1939–1945*. Toronto: University of Toronto Press, 2012.

Patrias, Carmela, and Larry Savage. *Union Power: Solidarity and Struggle in Niagara*. Edmonton: Athabasca University Press, 2012.

Penner, Norman. *Canadian Communism: The Stalin Years and Beyond*. Toronto: Methuen, 1988.

Pickersgill, J.W. *The Mackenzie King Record*. Vol. 1, *1939–1944*. Toronto: University of Toronto Press, 1960.

– *Seeing Canada Whole: A Memoir*. Markham, ON: Fitzhenry & Whiteside, 1994.

Pierson, Ruth Roach. *"They're Still Women After All": The Second World War and Canadian Womanhood*. Toronto: McClelland & Stewart, 1986.

Pigden, Garnet, and Ardith McKinnon. *"Way Back When": Reflections of Madoc Village and Madoc County*. Madoc, ON: Privately Printed, 1975.

Plato. *The Republic*. Translated by Benjamin Jowett. New York: Modern Library, 1941.

Plotke, David. *Building a Democratic Political Order: Reshaping American Liberalism in the 1930s and 1940s*. New York: Cambridge University Press, 1996.

Power, Charles G. *A Party Politician: The Memoirs of Chubby Power*. Edited by Norman Ward. Toronto: Macmillan, 1966.

Prentice, Alison, Paula Bourne, Gail Cuthbert Brandt, Beth Light, Wendy Mitchinson, and Naomi Black. *Canadian Women: A History*. Toronto: Harcourt Brace Jovanovich, 1988.

Queen's University, Industrial Relations Centre. *Industrial Relations at Queen's: The First Fifty Years*. Kingston, ON: Queen's University, 1987. Accessed 22 July 2011. http://irc.queensu.ca/sites/default/files/articles/industrial-relations-at-queens-the-first-fifty-years.pdf.

Queen's University, School of Commerce and Administration, Industrial Relations Section. *The Right to Organize: Recent Canadian Legislation*. Bulletin No. 8. Kingston, ON: Queen's University, 1943.

Radforth, Ian. *Bush Workers and Bosses: Logging in Northern Ontario, 1900–1980*. Toronto: University of Toronto Press, 1987.

Recchiuti, John Lewis. *Civic Engagement: Social Science and Progressive-Era Reform in New York City*. Philadelphia, PA: University of Pennsylvania Press, 2007.

Risk, R.C.B. *A History of Canadian Legal Thought: Collected Essays*. Toronto: University of Toronto Press, 2006.

Robinson, David M. *Emerson and the Conduct of Life: Pragmatism and Ethical Purpose in the Later Work*. New York: Cambridge University Press, 1993.

Ross, Dorothy. *The Origins of American Social Science*. New York: Cambridge University Press, 1991.

Russell, Bob. *Back to Work? Labour, State, and Industrial Relations in Canada*. Toronto: Nelson Canada, 1990.

Russell, Peter, ed. *Leading Constitutional Decisions: Cases on the British North America Act*. 1965. Reprint. Toronto: McClelland & Stewart, 1976.

Salutin, Rick. *Kent Rowley, the Organizer: A Canadian Union Life*. Toronto: James Lorimer & Co., 1980.

Sangster, Joan. *Earning Respect: The Lives of Working Women in Small-Town Ontario, 1920–1960.* Toronto: University of Toronto Press, 1995.

– *Transforming Labour: Women and Work in Postwar Canada.* Toronto: University of Toronto Press, 2010.

Saywell, John T. *"Just Call Me Mitch": The Life of Mitchell F. Hepburn.* Toronto: University of Toronto Press, 1991.

Sharp, Mitchell. *Which Reminds Me: A Memoir.* Toronto: University of Toronto Press, 1993.

Smith, Doug. *Cold Warrior: C.S. Jackson and the United Electrical Workers.* St. John's, NL: Canadian Committee on Labour History, 1997.

– *Let Us Rise! A History of the Manitoba Labour Movement.* Vancouver, BC: New Star Books, 1985.

Smock, Raymond W., ed. *Booker T. Washington in Perspective: Essays of Louis R. Harlan.* Jackson, MS: University Press of Mississippi, 1988.

Stacey, C.P. *Arms, Men and Governments: The War Policies of Canada, 1939–1945.* Ottawa: Supply and Services, 1970.

Stanton, John. *My Past Is Now: Further Memoirs of a Labour Lawyer.* St. John's, NL: Canadian Committee on Labour History, 1994.

– *Never Say Die! The Life and Times of a Pioneer Labour Lawyer.* Ottawa: Steel Rail Publishing, 1987.

Stephen, Jennifer A. *Pick One Intelligent Girl: Employability, Domesticity, and the Gendering of Canada's Welfare State, 1939–1947.* Toronto: University of Toronto Press, 2007.

Struthers, James. *"No Fault of Their Own": Unemployment and the Canadian Welfare State, 1914–1941.* Toronto: University of Toronto Press, 1983.

Sugiman, Pamela. *Labour's Dilemma: The Gender Politics of Auto Workers in Canada, 1937–1979.* Toronto: University of Toronto Press, 1994.

Thompson, John Herd, and Stephen J. Randall. *Canada and the United States: Ambivalent Allies.* 4th ed. Athens, GA: University of Georgia Press, 2008.

Thompson, John Herd, with Allen Seager. *Canada, 1922–1939: Decades of Discord.* Vol. 15 of The Canadian Centenary Series. Reprint. Toronto: McClelland & Stewart, 1986.

Tomlins, Christopher. *The State and the Unions: Labor Relations, Law, and the Organized Labor Movement in America, 1880–1960.* New York: Cambridge University Press, 1985.

Tuohy, Carolyn J. *Policy and Politics in Canada: Institutionalized Ambivalence.* Philadelphia, PA: Temple University Press, 1992.

Van Loon, Richard, and Michael S. Whittington. *The Canadian Political System: Environment, Structure, and Process.* 3rd ed. rev. Toronto: McGraw-Hill Ryerson, 1981.

Vittoz, Stanley. *New Deal Labor Policy and the American Industrial Economy*. Chapel Hill, NC: University of North Carolina Press, 1987.

Wardhaugh, Robert A. *Behind the Scenes: The Life and Work of William Clifford Clark*. Toronto: University of Toronto Press, 2010.

Wartzman, Rick. *The End of Loyalty: The Rise and Fall of Good Jobs in America*. New York: Public Affairs, 2017.

Weiler, Paul. *Governing the Workplace: The Future of Labor and Employment Law*. Cambridge, MA: Harvard University Press, 1990.

– *Reconcilable Differences: New Directions in Canadian Labour Law*. Toronto: Carswell, 1980.

Whitaker, Reginald. *The Government Party: Organizing and Financing the Liberal Party of Canada, 1930–58*. Toronto: University of Toronto Press, 1986.

Woods, H.D. *Labour Policy in Canada*. 2nd ed. Toronto: Macmillan, 1973.

Young, Walter D. *The Anatomy of a Party: The National CCF, 1932–61*. Toronto: University of Toronto Press, 1969.

Zieger, Robert H. *American Workers, American Unions*. 2nd ed. Baltimore, MD: Johns Hopkins University Press, 1994.

– *The CIO: 1935–1955*. Chapel Hill, NC: University of North Carolina Press, 1995.

Articles

Abbott, Kirby. "The Coal Miners and the Law in Nova Scotia: From the 1864 Combination of Workmen Act to the 1947 Trade Union Act." In *Workers and the State in Twentieth Century Nova Scotia*, edited by Michael Earle, 24–46. Fredericton, NB: Acadiensis Press, 1989.

Abella, Irving Martin. "Oshawa 1937." In *On Strike: Six Key Labour Struggles in Canada, 1919–1949*, edited by Irving Abella, 93–128. Toronto: James Lewis and Samuel, 1974.

Adair, Kim, Peter Pautler, and David Strang. "The URWA and the Struggle for Union Recognition, 1937–39." In *Industrial Unionism in Kitchener, 1937–47*, edited by Terry Copp, 1–29. Elora, ON: Cumnock Press, 1976.

Akyeampong, Ernest B. "A Statistical Portrait of the Trade Union Movement." Statistics Canada, Catalogue no. 75-001-XPE. *Perspectives on Labour and Income* (Winter 1997): 45–54.

Angus, H.F. "Review of *The Incredible Canadian: A Candid Portrait of Mackenzie King*, by Bruce Hutchinson." *Canadian Journal of Economics and Political Science* 20, no. 1 (February 1954): 121.

Armstrong, D.E., and Muriel Armstrong. "Third Party Intervention in the Alberta Coal Industry, 1900–1951." In *Patterns of Industrial Dispute Settlement in Five Canadian Industries*, edited by H.D. Woods, 25–88. Montreal: McGill University Press, 1958.

Belisle, Donica. "Negotiating Paternalism: Women and Canada's Largest Department Stores, 1890–1940." *Journal of Women's History* 19, no. 1 (Spring 2007): 58–81.

Biel, Steven. "The Left and Public Memory." *Reviews in American History* 23 (December 1995): 704–9.

Brandt, Gail Cuthbert. "Pigeon-Holed and Forgotten: The Work of the Subcommittee on the Post-War Problems of Women, 1943." *Histoire sociale/ Social History* 15, no. 29 (May 1982): 239–59.

Brattain, Michelle. "A Town as Small as That: Tallapoosa, Georgia and Operation Dixie, 1945–1950." *Georgia Historical Quarterly* (Summer 1997): 395–425.

Bray, Bonita. "Against All Odds: The Progressive Arts Club's Production of *Waiting for Lefty*." In *Canadian Working-Class History: Selected Readings*, edited by Laurel Sefton MacDowell and Ian Radforth, 253–66. 3rd ed. Toronto: Canadian Scholars Press, 2006.

Brecher, Michael. "Patterns of Accommodation in the Men's Garment Industry of Quebec, 1914–1954." In *Patterns of Industrial Dispute Settlement in Five Canadian Industries*, edited by H.D. Woods, 91–186. Montreal: McGill University Press, 1958.

Brody, David. "The Breakdown of Labor's Social Contract: Historical Reflection, Future Prospects." *Dissent* (Winter 1992): 32–41.

– "Labor Elections: Good for Workers," *Dissent* (Summer 1997): 71–7.

– "Moving Past EFCA," *Labor* 7, no. 3 (2010): 25–8.

– "A Question of Rights." *New Labor Forum* (Fall–Winter, 1998): 129–37.

– "Workplace Contractualism in Comparative Perspective." In *Industrial Democracy in America: The Ambiguous Promise*, edited by Nelson Lichtenstein and Howell John Harris, 176–205. New York: Cambridge University Press, 1993.

Bronfenbrenner, Kate. "No Holds Barred: The Intensification of Employer Opposition to Organizing." Economic Policy Institute, Briefing Paper # 235, 20 May 2009. http://www.epi.org/files/page/-/pdf/bp235.pdf.

Brooks, Stephen. "Imagining Each Other." In *Canada and the United States: Differences That Count*, edited by David M. Thomas and David N. Biette, 23–45. 4th ed. Toronto: University of Toronto Press, 2014.

Budd, John W. "Union Wage Determination in Canadian and U.S. Manufacturing, 1964–1990: A Comparative Analysis." *Industrial and Labor Relations Review* 49 (July 1996): 672–89.

Buse, Dieter K., and Mercedes Steedman. "Reviewing the Past and Looking to the Future: Activists Reminisce at the Mine Mill Conference Sudbury, May 1993." *Labour/Le Travail* 33 (Spring 1994): 195–252.

Calvert, John R. "The Divergent Paths of the Canadian and American Labour Movements." *The Round Table* 303 (1987): 378–92.

Canada, Advisory Committee on Reconstruction, Subcommittee on Post-War Problems of Women. *Post-War Problems of Women: Final Report of the Subcommittee.* 30 November 1943. Ottawa: King's Printer, 1944.

Canada, Department of Labour. "Wartime Labour Relations Order." *Labour Gazette* 44, no. 2 (1944): 135–43. Accessed July 2012. https://archive.org/stream/labourgazette1944cana#page/134/mode/2up.

Canadian Broadcasting Corporation. *CBC Program Schedule.* 27 May 1945. Accessed 18 January 2016. http://www.otrr.org/FILES/Magz_pdf/CBC%2Program%20Schedule/CBC%20Program%20Schedule%20450527.PDF.

– "The Red Scare." Accessed 24 July 2016. http://www.cbc.ca/history/EPISCONTENTSE1EP15CH1PA2LE.html.

– "The Soldier's Return: A Digest of the Series Broadcast on the CBC Trans-Canada Network during the Winter of 1944–45." Toronto: CBC Publications, 1945.

Cassidy, Keith. "Mackenzie King and American Progressivism." In *Mackenzie King: Widening the Debate*, edited by John English and J.O. Stubbs, 105–29. Toronto: Macmillan, 1977.

Chaison, Gary N. "Union Growth, Structure, and Internal Dynamics." In *Union-Management Relations in Canada*, edited by John C. Anderson and Morley Gunderson, 147–70. Toronto: Addison-Wesley, 1982.

Charpentier, Alfred. "La conscience syndicale lors des grèves du textile en 1937 et de l'amiante en 1949." *Labour/Le Travail* 3 (1978): 202–20.

– "La Grève du Textile dans le Québec en 1937." *Relations industrielles* 20, no. 1 (January 1965): 86–127.

Chaykowski, Richard P., and Anil Verma. "Adjustment and Restructuring in Canadian Industrial Relations: Challenges to the Traditional System." In *Industrial Relations in Canadian Industry*, edited by Richard P. Chaykowski and Anil Verma, 1–38. Toronto: Holt, Rinehart and Winston, 1992.

Chouinard, Denys. "Alfred Charpentier face au gouvernment du Québec, 1935–1946." *Revue d'histoire de l'Amérique française* 31, no. 2 (September 1977): 211–27.

Coats, R.H. "Statistical Survey, 1937 and 1938, of Economic and Social Conditions." In *The Dirty Thirties: Canadians in the Great Depression*, edited by Michiel Horn, 78–80. Toronto: Copp Clark Publishing, 1972.

Cohen, J.L. "Dominion Has the Power to Legislate for Labour." *Saturday Night*, 14 December 1946.

Colling, Herb. "Excerpts from *99-Days, the Ford Strike in Windsor, 1945.*" *Walkerville Times Magazine.* Accessed 12 July 2015. http://www.walkervilletimes.com/27/ford-strike.html.

Copp, Terry. "The Rise of Industrial Unions in Montréal 1935–1945." *Relations industrielles/Industrial Relations* 37, no. 4 (1982): 843–75.

Copp, Terry, and Blake Weller. "Introduction." In *Industrial Unionism in Kitchener, 1937–47*, edited by Terry Copp, i-vii. Elora, ON: Cumnock Press, 1976.

Cox, Mark. "The Limits of Reform: Industrial Regulation and Management Rights in Ontario, 1930–7." *Canadian Historical Review* 68 (December 1987): 552–75.

Craven, Paul. "King and Context: A Reply to Whitaker." *Labour/Le Travail* 4 (1979): 165–186.

Cruikshank, Douglas, and Gregory S. Kealey. "Strikes in Canada, 1891–1950." *Labour/Le Travail* 20 (Fall 1987): 84–145.

DeLong, Brad. "Debate: Is There a Substitute for Unions in Achieving Equitable Growth? And Can Unions Be Saved?" Washington Center for Equitable Growth, 28 February 2014. Accessed 5 August 2015. http://equitablegrowth.org/equitablog/debate-is-there-a-substitute-for-unions-in-achieving-equitable-growth-and-can-unions-be-saved/.

Earle, Michael. "'Down With Hitler and Silby Barrett': The Cape Breton Miners' Slowdown Strike of 1941." In *Workers and the State in Twentieth Century Nova Scotia*, edited by Michael Earle, 109–43. Fredericton, NB: Acadiensis Press, 1989.

Earle, M., and H. Gamberg. "The United Mine Workers and the Coming of the CCF to Cape Breton." In *Workers and the State in Twentieth Century Nova Scotia*, edited by Michael Earle, 85–108. Fredericton, NB: Acadiensis Press, 1989.

Edwards, Alfred. "The Mill: A Worker's Memoir of the 1930s and 1940s." *Labour/Le Travail* 36 (Fall 1995): 253–98.

Elliot-Meisel, Elizabeth R.B. "A Grand and Glorious Thing … the Team of Mackenzie and Roosevelt." In *Franklin D. Roosevelt and the Formation of the Modern World*, edited by Thomas C. Howard and William D. Pederson, 138–56. Armonk, NY: M.E. Sharpe, 2003.

England, Dan, Robert England, and Del Stewart. "The 1946 Rubber Workers' Strike." In *Industrial Unionism in Kitchener, 1937–47*, edited by Terry Copp, 79–98. Elora, ON: Cumnock Press, 1976.

English, John. "Canada's Road to 1945." *Journal of Canadian Studies* 16 (Fall–Winter 1981): 100–9.

Farr, James. "The Historical Science(s) of Politics: The Principles, Association, and Fate of an American Discipline." In *Modern Political Science: Anglo-American Exchanges since 1880*, edited by Robert Adcock, Mark Bevir, and Shannon C. Stimson, 66–96. Princeton, NJ: Princeton University Press, 2007.

Feeney-Gallagher, Douglas J. "Battle on the Benches: The Wagner Act and the Federal Circuit Courts of Appeals, 1935–1942." *Seattle University Law Review* 23, no. 3 (2000): 503–48.

Finkel, Alvin. "The Cold War, Alberta Labour, and the Social Credit Regime." *Labour/Le Travail* 21 (Spring 1988): 123–52.
– "Paradise Postponed: A Re-examination of the Green Book Proposals of 1945." *Journal of the Canadian Historical Association* 4 (1993): 120–42.
Fisher, Robin. "The Decline of Reform: British Columbia Politics in the 1930s." *Journal of Canadian Studies* 25 (Autumn 1990): 74–89.
Forrest, Anne. "Hidden in the Past: How Labour Relations Policy and Law Perpetuate Women's Economic Inequality." *Canadian Woman Studies* 23, nos. 3–4 (2004): 65–71.
Fox, Bonnie J., and John Fox. "Women in the Labour Market, 1931–81: Exclusion and Competition." *Canadian Review of Sociology and Anthropology* 23, no. 1 (1986): 1–21.
Frager, Ruth. "Mixing with People on Spadina: The Tense Relations between Non-Jewish Workers and Jewish Workers." In *The History of Immigration and Racism in Canada: Essential Readings*, edited by Barrington Walker, 142–57. Toronto: Canada Scholars' Press Inc., 2008.
– "No Proper Deal: Women Workers and the Canadian Labour Movement, 1870–1940." In *Union Sisters: Women in the Labour Movement*, edited by Linda Briskin and Lynda Yanz, 44–64. Toronto: Women's Educational Press, 1983.
Fudge, Judy. "After Industrial Citizenship: Market Citizenship or Citizenship at Work?" *Relations industrielles/Industrial Relations* 60, no. 4 (2005): 631–56.
– "Rungs on the Labour Law Ladder: Using Gender to Challenge Hierarchy." *Saskatchewan Law Review* 60, no. 2 (1996): 237–64.
Fudge, Judy, and Eric Tucker. "Pluralism or Fragmentation? The Twentieth Century Employment Law Regime in Canada." *Labour/Le Travail* 46 (Fall 2000): 251–306.
Galenson, Walter, and Arnold Zellner. "International Comparison of Unemployment Rates." In *The Measurement and Behavior of Unemployment*, edited by the National Bureau Committee for Economic Research, 439–584. Princeton, NJ: Princeton University Press, 1957. http://www.nber.org/chapters/c2649.pdf.
Goddard, John. "Labour Law and Union Recognition in Canada: A Historical-Institutionalist Perspective." *Queen's Law Journal* 38, no. 2 (2013): 391–417.
Goldfield, Michael, and Bryan D. Palmer, "Canada's Workers Movement: Uneven Developments." *Labour/Le Travail* 59 (Spring 2007): 149–77.
Guard, Julie. "Fair Play or Fair Pay? Gender Relations, Class Consciousness, and Union Solidarity in the Canadian UE." *Labour/Le Travail* 37 (Spring 1996): 149–77.
– "Womanly Innocence and Manly Self-Respect: Gendered Challenges to Labour's Postwar Compromise." In *Labour Gains, Labour Pains: 50 Years of PC 1003*, edited by Cy Gonick, Paul Phillips, and Jesse Vorst, 119–37. Winnipeg: Fernwood Publishing, 1995.

Hanson, S.D. "Estevan 1931." In *On Strike: Six Key Labour Struggles in Canada, 1919–1949*, edited by Irving Abella, 33–77. Toronto: James Lewis and Samuel, 1974.

Harris, Howell John. "The Snares of Liberalism? Politicians, Bureaucrats, and the Shaping of Federal Labor Relations Policy in the United States, ca. 1915–47." In *Shop Floor Bargaining and the State: Historical and Comparative Perspectives*, edited by Steven Tolliday and Jonathan Zeitlin, 148–91. Cambridge: Cambridge University Press, 1985.

Heeney, A.D.P. "Cabinet Government in Canada: Some Recent Developments in the Machinery of the Central Executive." *Canadian Journal of Economics and Political Science* 12 (August 1946): 282–301.

Heron, Craig. "Afterword: Male Wage-Earners and the State in Canada." In *Workers and the State in Twentieth Century Nova Scotia*, edited by Michael Earle, 241–64. Fredericton, NB: Acadiensis Press, 1989.

– "Boys Will Be Boys: Working-Class Masculinities in the Age of Mass Production." *International Labour and Working-Class History* (Spring 2006): 6–34.

Heron, Craig, and Robert Storey. "Work and Struggle in the Canadian Steel Industry, 1900–1950." In *On the Job: Confronting the Labour Process in Canada*, edited by Craig Heron and Robert Story, 210–44. Kingston and Montreal: McGill-Queen's University Press, 1986.

Hollander, Taylor. "Making Reform Happen: The Passage of Canada's Collective-Bargaining Policy, 1943–1944." *Journal of Policy History* 13, no. 3 (2001): 299–328.

How, Douglas. "One Man's Mackenzie King." *The Beaver* 78, no. 5 (October/November 1998): 31–7.

Hurd, Richard W. "Moving Beyond the Critical Synthesis: Does the Law Preclude a Future for US Unions?" *Labor History* 54, no. 2 (2013): 193–200.

Huxley, Christopher, David Kettler, and James Struthers. "Is Canada's Experience 'Especially Instructive'?" In *Unions in Transition: Entering the Second Century*, edited by Seymour Martin Lipset, 113–32. Los Angeles: Institute for Contemporary Studies, 1986.

Industrial Relations Counselors, Inc. "The Birth of IRC." In *The Roots of Industrial Democracy*. Accessed 18 July 2007. http://ircounselors.org/history/history06.html.

Jacoby, Sanford. "Masters to Managers: An Introduction." In *Masters to Managers: Historical and Comparative Perspectives on American Employers*, edited by Sanford Jacoby, 1–15. New York: Columbia University Press, 1991.

– "Reckoning with Company Unions: The Case of Thompson Products, 1934–1964." *Industrial and Labor Relations Review* 43 (October 1989): 19–40.

Jamieson, Stuart. "Industrial Relations and Government Policy." *Canadian Journal of Economics and Political Science* 17 (February 1951): 25–38.

Jenson, Jane. "'Different' But Not 'Exceptional': Canada's Permeable Fordism." *Canadian Review of Sociology and Anthropology* 26, no. 1 (1989): 68–94.

Jenson, Jane, and Rianne Mahon. "Legacies for Canadian Labour of Two Decades of Crisis." In *The Challenge of Restructuring: North American Labour Movements Respond*, edited by Jane Jenson and Rianne Mahon, 72–92. Philadelphia, PA: Temple University Press, 1993.

Kaplan, William. "How Justice Rand Devised His Famous Formula." In *Work on Trial: Canadian Labour Law Struggles*, edited by Judy Fudge and Eric Tucker, 77–109. Toronto: Irwin Law, 2010.

Kaufman, Bruce. "Accomplishments and Shortcomings of Nonunion Employee Representation in the Pre-Wagner Act Years: A Reassessment." In *Nonunion Employee Representation: History, Contemporary Practice, and Policy*, edited by Bruce Kaufman and Daphne Gottlieb Taras, 21–60. New York: M.E. Sharpe, 2000.

Kealey, Gregory S. "The Canadian State's Attempt to Manage Class Conflict, 1900–1948." In *Social Welfare, 1850–1950: Australia, Argentina, and Canada Compared*, edited by D.C.M. Platt, 125–47. London: Macmillan Press, 1989.

Keshen, Jeffrey A. "Revisiting Canada's Civilian Women during World War II." *Histoire sociale/Social History* 30, no. 60 (1997): 239–66.

Kessler-Harris, Alice. "Treating the Male as 'Other': Redefining the Parameters of Labor History." *Labor History* 34 (Spring–Summer 1993): 190–204.

Kettler, David, James Struthers, and Christopher Huxley. "Unionization and Labour Regimes in Canada and the United States: Considerations for Comparative Research." *Labour/Le Travail* 25 (Spring 1990): 161–87.

King, W.L. Mackenzie. "The Practice of Liberalism." In *The Dirty Thirties: Canadians in the Great Depression*, edited by Michiel Horn, 489–496. Toronto: Copp Clark Publishing, 1972.

Klare, Karl. "Judicial Deradicalization of the Wagner Act and the Origins of Modern Legal Consciousness, 1937–1941." *Minnesota Law Review* 62 (1978): 265–339.

Klee, Marcus. "'Hands-off Labour Forum': The Making and Unmaking of National Working-Class Radio Broadcasting in Canada, 1935–1944." *Labour/Le Travail* 35 (Spring 1995): 107–32.

Lahey, William. "Canada Temperance Act." In *Alcohol and Temperance in Modern History: An International Encyclopedia*, edited by Jack S. Blocker, David M. Fahey, and Ian R. Tyrrell, 1:130–1. Santa Barbara, CA: ABC-CLIO, 2003.

Lalande, Léon. "The Status of Organized Labour: An Outline of the Development of the Law in Great Britain, the United States, and Canada." *The Canadian Bar Review* 19 (November 1941): 638–81.

Laskin, Bora. "Labour Law: 1923–1947." *The Canadian Bar Review* 26 (1948): 286–307.

– "The Legal Status of Trade Unions." In *Problems in Canadian Unity: Lectures Given at the Canadian Institute on Economics and Politics, August 6 to 19, 1938*, edited by Violet Anderson, 90–102. Toronto: Thomas Nelson and Sons, 1938.

Lehmbruch, Gerhard. "Liberal Corporatism and Party Government." *Comparative Political Studies* 10 (April 1977): 91–126.

Li, Peter S. "Cultural Diversity in Canada: The Social Construction of Racial Differences." Department of Justice Strategic Issues Series, rp02-8e. Ottawa: Research and Statistics Division, 2000. http://www.justice.gc.ca/eng/rp-pr/csj-sjc/jsp-sjp/rp02_8-dr02_8/rp02_8.pdf.

Licht, Walter. "Studying Work: Personnel Policies in Philadelphia Firms, 1850–1950." In *Masters to Managers: Historical and Comparative Perspectives on American Employers*, edited by Sanford Jacoby, 43–73. New York: Columbia University Press, 1991.

Lichtenstein, Nelson. "From Corporatism to Collective Bargaining: Organized Labor and the Eclipse of Social Democracy in the Postwar Era." In *The Rise and Fall of the New Deal Order, 1930–1980*, edited by Steve Fraser and Gary Gerstle, 122–52. Princeton, NJ: Princeton University Press, 1989.

Logan, H.A. "Government Control of Labour Relations." *Behind the Headlines* 2 (October 1941): 1–29.

Logan, John. "How 'Anti-Union' Laws Saved Canadian Labour: Certification and Striker Replacements in Post-War Industrial Relations." *Relations industrielles/Industrial Relations* 57, no. 1 (2002): 129–58.

– "Permanent Replacements and the End of Labor's 'Only True Weapon.'" *International Labor and Working Class History* (Fall 2008): 171–92.

– "The Union Avoidance Industry in the United States." *British Journal of Industrial Relations* 44 (December 2006): 651–75.

Loney, E.D. "Momentum." In *The Dirty Thirties: Canadians in the Great Depression*, edited by Michiel Horn, 65–6. Toronto: Copp Clark Publishing, 1972.

Macaray, David. "Union Strikes and Replacement Workers." *Counterpunch* (16 April 2008). Accessed 25 November 2017. https://www.counterpunch.org/2008/04/16/union-strikes-and-replacement-workers/.

MacDonald, Hugh P. "Principles: The Principles of Principles." *The Pluralist* 4, no. 3 (Fall 2009): 98–126.

MacDowell, Laurel Sefton. "Company Unionism in Canada, 1915–1948." In *Nonunion Employee Representation: History, Contemporary Practice, and Policy*, edited by Bruce E. Kaufman and Daphne Gottlieb Taras, 96–120. New York: M.E. Sharpe, 2000.

– "The Formation of the Canadian Industrial Relations System during World War Two." *Labour/Le Travail* 3 (1978): 175–96.

– "The 1943 Steel Strike against Wartime Wage Controls." *Labour/Le Travail* 10 (Fall 1982): 65–85.

Mahn, Bryan, and Ralph Schaffner. "The Packinghouse Workers in Kitchener: 1940–47." In *Industrial Unionism in Kitchener, 1937–47*, edited by Terry Copp, 30–52. Elora, ON: Cumnock Press, 1976.

Makahonuk, Glen. "Trade Unions in the Saskatchewan Coal Industry, 1907–1945." *Saskatchewan History* 31 (Spring 1978): 51–68.

Manley, John. "Communists and Auto Workers: The Struggle for Industrial Unionism in the Canadian Automobile Industry, 1926–36." *Labour/Le Travail* 17 (Spring 1986): 105–33.

Martin, Lawrence. "The Weirdo PM Who Showed the Way." *Globe and Mail*, 8 November 2011. https://beta.theglobeandmail.com/news/politics/the-weirdo-pm-who-showed-the-way/article4182988/?ref=http://www.theglobeandmail.com&.

Maynard, Steven. "Rough Work and Rugged Men: The Social Construction of Masculinity in Working-Class History." *Labour/Le Travail* 23 (Spring 1989): 159–69.

McCall, Leslie. "The Complexity of Intersectionality." *Signs* 230, no. 3 (2005): 230–43.

McCallum, Margaret E. "Corporate Welfarism in Canada, 1919–39." *Canadian Historical Review* 71 (March 1990): 46–79.

McIlroy, John, and Richard Croucher. "The Turn to Transnational Labor History and the Study of Global Trade Unionism." *Labor History* 54, no. 5 (2013): 491–511.

McInnis, Peter S. "Teamwork for Harmony: Labour-Management Production Committees and the Postwar Settlement in Canada." *Canadian Historical Review* 77 (September 1996): 317–52.

McKay, Ian. "Review of *'An Impartial Umpire': Industrial Relations and the Canadian State, 1900–1911*, by Paul Craven." *Labour/Le Travail* 8/9 (Autumn 1981–Spring 1982): 364–70.

Meltz, Noah. "Labor Movements in Canada and the United States." In *Challenges and Choices Facing American Labor*, edited by Thomas A. Kochan, 315–34. Cambridge, MA: MIT Press, 1985.

– "Unionism in Canada, U.S.: On Parallel Treadmills?" *Forum for Applied Research and Public Policy* (Winter 1990): 46–52.

Mercier, Laurie. "Gender, Labour, and Place: Reconstructing Women's Spaces in Industrial Communities of Western Canada and the United States." *Labour History* 53, no. 3 (2012): 389–407.

Morton, Desmond. "Aid to Civil Power: The Stratford Strike of 1933." In *On Strike: Six Key Labour Struggles in Canada, 1919–1949*, edited by Irving Abella, 79–91. Toronto: James Lewis and Samuel, 1974.

Moulton, David. "Ford Windsor 1945." In *On Strike: Six Key Labour Struggles in Canada, 1919–1949*, edited by Irving Abella, 129–61. Toronto: James Lewis and Samuel, 1974.

Muszynski, Alicja. "The Organization of Women and Ethnic Minorities in a Resource Industry: A Case Study of the Unionization of Shoreworkers in the B.C. Fishing Industry, 1937–1949." *Journal of Canadian Studies* 19, no. 1 (Spring 1984): 89–107.

National Council of State Legislatures. "Right to Work Resources." Accessed 11 January 2014. http://www.ncsl.org/research/labor-and-employment/right-to-work-laws-and-bills.aspx.

Panitch, Leo. "Corporatism in Canada." *Studies in Political Economy* 1 (1979): 43–92.

– "The Development of Corporatism in Liberal Democracies." *Comparative Political Studies* 10 (April 1977): 61–90.

Parr, Joy. "Gender History and Historical Practice." *Canadian Historical Review* 76 (September 1995): 354–76.

Plotke, David. "The Wagner Act, Again: Politics and Labor, 1935–37." *Studies in American Political Development: An Annual* 3 (1989): 105–56.

Princeton University, Industrial Relations Section. Selected References. No. 14. "Union Security." 1 March 1947. http://dataspace.princeton.edu/jspui/handle/88435/dsp0112579s27z.

Radforth, Ian, and Joan Sangster. "'A Link between Labour and Learning': The Workers Educational Association of Ontario, 1917–1951." *Labour/Le Travail* 8/9 (Autumn/Spring 1981/1982): 41–78.

Ramirez, Bruno. "U.S. Response to the Canadian Industrial Disputes Investigation Act." *Relations industrielles/Industrial Relations* 29, no. 3 (1974): 541–59.

Rashid, Abdul. "Seven Decades of Wage Changes." *Perspectives on Labour and Income* 5, no. 2 (Summer 1993): 9–21.

Riddell, Craig, Gideon Rosenbluth, and Mark Thompson. "Tribute to Stuart Marshall Jamieson, 1914–2002." *Relations industrielles/Industrial Relations* 59, no. 2 (2004): 231.

Roberts, Wayne, and John Bullen. "A Heritage of Hope and Struggle: Workers, Unions, and Politics in Canada, 1930–1982." In *Modern Canada, 1930–1980s*, edited by Michael S. Cross and Gregory S. Kealey, 105–40. Toronto: McClelland & Stewart, 1984.

Robinson, Ian. "Economic Unionism in Crisis: The Origins, Consequences, and Prospects of Divergence in Labour-Movement Characteristics." In *The Challenge of Restructuring: North American Labour Movements Respond*, edited by Jane Jenson and Rianne Mahon, 19–47. Philadelphia, PA: Temple University Press, 1993.

Robson, Robert S. "Strike in the Single Enterprise Community: Flin Flon, Manitoba – 1934." In *Canadian Labour History: Selected Readings*, edited by David J. Bercuson, 159–178. Toronto: Copp Clark Pitman, 1987.

Rose, Joseph B., and Gary N. Chaison. "Linking Union Density and Union Effectiveness: The North American Experience." *Industrial Relations* 35 (January 1996): 78–105.

– "The State of the Unions: United States and Canada." *Journal of Labor Research* 6 (Winter 1985): 97–111.

Rouillard, Jacques. "Le militantisme des travailleurs au Québec et en Ontario, niveau de syndicalisation et mouvement de grèves (1900–1980)." *Revue d'histoire de l'Amérique française* 37 (Septembre 1983): 201–25.

– "Major Changes in the Confédération des travailleurs catholiques du Canada, 1940–1960." Translated by Henri Malebranche. In *Quebec Since 1945: Selected Readings*, edited by Michael D. Behiels, 111–32. Toronto: Copp Clark Pitman, 1987.

Russell, Bertrand. "A Philosophy for You in These Times." *Reader's Digest* 39 (October 1941): 5–7.

Russell, Bob. "Labour's *Magna Carta*? Wagnerism in Canada at Fifty." In *Labour Gains, Labour Pains: 50 Years of PC 1003*, edited by Cy Gonick, Paul Phillips, and Jesse Vorst, 177–92. Winnipeg: Fernwood Publishing, 1995.

Sangster, Joan. "The Softball Solution: Female Workers, Male Managers, and the Operation of Paternalism at Westclox, 1923–60." *Labour/Le Travail* 32 (Fall 1993): 167–99.

– "'We No Longer Respect the Law': The Tilco Strike, Labour Injunctions, and the State." *Labour/Le Travail* 53 (Spring 2004): 47–88.

Schatz, Ronald. "From Commons to Dunlop: Rethinking the Field and Theory of Industrial Relations." In *Industrial Democracy in America: The Ambiguous Promise*, edited by Nelson Lichtenstein and Howell John Harris, 87–112. New York: Cambridge University Press, 1993.

Scheinberg, Ellen. "The Tale of Tessie the Textile Worker: Female Textile Workers in Cornwall during World War II." *Labour/Le Travail* 33 (Spring 1994): 153–81.

Scheinberg, Stephen. "Invitation to Empire: Tariffs and American Economic Expansion in Canada." *Business History* 47 (Summer 1973): 218–38.

Schiller, Reuel E. "From Group Rights to Individual Liberties: Post-War Labor Law, Liberalism, and the Waning of Union Strength." *Berkeley Journal of Employment and Labor Law* 20, no. 1 (1999): 1–73.

Schmitter, Philippe C. "Modes of Interest Intermediation and Models of Societal Change in Western Europe." *Comparative Political Studies* 10 (April 1977): 7–38.

Scott, F.R. "Federal Jurisdiction over Labour Relations: A New Look." *The McGill Law Journal* 6, no. 3 (1960): 153–67.

– "W.L.M.K." Canada Poetry Online. Accessed 24 May 2015. http://canpoetry.library.utoronto.ca/scott_fr/poem5.htm.

Seager, Allen. "Minto, New Brunswick: A Study in Canadian Class Relations between the Wars." *Labour/Le Travail* 5 (Spring 1980): 81–132.

Sharpe, Christopher A., and Lynne Marks. "The Home Front in the Second World War." In *Historical Atlas of Canada III: Addressing the Twentieth Century, 1891–1961*, edited by Donald Kerr and Deryck W. Holdsworth, Plate 48. Toronto: University of Toronto Press, 1990.

Siemiatycki, Myer. "Munitions and Labour Militancy: The 1916 Hamilton Machinists' Strike." In *Canadian Labour History: Selected Readings*, edited by David J. Bercuson, 119–37. Toronto: Copp Clark Pitman, 1987.

Skocpol, Theda, and Kenneth Finegold. "Explaining New Deal Labor Policy." *American Political Science Review* 84, no. 4 (December 1990): 1297–1315.

Smith, Helen, and Pamela Wakewich. "'Beauty and the Helldivers': Regulating Women's Work and Identities in a Warplant Newspaper." *Labour/Le Travail* 44 (Fall 1999): 71–107.

– "Regulating Body Boundaries and Health during Wartime: Nationalist Discourse, Media Representations and the Experiences of Canadian Women War Workers." *Gender and History* 24, no. 1 (April 2012): 56–73.

– "Trans/Forming the Citizen Body in Wartime: National and Local Public Discourse on Women's Bodies and 'Body Work' for Women during the Second World War." In *Contesting Bodies and Nation in Canadian History*, edited by Patrizia Gentile and Jane Nicholas, 305–27. Toronto: University of Toronto Press, 2013.

Soltas, Evan. "Is the U.S. Better Off without Unions?" *Bloomberg View* (19 February 2014). Accessed 5 August 2015. https://www.bloomberg.com/view/articles/2014-02-19/is-the-u-s-better-off-without-unions-.

Stanton, John. "Government Internment Policy, 1939–1945." *Labour/Le Travail* 31 (Spring 1993): 203–41.

Stewart, Bryce M. "War-Time Labour Problems and Policies in Canada." *Canadian Journal of Economics and Political Science* 7 (August 1941): 426–46.

Storey, Robert. "The Struggle to Organize Stelco and Dofasco." *Relations industrielles/Industrial Relations* 42 (Spring 1987): 366–84.

– "Unionization versus Corporate Welfare: The 'Dofasco Way.'" *Labour/Le Travail* 12 (Fall 1983): 7–42.

Sugiman, Pamela. "Privilege and Oppression: The Configuration of Race, Gender, and Class in Southern Ontario Auto Plants, 1939 to 1949." *Labour/Le Travail* 47 (Spring 2001): 83–113.

Taras, Daphne G. "Portrait of Nonunion Employee Representation in Canada: History, Law, and Contemporary Plans." In *Nonunion Employee Representation: History, Contemporary Practice, and Policy*, edited by Bruce Kaufman and Daphne Gottlieb Taras, 121–48. New York: M.E. Sharpe, 2000.

– "Voice in the North American Workplace: From Employee Representation to Employee Involvement." In *Industrial Relations to Human Resources and Beyond: The Evolving Process of Employee Relations Management*, edited Bruce E. Kaufman, Richard A. Beaumont, and Roy B. Helfgott, 293–329. New York: M.E. Sharpe, 2003.

Tillett-Saks, Andrew. "Why the Labor Movement Must Join the Anti-Racist Struggle to Make Black Lives Matter." *Working In These Times* (*In These Times* blog), 6 April 2016. http://inthesetimes.com/working/entry/19038/unions-labor-black-lives-matter-anti-racist-racial-justice.

Tomlins, Christopher L. "AFL Unions in the 1930s: Their Performance in Historical Perspective." *Journal of American History* 65 (March 1979): 1021–42.

– "The New Deal, Collective Bargaining, and the Triumph of Industrial Pluralism." *Industrial and Labor Relations Review* 39 (October 1935): 19–34.

Traves, Tom. "Security without Regulation." In *The Consolidation of Capitalism, 1896–1929*, edited by Michael S. Cross and Gregory S. Kealey, 19–44. Toronto: McClelland & Stewart, 1983.

Troy, Leo. "Is the U.S Unique in the Decline of Private Sector Unionism?" *Journal of Labor Research* 11 (Spring 1990): 111–43.

Tucker, Eric M. "Shall Wagnerism Have No Dominion?" Research Paper No. 30. *Osgoode Legal Studies Research Paper Series* 10, no. 8 (2014): 1–20.

United States Government, Department of Commerce and Labor. *Bulletin of the Bureau of Labor.* Washington, DC: Government Printing Office, 1911.

Vinel, Jean-Christian. "Christopher Tomlins' *The State and the Unions* Today: What the Critical Synthesis Can Teach Us Now That the Unions Have Gone." *Labor History* 54, no. 2 (2013): 177–92.

Wakewich, Pamela, and Helen Smith. "The Politics of 'Selective' Memory: Re-visioning Canadian Women's Wartime Work in the Public Record." *Oral History* (Autumn 2006): 56–68.

Walter P. Reuther Library, Wayne State University. "(6647) Ford, UAW, 1945 Strike Agreement, Windsor, Ontario." Accessed 12 July 2015. http://reuther.wayne.edu/node/3408.

Warner, Kris. "Protecting Fundamental Labor Rights: Lessons from Canada for the United States." Working Paper, Center for Economic and Policy Research, August 2012. http://cepr.net/documents/publications/canada-2012-08.pdf.

Webber, Jeremy. "Compelling Compromise: Canada Chooses Conciliation Over Arbitration, 1900–1907." *Labour/Le Travail* 28 (Fall 1991): 15–57.

– "The Malaise of Compulsory Conciliation: Strike Prevention in Canada during World War II." In *The Character of Class Struggle: Essays in Canadian Working-Class History, 1850–1985*, edited by Bryan D. Palmer, 138–59. Toronto: McClelland & Stewart, 1986.

– "The Mediation of Ideology: How Conciliation Boards through the Mediation of Particular Disputes Fashioned a Vision of Labour's Place within Canadian Society." *Law in Conflict* 7 (1989): 1–23.

Weiler, Paul. "Promises to Keep: Securing Workers' Rights to Self-Organization under the NLRA." *Harvard Law Review* 96 (June 1983): 1769–1827.

Wells, Don. "Autoworkers on the Firing Line." In *On the Job: Confronting the Labour Process in Canada*, edited by Craig Heron and Robert Storey, 327–52. Kingston and Montreal: McGill-Queen's University Press, 1986.

– "The Impact of the Postwar Compromise on Canadian Unionism: The Formation of an Auto Worker Local in the 1950s," *Labour/Le Travail* 36 (Fall 1995): 147–73.

Westhues, Kenneth. "Sociology for a New Century: Mackenzie King's First Career." In *Mackenzie King: Citizenship and Community: Essays Marking the 125th Anniversary of the Birth of William Lyon Mackenzie King*, edited by John English, Kenneth McLaughlin, and P. Whitney Lackenbauer, 186–210. Montreal: Robin Brass Studio, 2002.

Whitaker, Reginald. "The Liberal Corporatist Ideas of Mackenzie King." *Labour/Le Travail* 2 (1977): 137–69.

– "Official Repression of Communism during World War II." *Labour/ Le Travail* 17 (Spring 1986): 135–66.

– "Political Thought and Political Action in Mackenzie King." *Journal of Canadian Studies* 13 (1978–79): 40–60.

White, Jay. "Pulling Teeth: Striking for the Check-Off in the Halifax Shipyards, 1944." In *Workers and the State in Twentieth Century Nova Scotia*, edited by Michael Earle, 144–70. Fredericton, NB: Acadiensis Press, 1989.

Williams, C. Brian. "Notes on the Evolution of Compulsory Conciliation in Canada." *Relations industrielles/Industrial Relations* 19 (1969): 298–324.

Wimmer, Hermann. "Catechism on Methods of Teaching." *American Journal of Education* 4 (1858): 233–44, 505–19.
Windscheffel, Ruth Clayton. "Politics, Religion, and Text: W.E. Gladstone and Spiritualism." *Journal of Victorian Culture* (Spring 2006): 1–29.
Winter, David G. "Measuring the Motives of Political Actors at a Distance." In *The Psychological Assessment of Political Leaders: With Profiles of Saddam Hussein and Bill Clinton*, edited by Jerrold M. Post, 153–77. Ann Arbor, MI: University of Michigan Press, 2003.
Wolfe, David A. "The Canadian State in Comparative Perspective." *Canadian Review of Sociology and Anthropology* 26, no. 1 (1989): 95–126.
– "The Rise and Demise of the Keynesian Era in Canada: Economic Policy, 1930–1982." In *Modern Canada, 1930–1980s*, edited by Michael S. Cross and Gregory S. Kealey, 46–78. Toronto: McClelland & Stewart, 1984.
Woods, H.D. "Canadian Collective Bargaining and Dispute Settlement Policy: An Appraisal." *Canadian Journal of Economics and Political Science* 21 (November 1955): 447–65.
Wright, Robert A . "The Canadian Protestant Tradition." In *The Canadian Protestant Experience, 1760–1990*, edited by George A. Rawlyk, 139–97. Montreal: McGill-Queen's University Press, 1990.

Unpublished Papers

Manley, John. "Canadian Communism, Revolutionary Unionism and the 'Third Period': The Workers Unity League, 1929–1935." Paper presented to the Canadian Historical Association, Calgary, AB, June 1994.
Thompson, John Herd. "'National Character' and United States-Canadian Differences: An Exploration of Seymour Lipset's Explanation of the *Continental Divide*." Paper presented to the Canadian Historical Association, Calgary, AB, June 1994.
Whitton, Charlotte. "'All That It Stands For': Some Notes on How Ban Righ Hall at Queen's Came to Be and the Role of the Alumnae Therein." Unpublished manuscript. September 1958.

Dissertations and Theses

Bedore, Margaret Elizabeth. "The Reading of Mackenzie King." PhD diss., Queen's University, 2008.
Coates, Daniel. "Organized Labor and Politics in Canada: The Development of a National Labor Code." PhD diss., Cornell University, 1973.

Fudge, Judy. "Voluntarism and Compulsion: The Canadian Federal Government's Intervention in Collective Bargaining from 1900 to 1946." PhD diss., University of Oxford, 1988.

Gray, Stephen C. "Woodworkers and Legitimacy: The IWA in Canada, 1937–1957." PhD diss., Simon Fraser University, 1989.

Hollander, Taylor. "'Down the Middle of the Road': The Canadian State and Collective Bargaining, 1935–1948." PhD diss., Binghamton University, 1998.

Isbester, Alexander Fraser. "A History of the National Catholic Unions in Canada, 1901–1965." PhD diss., Cornell University, 1968.

Matheson, David W.T. "The Canadian Working-Class and Industrial Legality, 1939–1949." Master's thesis, Queen's University, 1989.

Millar, Frederick David. "Shapes of Power: The Ontario Labour Relations Board, 1944 to 1960." PhD diss., York University, 1980.

Warrian, Peter Jon. "'Labour Is Not a Commodity': A Study of the Rights of Labour in the Canadian Postwar Economy, 1944–48." PhD diss., University of Waterloo, 1986.

Wilson, Jeffrey. "Charles Millard and the Canadian Labour Movement." Master's thesis, Wilfrid Laurier University, 1990.

Wolfe, David A. "The Delicate Balance: The Changing Economic Role of the State in Canada." PhD diss., University of Toronto, 1980.

Index

www.ingramcontent.com/pod-product-compliance
Lightning Source LLC
LaVergne TN
LVHW040756070826
844660LV00025B/1156

* 9 7 8 1 4 8 7 5 2 1 9 3 6 *